CW01198441

REINVENTING LEGAL EDUCATION

European legal teaching – historically formalistic, doctrinal, hierarchical, and passive – is coming under increasing pressure to reimagine itself as pragmatic, policy-aware, and action-oriented. Out of this context, a bottom-up movement of university law clinics appears to be emerging in Europe. Although intellectually indebted to the US model, the European variant reflects legal education and practice in Europe, specifically the multi-layered and multi-genetic legal landscape resulting from the Europeanization and internationalization of national legal systems, the globalization of European legal markets, and the growing demand for civic engagement in view of increasingly powerful supranational institutions. Through the prism of clinical legal education, *Reinventing Legal Education* is the first attempt to gather scholarly and systematic reflections on the developments taking place in European legal teaching and practice. This groundbreaking book should be read by anyone interested in how clinical legal education is reinventing legal education in Europe.

Alberto Alemanno is Professor of Law at HEC Paris, where he holds the Jean Monnet Chair in European Union Law. Alemanno is also Global Professor of Law at New York University in Paris, where he established and directs the EU Public Interest Clinic. Alemanno is the co-founder and director of The Good Lobby, an advocacy skill–sharing community, and is a Young Global Leader at the World Economic Forum.

Lamin Khadar is the Pro Bono Associate for Europe at DLA Piper. He has co-founded The Good Lobby with Alberto Alemanno. He was previously the executive director of the HEC-NYU EU Public Interest Clinic in Paris. He is a former Fulbright Award Winner and spent time working with the Global Public Interest Law Network in New York and as a research student at New York University and the University of California, Los Angeles.

Reinventing Legal Education

HOW CLINICAL EDUCATION IS REFORMING
THE TEACHING AND PRACTICE OF LAW IN EUROPE

Edited by

ALBERTO ALEMANNO

New York University School of Law

LAMIN KHADAR

DLA Piper

CAMBRIDGE
UNIVERSITY PRESS

CAMBRIDGE
UNIVERSITY PRESS

University Printing House, Cambridge CB2 8BS, United Kingdom

One Liberty Plaza, 20th Floor, New York, NY 10006, USA

477 Williamstown Road, Port Melbourne, VIC 3207, Australia

314–321, 3rd Floor, Plot 3, Splendor Forum, Jasola District Centre, New Delhi – 110025, India

79 Anson Road, #06–04/06, Singapore 079906

Cambridge University Press is part of the University of Cambridge.

It furthers the University's mission by disseminating knowledge in the pursuit of education, learning, and research at the highest international levels of excellence.

www.cambridge.org
Information on this title: www.cambridge.org/9781107163041
DOI: 10.1017/9781316678589

© Cambridge University Press 2018

This publication is in copyright. Subject to statutory exception and to the provisions of relevant collective licensing agreements, no reproduction of any part may take place without the written permission of Cambridge University Press.

First published 2018

Printed in the United States of America by Sheridan Books, Inc.

A catalogue record for this publication is available from the British Library.

ISBN 978-1-107-16304-1 Hardback

Cambridge University Press has no responsibility for the persistence or accuracy of URLs for external or third-party internet websites referred to in this publication and does not guarantee that any content on such websites is, or will remain, accurate or appropriate.

Contents

List of Contributors — page viii

Introduction — 1
Alberto Alemanno and Lamin Khadar

PART I WHERE HAVE WE COME FROM AND WHAT HAVE WE LEARNED? REFLECTIONS ON THE FIRST WAVE OF CLINICAL LEGAL EDUCATION IN EUROPE (MID-1990S TO MID-2000S) — 27

1 Reflections on US Involvement in the Promotion of Clinical Legal Education in Europe — 29
Philip M. Genty

2 Poland as the Success Story of Clinical Legal Education in Central and Eastern Europe: Achievements, Setbacks, and Ongoing Challenges — 44
Katarzyna Wazyńska-Finck

PART II WHERE ARE WE NOW AND WHERE ARE WE GOING? INSIGHTS INTO THE SECOND WAVE OF CLINICAL LEGAL EDUCATION IN EUROPE (MID-2000S TO THE PRESENT) — 57

Part IIA National Perspectives on Clinical Legal Education in Europe: Exploring the Strength and Diversity of National Clinical Movements — 58

3 The Emergence of an Italian Clinical Legal Education Movement: The University of Brescia Law Clinic — 59
Marzia Barbera

4	A New Dawn in the Czech Clinical Movement: The Clinical Programme at the Law School of Palacký University in Olomouc *Veronika Tomoszková and Maxim Tomoszek*	76
5	Towards the Institutionalization of Legal Clinics in Spain: The Environmental Law Clinic at Rovira I Virgili University *Maria Marquès i Banqué*	93
6	Law Clinics in France through the Prism of the Fundamental Rights Law Clinic, University of Caen Normandy *Xavier Aurey*	110

	Part IIB	The Europeanization of Clinical Legal Education: How Clinical Legal Education Is Being Adapted for European Law and European Issues	126

7	On the Front Line of the Migrant Crisis: The Human Rights and Migration Law Clinic (HRMLC) of Turin *Ulrich Stege and Maurizio Veglio*	127
8	The Refugee Rights Movement and the Birth of Clinical Legal Education in Germany: Humboldt Law Clinic Human and Fundamental Rights, Berlin, and Refugee Law Clinic, Hamburg *Nora Markard*	145
9	The EU Public Interest Clinic and the Case for EU Law Clinics *A. Alemanno and L. Khadar*	163
10	The EU Rights Clinic at the University of Kent in Brussels: EU Free Movement Law in Action *Anthony Valcke*	187

	Part IIC	Between Europe and the World: Exploring Internationalization within the European Clinical Movement	208

11	The Human Rights Law Clinic at Ghent University *Eva Brems and Stijn Smet*	209
12	Clinical Legal Education at Central European University, Budapest: A Small Project with Big Ambitions in a Supportive Institution *Renáta Uitz and Eszter Polgári*	230

13	The International Human Rights Clinic at SOAS *Lynn Welchman*	247
14	The Experience of the Åbo Akademi University International Human Rights Law Clinic, Finland *Juan-Pablo Pérez-León-Acevedo*	272
15	The International Economic Law Clinic at the Graduate Institute in Geneva *Joost Pauwelyn and Mattia Salamanca Orrego*	292
16	The Amsterdam International Law Clinic *Hege Elisabeth Kjos and André Nollkaemper*	309
	Conclusion *Alberto Alemanno and Lamin Khadar*	322

Contributors

Alberto Alemanno HEC Paris/NYU Law

Xavier Aurey University of Essex

Marzia Barbera University of Brescia

Eva Brems Ghent University

Katarzyna Wazynska-Finck European University Institute

Phillip Genty Columbia Law School

Lamin Khadar DLA Piper

Hege Elisabeth Kjos University of Amsterdam

Nora Markard University of Hamburg / Humbult University Berlin

Maria Marquès Universitat Rovira i Virgili

André Nollkaemper University of Amsterdam

Joost Pauwelyn The Graduate Institute

Juan Pablo Pérez Åbo Akademi University

Eszter Polgári Central European University

Mattia Salamanca Orrego The Graduate Institute

Stijn Smet University of Melbourne

Ulrich Stege International University College of Turin

Maurizio Veglio International University College of Turin

Maxim Tomoszek Palacký University Olomouc

Veronika Tomoszková Palacký University Olomouc

Renáta Uitz Central European University

Anthony Valcke University of Kent in Brussels

Katarzyna Ważyńska-Finck European University Institute

Lynn Welchman School of Oriental and African Studies

Introduction

Alberto Alemanno and Lamin Khadar

Given the dramatic recent transformations to legal professions and justice systems globally, one might expect to witness parallel developments in legal education. Yet despite the urgent need to reform the legal curriculum in light of these unprecedented, seismic developments, the curricula of law schools continue, in many respects, to resemble curricula in the time of law students' ancestors.[1] Despite the massive internationalization of legal practice and culture, law continues to be presented as a predominantly domestic affair. At a time in which individuals, businesses, and other organizations increasingly operate across jurisdictional lines,[2] we continue training law students to think as domestic lawyers. While the traditionally local nature of the law partly explains this situation,[3] there is a considerable risk that, by privileging the domestic perspective over an international perspective, the law curriculum remains largely insulated from major societal transformations, such as the democratization of knowledge through technological development or the disruptive effects brought about by the sharing-economy.[4] These are some of the forces that are reshaping all professions, including the legal profession.[5] The legal market is in a state of flux, and the legal professions are reluctantly undergoing radical

---

[1] Ernst van Bemmelen van Gent, *Legal Education: A New Paradigm*, BYNKERSHOEK LAW REVIEW 2–18 (2012), http://ssrn.com/abstract=1273683. (Arguing that "The curriculum and teaching techniques have remained largely the same as in the 1800 to 1950 era"); Aalt Willem Heringa, *Towards a Truly European Legal Education. An Agenda for the Future*, in Educating European Lawyers (Aalt Willem Heringa, and Bram Akkermans, eds., Antwerp: Intersentia, 2011), 3–18.

[2] Francis Snyder, *Economic Globalisation and the Law in the 21st Century*, in THE BLACKWELL COMPANION TO LAW AND SOCIETY, BLACKWELL COMPANIONS TO SOCIOLOGY (Austin Sarat, ed., Blackwell Publishing, 2004), 624–40.

[3] Carole Silver. EDUCATING LAWYERS FOR THE GLOBAL ECONOMY: NATIONAL CHALLENGES. (2009), 2. "This local nature of law, then, means that we cannot resolve the challenge of educating lawyers to work in a global economy simply by teaching global law. And we surely cannot teach the law of each nation; there are too many and too many differences among them. We probably cannot even accurately anticipate which national legal regimes will assume importance in the career of any particular student."

[4] *See, e.g.*, Susan McClellan, *Externships for Millennial Generation Law Students: Bridging the Generation Gap*, 15 CLINICAL L. REV. 255 (2009), http://digitalcommons.law.seattleu.edu/faculty/157.

[5] Richard Susskind and Daniel Susskind, THE FUTURE OF THE PROFESSIONS: HOW TECHNOLOGY WILL TRANSFORM THE WORK OF HUMAN EXPERTS (Oxford University Press, 2015).

transformation. In the meantime, we are assisting a progressive industrialization of the legal profession.

The gap between legal education and legal realities appears particularly striking in Europe, where legal scholars and their academic institutions persist with their historical reluctance to engage in self-reflection.[6] Due to their traditionalist, corporatist reflex to police disciplinary borders, European lawyers and scholars engage more frequently in "siloed debate" than in deeper, methodological thinking. In other words, the European legal academy remains more interested in debating *what* to teach than *how* to teach.[7] Concern for and interest in a debate on legal research methods is not necessarily greater.[8] Moreover, the overall contribution by European universities to community engagement is embarrassingly modest, especially if compared with their long-standing ties with their communities.[9]

As a result, by prioritizing a positivist and formalist approach to law and lawyering, Europe continues to shy away from self-reflection in legal education. In the absence of an Oliver Wendell Holmes Jr. or a Karl Llewellyn[10] or even anything similar to a "Langdell revolution,"[11] there is very little tradition of soul-searching and thinking beyond the classroom and beyond legal texts, in Europe.

Reinventing Legal Education responds to a desire to fill up a gap existing between the millenarian history of European legal education and the realities of today's practice. But there is more. The need for law schools to teach students to understand the complexity of the law as it takes shape through practice appears heightened at unprecedented times characterized by social and economic turmoil across the continent.

This book is an initial attempt at promoting awareness about the importance of self-examination in European legal academia and teaching by shedding some light on some of the most promising transformations currently spreading across the continent. Indeed, behind the apparent status quo bias cloaking European legal academia, something is moving (in the legal curriculum). The major novelty of European legal education is the emerging, pan-European phenomenon of *clinical legal education* (CLE).

---

[6] See, e.g., Bruno De Witte, *European Union Law: A Unified Academic Discipline*, 1 CROATIAN YEARBOOK OF EUROPEAN LAW & POLICY 4 CROATIAN Y.B. E (2008); Miguel Poiares Maduro, *Legal Education and the Europeanisation and Globalisation of Law [editorial note]*, CROATIAN YEARBOOK OF EUROPEAN LAW & POLICY 4 CROATIAN Y.B. E (2008); Julie Dickson and Petros Eleftheriadis, eds., PHILOSOPHICAL FOUNDATIONS OF EUROPEAN UNION LAW (Oxford University Press, 2012).
[7] *Id.*
[8] R. van Gestel and H.-W. Micklitz, *Why Methods Matter in European Legal Scholarship*, 20 (3) EUROPEAN LAW JOURNAL 292–316 (2014).
[9] P. Benneworth and M. Osborne, KNOWLEDGE ENGAGEMENT AND HIGHER EDUCATION IN EUROPE (Global University Network for Innovation, 2014).
[10] For a detailed review of the evolutions if US legal education see Paul D. Carrington, *Hail! Langdell!*, 20 (3) LAW & SOCIAL INQUIRY 691–760 (1995).
[11] For an insightful account of the "Langdell revolution," *see* Daniel R. Coquillette and Bruce A. Kimball, ON THE BATTLEFIELD OF MERIT: HARVARD LAW SCHOOL, THE FIRST CENTURY (Harvard University Press, 2015).

Introduction 3

Although largely an American invention,[12] today CLE is afoot in Europe. While legal clinics have been a consistent feature of legal education in Eastern and Central Europe since the mid-1990s – largely prompted by the fall of the Berlin Wall[13] – and in Britain, Norway, and the Netherlands since the early 1970s, they have developed much more slowly in the bulk of Western continental Europe.[14] However, the past five to ten years has seen a boom in CLE, first in Spain, then in Italy, France, and Germany. With the birth of the European Network for Clinical Legal Education[15] (ENCLE) in 2012 – whose goal is uniting clinics across the continent – CLE is now a truly pan-European phenomenon.[16] Over the past decade, a handful of specialist European Union (EU), European Convention of Human Rights (ECHR) and international law and advocacy clinics have begun to emerge. To name just a few, clinics such as the EU Rights Clinic in Brussels,[17] the European Human Rights and Migration Law Clinic in Turin,[18] the EU Public Interest Clinic in Paris,[19] or the Clinical Programme of the Graduate Institute in Geneva.[20]

The urgent need to reform legal education in light of the Europeanization and internationalization of national legal systems, the globalization of legal practice, and the equal demand for civic engagement in view of increasingly powerful supranational institutions and international actors appear among a number of catalysts and incentives for the emergence of university law clinics in Europe. Through the

---

[12] Although there exist early examples of clinics in European law schools, clinical education blossomed in the United States beginning in the 1960s. *See, e.g.*, J. P. "Sandy" Ogilvy, *CLEPR's 40th Anniversary: Papers and Speeches from the AALS-ABA-CLEA Celebration of CLEPR: Celebrating CLEPR's 40th Anniversary: The Early Development of Clinical Legal Education and Legal Ethics Instruction in U.S. Law Schools*, 16 (1) CLINICAL L. REV. 9–18 (Fall 2009); Richard J. Wilson, CLINICAL LEGAL EDUCATION IN DUTCH LEGAL CULTURE: CLASHES OF TRADITION, TOLERANCE AND PROGRESS IN GLOBAL LAW'S CAPITAL. Digital Commons@ American University Washington College of Law (Working Paper 1-1-2010), 29. In addition, Edwin Rekosh cites even earlier examples in Copenhagen, Denmark, and Rostock, Germany. *See* Edwin Rekosh, *Constructing Public Interest Law: Transnational Collaboration and Exchange in Central and Eastern Europe*, 13 UCLA J. INT'L L. & FOREIGN AFF.56, 84 (2008); Ł. Bojarski, *Społeczny aspect działania poradni*, in STUDENCKA PORADNIA PRAWNA. IDEA, ORGANIZACJA, METODOLOGIA (Warsaw: Fundacja Uniwersyteckich Poradni Prawnych 2005), 1–16.

[13] For an account of the drivers leading to the development of CLE in Central and Eastern Europe, *see, e.g.*, Dubravka Aksamovic and Philip Genty, *An Examination of the Challenges, Successes and Setbacks for Clinical Legal Education in Eastern Europe*, 20 INT'L J. CLINICAL LEGAL EDUC. 427, 429–30 (2014).

[14] For an account of the late development of CLE in Western Europe, *see*, Richard Wilson, *Western Europe: Last Holdout in the Worldwide Acceptance of Clinical Legal Education*, 10 GERMAN LAW JOURNAL 825 (2009).

[15] See http://encle.org/.   [16] *See* Chapter 7 in this volume.

[17] *See* Chapter 10 by Anthony Valcke in this volume, and, for a brief overview, http://blogs.kent.ac.uk/eu-rights-clinic/.

[18] *See* Chapter 7 by Ulrich Stege and Maurizio Veglio in this volume, and, for a brief overview, http://www.iuctorino.it/content/clinical-programme-0.

[19] *See* Chapter 9 by Alberto Alemanno and Lamin Khadar in this volume, and, for a brief overview, http://elabeurope.eu/hec-nyu-clinic/.

[20] *See* Chapter 15 by Joost Pauwelyn and Mattia Salamanca Orrego in this volume, and, for a brief overview, http://graduateinstitute.ch/home/executive/masters_executive/llm/llm_programme/llm-clinic-programme.html.

European clinical movement, spurred on by this restructuring of the European legal field, European legal teaching – historically formalistic, doctrinal, hierarchical, and passive (lecture- and textbook-based)[21] – is coming under increasing pressure to reimagine itself as pragmatic, policy-aware, and action-oriented. In line with its genesis and development in the United States, European CLE emerges today in response to the limits of traditional legal education to teach students in the complex ways of thinking and acting increasingly required of lawyers if they are to fulfil their vital roles in society.

Reinventing Legal Education is a first attempt to gather, in a scholarly and systematic manner, reflections on the fascinating and rapid developments taking place in European legal teaching and practice as witnessed through the prism of CLE. It examines the various and typically entrepreneurial academic efforts touching in various ways on the practice and teaching of European and international law. It thus presents a range of views from practicing European legal clinicians and practitioners reflecting on how they are challenging the *status quo* of law teaching and lawyering. In particular, it collects a series of guides and narratives that offer insights into how this emerging phenomenon is impacting legal teaching and practice in Europe. The open, provocative question addressed by this volume is whether CLE might contribute to reinventing legal education in Europe.

CONTEXTUALIZING CLINICAL LEGAL EDUCATION IN EUROPE

Recent years witnessed a rapid diffusion of legal clinics within law schools across the globe, leading some to talk of a "global clinical movement."[22] Although far from becoming an essential component of legal education across the globe, CLE and its method of exposing law students to their future professional role has witnessed over the past half a century a notable expansion.

Unlike traditional legal education, clinics provide hands-on, professional skills training that relies on experiential learning methods. The aim is to place students in the role of lawyers, generally in real-life scenarios, forcing them to not only face but also react to a concrete problem. Although several accounts exist about its origins and evolution, it appears undisputed that CLE finds its roots in the establishment of the university-based legal aid bureau (i.e. legal services aimed

---

[21] See, e.g., R. van Gestel and H-W. Micklitz, Why Methods Matter in European Legal Scholarship, 20 (3) EUROPEAN LAW JOURNAL 294 (2014). Richard Ball and Christian Dadomo, UKCLE Law Subject Survey: European Union Law (2010), 89 and 104. Project Report. Unpublished. http://eprints.uwe.ac.uk/14747. This survey related to EU law teaching in the UK and found that such teaching (at least at universities) was primarily conservative and doctrinal. However, anecdotal evidence suggests that this would be even more so for continental Europe, which is traditionally far more conservative in its approach to legal education.

[22] See, generally, Frank S. Bloch, ed. THE GLOBAL CLINICAL MOVEMENT: EDUCATING LAWYERS FOR SOCIAL JUSTICE (Oxford University Press, 2010). See also Jocelyn Kestenbaum Getgen, Esteban Hoyos-Ceballos, and Melissa C. del Aguila Talvadkar. *Catalysts for Change: A Proposed Framework for Human Rights Clinical Teaching and Advocacy*, 18 CLINICAL L. REV. 462 (2011).

at the unprivileged).[23] From the outset, legal clinics have been characterized by two major aims: to enable law students to put into practice what they learn and – while doing so – to serve the public interest so as to pursue social justice objectives.

It is during the American civil rights and public interest law movements of the 1960s and 1970s that CLE went through a period of rapid expansion in the United States, largely spearheaded by the Ford Foundation. During this period, the Ford Foundation provided extensive financial support towards the establishment of university legal clinics. In concrete terms, just short of $12.5 million was granted to US law schools towards CLE between 1959 and 1978.[24] This was followed up by an $87 million investment by the US Congress geared towards institutionalizing CLE in the United States between 1978 and 1997.[25] Law clinics are now a feature of virtually every US law school and are growing in number and acceptance.[26] Today, around 75% of students enrolled at Harvard Law School experience clinical teaching in their curriculum.[27]

In parallel to the US clinical experience, clinics emerged in the 1960s and 1970s in other countries such as Australia, Canada, and the United Kingdom[28] (see Chapter 13 by Lynn Welchman in this volume for more on the evolution of CLE in the UK). In 1973, the Ford Foundation sponsored a conference on legal aid held at the University of Natal in Durban, South Africa. This proved to be the spark of a South African CLE movement, which resulted in clinical programmes being established in sixteen of the (then) twenty-one South African universities.[29] The mid-1970s through the 1980s was perhaps the starting point and initial phase of the global clinical movement as it also saw the emergence of clinical programmes in India, Botswana, Tanzania, Australia, Chile, Peru, and Argentina.[30]

Meanwhile, in Europe, there was some very early experimentation with "CLE" (or at least similar practices) in the late nineteenth and early twentieth centuries in Russia, Germany, Denmark, Scotland, Norway, and no doubt other countries across Europe.[31] Subsequently, the mid-60s through the early 70s witnessed reinvigorated interest in transforming the provision of legal services in Europe. Emboldened by

---

[23] Marshall J., Breger, *Legal Aid for the Poor: A Conceptual Analysis*, 60 N.C. L. REV. 281 (1981–1982).
[24] See Margaret Martin Barry, Jon C. Dubin, and Peter A. Joy. *Clinical Education for this Millennium: The Third Wave*, 7 CLINICAL L. REV. 18–19 (2000).
[25] *Id.*
[26] Robert R. Kuehn and David A. Santacroce. *The 2010-11 Survey of Applied Legal Education* (Center for the Study of Applied Legal Education 2012), 7.
[27] See Harvard Law School Clinics, http://hls.harvard.edu/dept/clinical/.
[28] Giddings et al., *The First Wave of Modern Legal Education*, in THE GLOBAL CLINICAL MOVEMENT: EDUCATING LAWYERS FOR SOCIAL JUSTICE (Frank S. Bloch, ed., Oxford University Press 2010), 4.
[29] Willem De Klerk, *University Law Clinics in South Africa*, 122 (4) SOUTH AFRICAN LAW JOURNAL 930 (2005).
[30] *Id.*, at 934; Richard J. Wilson, *Training for Justice: The Global Reach of Clinical Legal Education*, 22 PENN STATE INT'L. L. REV. 421 (2004).
[31] A clinic was apparently established by Professor Rudolf von Jhering in Rostock in 1847; a clinic was established by Professor Dmitrij Mejer in Kazan at around the same time; the Copenhagen University Student Union Legal Aid for the Poor organization was founded in 1885 and is still in operation today;

the rebellious spirit of the 1970s and often taking inspiration from the US Office of Economic Opportunities Legal Services Programme, legal aid organizations typically staffed by students and academics were established in Norway, the Netherlands, Belgium, and the UK. For example, *rechtswinkels* ("law shops") were established throughout the Netherlands starting at the University of Tilburg in 1969. *Wetswinkels* and *boutiques de droit* were established throughout Belgium starting in 1972, in Ghent and Louvain. Meanwhile, in Norway, the *Juss-Buss* ("law bus") was launched at the University of Oslo in 1971, literally bussing law students out to the suburbs of Oslo to provide free legal advice.[32]

Finally, in the mid-1990s, following the fall of the Berlin Wall (and through to the early 2000s), the CLE movement reached Europe in a significant way (see Chapter 1 by Philip Genty and Chapter 2 by Katarzyna Ważyńska-Finck in this volume for a more detailed reflection on this). However, these developments were exclusively confined to Central and Eastern Europe (CEE), where not only the Ford Foundation, but various other mainly US donor organizations – including most notably the Open Society Institute (through the Constitutional Law and Policy Institute (COLPI)) and the American Bar Association Central European and Eurasian Law Initiative (ABA CEELI) but also USAID, the German Marshall Fund, the MacArthur Foundation, and even UNHCR and the OSCE – collectively invested significant resources into the establishment of legal clinics in the region.[33] COLPI and the Columbia University, Public Interest Law Initiative (PILI; now PILnet) helped to set up more than seventy-five law school clinical programmes in several Central and Eastern European countries,[34] while CEELI helped to establish more than one hundred law school clinics in Russia.[35] To get a sense of the scale of the investment, funding for individual clinics typically ranged from $10,000 to $25,000 annually. In addition the funders paid for regional conferences and colloquia, training events, and educational exchanges. Open Society alone was investing in the region of $1,000,000 annually into CLE in CEE between around 1998 and 2002.[36] Meanwhile, the Ford Foundation invested

---

and the Edinburgh Legal Dispensary was founded in 1900. See Rekosh, *supra* note 12; and Hector Lewis MacQueen, *Lawyers' Edinburgh 1908–2008*, 8 BOOK OF THE OLD EDINBURGH CLUB (NEW SERIES) 11 (2010). Meanwhile, legal clinics have reportedly existed in Norway since at least 1920. See Jon T. Johnsen, *Nordic Legal Aid*, 5 (2) MARYLAND J. CONTEMP. LEGAL ISSUES 305 (1994).

[32] Bryant G. Garth, NEIGHBORHOOD LAW FIRMS FOR THE POOR: A COMPARATIVE STUDY OF RECENT DEVELOPMENTS IN LEGAL AID AND IN THE LEGAL PROFESSION, BRILL 118–29 (1980); unpublished 2011 article on the origins of the Juss-Buss written by Jon T. Johnsen on file with authors.

[33] Rekosh, *supra* note 12 at 75.

[34] Armenia, Belarus, Bosnia, Bulgaria, Croatia, Czech Republic, Estonia, Georgia, Hungary, Kazakhstan, Kyrgyzstan, Latvia, Lithuania, Macedonia, Moldova, Montenegro, Poland, Romania, Russia, Serbia, Slovenia, Slovakia, and Ukraine. See Mariana Berbec-Rostas, Arkady Gutnikov, and Barbara Namyslowska-Gabrysiak, *Clinical Legal Education in Central and Eastern Europe: Selected Case Studies*, in THE GLOBAL CLINICAL MOVEMENT: EDUCATING LAWYERS FOR SOCIAL JUSTICE (Frank S. Bloch, ed., Oxford University Press 2010), 55.

[35] Wilson, *supra* note 30 at 426.

[36] Stephen Golub, Forging the Future: Current and Potential Soros Foundations Network Support for Clinical Legal Education and Related Law Programmes (2002).

nearly $1 million into one clinic alone (at Jagiellonian University Law School) between 1998 and 2004.[37] Collectively, the investment made by donors into CLE in this period (1998 to 2004) was likely in the tens of millions of dollars.

However, as funding for CLE in CEE declined in the mid-2000s, largely as a result of shifting priorities of the donors and a mistaken belief (or justification) that the EU would take over funding CLE in CEE following accession, most of these law school clinics proved to be unsuccessful or unsustainable over the long term.[38] Many of them closed almost immediately when the funding dried up, and, arguably, some of the funders did not have an adequate sustainability strategy. However, there are a few success stories, most notably in Poland, where CLE is now institutionalized in much the same way as it is in the United States (there being a clinic in every Polish law school), and this largely the result of a national funding organization, Fundacja Uniwersyteckich Poradni Prawnych, which took it upon itself to plan for and implement a sustainability strategy that gradually shifted funding responsibility away from foreign donors and onto Polish law departments themselves.[39] Other success stories, albeit to a much to a lesser degree, are Russia, where ABA CEELI was most active and scores if not hundreds of clinics (or clinic-like structures) have survived to this day, and the Czech Republic, where CLE has had something of resurgence in recent times (see Chapter 4 by Veronika Tomoszková and Maxim Tomoszek in this volume for more on this).

Presently (in the past five to ten years), after much inactivity, we are witnessing a CLE boom in Western Europe. In spite of persistent claims that CLE is incompatible with[40] or rendered redundant by civil law legal systems,[41] Western European universities are turning to CLE at an astonishing pace. Recent ENCLE and Open Society Justice Initiative surveys (recording more or less formalized clinics; i.e. with some degree of academic oversight/supervision) suggest that there are more than thirty clinics in Germany alone (at separate universities), more than twenty in Italy, more than twenty in the UK, at least five in France, at least five in Spain, between three and six apiece in the Netherlands and Belgium, and several others dotted across Scandinavia and southern Europe.[42] Counting clinics is a notoriously difficult exercise, and so there are likely many more than these surveys reveal. Considering that just ten or even five years ago these figures (certainly in continental Western Europe) would have been at or near zero, this is a significant increase.

[37] Ford Foundation grant reports for Jagiellonian University (1998–2002) on file with authors.
[38] See Rekosh, *supra* note 12 at 92; *see* Irina Gross Grudzinska, Reflection Memo (2002), on file with author, reshifting funding priorities of donors; interview with Filip Czernicki, June 23, 2016.
[39] Interview with Filip Czernicki, June 23, 2016.
[40] E.g. because of the more formalist or positivist conceptions of law in the civil law traditions or the unique role of the civil law professoriate in the formation of law. *See* Wilson, *supra* note 14.
[41] E.g. because of the apprenticeship system that dominates civil law jurisdictions or the generous state legal aid systems found in Western European civil law jurisdictions. *Id.*
[42] *See* Clelia Bartoli, *Legal Clinics in Europe: For a Commitment of Higher Education to Social Justice*, Special Issue DIRITTO E QUESTIONI PUBBLICHE (2016) and records kept by the Open Society Justice Initiative on file with the authors.

Moreover, networks of law clinics are emerging in France (Réseau Francophone pour l'enseignement Clinique du Droit) and Italy (Rete Cliniche legali in Italia) and at the pan-European level (European Network for Clinical Legal Education).

Unlike the first generation of CLE in (Eastern) Europe, the recent boom does not seem to have US donor organizations as the primary engines of growth, although Open Society continues to fund a handful of clinics in Italy, France, and Germany.[43] While often still partially US-inspired or involving collaboration with US universities – as in the case of the EU Public Interest Clinic in Paris – these clinics seem to be European initiated, highly entrepreneurial, and even, in a few exceptional instances, also EU funded (e.g. the European Social Fund or the Jean Monnet action of the EU's Lifelong Learning Programme) affairs, thus proving the theory (or hope) of the exiting US funders in the mid-2000s not entirely without merit.[44] The reasons for this recent growth are, however, unclear and are explored for the first time in this volume. Maxim Tomoszek, co-founder and president of the European Network for Clinical Legal Education and director of the Olomouc Law School Clinic (and a contributor to this volume) speculates that it may be due to a gradual realization of the merits of CLE (both in terms of teaching law and in terms of advancing social justice), or indeed – he goes on to say – it may simply be a fad.[45] Whatever the case, European CLE literature points towards the so-called *Bologna Process*, which has prompted a pragmatic reconsideration of *inter alia* higher legal education, as a major source of inspiration (or justification) for change.[46] Many authors see CLE as an answer to the Bologna Process's call for "increased attention to competences and skills in university education" (so that graduates may better participate in economy and society following graduation).[47] Other authors point towards globalization, East–West European integration, domestic reform of the regulation of the legal professions, and even the recent economic crisis as factors energizing the recent take-up of CLE in Western Europe.[48]

---

[43] Interview with Zaza Namordaze, director of the Open Society Justice Initiative's Budapest office, June 22, 2016.
[44] Maxim Tomoszek, *The Growth of Legal Clinics in Europe–Faith and Hope, or Evidence and Hard Work?*, 21 (1) INT'L. J. CLINICAL LEGAL EDUC. 96 (2014). *See also* Chapter 4, co-authored with Veronika Tomoszková, in this volume.
[45] Id., at 97–100.
[46] *See, e.g.*, Lusine Hovannisian, *Clinical Legal Education and the Bologna Process*, 2 PILI PAPERS (2006); Andreas Bucker and William A. Woodruff. *The Bologna Process and German Legal Education: Developing Professional Competence through Clinical Experiences*, 9 GERMAN L. J. 575 (2008); Marie-Luce Paris and Lawrence Donnelly, *Legal Education in Ireland: A Paradigm Shift to the Practical*, 11 GERMAN L. J. 1067 (2010); and Diego Blázquez-Martín, *The Bologna Process and the Future of Clinical Education in Europe: A View from Spain*, in THE GLOBAL CLINICAL MOVEMENT: EDUCATING LAWYERS FOR SOCIAL JUSTICE (Frank S. Bloch, ed., Oxford University Press 2010); Jeremy Perelman, *Transnational Human Rights Advocacy, Clinical Collaborations, and the Political Economies of Accountability: Mapping the Middle*, 16 YALE HUM. RTS. & DEV. L. J. 89(2013).
[47] Id.; *see also* Bucker and Woodruff, *supra* note 46, at 614–17.
[48] Dubravka Askamovic, Philip Genty, and Ulrich Stege, Evidence of Successes and Challenges in Clinical Legal Education in Europe (unpublished, on file with author) (2015), 8.

CONTEXTUALIZING THE STUDY OF CLINICAL EDUCATION IN EUROPE

In the midst of these sometimes institutionalized and sometimes sporadic efforts at establishing legal clinics in Europe over the past twenty years, a growing body of literature has emerged in relation to university law clinics in Europe. Initially, these articles were primarily written by American clinicians who were directly involved in running and establishing clinics in CEE.[49] More recently, we have seen articles produced by local (European) clinicians – as mentioned in the preceding section– and relating also to law clinics in Western Europe.[50]

However, much like the efforts at establishing clinics themselves, this literature is often sporadic, generally a mosaic of introspective accounts with the inevitable result that authors talk past one another. To the extent that a real conversation has emerged, it largely concerns legal imperialism/US legal transplants.[51] Authors tend to seek to downplay the importance of US actors in the development of legal clinics in Europe and aim to establish the European credentials of CLE. While US authors obsess over the scale and appropriateness of American involvement, European authors are overly keen to justify and promote the growth of CLE in Europe by reference to the local context. However, this conversation somewhat misses the point that great changes are taking place in European legal education and legal practice, and CLE is intimately bound up in these changes. The simple question that commentators have universally failed to ask is: *"What does the emergence and growth of CLE mean for European law teaching and practice?"* This is the leading research question that we intend to address in this volume and which will be central to the set of queries addressed by our contributors.

[49] Philip M. Genty, *Overcoming Cultural Blindness in International Clinical Collaboration: The Divide Between Civil and Common Law Cultures and Its Implications for Clinical Education*, 15 (1) CLINICAL L. REV. (2008); Leah Wortham, *Aiding Clinical Education Abroad: What Can Be Gained and The Learning Curve on How to Do So Effectively*, 12 CLINICAL L. REV. 615 (2006); Wilson, *supra* note 30 at 421, 428; Emilija S. Karajovic, *ABA/CEELI's Clinical Legal Education Programme in Serbia*, 4 INT'L. J. CLINICAL LEGAL EDUC. (2004); Steven Austermiller, *ABA/CEELI's Law Clinic Programmes in Croatia*, 3 INT'L. J. CLINICAL LEGAL EDUC. (2003); John M. Burman, *The Role of Clinical Legal Education in Developing the Rule of Law in Russia*, 2 WYO. L. REV. 89 (2002); Lawrence M. Grosberg, *Clinical Education in Russia: "Da and Nyet,"* 7 CLINICAL L. REV. (2001); Stephan Anagnost, *The Challenge of Providing High Quality, Low Cost Legal Aid for Asylum Seekers and Refugees*, 12 INT'L. J. REFUGEE L. 577 (2000); Rodney J. Uphoff, *Why in-House Live Client Clinics Won't Work in Romania: Confessions of a Clinician Educator*, 6 CLINICAL L. REV. 315 (1999); James C. May, *Creating Russia's First Law School Legal Clinic*, 23 VERMONT BAR J. L. DIGEST 43 (Aug. 1997); and C. Nicholas Revelos, *Teaching Law in Transylvania: Notes from a Different Planet*, 45 J. LEGAL EDUC. 597 (1995). For an overview of this literature, see Chapter 1 by Philip Genty in this volume.

[50] See, e.g., Bartoli, *supra* note 42; Askamovic, Genty, and Stege, *supra* note 48; Askamovic and Genty, *supra* note 13; Berbec-Rostas, Gutnikov, and Namyslowska-Gabrysiak, *supra* note 34; Blázquez-Martín, *supra* note 46; Paris and Donnelly, *supra* note 46 at 1067; and Bucker and Woodruff, *supra* note 46 at 575.

[51] See, e.g., Richard J. Wilson, *Beyond Legal Imperialism: US Clinical Legal Education and New Law and Development*, in THE GLOBAL CLINICAL MOVEMENT: EDUCATING LAWYERS FOR SOCIAL JUSTICE (Frank S. Bloch, ed., Oxford University Press 2010), 135 ss.

In 2014, the European Network for Clinical Legal Education teamed up with a Member of the European Parliament (Cécile Kyenge) to embark on a survey-based project aimed at mapping CLE in Europe (i.e. identifying which legal clinics are currently in operation and what activities they are engaged in).[52] As useful as this preliminary effort may be, particularly for engaging the EU in the promotion of CLE, what is also needed is a systematic scholarly review of CLE in Europe – specifically in the context of reforming the teaching and practice of European law, especially as it relates to EU law, ECHR law, and international law – that goes beyond merely the tracing of history and mapping of current practice and reflects normatively on these developments and places them in the broader context of reforming legal education and legal practice in Europe.

AIMS AND STRUCTURE

The major aim of the volume is to deepen our theoretical understanding of the rapid diffusion of CLE and measure its impact on the teaching and practice of law in Europe. In other words, we are interested in exploring how CLE is transforming law teaching and practice in Europe. Other, ancillary aims are to promote self-reflection in European legal education, to disseminate new ideas about legal education and research to build a case for European law clinics, and to do so well beyond traditional academic audiences.

To unpack the multifarious phenomenon of CLE in Europe, we have asked leading clinicians and practitioners based and active across the continent to share their experience in their individual chapters.[53] Therefore, in addition to a first introductory set of chapters setting the historical scene, the second part builds upon the experiences and reflections of leading clinicians in Europe. To frame their contributions and align them to the aims pursued by this volume, our contributors have followed a set of questions – that were originally organized in the form of a survey. This served to structure their contributions, thus facilitating comparability and learning.

METHODOLOGY

To further deepen our methodological reflection, we have encouraged each contributor to the volume to address the growing European phenomenon of CLE as if it were a biological process. At a first glance, given its major indebtedness to the United

---

[52] Bartoli, *supra* note 42.
[53] To make the edited volume coherent, the scope has been limited to contributions from clinicians and practitioners based in Europe and engaged (broadly speaking) in the teaching and practice of EU, ECHR, and international law. Clinics with a domestic focus were included only so far as they are engaging, to some extent, with supranational and international law and legal institutions. Clinics focusing *purely* on domestic law fall beyond the scope of this volume.

States, the phenomenon of CLE in Europe (certainly Central and Eastern Europe) may be seen as a process of transplantation of that model to other parts of the world.[54] Even in Western Europe, as the chapters of this volume will reveal, the indebtedness to the United States cannot be denied. When examined from this perspective, there appears to be merit when addressing our initial research question (i.e. how CLE is transforming legal education in Europe), to reflect on two questions:

- How is the practice and theory of CLE adapting in European soil ("adaptation")?
- What are the fruits of the emerging, "Europeanized" CLE practice ("blossoming")?

The *adaptation* inquiry serves us to explore how CLE (as it is understood today), which, at least historically, is not a European practice, is transforming itself in order to thrive. In particular, we are interested in examining several questions: How have/are European clinics adopting aims, models, structures, or methods or engaging in issues which are context-specific (endogenous or unique to Europe)? Are they embracing European institutions and European issues? Are they forming European networks and pursing Pan-European collaboration? How are they adapting CLE to fit the demands of European legal education? Is the resulting model(s) of CLE characterized by convergence, divergence, or hybridization?

The *blossoming* question, in turn, aims at gauging the transformative impact CLE is having on legal education in Europe. We ask the following questions: Are clinics training better lawyers and thus satisfying the legal market's demand? Are they manufacturing "European"/"international" lawyers (as opposed to domestic ones)? Are they changing what it means to be a "domestic" lawyer? Are they facilitating the globalization of the market for legal education? Are they transforming the role and self-identity of European law schools and European legal teaching? Are they instilling values, such as social justice, in students in a way that was not done in the past?[55]

In the individual contributions to this volume, the phenomena of CLE's adaptation and blossoming are explored by trying to situate CLE in Europe within a number of ongoing and variously overlapping discourses, narratives, and processes that form the background context to the emergence of CLE in Europe. These include:

- The Europeanization and internationalization of domestic legal fields (i.e. law and legal practice)
- The emergence of supranational and international jurisdictions and tribunals
- The emergence of a European and global market for legal education

---

[54] See, e.g., Wilson, *supra* note 51, at 135 ss; Wortham, *supra* note 49; Austermiller, *supra* note 49; Burman, *supra* note 49; Uphoff, *supra* note 49; May, *supra* note 49; and Revelos, *supra* note 49.

[55] This largely coincides with what Frank Bloch defines as "socially relevant legal education." *See*, Frank S. Bloch, ed. THE GLOBAL CLINICAL MOVEMENT: EDUCATING LAWYERS FOR SOCIAL JUSTICE (Oxford University Press, 2010), xxii.

- Increasing demands for relevance in law school education
- The emergence of a CSR/service learning/community engagement ethic within European higher education institutions
- Increased focus on innovation and practical skill-based education within European higher education institutions

The purpose of this list of themes, to be treated as a set of hypotheses, is to nudge European clinicians to objectify whether the justifications, aims, drivers, and catalysts behind the process of clinic formation fit within or emerge from the identified ongoing discourses, narratives, and processes. It also aims at gauging the extent to which an advocate of CLE may strategically rely on these discourses or take advantage of these process to advance CLE in Europe.

MAJOR THEMES/HYPOTHESIS IN EUROPEAN CLINIC FORMATION

To clarify the meaning of the themes that we identified as hypotheses to be tested by our contributors as they reflect on their own individual clinic formation, this section offers an introductory analysis for each of those narratives. By creating a common language throughout the volume, they enable collective reflection and feed into the concluding remarks contained in the final chapter.

The Internationalization and Europeanization of Domestic Legal Fields

Law has gained growing international recognition and effect over the past few decades. It is almost a truism to observe that the legal system continues to undertake profound transformations in a world where national borders are less important than ever (they no longer exist in most of the EU) and the interconnectedness of societies is part of daily life.[56] As international law has expanded from its traditional subjects and sources, thus penetrating the national sphere, domestic law continues to increasingly converge amid regulatory cooperation efforts.[57] This phenomenon, often referred to as the *internationalization of law*, reveals important features of the contemporary legal system.[58] First, legal problems are no longer neatly confined to national jurisdictions, exclusively governed by domestic law. International law increasingly controls what might have been previously labelled as purely internal or domestic situations. In this way, state sovereignty is continually

---

[56] For a first substantial treatment of law and globalisation, see D. M. Trubek, Y. Dezalay, R. Buchanan, and J. R. Davis, *Global Restructuring and the Law: Studies of the Internationalization of Legal Fields and the Creation of Transnational Arenas*, 44 CASE WESTERN RESERVE L. REV. 407–98 (1994).

[57] Jonathan B. Wiener and Alberto Alemanno, *The Future of International Regulatory Cooperation: TTIP as a Learning Process Toward a Global Policy Laboratory*, LAW AND CONTEMPORARY PROBLEMS (2015).

[58] For a theory of legal globalization, *see* W. Twining, GENERAL JURISPRUDENCE– UNDERSTANDING LAW FROM A GLOBAL PERSPECTIVE (Cambridge University Press, 2009).

undermined. Second, principles, norms, and rules emanating from diverse sources and operationalized by a panoply of public and private actors at local, national, regional, and global levels populate a complex and globalized legal world. Third, this process of internationalization occurs – although to a different extent – within and across legal fields, such as commercial, environmental, human rights, financial, criminal, and labour law.[59] As such, it contributes to the development of a postnational law characterized by different actors, sources of law, and modes of operation.[60] As stated, "internationalization is a process of operationalization of the law accomplished by diverse actors in multiple territories."[61]

By calling into question the idea of law as a coherent system of norms within a given national jurisdiction, internationalization raises ontological questions for the law. These have to do with its authority and the proliferation of its sources, as well as of its fragmentation. As such, internationalization of law is prone to generate two major problems: first, the emancipation of entire subsystems (e.g. niche areas and emerging practices of law) from the traditional legal framework, and, second and consequently, a loss in the predictive value of the legal system (as its subsystems provide different, often dissonant responses).[62]

Today's internationalization of law affects all dimensions of the legal system, whether it is in law teaching, legal research, legislation, regulation, or – as illustrated in the following section – adjudication.

As a result, any lawyer, regardless of the geographical scope of her practice, is increasingly expected to work and research across countries and regions with differing legal traditions. It appears indisputable that, given the rapid internationalization of domestic legal fields, it is no longer possible to teach consumer law, tax law, or environmental law, to name just a few, without at least some basic notions of international law. Yet the progressive internationalization of the law has not been followed up by a parallel internationalization of legal education.[63] In other words, the traditional legal curriculum has not been denationalized.

The imperative for mainstreaming nondomestic sources of law into the legal curriculum appears all the more self-evident when examined from the perspective of the EU. The approximation of the member state national legal orders both at the procedural and substantive levels as a result of European integration has led not only to an expansion of EU law, but also to a compenetration of the EU and national legal orders. Given the intertwined nature of national and EU law, it appears artificial

---

[59] Snyder, *supra* note 2, at 627 (arguing that some legal fields have always been more internationalized than others).
[60] For a nuanced perspective on the impact of globalization on legal thought, *see* Ralf Michaels, *Globalization and Law: Law Beyond the State* in LAW AND SOCIAL THEORY (Banakar and Travers, eds., Hart Publishing, 2013).
[61] Marcelo Dias Varella, INTERNATIONALISATION OF LAW (Springer 2014), 1.   [62] *Id.*
[63] Jürgen Basedow, *Breeding Lawyers for the Global Village – the Internationalisation of Law and Legal Education*, in THE INTERNATIONALISATION OF LEGAL EDUCATION, THE FUTURE PRACTICE OF LAW (William van Caenegem and Mary Hiscock, eds., Edward Elgar 2015).

today (as well as ill-considered) to learn about national law without discussing the nature, function, constitutional and institutional system, general principles, and method of interpretation of EU law. Today EU law affects virtually all areas of the national legal systems, including constitutional and administrative law and private law, as well as criminal law.

Yet, despite the deeply existential and legally well-defined bond between national and EU law, most law schools in Europe still present EU law as an autonomous, detached discipline that is often offered as an elective.[64]

Some resistance against the mainstreaming of international and EU law may have to do with their potential to question domestic legal systems. These legal orders oblige the lawyer to be critical via-à-vis her own domestic systems: both international and EU law may act as a sword and as a shield against national legal system.[65]

What is more, the internationalization of the law is in turn shaping the practice of the law. The late 1980s into the early 2000s saw extensive international expansion among large American and English law firms. The Table 1 illustrates the incredible rate of internationalization among six leading global law firms. Across the six firms, there was an average of more than a 300% increase in the number of foreign offices between 1987 and 2016.

If the legal system can no longer be taught along jurisdictional lines, it is not only because domestic law and international law are difficult to distinguish today, but also because the international legal practice of Big Law does not really care about national categories and boxes. Thus, for example, the practice of international

TABLE 1 *International Expansion among Large UK/US Corporate Law Firms*[66]

Firm	Number of Foreign Offices			
	1987	2002	2016	% Increase – 1987 to 2016
Baker & MacKenzie (US)	30	68	69	+130
Clifford Chance (UK)	12	33	34	+183
Jones Day (US)	5	29	24	+380
Freshfields (UK)	4	28	26	+550
Sidley & Austin (US)	3	8	10	+233
Skadden & Arps (US)	2	22	14	+600

[64] For a notable exception, see Nicole Kornet, *Future-Minded Legal Education in Europe: The European Law School*, MEPLI Working Paper Series 2013-10.
[65] See Chapter 4 by Maxim Tomoszek in this volume.
[66] J. Faulconbridge, J. Beaverstock, D. Muzio, and P. Taylor, *Global Law Firms: Globalization and Organizational Spaces of Cross-Border Legal Work*, 28 (3) NORTH WESTERN J. INT'L. L. & BUSINESS 459 (2007–2008); *See also* J. Beverstock et al., *The Long Arm of the Law: London's Law Firms in a Globalising World Economy*, A 31 ENVIRONMENT AND PLANNING (1999); and J. Bauman, PIONEERING A GLOBAL VISION: THE STORY OF BAKER & MCKENZIE (Gilberts Law Summaries, 1999).

contract law has witnessed a progressive internationalization[67] over the years and is prompting domestic laws to reform themselves so as to accommodate the new dominant practices.[68]

The internationalization of law is also producing new legal professions. Today, any individual who is expected in her day job to produce legal products and regard herself as jurist should be considered a legal professional. The new legal professions include compliance officers, regulatory affairs specialists, and in-house lawyers, as well as policy-makers and legal consultants (e.g. tax experts, lobbyists, regulatory affairs).

Our hypothesis, which is explored by the individual contributions to this volume, is that CLE in Europe, has emerged in part as a response to this process of internationalization. By confronting law students with the reality of legal practice in all its complexity, CLE is at the forefront of a reimaging within legal teaching that aims to produce lawyers who are better equipped to operate as translators at the domestic level between international norms and domestic legal systems, institutions, and bureaucracies. By exposing students to an increasingly multisource and transdisciplinary "law in action," CLE may contribute to the denationalization of the law curriculum. This may in turn provide global fluency to young lawyers and upgrade legal education to reflect legal reality.

(See in particular Chapter 10 by Anthony Valcke, Chapter 4 by Veronika Tomoszková and Maxim Tomoszek, Chapter 11 by Eva Brems and Stijn Smet, and Chapter 7 by Ulrich Stege and Maurizio Veglio to explore this theme further.)

The Emergence of Supranational and International Jurisdictions and Tribunals

More than a century ago, The Hague Convention on the Pacific Settlement of International Disputes established the Permanent Court of Arbitration, the first standing state-to-state dispute settlement system in history. Since then, the creation of international and supranational courts has been advancing rapidly. Today, we count more than twenty permanent international courts and tribunals that solve disputes between states, sometimes international organizations, and whose decisions are binding between the parties.[69] On top of those courts, there are least seventy other international institutions that exercise judicial or quasi-judicial functions.

---

[67] *See, e.g.*, Francisco Orrego Vicuña, OF CONTRACTS AND TREATIES IN THE GLOBAL MARKET I. THE PARADOXES OF GLOBAL CHANGE IN THE LAW : THE INTERNATIONALIZATION OF PRIVATE CONTRACTS (May Planck UNYB, 2004).

[68] The reform of French contract law of February 2016 was presented reinforcing its economic efficiency and its attractiveness. *See* Oxford Law Blog, The Transformation of French Contract Law, https://www.law.ox.ac.uk/news/2015-11-02-transformation-french-contract-law-government-decree-%E2%80%93-and-translated–english.

[69] *See, e.g.*, C. Romano, K. Alter, and Y. Shany, eds., THE OXFORD UNIVERSITY PRESS HANDBOOK OF INTERNATIONAL ADJUDICATION (Oxford University Press, 2014).

This rapid multiplication of international fora, which has been characterized by a lack of coordination, has given rise to a number of transformational effects not only on the practice but also on the nature of law.

The transnational judicial dimension of legal practice is today epitomized by the EU, a legal order characterized by a plurality of sources, judicial authorities, and the introduction of new modes of governance that have profoundly shaped the nature and practice of the law. This constellation is further complexified by the numerous agreements concluded by the EU with third countries as well as international organizations (such as the World Trade Organization [WTO]) that entail the operation of dispute settlement mechanisms, or by the existence of legal sources, also operationalized by dedicated judicial bodies, such as the ECHR.

This exceptional growth of the international judicial sector is raising new challenges for legal education both in Europe and elsewhere. In the old days, lawyers were expected to know how to litigate before national courts according to the relevant procedural rules, and a very small group of them might have been exposed to the application of private international law rules to determine the competent forum and applicable law. Only an elite group of lawyers knew about the existence, operation, and potential for legal practice and representation before international and supranational courts. Today, the multiplication of international and supranational courts has considerably changed the judicial ecosystem, and it has become expected that, for example, any European lawyer must understand the jurisdictional competences of different international courts such as the ECHR and the Court of Justice of the EU (CJEU) or master conflict of law rules in her daily practice. At the EU level, the establishment of the preliminary reference proceeding has democratized access to international court dispute settlement systems by rendering any European-based lawyer susceptible to plead a case before the CJEU.[70] Should a national judge refer a matter – be it on a point of interpretation or validity – before the CJEU, the lawyers in the main, national dispute may be called upon to represent their clients by presenting their observations in front of the "Supreme Court of the land." Analogously, at the level of the Council of Europe, a lawyer invoking the European Convention of Human Rights on behalf of a client before a domestic court could end up – after having exhausted all domestic remedies – representing her client in front of the ECHR in Strasbourg. While the judicial practice developed by both European Courts has inevitably paved the way to the establishment of dedicated communities of lawyers specializing in EU and ECHR law litigation, it remains common to witness nonspecialized, domestic lawyers to plead for the first – and in most cases last – time in front of these international courts.

But the internationalization of the judicial architecture is not only affecting the bar. Other actors, such as in-house lawyers, policy-makers (e.g. think of the agents

---

[70] See, e.g., Daniel Sarmiento, *Amending the Preliminary Reference Procedure for the Administrative Judge*, 2 (1) REVIEW OF EUROPEAN AND ADMINISTRATIVE LAW 29–44 (2009).

working for the EU institutions), and legal consultants (e.g. tax experts, lobbyists, regulatory affairs) are also increasingly exposed to rulings coming from different, multifarious judicial authorities.

Our hypothesis, which has been tested in the individual contributions to this volume, is that CLE in Europe in some way aims to embrace these changes to the legal system and, by exposing students to a multiplicity of fora, may familiarize current graduates with the many, often competing, judicial legal dispute settlement systems. In particular, by pursuing interaction with public authorities and supranational and international bodies, prompting strategic thinking on legal remedies and avenues, CLE can render students more comfortable with an increasingly multilayered and – as a result – multijurisdictional legal landscape.

(See in particular Chapter 14 by Juan-Pablo Pérez-León-Acevedo, Chapter 15 by Joost Pauwelyn and Mattia Salamanca Orrego, Chapter 16 André Nollkaemper and Hege Elisabeth Kjos, Chapter 12 by Renáta Uitz and Eszter Polgári, and Chapter 9 Alberto Alemanno and Lamin Khadar to explore this theme in more detail.)

The Emergence of a European and a Global Market for Legal Education

Educating law students to work in an increasingly global context is emerging as a challenge for traditional legal education. The history of legal education shows that teaching has relied on a model that – for more than a century of law school teaching – privileges theory over practice but also domestic law over international law. Even today, law schools provide minimal opportunity for students to study abroad, acquire language fluency, and learn how to apply the practical problem-solving skills critical to becoming a competent lawyer in real-world settings.[71] Traditionally, European law schools focus on defining and teaching the content of the law and leave the practice-related study to postgraduate courses or apprenticeships, whereby practicing lawyers, sometimes judges, share information about how to practice law, in most case through informal interaction.

Amid the implementation of the Bologna Process and the pervasive internationalization of the legal market, some changes are, however, taking place today. Those reflect the need of both internationalizing, professionalizing, and rendering more practical the legal educational experience. A few incipient signs suggest the emergence of a European and a global market for legal education.

First, European law schools are progressively embracing – over the years – a two-degree model with the bachelor's level education focusing on domestic law (and aimed at preparing for the national bar) and the master's level concentrating on providing a legal specialization (e.g. EU law, tax law, or intellectual property law). By targeting essentially nationals, the legal education market at the bachelor's level remains domestic, whereas that of legal masters has increasingly become a European and international market.

---

[71] See, e.g., Gene R. Shreve, *History of Legal Education*, 97 (2) HARVARD L. REV. 597–606 (1983).

Amid the emergence of numerous LLM programmes across Europe,[72] the ensuing competition among European law schools' master's programmes has led some observers to qualify this process as a form of Americanization of legal education.[73] Indeed, historically, European top (or at least wealthy) law graduates – predominantly from continental Europe – have been admitted to US LLM programmes (initially established by Ivy Leagues law schools) to gain an exposure to the US legal system. This remains the case today. An LLM from a top US law school is one of the credentials certifying the pedigree of the "global lawyer" and is, as such, one of the must-haves that "indicate elite status in the market for legal advice around the world."[74] Yet if having an international LLM degree used to be a guarantee of employability, today – amid a significant commodification of legal masters' programmes[75] – more is required from a young, entry-level lawyer to impress the hiring partners.

In the meantime, an increasing number of European law schools compete to attract law students from all over the continent and beyond and invite them to spend one academic year gaining an exposure to a new legal order and/or a particular field of law. The growth of the domestic market for LLM has to do with the fact that, in some European jurisdictions, the "master of laws" has become the basic professional degree for admission into legal practice (e.g. Spain, Denmark, Sweden, Cyprus, Italy, and Switzerland). That LLM market is, however, predominantly international[76]: there is considerable mobility among European LLMs. We should note, however, that while LLMs are extremely valuable to law school budgets in the United States and the United Kingdom, this is less the case in continental European countries.

Second, as the knowledge and skill-set required in the legal profession are changing, the legal curricula – in particular those of LLM programmes – increasingly reflect the demand of "Big Law," that is, large multinational commercial law firms.[77] They – either directly (via sponsorships, moot courts, etc.) or indirectly (via their hiring procedures) determine the content and scope of legal training during and prior to the apprenticeship stage.[78]

---

[72] Poiares Maduro, *supra* note 6, at vi.   [73] *Id.*
[74] Carole Silver, *The Variable Value of U.S. Legal Education in the Global Legal Services Market*, 24 GEORGETOWN J. LEGAL ETHICS 1 (2011).
[75] Poiares Maduro, *supra* note 6 at vi (citing more than one hundred European law schools offering some form of LLM open to foreign students).
[76] There exist around 1,000 LLM programmes worldwide, according to the Study Portals Intelligence.
[77] "Big Law refers to the enormous, multi-national law firms – firms that have globalized in every sense of the word – and the economic power they exert in every country in which they operate. These law firms manage the legal aspects of gigantic corporate mergers and acquisitions; they litigate and arbitrate before domestic and international bodies for stakes involving billions of dollars." See Richard J. Wilson, *Practical Training in Law in the Netherlands: Big Law Model or Clinical Model, and the Call of Public Interest Law*, 8 (1) UTRECHT LAW REVIEW 179 (2012).
[78] Silver, *supra* note 74.

International law firms seem to have identified a set of common characteristics and credentials that define a "global lawyer": or at least a lawyer for the future. In the UK, consortiums of large law firms, each taking on up to one hundred trainee lawyers a year, have recently come together to develop their own "accelerated" legal practice course (the accelerated LPC – which one of the authors, Lamin Khadar, graduated from) which all of their recruits are required to undertake.[79] Similarly, in the Netherlands, fourteen large firms came together to create the "Law Firm School" in 2009 to provide vocational training to their recruits.[80] These training programmes have been devised to provide, in tandem with the apprenticeship period they are linked to, an extensive socialization period for young commercial lawyers. The sponsoring firms also seek to make the vocational stage of legal education (for their recruits) more relevant to commercial law practice.

The selective, elitist nature of these forms of legal training combined with their corporate focus seem to largely neglect the broad societal commitments that should drive the activities of all lawyers, in particular those who wield the most influence.

The time seems ready to change legal education drastically. This appears all the more true should one consider that the internationalization of the teaching and practice of law is also producing new legal professions. If, until a few decades ago, a legal professional was essential an attorney, notary, or in-house lawyer, today we see an expansion of the definition of the legal profession. One can consider that all individuals whose normal day job produces legal products (objective criterion) and who regard themselves as jurist (subjective criterion) may be considered Legal Professionals. When framed under these new terms, the demand for legal education appears redefined.

Whatever the case, European CLE literature points towards the Bologna Process as a major source of inspiration (or justification) for change.[81] Many authors see CLE as an answer to the Bologna Process's call for "increased attention to competences and skills in university education: so that graduates may better participate in the economy and society following graduation."[82] This is the hypothesis that our contributors test in their individual chapters.

(See in particular Chapter 6 by Xavier Aurey, Chapter 14 by Juan-Pablo Pérez-León-Acevedo, Chapter 16 by André Nollkaemper and Hege Elisabeth Kjos, Chapter 9 by Alberto Alemanno and Lamin Khadar, and Chapter 7 by Ulrich Stege and Maurizio Veglio to explore this theme in more detail.)

---

[79] See, e.g., Freshfields Bruckhaus Deringer, Herbert Smith Freehills, Hogan Lovells, Norton Rose or Slaughter and May, see http://www.bpp.com/accelerated-lpc (25/11/2015).

[80] Wilson, supra note 77 at 178–79. See also http://thelawfirmschool.nl/ (25/11/2015).

[81] See e.g., Hovannisian, supra note 46; Bucker and Woodruff, supra note 46 at 575; Paris and Donnelly, supra note 46 at 1067; Blázquez-Martín, supra note 46; Perelman, supra note 46 at 89.

[82] Id.; see also Bucker and Woodruff, supra note 46 at 614–17.

Increasing Demands for Relevance in Law School Education

CLE blossomed in the United States in the 1960s and 1970s during the so-called second wave of the CLE movement.[83] The fact that interest in CLE reached boiling point during the tumultuous 1960s and 1970s is far from coincidental. The riotous spirit of these decades seized law students, law teachers, and law schools. There were increased demands for relevance within legal education in light of the civil rights movement and, *inter alia*, the work of the US National Association for the Advancement of Colored People (NAACP) Legal Defense Fund (culminating in *Brown v. Board of Education*).[84] In the words of one commentator, there was at the time "a desire on the part of a significant number of law students to help make the law serve the needs of the poor."[85] A leading figure in the CLE movement, Arthur Kinoy, writing in 1969, put it another way. There was, in his view, a crisis gripping American legal education; a crisis which left no major law school untouched and revealed itself in the form of "deep malaise, boredom, frustration, and dissatisfaction."[86] Students apparently began to question the relevance of law school to such an extent that many of them even dropped out. He described the crisis in these terms: "How can law and a profession whose life is based upon law's existence, remain relevant to the pressing and fundamental problems of contemporary American society."[87]

In response to this crisis, he implored legal educators of the day to "tak[e] on major cases and situations involving the relationship of the processes of the law to the fundamental problems of contemporary society."[88]

These demands for greater relevance continued and evolved in the subsequent years as a consequence of the work of Ralph Nader, which aimed at bringing accountability to the unwieldy and Kafkaesque US agencies and the corporations they were mandated to regulate.[89] During this period, clinical programmes began to specialize, moving separately into the civil rights, consumer rights, environmental rights, and poverty rights movements (collectively "the public interest law movement"). These demands for relevance were felt not only in law schools but also within the profession. The public interest law movement inspired elite law students across the country, and public interest law firms[90] began to attract the best students

---

[83] Barry, Dubin, and Joy, *supra* note 24 at 12, 13.
[84] Brown v Board of Education of Topeka, 347 U.S. 483 (1954).
[85] Charles E. Ares, *Legal Education and the Problem of the Poor*, 17 (3) J. LEGAL EDUC. 310 (1965), cited in Barry, Dubin, and Joy, *supra* note 24 at 12.
[86] Arthur Kinoy, *The Present Crisis in American Legal Education*, 24 RUTGERS L. REV. 1 (1969).
[87] *Id.*, at 2, 3.   [88] *Id.*, at 7.
[89] Barry, Dubin, and Joy, *supra* note 24 at 12; see also Robert L. Rabin, *Lawyers for Social Change: Perspectives on Public Interest Law*, STANFORD L. REV. 207–61 (1976).
[90] Small, typically foundation-funded law firms promoting specific "public interests" such as the environment, minority rights, or the poor.

and sap the talent pool of large commercial law firms.[91] A 1969 memo from one law firm read:

> It has become increasingly evident that there is a tendency among younger lawyers, particularly those with highest academic qualification, to seek out public service-oriented careers as an alternative to practice in the larger metropolitan law firm.[92]

The firms responded by setting up *pro bono* programmes. One study suggested that, by 1973, at least twenty-four large US law firms had formalized *pro bono* programmes aimed at involving their lawyers, on a *pro bono* basis, in working for needy clients and public interest causes.[93] Some firms, such as Hogan & Hartson, even established entire public interest law departments with several full-time staff dedicated to *pro bono* work.[94] During the 1990s and through to the present day, such demands for relevance (which, it should be clear, do not arise only from students), far from disappearing, have resulted in the emergence of scores of international human rights clinics across the United States and across the globe.[95]

Turning now back to Europe, at least since the end of the past decade, we have a heightened sense of crisis that also penetrates our law schools to a palpable extent, among them the sovereign debt crisis, the migrant crisis, the terror threat, and the constant threat (now partial reality) of European disintegration: Brexit and Grexit. There are the crises *in* Europe and there is the crisis *of* Europe. Our hypothesis, which is tested in some of the contributions in this volume, is that as we pass through our very own tumultuous period in Europe (particularly but not exclusively in the form of the migrant crisis), students and law teachers are demanding greater relevance in law school education.[96] The economic crisis may not lead to boredom and malaise in European law school classrooms (far from it!), but it may have led to an increased concern with professionalization, securing jobs, and acquiring the practical professional experience valued by employers.[97] The migrant crisis might have led to greater demands for relevance in the form a desire on the part of many European law students and teachers to play a role, to help out, to get involved.[98] While the democratic and constitutional crisis, the crisis *of* Europe, may furnish

---

[91] Steve Allen Boutcher, The Institutionalization of Pro Bono Publico in Large Law Firms: An Analysis of the Causes and Consequences of Large Firm Pro Bono Programmes, Dissertation submitted in partial satisfaction of the requirements for the degree of Doctor of Philosophy in Sociology (2010), 22.

[92] *Id.*, at 22–23.

[93] Joel F. Handler, Ellen Jane Hollingsworth, and Howard S. Erlanger. LAWYERS AND THE PURSUIT OF LEGAL RIGHTS (Academic Press, 1978), 123.

[94] S. Cummings, *The Politics of Pro Bono*, 52 (1) UCLA L. REV. 36 (2004).

[95] Deena R. Hurwitz, *Lawyering for Justice and the Inevitability of International Human Rights Clinics*, 28 YALE J. INT'L L. 505 (2003);, Jocelyn Getgen Kestenbaum, Esteban Hoyos-Ceballos, and Melissa C. del Aguila Talvadkar, *Catalysts for Change: A Proposed Framework for Human Rights Clinical Teaching and Advocacy*, 18 CLINICAL L. REV. (2011).

[96] See esp. Chapter 7 by Ulrich Stege and Maurizio Veglio, Chapter 8 by Nora Markard, Chapter 9 by A. Alemanno and L. Khadar, and Chapter 10 by Anthony Valcke.

[97] *See* Chapter 13 by Lynn Welchman and Chapter 14 Juan-Pablo Pérez-León Acevedo in this volume.

[98] *See* Chapter 8 by Nora Markard and Chapter 7 by Ulrich Stege and Maurizio Veglio in this volume.

students with a greater desire to understand the EU and how it works in practice,[99] we suspect that CLE in Europe may be arising in response to such demands for greater relevance, or at the very least, capitalizing on them for its growth.

(See in particular Chapter 8 by Nora Markard, Chapter 3 by Marzia Barbera, Chapter 13 by Lynn Welchman, and Chapter 7 by Ulrich Stege and Maurizio Veglio to explore this theme in more detail.)

The Emergence of a CSR/Service Learning/Community Engagement Ethic within European Higher Education Institutions

The idea that universities produce knowledge for the sake of knowledge alone, that academics as a whole are monks residing in cloisters or sheltered elites hiding away in ivory towers is untenable and has always been untenable. Universities have been intimately bound up with the respective societies in which they found themselves from the very beginning, serving public needs and private interests.[100]

Whether you call it community engagement, service learning, the third mission or even CSR, in their modern form, such practices in Europe began in the 1960s and '70s, when we have many examples of community engagement across Europe.[101] Particularly in the field of law, as noted earlier, we can find the *rechtswinkels* or law shops in the Netherlands and Belgium, the *Juss Buss* or law bus in Norway, and even fully fledged legal clinics in the UK during this period.[102] But also beyond law there was the "science shop" movement developed in the Netherlands and deployed throughout Europe whereby academics acted as consultants to community groups with specific questions in the context of community problem-solving.[103]

However, the 1980s saw modernization and rationalization within higher education, and value engagement beyond the university was increasingly defined in financial terms such that engagement with the private sector, with business, or with the organized public sector (hospitals, local governments, etc.) began to be

---

[99] See Chapter 10 by Anthony Valcke and Chapter 9 by Alberto Alemanno and Lamin Khadar in this volume.

[100] P. Benneworth and M. Osborne, Knowledge engagement and higher education in Europe, 2014, 219; Paul Benneworth and Lynne Humphrey, *Universities' Perspectives on Community Engagement*, in UNIVERSITY ENGAGEMENT WITH SOCIALLY EXCLUDED COMMUNITIES (Paul Benneworth, ed., Springer Netherlands 2013), 165–87.

[101] P. Benneworth and M. Osborne, Knowledge engagement and higher education in Europe, 2014, 220; Juliet Millican and Tom Bourner, *Student-Community Engagement and the Changing Role and Context of Higher Education*, 53 (2/3) EDUCATION+ TRAINING 89–99 (2011); Hans G. Schuetze, *Universities and Their Communities: Engagement and Service as Primary Mission*, in HIGHER EDUCATION AND CIVIC ENGAGEMENT (Lorraine McIlrath and Ann Lyons, eds., Palgrave Macmillan US, 2012), 61–77.

[102] *Supra* note 33.

[103] Loet Leydesdorff and Janelle Ward, *Science Shops: A Kaleidoscope of Science–Society Collaborations in Europe*, 14 (4) PUBLIC UNDERSTANDING OF SCIENCE 353–72 (2005); Henk Mulder, et al., *Science Shops as Science-Society Interfaces*, in INTERFACES BETWEEN SCIENCE AND SOCIETY (Greenleaf Publishing, 2006).

prioritized over other forms of engagement.[104] This trend, to an extent, continues to this day, where innovation, employability, and research impact dominate discussions around university objectives beyond the core functions of knowledge production and dissemination.[105] The Bologna Process and the REF system, discussed further later, are examples of this trend.

Nevertheless, in varying degrees and in different ways, the imperative to engage with local communities and civil society in a constructive way has filtered into the objectives of universities at both regional and domestic levels across Europe.[106] Engagement might happen in the form of research collaboration, service provision, knowledge exchange in the form of capacity building, or teaching beyond the university.

Our hypothesis is that, in some way, the idea of community engagement can and has in some cases served as a narrative to justify CLE in Europe and win support from university administrations.[107] We believe that, to some extent, clinicians may be relying on these narratives strategically to pursue the institutionalization of law clinics at their respective universities. Alternatively, these higher education missions might inspire law teachers to set up clinics.

(See in particular Chapter 5 by Maria Marquès, Chapter 11 by Eva Brems and Stijn Smet, and Chapter 7 by Ulrich Stege and Maurizio Veglio to explore this theme in more detail.)

Increased Focus on Innovation and Practical Skill-Based Education within European Higher Education Institutions

In apparent contradiction with the European member states' traditional resistance to any harmonization policy in education, the Bologna Process declared that

> the European process, thanks to the extraordinary achievements of the last few years, has become an increasingly concrete and relevant reality for the Union and its citizens ... we are witnessing a growing awareness in large parts of the political and academic world and in public opinion of the need to establish a more complete and

---

[104] P. Benneworth and M. Osborne, Knowledge engagement and higher education in Europe, 2014, 220.

[105] Rómulo Pinheiro, Patricio V. Langa, and Attila Pausits, *The Institutionalization of Universities' Third Mission: Introduction to the Special Issue*, 5 (3) EUROPEAN JOURNAL OF HIGHER EDUCATION 227–32 (2015); Arend Zomer, and Paul Benneworth, *The Rise of the University's Third Mission*, in REFORM OF HIGHER EDUCATION IN EUROPE (Jürgen Enders, ed., Sense Publishers, 2011) 81–101; Magnus Gulbrandsen and Stig Slipersaeter, *The Third Mission and the Entrepreneurial University Model*, in UNIVERSITIES AND STRATEGIC KNOWLEDGE CREATION (Andrea Bonaccorsi and Cinzia Daraio, eds., Edward Elgar Publishing, 2007), 112–43.

[106] P. Benneworth and M. Osborne, Knowledge engagement and higher education in Europe, 2014, 222–24; Stefano Paleari, Davide Donina, and Michele Meoli, *The Role of the University in Twenty-First Century European Society*, 40 (3) THE JOURNAL OF TECHNOLOGY TRANSFER 369–79 (2015).

[107] See Chapter 5 by Maria Maquès i Banqué, and Chapter 11 by Eva Brems and Stijn Smet in this volume.

far-reaching Europe, in particular building upon and strengthening its intellectual, cultural social and scientific and technological dimensions.[108]

The Bologna Declaration seeks to create a "European space for higher education" with three main goals: international competitiveness, mobility, and employability. Despite the declared ambition, such a Declaration does not lead to an harmonization of higher education in Europe as such, but rather intends to promote transparency via comparability of educational curricula so as to increase the mobility of students and professors. In particular, it recognizes the link between education and employment, and it presents its reforms as a way to increase the labour market for graduates in a "globalized market for a high-grade work force."

It is generally recognized that the Bologna Process not only opened a space to introduce practical approaches into traditional legal education, but, more importantly, it also contributed to put on the agenda – and therefore instil into legal academia – the urgent need for better preparation of students.[109] Due to the traditional reluctance of European legal academia to rethink and reform the legal curricula existing across European countries, the Bologna Process had the effect of opening a Pandora's Box : should the law schools limit themselves to teaching domestic law or also other legal systems? Should students study in their own native language or a foreign one? How can schools better prepare students for the market of the legal professions?

Our working hypothesis is that the Bologna Process, by the mere fact of asking this set of questions, has played a role in preparing the ground for the dissemination of CLE in Europe. We believe that, to some extent, clinicians have borrowed this language in order to "sell" their CLE project to their universities, or at least have indirectly benefited from the new Zeitgeist instilled by the Bologna Process.

(See in particular Chapter 6 by Xavier Aurey and Chapter 16 by André Nollkaemper and Hege Elisabeth Kjos to explore this theme in more detail.)

CONCLUSION

Legal education is a subject that is more often practiced than reflected upon. This is all the more so in Europe, where legal academia demonstrated a historical reticence to engage in self-reflection, self-critique, and soul-searching. Despite its rapidly changing landscape, European legal academia proved extremely resilient in protecting its traditional legal curriculum and teaching methods against disruptive and pervasive phenomena such as digitalization. "Who should I become and why?" or "how should I teach and why?" are both questions that have traditionally been set

---

[108] Bologna declaration, 1998.
[109] See, e.g., Frans J. Vanistendael, *Blitz Survey of the Challenges for Legal Education in Europe, Symposium: Emerging Worldwide Strategies in Internationalizing Legal Education*, 18 DICKINSON J. INT'L. L. 457 (2000).

aside in European legal education in favour of "what should I learn?" and "what should I teach?"

Yet, as epitomized by the emergence of CLE – first in Central and Eastern Europe, then in the West[110] – some transformations are occurring in the legal curricula which suggest that the time is ripe for more collective introspection in European legal education.

The developments are not fortuitous and seem to respond to significant changes in the European academic and professional legal fields. We have witnessed the ascendance of powerful and highly legalized supranational European and international institutions which seem capable of providing solutions but often remain distant, undecipherable, and apparently unaccountable to ordinary citizens and those at the bottom of the power pyramid. This dynamic has fostered (and perhaps demands) a new brand of European legal practitioners and academics who are more inclined towards seeing legal practice and scholarship as a form of civic engagement or political activism, mediating between ordinary citizens (and noncitizens), pressing political and social issues, and the power centres in Brussels, Strasbourg, Luxembourg, and Geneva.[111]

On the demand side, the internationalization and Europeanization of national legal orders in Europe and the attendant regionalization and globalization of legal practice is drastically changing what it means to be a practicing lawyer in Europe and the requisite skill-set that is needed (e.g. multilingualism, multijurisdictionalism).[112]

The globalization of legal education in Europe is placing pressure on law schools to revise their teaching practices and student offerings to stay competitive on the international market.[113] Within the academic job market, this process has resulted in intensified competition, especially at the top schools, which has given rise to a highly cosmopolitan, innovative, and entrepreneurial class of legal academics who are keen to learn from other parts of the globe and experiment with novel pedagogies.

---

[110] See Chapter 1 by Philip Genty in this volume.
[111] Lamin Khadar, *University Law Clinics and the Growing Demand for EU Law*, Open Society Foundation Voices, www.opensocietyfoundations.org/voices/university-law-clinics-and-growing-demand-eu-law; and Alberto Alemanno, Public Interest Lawyering as Vocation, 1st Falcon Public Lecture, Leuven University, December 2014.
[112] Poiares Maduro, *supra* note 6; Aalt Willem Heringa, *European Legal Education or Legal Education in Europe [editorial]*, 18 (3) MAASTRICHT JOURNAL OF EUROPEAN AND COMPARATIVE LAW 221–22 (2011).
[113] See Karsten Schmidt, *New Challenges for Law Faculties: The View of a Private Law School*, 6 (1) EUROPEAN JOURNAL OF LEGAL EDUCATION 4, 5 (2011); Vincenzo Ferrari, *Doctoral Education in an International Perspective*, 5 (2) EUROPEAN JOURNAL OF LEGAL EDUCATION 10 (2009); Marie-Luce Paris-Dobozy, *Challenging Exchange Programmes: Studying the Common Law and Civil Law Systems in a Joint Law Degree*, 5 (1) EUROPEAN JOURNAL OF LEGAL EDUCATION 47, 49, 56 (2009); Simon Marginson, and Marijk van der Wende, *Europeanisation, International Rankings and Faculty Mobility: Three Cases in Higher Education Globalisation*, OECD, IN CENTRE FOR EDUCATIONAL RESEARCH AND INNOVATION, HIGHER EDUCATION TO 2030, VOLUME 2: GLOBALIZATION (Paris, 2009), 110; and Carel Stolker, RETHINKING THE LAW SCHOOL: EDUCATION, RESEARCH, OUTREACH AND GOVERNANCE (Cambridge University Press, 2014), 267–68.

Simultaneously, there is increasing salience in the European public consciences of the complex crises that entangle our societies (financial and economic, social and political) and that give rise to demands for increased relevance in law school teaching. Last, but not least, it is widely recognized that the Bologna Process not only opened a space to introduce practical approaches into traditional legal education, but, more critically, it also contributed to put on the agenda the urgent question of how better to prepare students for the market of the legal professions.

We submit at the beginning of this volume that all of these processes and structural adjustments are central to understanding the emergence of the European CLE movement. They both sustain the movement and offer glimpses of what it could achieve. Growing out of this context, Europe's new legal clinics seem capable of radically reinventing traditional European approaches to legal education and practice. Through the European clinical movement, spurred on by this restructuring of the European legal field, European legal teaching – historically formalistic, doctrinal, hierarchical, and passive[114] – is coming under increasing pressure to reimagine itself as pragmatic, policy-aware, and action-oriented.

As CLE is emerging as a badly needed bridge between teaching and the practice of the law, as well as between academia and society, this volume provides a sense of the new directions undertaken by a growing community of entrepreneurial academics.

The following chapters bring to light valuable legal education realities that, due to their innovative and therefore antagonistic nature to mainstream education, have not attracted yet the attention they deserve.

---

[114] Ball and Dadomo, *supra* note 21.

PART I

Where Have We Come from and What Have We Learned?

Reflections on the First Wave of Clinical Legal Education in Europe (Mid-1990s to Mid-2000s)

1

Reflections on US Involvement in the Promotion of Clinical Legal Education in Europe

Philip M. Genty

What is the influence of the United States on European clinical legal education? The first reaction of many would be that this is not a particularly difficult question to answer. After all, clinical legal education is largely a US invention. Although one can find early examples of clinics in European law schools,[1] the large-scale development of law school clinical education happened in the United States beginning in the 1960s.[2] At present, there are clinical programs in each of the 207[3] American Bar Association (ABA)-approved US law schools. The Clinical Legal Education Association now lists 1,325 clinical teachers in its membership directory.[4] So how could the United States *not* be a major influence on clinical legal education in Europe and elsewhere?

This chapter will suggest, however, that the story is more complicated than it might at first appear: in the most visible areas – especially funding – the US contributions have had less of an impact than commonly thought. But, at the same time, the USA has contributed in ways that are both subtler and more enduring.

The chapter proceeds as follows. Section I recounts some of the history of US support for European clinical legal education, particularly in Central and Eastern Europe. Section II describes the failure of many US-supported programs to achieve sustainability and the ensuing temporary decline of clinical legal education in Europe. Section III describes the "rebirth" of European clinical education in Central and Eastern Europe and discusses its spread to Western Europe, which has

---

[1] For example, the University of Tilburg in the Netherlands had a version of a law clinic as early as 1969. See Richard J. Wilson, *Clinical Legal Education in Dutch Legal Culture: Clashes of Tradition, Tolerance and Progress in Global Law's Capital*. Digital Commons@American University Washington College of Law, Working Paper 1-1-2010, p. 29. In addition, Edwin Rekosh cites even earlier examples in Copenhagen, Denmark, and Rostock, Germany. See Edwin Rekosh, *Constructing Public Interest Law: Transnational Collaboration and Exchange in Central and Eastern Europe* (hereinafter "Rekosh, *Constructing Public Interest Law*"), 13 UCLA J. INT'L L. & FOREIGN AFF. 56, 84 (2008).
[2] See J. P. "Sandy" Ogilvy, *CLEPR's 40th Anniversary: Papers and Speeches from the AALS-ABA-CLEA Celebration of CLEPR: Celebrating CLEPR's 40th Anniversary: The Early Development of Clinical Legal Education and Legal Ethics Instruction in US Law Schools*, 16 CLINICAL L. REV. 1, 9–18 (Fall 2009).
[3] See www.americanbar.org/groups/legal_education/resources/aba_approved_law_schools.html.
[4] See www.cleaweb.org/ClinicianLocator.

been due, at least in part, to the delayed, indirect effects of earlier US efforts. Section IV concludes with reflections about the value of US contributions, past and future.

THE "UNITED STATES INVASION": US SUPPORT FOR EUROPEAN CLINICAL LEGAL EDUCATION IN THE LAST YEARS OF THE TWENTIETH CENTURY

The years after the fall of the Berlin Wall brought a flood of US funding and academic visits. The Ford Foundation, the American Bar Association Central and East European Law Initiative[5] (ABA-CEELI), and the Soros-funded foundations provided significant funding. The support was not limited to clinical legal education but extended to legal education more broadly. The Chair of the ABA Section of International Law during this period describes CEELI's contributions:

By the end of 1992, CEELI had:

- conducted 27 technical assistance workshops in Bulgaria, Romania, the Czech and Slovak Republics, Poland, Hungary, Yugoslavia, Albania, Lithuania, Armenia, Russia, Ukraine, Belarus, and Kazakhstan;
- held 4 legal training seminars;
- assessed over 120 draft laws from 17 different countries;
- placed 21 long-term Liaisons and 25 Legal Specialists in the field, from Brno to Bishkek;
- hosted 41 law school deans from Central and Eastern Europe at 120 US "sister law schools";
- coordinated with the Soros Foundation in placing 27 students from the former Soviet Union in LLM programs in the United States; and
- employed over 600 American lawyers and judges as CEELI volunteers.[6]

A significant portion of the support went to clinical legal education programs. Edwin Rekosh, founder and former Executive Director of PILnet (which was then the Public Interest Law Initiative in Transitional Societies, or PILI) summarizes the combined work of these funders: "Collectively, the clinical programs supported by these three donors numbered well over one hundred in the roughly 25 post-communist countries. The Soros network alone supported the development of 75 university-based clinics in Central and Eastern Europe and the former Soviet Union between 1997 and 2002."[7]

In addition to funding clinical programs, these donors hosted a number of academic conferences focusing on clinical legal education. PILnet was particularly

---

[5] This name was later changed to reflect a shift in geographical focus. See infra note 18.
[6] James R. Silkenat, *The American Bar Association and the Rule of Law*, 67 SMU L. REV. 745, 751–52 (2014) (citations omitted).
[7] See Rekosh, *Constructing Public Interest Law*, supra note 1, at 88 n. 101.

active. In collaboration with the Constitutional and Legal Policy Institute (COLPI) of the Soros Foundation, PILnet organized a series of annual colloquia in the US (1998), Poland (1999), Bulgaria (2000), and Latvia (2001).[8] These were wonderfully well-attended – for example, the 2000 colloquium in Sofia and Varna, Bulgaria, drew fifty-seven participants from nineteen countries, in addition to the American facilitators.[9] PILnet also organized a number of smaller regional conferences and training sessions. I participated in many of these,[10] as did other US clinical law teachers. In addition to these formal gatherings, there was a literal invasion of American academics, both clinical and doctrinal, spending their sabbaticals in Europe or doing study visits there. Upon their return, many wrote about their interactions with European faculty members and students.[11] Indeed, a survey of clinical teachers lists 50 faculty members from 35 different law schools who have taught in Central and Eastern Europe.[12]

---

[8] *See* Leah Wortham, *Aiding Clinical Education Abroad: What Can Be Gained and the Learning Curve on How to Do So Effectively* (hereinafter "Wortham, *Aiding Clinical Education Abroad*"), 12 CLINICAL L. REV. 615, 621 n. 20 (2006).

[9] *See* Colloquium Program, on file with the author.

[10] Workshop and Meetings on Clinical Legal Education, Tbilisi State University, Faculty of Law, Tbilisi, Georgia, April 2009; Skopje Conference on Clinical Education, Republic of Macedonia, November 2008; "Developing University-Based Legal Clinics in Serbia and Montenegro: Workshop for Clinical Teachers," University of Belgrade Faculty of Law, April 2006; "2004 Intensive Teacher Training for New Clinical Educators: Pedagogical Challenges of Supervision," Faculty of Law Justinianus Primus, Ss. Cyril and Methodius University, Skopje, Republic of Macedonia, November 2004; Intensive teacher training: "Developing Live-Client Clinics: Challenges and Strategies," Belgrade, Serbia and Montenegro, April 2004; "2003 Intensive Teacher Training: Incorporating Practical Experience into the Clinical Classroom and Techniques of Self-Critique," Prague, Czech Republic, November 2003; Clinical Legal Education Interactive Teaching Methods Training, Belgrade, Serbia, and Montenegro, May 2003; "Reforming Legal Education with Special Emphasis on Legal Clinics," Osijek, Croatia, May 2003; Workshop on Clinical Legal Education, Tirana Law School Legal Clinic, Tirana, Albania, March 2001; Meeting on Clinical Legal Education for the Countries of the Former Yugoslavia, Ohrid, Macedonia, November 2000.

[11] *See, e.g.*, John Burman, Teaching in Russia: You Don't Know What You've Got Till It's Gone, WYOMING LAWYER (June 1999); George A. Critchlow, *Teaching Law in Transylvania: Notes on Romanian Legal Education*, 44 J. LEGAL EDUC. 157 (1994); Lawrence M. Grosberg, *Clinical Education in Russia: "Da and Nyet"*, 7 CLINICAL L. REV. 469 (Spring 2001); Jeremy T. Harrison, *Legal Education in an Eastern European Law School*, 7 JOURNAL OF INTERNATIONAL LAW AND PRACTICE 263 (1998); Katalin Kolláth and Robert Laurence, *Teaching Abroad: Or, "What Would That Be in Hungarian?"* 43 J. LEGAL EDUC. 85 (1993); James C. May, Creating Russia's First Law School Legal Clinic, VERMONT BAR JOURNAL & LAW DIGEST, August 1997; William D. Meyer, *Remnants of Eastern Europe's Totalitarian Past: The Example of Legal Education in Bulgaria*, 43 J. LEGAL EDUC. 228 (1993); C. Nicholas Revelos, *Teaching Law in Transylvania: Notes from a Different Planet*, 45 J. LEGAL EDUC. 597 (December 1995); Lee Dexter Schnasi, *Globalizing: Clinical Legal Education: Successful Under-Developed Country Experiences*, 6 T.M. COOLEY J. PRAC. & CLINICAL L. 129 (2003); Rodney J. Uphoff, *Why In-House Live Client Clinics Won't Work in Romania: Confessions of a Clinical Educator*, 6 CLINICAL L. REV. 315 (Fall 1999).

[12] *See* Compilation of Clinical Law Teachers with International Teaching or Consulting Experience, compiled by J. P. "Sandy" Ogilvy, Columbus School of Law, The Catholic University of America (originally compiled by Roy T. Stuckey, Faculty Emeritus, University of South Carolina). Updated: February 27, 2012, www.law.edu/res/docs/INTERNATIONAL_TEACHING_Survey_revo8-23 -12.pdf.

A particularly fruitful international collaboration is the partnership between Columbus School of Law of the Catholic University of America and the Jagiellonian University in Kraków, Poland. The collaboration began in 1992 and expanded in 1997, with the help of a Ford Foundation grant.[13] The two schools now cooperate in American law certificate and LL.M. programs taught by Catholic University faculty, primarily in Jagiellonian University's facilities in Poland.[14]

With the support of funding and American consultants, many clinical programs were established in Central and Eastern European countries. In Chapter 2, Katarzyna Ważyńska-Finck describes this history in detail.[15] This growth of clinical education was largely confined to Eastern Europe, however, with the exception of the United Kingdom. Western (Continental) European countries were much slower to adopt clinical education as part of their curricula.[16]

The late 1990s and early 2000s were therefore a boom period for the infusion of US resources into clinical legal education programs in Central and Eastern Europe. But as in any "boom-and-bust" cycle, everything changed very suddenly. Funding priorities shifted, and the money began to move to other regions, including Asia,[17] Africa, and Latin America.

The Soros-funded Open Society Institute announced this shift in its 2002 annual report:

> The Open Society Institute and the Soros foundations network in 2002 pushed forward with geographic diversification and intensified efforts in public policy advocacy. Increased diversification and advocacy were accompanied by significant funding cutbacks in certain regions, namely, the Central European countries that are candidates for accession to the European Union (EU) in 2004 and Russia.... Cutbacks in these regions ... were made because we believe that our efforts have largely found fertile ground.[18]

The 2002 report also described the launch of the Open Society Justice Initiative, "a legal program with global reach that replaces the regional legal reform programs

---

[13] See Wortham, *Aiding Clinical Education Abroad*, supra note 8, at 619.   [14] See id. at 620.
[15] Hereinafter "Wazynska-Finck, *Poland as the Success Story of Clinical Legal Education.*"
[16] See Richard J. Wilson, *Western Europe: Last Holdout in the Worldwide Acceptance of Clinical Legal Education*, 10 GERMAN LAW JOURNAL 825 (2009). For discussions of the reasons for the greater enthusiasm for clinical legal education in the East, see Ważyńska-Finck, *Poland as the Success Story of Clinical Legal Education*, Chapter 2 in this volume; and Dubravka Akšamović and Philip Genty, *An Examination of the Challenges, Successes and Setbacks for Clinical Legal Education in Eastern Europe* (hereinafter "Akšamović and Genty, *Clinical Legal Education in Eastern Europe*"), 20 INT'L J. CLINICAL LEGAL EDUC. 427, 429–30 (2014).
[17] One indication of this shift was that ABA-CEELI, formerly the Central and Eastern European Law Initiative, became the Central European *and Eurasian* Law Initiative. See Silkenat, *The American Bar Association and the Rule of Law*, supra note 6 at 747.
[18] Soros Foundations Network 2002 Report, BUILDING OPEN SOCIETIES, 14, https://www.opensocietyfoun dations.org/sites/default/files/a_complete_report_0.pdf.

of the Constitutional and Legal Policy Institute" [COLPI].[19] The 2002 report included discussions of regional work in Africa, Southeast Asia, and the Americas.[20]

By 2007, the Justice Initiative could boast of having "assisted in the development of university-based legal clinics ... in more than 50 countries in Africa, Eastern Europe, Latin America, the Middle East, Southeast Asia, and the former Soviet Union."[21] Among the projects supported by the Open Justice Initiative was the First Southeast Asia Clinical Legal Education Training of Trainers Workshop in 2007.[22] This broader mission, paid for out of the same limited pool of funding, meant that less money was available for the European educational programs that had previously depended on this support.[23]

Like the Open Society Institute, PILnet began to shift its focus away from Europe. Although the organization continues to be involved in Central and Eastern Europe, it expanded to China in 2003 and now has offices in Hong Kong and Beijing.[24]

The immediate effect of this shift in priorities was profound. As discussed in the next section, with the loss of funding, many of the new clinical programs in Central and Eastern European law schools proved to be unsustainable.

EARLY PROMISE UNFULFILLED: THE INITIAL DECLINE OF CLINICAL LEGAL EDUCATION AFTER THE WITHDRAWAL OF US FUNDING

A central goal of the US efforts described in Section I was to effect a lasting transformation of European legal education through the creation of sustainable clinics at European law schools. But the loss of outside funding revealed the fragility of the new European clinical "infrastructure." Many of the clinical programs that had been established in the late 1990s and early 2000s failed to survive.[25] No catalogue of the clinical programs that were started during that period has been created, so it is impossible to document precisely which of the programs ceased to exist. Without these data, it is also impossible to know for certain why many programs failed while others continued to function.

What we do know is that Poland was one country where clinics continued to flourish despite the shifts in funding. In Chapter 2 Katarzyna Ważyńska-Finck

[19] Id. at 15. See also Patricia M. Wald, Launching the Justice Initiative, OPEN SOCIETY JUSTICE INITIATIVE 2003 ACTIVITIES REPORT 6.
[20] Soros Foundations Network, supra note 18.
[21] OPEN SOCIETY JUSTICE INITIATIVE REPORT ON DEVELOPMENTS 2005–2007, 9, https://www.opensociety foundations.org/sites/default/files/developments_20071221.pdf.
[22] See Bruce Avery Lasky and Shuvro Prosun Sarker, Introduction: Clinical Legal Education and Its Asian Characteristics, in CLINICAL LEGAL EDUCATION IN ASIA: ACCESSING JUSTICE FOR THE UNDERPRIVILEGED 8 (Shuvro Prosun Sarker ed. 2015).
[23] The 2002 annual report explicitly acknowledged as much. See Soros Foundations Network, supra note 18.
[24] See www.pilnet.org/public-interest-lawyers.html.
[25] See Rekosh, Constructing Public Interest Law, supra note 1, at 88.

describes some of the factors for the sustainability of Polish clinical legal education.[26]

For other countries, several reasons may be offered for the failure of many clinics to survive the loss of outside funding. The first and most obvious reason is that many universities proved unwilling to pay for clinical legal education. Once outside resources were withdrawn, universities often declined to assume responsibility for funding and staffing the clinical programs.

Second, many of the clinics were dependent on particular individuals, typically young, junior faculty with a special interest in clinical legal education. These individuals attended the international conferences described in Section I and actively engaged with colleagues from the United States. They were committed to the clinical teaching mission, but this commitment did not necessarily extend to the rest of the law faculty. If these individuals left their positions at the university, there was no guarantee that anyone would take their places in the clinics.[27] In addition, some of the clinical teachers did not have formal academic status, especially those who had come to the universities from nonprofit, nongovernmental organizations (NGOs). Their jobs in the law faculty depended on "soft money" from outside funding sources; when the funding ended, the jobs did as well.

Third, because professors in many European countries are not admitted to practice law, European "live-client" clinics in these countries must hire private attorneys to handle the court proceedings in clinic cases. These lawyers need to be paid, and the universities were likewise unwilling to pick up this expense once the outside funding ended. Thus, these clinics could no longer function. Some were transformed into simulation programs in which students worked in the classroom with materials from actual past cases that were no longer active, but some simply ended.

Fourth, some of the clinics that were created existed in name only. I remember vividly one visit to an Eastern European country where our group was proudly led to the "new clinic." This consisted of a single, shiny, expensive new room, complete with the latest computers and a large collection of books, but with not a single student or client in sight. Further conversation revealed that the "clinic" was a kind of "Potemkin Village," designed to impress foreign visitors and attract additional funding that could be diverted for other purposes. Once the funding was no longer available, there was no need to keep such "clinics" open.

---

[26] See Wazynska-Finck, *Poland as the Success Story of Clinical Legal Education*.

[27] Edwin Rekosh describes the first attempt to establish a law clinic at Palacký University, Olomouc, Czech Republic as one such example. The original clinic was dependent on a supportive dean who passed away, which led to the demise of the clinic. See Rekosh, *Constructing Public Interest Law*, supra note 1, at 87–88, n. 98. The story has a happy ending, however, because the clinic was eventually reborn and has continued to thrive. See also Veronika Tomosková and Maxim Tomoszek, *The Clinical Programme at the Law School of Palacký University in Olomouc*, Chapter 4 in this volume; and Akšamović and Genty, *Clinical Legal Education in Eastern Europe*, supra note 16, at 433.

Fifth, and perhaps most important, the American models that were "transplanted" failed to take account of the significant structural and cultural differences between the United States and Europe, particularly the distinct common law and civil law traditions in which legal education in the United States and Europe, respectively, is grounded.[28] Beyond legal culture, an important practical difference between the US and European systems is that clinical legal education is not typically part of the formal, doctrinal European law curriculum. This means that law clinics are treated as a kind of extracurricular activity for both professors and students: professors teach clinics on an "overload" basis (i.e. in addition to their already demanding doctrinal classroom responsibilities), and students do not receive academic credit for the clinic. As Edwin Rekosh has observed,

> Even where law school administrators appreciate the intensive supervision demands of a clinic, and the pedagogical value associated with it, they generally do not have the resources or are not willing or able to fight the necessary political battles to decrease other demands on the time of the professors involved.[29]

The loss of outside funding made it less likely that supporters of clinical legal education in European universities would have the resources to fight these battles.

In short, on the basis of the experiences just described, one might conclude that the influence of the United States on European clinical legal education has been much less than is commonly believed. The most visible sources of potential US influence – funding and educational consultants – failed to have a direct, lasting impact on European legal education. Much of the early growth of European clinical education that occurred in the 1990s and 2000s was reversed once the outside foundation funding moved to other regions. But, as discussed in Section III, that turned out not to be the end of the story.

THE INDIRECT US ROLE IN THE RESURGENCE OF CLINICAL LEGAL EDUCATION IN EUROPE

Just as a fire is not truly extinguished while a few embers continue to glow, the European clinical legal education movement, though diminished, did not actually die with the end of outside US foundation funding. Or, to use another metaphor, seeds had been planted, and these soon began to bear fruit.

---

[28] For an examination of these differences and the way they play out in the context of clinical legal education, *see* Philip M. Genty, *Overcoming Cultural Blindness in International Clinical Collaboration: The Divide Between Civil and Common Law Cultures and Its Implications for Clinical Education* (hereinafter "Genty, *Overcoming Cultural Blindness*"), 15 CLINICAL L. REV. 131 (Fall 2008). For a discussion of additional differences between the US and European clinical education, *see* Akšamović and Genty, *Clinical Legal Education in Eastern Europe*, *supra* note 16, at 435–36.

[29] *See* Rekosh, *Constructing Public Interest Law*, *supra* note 1, at 89.

While the influence of US funding and clinical consultants had failed to have the hoped-for *direct* impact on European legal education, there were at least three *indirect* impacts that were actually more meaningful and lasting. First, while law clinics, especially "live-client" clinics, at first failed to take hold, this was not true of interactive teaching methods. The interactive techniques modeled by clinical teachers and others in international conferences and training sessions excited the European educators who were exposed to them. The European faculty members who had experienced only the lecture as a teaching method saw the potential for a more dynamic classroom experience. They began to experiment with interactive teaching methods in their doctrinal classes, and they saw how engaged the students became. While lecturing surely continued to be an important teaching technique, the more innovative teachers began to mix their lectures with more interactive methods and saw how much the students benefited from this new classroom experience.[30]

The second important indirect US influence was perhaps even more significant. The interactions between US clinical educators and their European counterparts had enduring benefits:

> [T]he support provided in the 1990s and 2000s by outside organizations (Ford Foundation, ABA, OSI, PILnet, etc.) planted seeds of "human capital" – the law teachers and *students* who attended the conferences and workshops have become an energetic new generation of clinical educators ...[31]

A third benefit, which is related to the second, is that the conferences and workshops that the US clinical educators conducted for European teachers enabled the Europeans to meet each other and create their own networks. This was probably most obvious in Poland, which from a very early stage had some clinical programs in schools throughout the country. In Chapter 2, Katarzyna Ważyńska-Finck describes the 20-year history and current vibrant status of clinical legal education in Poland.[32] The international conferences gave the Polish teachers an opportunity to connect with one another, and this led to a strong national community of clinical educators.[33]

I was privileged to be involved in two such Polish conferences. In 2004, along with a number of US colleagues, I participated in the Third International Conference organized by the Global Alliance for Justice Education (GAJE) in Kraków, Poland.[34]

---

[30] For a discussion of the distinction between "clinical education" and "interactive teaching" and the adoption of the latter in European legal education, *see* Genty, *Overcoming Cultural Blindness*, *supra* note 28 at 146–49.
[31] Akšamović and Genty, *Clinical Legal Education in Eastern Europe*, *supra* note 16, at 436–37.
[32] *See* Ważyńska-Finck, *Poland as the Success Story of Clinical Legal Education*, Chapter 2 in this volume.
[33] For a detailed description of the activities of this community, *see* Ważyńska-Finck, *Poland as the Success Story of Clinical Legal Education*, Chapter 2 in this volume.
[34] *See* conference report, www.gaje.org/wp-content/uploads/2011/01/GAJE-Conf04-Report.pdf.

Although forty-three countries were represented, the conference brought together educators from law schools throughout Poland. The conference gave them the opportunity to establish or renew acquaintances and, most significantly, created an opportunity for exchanging teaching materials and stimulating the development of additional collaborative projects.

In 2007, two Columbia colleagues and I conducted workshops for the VIIIth Annual Colloquium on Clinical Legal Education in Poland at the University of Bialystok.[35] As with the GAJE conference, the colloquium brought together educators from universities throughout Poland. The majority of the participants were Polish, but there were a number of attendees from other European countries, including the Czech Republic, Armenia, Georgia, Kyrgyzstan, Moldova, and Ukraine. Again, I was able to observe the ways in which the gathering created "spaces" (both literally and figuratively) for important professional collaboration, community-building, and spirited social interaction among the Polish educators.

These benefits were not limited to the Poles, however. For teachers from other countries, the cross-national exchanges that occur at these international conferences have had similar value. For example, the relationships that developed at these conferences were probably a significant factor contributing to the eventual birth of the European Network for Clinical Legal Education (ENCLE), which is discussed later. In addition, the international conferences and workshops exposed European educators to the interactive, small-group model that is characteristic of American clinical conferences and gave these educators the experience of working together in intensive exercises and discussions focused on pedagogy. Many of these European educators then went on to host their own national, inter-European, and even international conferences.

For example, through a project co-funded by the EU's European Social Fund and the state budget of the Czech Republic, the faculty of Palacký University, Olomouc, hosted a series of three conferences on practical legal education, including clinical teaching, legal ethics, and skills training, in 2008, 2011, and 2012. These conferences were primarily for educators from the Czech Republic, as well as some other European participants, but several of my US colleagues and I were also invited to participate.[36] Because of the success of these conferences, Palacký University was ultimately chosen to host the 12th International Journal of Clinical Legal Education Conference in 2014.[37] The history of the clinical program and the impressive array of

---

[35] See Colloquium Report, www.fupp.org.pl/en/legal-clinics/conferences/173-viiith-annual-colloquium-on-clinical-legal-education-in-poland. Some of my US colleagues had participated in earlier colloquia. See, e.g., report on Fifth Annual Colloquium on Clinical Legal Education, Warsaw, Poland, 2002, www.fupp.org.pl/en/legal-clinics/conferences/172-2002-fifth-annual-colloquium-on-clinical-legal-education-15-16-november-2002-warsaw-poland.

[36] See, e.g., description of project and 2012 conference, http://lawforlife.upol.cz/en/.

[37] See conference brochure, http://unn-mlifi.newnumyspace.co.uk/school_of_law/IJCLE/documents/brochure.pdf.

curricular offerings that are part of that program are discussed in this volume in Chapter 4 by Veronika Tomosková and Maxim Tomoszek.[38]

The indirect influence of the United States in stimulating the development of European clinical legal education has therefore been profound and, it appears, lasting. It is important to note, however, that this was helped along significantly by forces that were purely European.

First and foremost is the "Bologna Process," which has transformed European legal education. Lusine Hovhannisian has described the Bologna Process as follows:

> In June 1999, the European Ministers of Education adopted the Bologna Declaration, in which the signatory countries pledged to reform the structures of higher education systems in a "convergent" way. Since the goal of the Bologna Process is to bring about convergence in higher education, including higher legal education, it has direct implications not only for the structure of legal education but also for its methodology and content. The Declaration seeks to create a "European space for higher education" ... with three main goals: international competitiveness, mobility and employability. The Declaration and the reforms it promotes focus not on the harmonization of higher education in Europe as such, but rather on the transparency necessary to increase the mobility of students and professors. It places great importance on the need for institutes of higher education in Europe to become more competitive internationally, so as to better rival American universities. It further recognizes the link between education and employment, casting the suggested reforms as a way to increase the labor market for graduates in a "globalized market for a high-grade work force."[39]

Additional requirements of the Bologna Process are "the introduction of a credit transfer system ... and other methods of encouraging student mobility, support for the mobility of faculty and staff, emphasis on European cooperation in quality assurance, and promotion of European dimensions in higher education itself."[40]

Hovhannisian's description highlights three aspects of the Bologna Process that have contributed to the development of interactive teaching generally and clinical legal education specifically in European law schools. First, linking education to the labor market means that a part of legal education must be focused on preparing students for the legal profession they will be entering. This is, of course, a central mission of clinical legal education.

Second, the adoption of the Bologna reforms, which apply throughout Europe, has stimulated the spread of interactive teaching and clinical education to Western Europe. Western European universities have had to modify their legal education

---

[38] See Veronika Tomosková and Maxim Tomoszek, *The Clinical Programme at the Law School of Palacký University in Olomouc,* Chapter 4 in this volume.

[39] Lusine Hovhannisian, *Clinical Legal Education and the Bologna Process,* PILI Papers, Number 2, Dec. 2006, at 5 (citations omitted), www.pilnet.org/public-interest-law-resources/25-clinical-legal-education-and-the-bologna-process.html. *See also* Laurel S. Terry, *The Bologna Process and Its Impact in Europe: It's So Much More than Degree Changes,* 41 VAND. J. TRANSNNAT'L 107 (2008).

[40] *See* Lusine Hovhannisian, Clinical Legal Education and the Bologna Process, *supra* note 39.

programs to remain competitive internationally. This has created an incentive to implement more innovative courses and interactive teaching methods that are designed to engage students and prepare them for global law practice. The past decade has therefore seen a significant growth in the number of clinical programs at Western European law schools.[41]

The third contribution of the Bologna Process is more subtle. The creation of a credit transfer system and the encouragement of student mobility have meant that classes for these "exchange students" must be taught in a common language. That language is typically English, and this makes it more likely that English-language teaching materials from the United States, the United Kingdom, and other common law countries will find their way into the curriculum. This creates a kind of "stealth" infiltration of US and common law approaches to teaching. The wide use of a common language also makes it easier to conduct intra-European teaching conferences.

Paralleling the role of the Bologna Process has been the "Europeanization" of legal systems through membership in the EU. The possibilities of a "European Law School" and a "European Common Law" were discussed in Western Europe as early as 1992,[42] but with the wave of Central and Eastern Europe countries joining or applying for EU membership since 2004, "Europeanization" has extended throughout this region as well.

But beyond the influence of Bologna and the European Union, an exciting development in European legal education has been the birth of a European-based clinical education community. This began in Poland and was initially concentrated in Central and Eastern Europe, but it has now spread throughout Europe.[43] The most visible manifestation of this trend was the founding, in 2012, of ENCLE, which now boasts more than 140 members from 30 countries.[44] ENCLE was built on the successful international networking model of GAJE.

European clinical teachers now host their own conferences, train their own teachers, publish their own resource materials, and develop their own clinical models. The US efforts of the 1990s and 2000s surely contributed in important ways to this process. So what conclusions can be drawn about the overall value of the past involvement of the United States in European clinical legal education? And is there still a role for the United States? These questions are taken up in the concluding section.

---

[41] The Western European clinical programs profiled in this volume provide vivid illustrations of this.
[42] See Jutta Brunnée, *The Reform of Legal Education in Germany: The Never-Ending Story and European Integration*, 42 J. LEGAL EDUC. 399, 423–26 (1992).
[43] The present volume describes a diverse array of clinical programs in Belgium, the Czech Republic, Finland, France, Germany, Hungary, Italy, the Netherlands, Poland, Spain, Switzerland, and the United Kingdom.
[44] See www.encle.org/membership-directories/mdir. See, also, PILnet Welcomes the European Network for Clinical Legal Education, 3 October 2012, www.pilnet.org/project-updates/166-pilnet-welcomes-the-european-network-for-clinical-education.html.

REFLECTIONS ON THE VALUE OF US INVOLVEMENT IN EUROPEAN CLINICAL LEGAL EDUCATION, PAST AND FUTURE

The foregoing discussion has described the ways in which the extensive US funding and consultative resources that were poured into Central and Eastern European legal education in the 1990s and 2000s yielded fewer *direct* benefits than might have been expected and, perhaps, than is commonly understood. Although clinical programs were established throughout the region, many of these did not survive when the outside funding ended and the consultants left.

What are the lessons from this? For one, those of us who were involved in these efforts probably did not spend enough time preparing ourselves *culturally*. We did not learn enough about the differences between US and European legal education and law practice. As a result, we sometimes focused on subjects that were of limited relevance to our audience. For example, there was an emphasis placed on the value of allowing students to take responsibility for cases even though the countries in which we were working did not have anything like our American student practice orders and were unlikely ever to move in this direction.

In addition, our choices of the specific skills we taught were probably misplaced.[45] The training sessions and exercises we designed focused on the dynamics of the attorney–client relationship, including developing interviewing and counseling skills, achieving an empathetic relationship with clients, and preparing for adversarial proceedings. However, these are *not* the skills at the core of European law practice, where the emphasis is more on presenting a case in writing to a judge who controls the flow of information. We probably should have been concentrating more on research, drafting of documents, and presentation skills, all of which are more relevant to practice in the inquisitorial civil law system.

On a practical level, we also failed to take sufficient account of the structural differences between European and US legal education. As discussed in Section II, in contrast to the United States, the European law curriculum is dominated by required doctrinal courses, which are dictated by the government departments responsible for higher education. This leaves little room for elective clinical courses. In addition, neither faculty nor students necessarily receive any credit for these courses. Furthermore, teaching loads in Europe are typically much heavier than in the United States,[46] and class size, at least in the European public universities, is also much larger. These factors make the highly individualized teaching that is characteristic of US clinical teaching difficult, if not impossible. European clinical education therefore needs to be structured around these practical constraints.

---

[45] For additional discussion of this point, including a summary of an exchange between the European and American co-authors, see Akšamović and Genty, Clinical Legal Education in Eastern Europe, *supra* note 16, at 434–36.

[46] For example, a European friend and colleague recently told me that she is expected to teach fifteen classroom hours *per week*. Most of my US colleagues would find this unimaginable.

Finally, there is no doubt that some of the funds were wasted on unnecessary clinical "infrastructure" (e.g. gleaming new spaces that actually served few, if any, functions). Funders probably paid too much attention to the physical aspects of law clinics and not enough to the development of the less visible "human capital" that has been such a crucial factor in the recent revival and growth of clinical legal education throughout Europe.

On the other hand, the *indirect* benefits show that some of the funds were very well spent indeed. The funds that paid for conferences and workshops exposed European teachers to interactive teaching methods that they were able to introduce in their own classroom teaching. In addition, the conferences and workshops created opportunities for interactions between the US and European educators and among the Europeans themselves. This "planted the seeds" for a new generation of European clinical teachers who had been inspired by what they had experienced in the conferences. Moreover, the interactions among the Europeans created new networks that have subsequently ripened into a vibrant European clinical teaching community. This community continues to thrive and embark on exciting, new – and distinctly European – models of clinics and clinical education.

Two noteworthy examples of such European clinical models are Roma rights clinics and the more recent EU law clinics. These models are distinctive because of their transnational character. Roma rights legal clinics are a type of human rights clinic, and, in that sense, they resemble other human right clinics throughout the world. But their distinctive feature is that they deal with a particular ethnic minority who experience economic and social hardship throughout Europe. Clinics on EU law, which have been initiated more recently, are distinctive in the way they address issues such as the free movement of EU citizens within the EU, the Common European Asylum System, EU human rights law, and EU consumer rights. EU clinics are discussed in Chapter 9.[47]

The European clinical programs have also been resourceful in adapting to some of the practical constraints imposed on them. For example, because of the general lack of student practice orders permitting students to appear and provide representation in judicial and administrative proceedings, European law schools have developed innovative "limited scope" models in which students provide legal advice and possibly draft documents for clients to use in their *pro se* appearances before the tribunals. A second approach is to have students work with NGOs, providing

---

[47] See the following chapters in this volume: Alberto Alemanno and Lamin Khadar, *The EU Public Interest Clinic and the Case for EU Law Clinics* (Chapter 9); Anthony Valcke, *The EU Rights Clinic at the University of Kent in Brussels* (Chapter 10); and Ulrich Stege and Maurizio Veglio, *On the Front Line of the Migrant Crisis: The Human Rights and Migration Law Clinic (HRMLC) of Turin* (Chapter 7). *See also* Lamin Khadar, Why the EU Should Take Note of the Europe's Newest Legal Clinics, October 2014, http://encle.org/news-and-events/news/25-why-the-eu-should-take-note-of-europe-s-newest-legal-clinics.

assistance on legislation and other matters in which the NGOs are involved.[48] The European programs have also made extensive use of the "street law clinic" model, in which law students teach practical legal concepts in secondary schools and other settings.[49]

Employing these and other approaches, clinical legal education programs have prospered throughout Europe. Much of the credit for this success goes to the Europeans themselves, but it is fair to say that the US efforts served as a catalyst for all that is happening today in European clinical legal education. On balance, then, the past involvement of US funders and clinical consultants had real value.

But what of the future? Is there still a role for the United States in European clinical legal education? The answer relates back to the benefits of the past collaboration between US and European clinical teachers. The Europeans learned from the Americans, but we surely learned from these exchanges as well. The Americans who worked with the Europeans were able to step outside our own environment and see ourselves in a fresh light. In responding to questions or explaining our teaching methods and goals to our European colleagues, we were able to understand ourselves better. And our colleagues often gave *us* ideas about how we might approach our own teaching and supervision differently. The experience was the equivalent of holding up a mirror and seeing one's own reflection in a new way.

I have experienced these benefits through my contacts with two different groups of clinical educators. The first group consists of legal academics who have added clinical teaching to their doctrinal teaching portfolio. It has been instructive to learn how they connect the theory about which they have written and taught throughout their careers to the practical context of the clinical courses and how they adapt their teaching styles to these different settings. These educators are also able to help the students see the relationships between their doctrinal and clinical courses.

The second group of clinical instructors are lawyers who came to clinical teaching from work in NGOs. I have admired the way they see their teaching as an extension of the activist work to which they have devoted their professional lives. Their approach to clinical pedagogy reflects this sense of mission.

Combining the experiences with these two groups of educators, I have been inspired by the example of people who "planted" new clinical models in an often hostile "soil." I have learned, or at least been reminded, that it is often necessary to adapt one's pedagogical goals to the particular environment in which one teaches.

---

[48] An example is the EU Clinic run jointly by NYU and HEC Paris, which is described in this volume. *See* Alberto Alemanno and Lamin Khadar, *The EU Public Interest Clinic and the Case for EU Law Clinics* (Chapter 9).

[49] *See, e.g., See* Veronika Tomosková and Maxim Tomoszek, *The Clinical Programme at the Law School of Palacký University in Olomouc*, Chapter 4 in this volume. *See also* Felisa Tibbitts, MANUAL ON STREET LAW-TYPE TEACHING CLINICS AT LAW FACULTIES PREPARED FOR CENTRAL AND EASTERN EUROPE, RUSSIA, THE SOUTH CAUCASUS, CENTRAL ASIA AND MONGOLIA, COLPI Paper No. 3 (Open Society Institute 2001).

More important, with the right sense of vision and motivation, it is *possible* to do so successfully. Many of my US colleagues have had similarly valuable experiences.[50]

This is why cooperation between clinical teachers in the United States and Europe continues to be so important for both parties. The Europeans have established a dynamic teaching community with a variety of clinical programs in schools throughout both the East and the West. But what they sometimes still lack is a self-conscious awareness of their own pedagogical choices and goals and the tradeoffs among these. And that is something we Americans, as outsiders, can give them. Just as the Americans profited from being able to see ourselves through the eyes of the Europeans and imagine other ways of approaching our work, the Europeans can derive important benefits from having this same experience. Ongoing collaboration is therefore to our great mutual advantage.

---

[50] See, e.g., Leah Wortham, *Aiding Clinical Education Abroad: What Can Be Gained and the Learning Curve on How to Do So Effectively*, 12 CLINICAL L. REV. 615, 623 n. 30 (2006) (citation omitted) (describing what she learned from working with several European colleagues and citing the similar experience of another US colleague).

2

Poland as the Success Story of Clinical Legal Education in Central and Eastern Europe

Achievements, Setbacks, and Ongoing Challenges

Katarzyna Ważyńska-Finck

Legal clinics as a method of teaching law and an important tool for social justice are an American invention,[1] which was received with lots of enthusiasm in Central and Eastern Europe in the past two decades. Curiously, it is the success of the clinical movement in the East (which would not be possible without US involvement and support)[2] that has contributed to the increased interest in clinics in the West.

This chapter discusses the history of clinical legal education (CLE) in Central and Eastern Europe by taking Poland as a case study. It sketches the specific context for the development of CLE in the region after the fall of communist regimes and analyses the degree of success measured by the sustainability of legal clinics.

The chapter scrutinizes both the reasons for the undoubted success in establishing legal clinics in Poland and the challenges and limitations CLE faces at present. The main focus will be on factors which have made clinics thrive and their impact on the teaching and practice of law. The chapter eventually makes a case for the Polish CLE experience as a scalable model and suggests a few avenues for further research and reflection.

THE 1990S: A TIME OF CHANGE AND INNOVATION

After the fall of the communist regimes and the decline of the Soviet Union, Central and Eastern Europe underwent fast and far-reaching changes, moving from centrally planned to free market economies and from authoritarian to democratic

---

[1] Czesław Znamierowski, a Polish legal philosopher, published in 1936 an article praising the idea of legal clinics and the role they could play in enhancing social justice. See Ł. Bojarski, *Społeczny aspect działania poradni*, in STUDENCKA PORADNIA PRAWNA. IDEA, ORGANIZACJA, METODOLOGIA (Fundacja Uniwersyteckich Poradni Prawnych, Warsaw 2005) at 1–16. E. Rekosh points to even earlier clinic-like projects in Europe in the nineteenth century. See E. Rekosh, *Constructing Public Interest Law: Transnational Collaboration and Exchange in Central and Eastern Europe*, 13 UCLA J. INT'L. L &. FOREIGN AFF. 83–84 (2008).

[2] *See* Chapter 1 in this volume.

governance. The role that lawyers could play in society during the transition increased significantly. The legal systems required profound changes, including the drafting of new democratic constitutions. The developing market economies necessitated not only new regulations, but also the services of lawyers proficient in corporate and commercial law. International law firms started to open their offices in the capitals of the region.

At the same time, radical free market reforms suddenly provoked high unemployment, which in turn fuelled growing social inequalities. Moreover, law students increasingly became aware of the challenges posed by the capitalist, competitive labour market. These new dynamics were combined with the rather hermetic attitude of local bar associations, which made it extremely difficult for the majority of law graduates to gain access to the bar.[3]

Simultaneously, education systems, including at the university level, were changing. Academic freedom rapidly replaced the ideological and institutional control of communist parties. However, according to some students and professors, the poor quality of teaching under communist rule could not be explained only by political pressure and censorship. It was the dominant academic culture which needed to be changed. The teaching methods were old-fashioned, based on lectures delivered to very big groups of students who were supposed to remain passive and absorb the purely theoretical knowledge. The relations between the faculty members and students were usually very distant and based on a strict hierarchy.[4] Critical thinking, including about the role of law and lawyers in society, was not encouraged.[5]

Many foreign organizations sought to facilitate the pro-democratic transition in Central and Eastern Europe through the provision of expertise, training, and funding. The assistance of US sponsors and academics with respect to the clinical movement in the region was an important aspect of this support.[6] The main idea was to strengthen the rule of law and human rights protection through the formation of new generations of lawyers (both teachers and future practitioners).

The history of CLE in Central and Eastern Europe has already generated a rich scholarship, including in relation to the diverse degree of success of clinical projects in various countries of the region.[7]

---

[3] For example, in Poland, the local bar associations controlled the entrance exams for the barrister apprenticeship, which enabled them to accept only very few candidates, often with family ties to the members of the bar. This regulation was successfully challenged by a young lawyer from the Law Clinic of the Jagiellonian University. See *infra* for details.

[4] For a more detailed description of legal education in the Soviet Union, *see* J. M. Burman, *The Role of Clinical Legal Education in Developing of the Rule of Law in Russia*, 2 WYOMING L. REV. 89–118 (2002).

[5] Although this problem cannot be explained only by the influence of the communist regimes because it has been also identified in some Western European countries, such as Germany or Italy. See Chapter 3 by Marzia Barbera and Chapter 8 by Nora Markard in this volume.

[6] See Chapter 1 by Philip Genty in this volume for a detailed account of the role of the US assistance for the clinics in the region.

[7] L. Wortham, *Aiding Clinical Education Abroad: What Can Be Gained and The Learning Curve on How to Do So Effectively*, 12 CLINICAL L. REV. 615–85 (2006); M. Berbec-Rostas, A. Gutnikov, and

The first university clinic in the region, which is still in activity,[8] was opened in 1995 at the Petrozavodsk State University in northeastern Russia with the help of Vermont Law School.[9] More programmes followed in the second half of the 1990s, supported by the American Bar Association Central European and Eurasian Law Initiative (ABA CEELI), the Ford Foundation, and various US law schools. Since then law clinics in Russia had known both periods of flourishing and decline.[10] By 2009, there were reportedly around 150 legal clinics in Russia. The idea of including clinical methods in law school curricula has become well-embedded in Russian universities, and legal clinics are recognized by law as providers of legal aid.[11]

In Poland, clinics began to emerge on the initiative of some faculty members who had become familiar with the idea during research visits to the United States, as well as of students dissatisfied with the traditional methods of teaching. The first clinic was established in October 1997, at Jagiellonian University in Krakow, with the support from the Ford Foundation, the Batory Foundation,[12] the American Embassy in Poland, and the Organization for Security and Cooperation in Europe (OSCE).[13] The clinic in Warsaw opened shortly afterwards, in 1998. At the beginning, the clinic had two sections dedicated to assisting prisoners and victims of gender violence and discrimination. The clinic collaborated with the Polish Helsinki Foundation and Women's Rights Centre. The two organizations supplied clients, and the clinic used their premises to meet them. In the following year, with assistance from the Ford Foundation, Constitutional and Legal Policy Institute (COLPI), and the Batory Foundation, the clinic started to develop both its scope of activity and facilities. An international conference on CLE was held in Warsaw and Krakow in 1999.[14] In the same year, with the assistance of the Batory Foundation, ten more clinics were established in Poland.[15]

Similarly, in Hungary, the first clinic started its activity in 1997, in Budapest at the Eötvös Loránd University (ELTE). It was a clinic specializing in refugee and asylum law, set up in cooperation with COLPI and the Hungarian Helsinki Committee. In 1999, the Legal Clinics and Street Law Foundation was established and the

---

B. Namyslowska-Gabrysiak, *Clinical Legal Education in Central and Eastern Europe: Selected Case Studies*, in THE GLOBAL CLINICAL MOVEMENT: EDUCATING LAWYERS FOR SOCIAL JUSTICE 52–67 (F. S. Bloch ed.); D. Aksamovic and P. Genty, An Examination of the Challenges, Successes and Setbacks for Clinical Legal Education in Eastern Europe, 20 INT'L. J. CLINICAL LEGAL EDUC. 427–38 (2014); I. Krasnicka, Legal Education and Clinical Legal Education in Poland, 13 INT'L. J. CLINICAL LEGAL EDUC. 47–55 (2008).

[8] http://urfak.petrsu.ru/klinika.htm (last visited June 22, 2016). [9] Burman, *supra* note 4, at 91.
[10] Berbec-Rostas, Gutnikov, and Namysłowska-Gabrysiak, *supra* note 7 at 64–65. [11] *Id.*
[12] The Batory Foundation was created in 1988 by George Soros and a group of Polish dissidents.
[13] K. Olechnowicz, *Historia Klinik Prawa*, 5 KLINIKA 18–21 (2008). For more information on the beginnings of the clinic in Cracow *see also* Wortham, *supra* note 7 at 620–21.
[14] E. Zielińska, *Klinika Prawa- Uniwersytecka Studencka Poradnia Prawna*, 1 KLINIKA 129–221 (1999).
[15] M. J. Skrodzka, *An interview with Filip Czernicki*, 11 EDUKACJA PRAWNICZA 26–28 (2013).

ELTE clinic extended its scope of activity to include sections dealing with criminal law, labour law, children's rights, nondiscrimination, and Roma rights and support for nongovernmental organizations (NGOs). In 2008, a new section dedicated to freedom of information was created in collaboration with the ELTE's Sociology of Law Department. There are also clinics in other towns, such as Miskolc, Debrecen, Pecs, and Szeged.[16]

In Belarus,[17] the first clinic, dedicated to women's rights, opened in 1998 at the European Humanity University. However, it ceased activity when the university itself was closed in 2004. The second initiative was the Street Law Clinic at the Law Faculty of Yanka Kupala State University of Grodno, launched in 1999, which was followed by a "classic" (live-client) legal clinic. Both programmes are still in activity. Two more clinics were established in 2000, but the movement received a new impetus in 2002, when clinical education gained legal recognition from the bar and nine more clinics were established. However, the clinics still lack a centralized structure and coordination.[18]

At a similar time, after 2000, clinics started to spring up also in Ukraine, Bulgaria, and Croatia.[19] In the Czech Republic, the first attempts undertaken in the 1990s ultimately failed, but the Olomouc clinic was reestablished in 2002 with assistance from the European Social Fund and has been in continuous activity ever since. It also had an influence on the law schools in Prague and Brno, which also included clinical or skills-oriented courses in their curricula.[20]

An important indicator of the progress made by the clinical movement in Central and Eastern Europe is the development of regional cooperation between the clinicians, evidenced by joint publications, conferences, and support in terms of expertise and training. For instance, the clinical movement in Belarus received assistance from ABA CEELI, but also from Polish, Russian, and Ukrainian clinicians.[21] Given the shared experience of political and economic transition, experts from the same region may have a better understanding of the needs and challenges faced by colleagues from a neighbouring country.[22]

---

[16] Berbec-Rostas, Gutnikov, and Namysłowska-Gabrysiak, *supra* note 7 at 59–60. See also Chapter 12 by Renáta Uitz and Eszter Polgári in this volume.

[17] K. Furman-Łajszczak, Y. Kvatshik, *Clinical Legal Education in Belarus and Polish Support for This Movement*, in: Klinika 2/2012, pp. 11–14.

[18] *Id.* 11–12.   [19] *Id.* 61–63.

[20] M. Tomoszek, *The Growth of Legal Clinics in Europe – Faith and Hope, or Evidence and Hard Work?*, 21, 1 INT'L. J. CLINICAL LEGAL EDUC. 93–102 (2014); also see Chapter 4 by Veronika Tomoszková and Maxim Tomoszek in this volume.

[21] Furman-Łajszczak and Kvatshik, *supra* note 17 at 13. Thanks to a grant from the Polish Mistry of Foreign Affairs and support of the LCF, a group of Belarussian clinical teachers came to Poland for a study visit, and a joint conference was organized in Minsk.

[22] F. Czernicki explained that the Polish history and experience made him more credible to listeners not only in the former Soviet sphere but also in Jordan and Lebanon, where clinics also started to develop after the Arab Spring. See Skrodzka, *supra* note 15 at 26.

THE POLISH SUCCESS: HOW CLE ADAPTED AND BLOSSOMED

The development of the clinical movement in Poland is considered a success story, in particular when measured by the sustainability of the clinics.[23] In academic year 2014/2015, there were twenty-five clinics in sixteen cities, although only twenty-two were considered as complying with standards developed by the Legal Clinics Foundation (LCF).[24] In total, 1,988 students, supervised by 351 teachers worked on 10,693 cases.[25] Polish clinicians created an umbrella organization, the LCF, which, since 2002, has worked to develop standards of quality for the clinics, elaborated clinical methodology, and provided funding and training.[26] The Foundation has published several books dedicated to clinical methodology, interactive teaching methods, and organizational matters. It also edits *Klinika*, a specialized review, and organizes two conferences per year. Polish lawyers provide training and advice to clinicians around the world.[27]

There were several reasons for a successful and relatively smooth development of the clinical movement in Poland. First, it was a heterogeneous and yet coherent movement composed of students (often members of the European Law Students Association), young legal scholars, and well-established law professors who shared, at least to some extent, the same ideas and convictions, such as the commitment to social justice and a sense of duty towards the less advantaged members of society.[28] The movement had its leaders, such as Filip Czernicki, one of the founders of the clinic at Warsaw University and the president of the LCF. However, it was the involvement of more than a few motivated individuals who guaranteed the sustainability of the clinics. A related factor was a certain social and cultural context. Despite more than four decades of a communist regime, a good dose of social sensibility and public responsibility among lawyers existed in Polish society which facilitated the establishment of legal clinics.

The role of the LCF was also pivotal, in particular as it partially took over the role of US sponsors (as they began to withdraw) through the operation of its grant programme. The Foundation has also fulfilled coordinating, supervisory, and standard-setting functions. Furthermore, thanks to the support of some senior faculty members, clinics quickly became integrated into the law school curriculum. For instance, since its inception, the Warsaw University clinic granted both students and

---

[23] Rekosh, *supra* note 1 at 89–90.
[24] See the annual report by the Foundation, www.fupp.org.pl/kliniki-prawa/publikacje/raporty (last visited June 28, 2016).
[25] *Id.*
[26] www.fupp.org.pl/en/foundation/history-mission (last visited June 28, 2016). The Foundation is based on the organization of legal clinics in South Africa, with which Polish clinicians became familiar after a study trip funded by the Ford Foundation.
[27] Skrodzka, *supra* note 15 at 26.
[28] Interview with Eleonora Zielińska, one of the founders of the Warsaw University Clinic, on file with the author.

teachers credits for clinic work.[29] Furthermore, many clinics in Poland have an individual administrative status of chair or institute within the law school.[30] Law schools in principle also cover at least part of the costs of clinical activities,[31] and teachers are, in most universities, paid for their clinical teaching just as they are paid for any other teaching. However, the degree of support, as symbolized by financial compensation or recognition of the teachers' work as part of their regular teaching duties, still varies from one university to another.[32] The point is that clinics are well-embedded in the law school structure.

This well-planned strategy in relation to the funding of the clinics, which consisted of a transition from external financial assistance to reliance on law schools to support clinics from their budgets, was probably the key reason for the sustainability of Polish clinics. In most other countries of Central and Eastern Europe, such strategic thinking was absent both on the part of local clinicians and their US partners. As a result, often, when the foreign funding was over, clinics were closed due to the lack of resources and staff. Some American actors assumed the European Union would take over as the main sponsor. However, CLE was almost unheard of in Western Europe, and the EU had no intention of stepping in.[33] Apart from largely resolving the financial issues, the LCF has provided Polish clinicians with a network of dedicated, competent, and like-minded people.

Another important element was the "proactive" approach to the US clinical model. Edwin Rekosh points to the capacity of local clinicians to adapt CLE to the local conditions as a major factor determining the clinics' prospects for survival.[34] Of course, the development of clinics in Poland would not have been possible without the support of American sponsors and scholars. Polish clinicians were willing to learn from American experts but, at the same time, knew that it was impossible to simply transplant the same methods to Poland.[35] The adaptation process involved the development of a pedagogical methodology that could fit with the local realities. Many legal scholars involved at the outset of the clinical movement combined academic work with legal practice and/or involvement with the local NGOs. This gave them a good understanding of the needs of potential clients and precise ideas about how law students could assist them.[36] Moreover,

---

[29] Zielińska, *supra* note 14.
[30] Skrodzka, *supra* note 15 at 26. Polish law schools are organized as a composition of chairs/institutes corresponding to the main areas of law. Each chair has its head, affiliated professors, lecturers, PhD students, etc. A clinic may have the same status (be the same organizational unit) as the chair/institute of criminal law or the chair of administrative law, which is a sign of recognition and gives it a certain position within the faculty.
[31] Law schools also hire one or two secretaries and provide offices and at least basic equipment.
[32] Interview with Katarzyna Syroka-Marczewska, on file with the author.
[33] Interview between Lamin Khadar and Filip Czernicki, June 23, 2016, on file with the author.
[34] Rekosh, *supra* note 1 at 88–90.
[35] Interview with the Fryderyk Zoll, one of the founders of the Jagiellonian University Clinic in Cracow, on file with the author.
[36] Interview with Eleonora Zielińska.

the participation of well-established law professors not only facilitated the implantation of clinics within law schools, but also provided the clinical movement with local experts. Relations with the US partners were friendly and egalitarian, and Polish clinicians did not perceive this assistance as the imposition of a foreign model.[37]

Despite the undisputed success of the clinical movement in Poland, certain obstacles, identified already at the outset, persist to this day. Some limitations are linked to the fact that students cannot represent their clients in court, with the exception of administrative proceedings,[38] and there is no legal regulation regarding clinics and their work. As a result, a student working on a case can prepare the documents and participate in the hearing as a member of the public (unless the hearing is held *in camera*) but cannot plead for the client. The fact that the student has no legal standing in the proceedings also prevents him or her from having access to court records. Furthermore, information obtained by students during the interviews with their clients is not covered by attorney–client privilege.[39] Several legislative proposals were put forward first by lawyers from the Jagiellonian University and then by the LCF in order to provide clinics with legal recognition and enable students to represent their clients in certain types of proceedings. Unfortunately, they were not adopted. Also, the recent law on free legal aid, which obliges local authorities to guarantee access to legal advice and assistance for disadvantaged members of society by hiring lawyers, does not foresee any role (or any funding) for legal clinics.[40]

CLE is well-embedded in law schools but has not yet managed to gain recognition as an important element within the legal system and to secure a regulatory framework governing its operation. Despite these limitations, Polish clinics have developed their own methods of action that enable them to function. In particular, students prepare requests for legal aid or direct clients towards a specialized NGO which may provide legal representation. Furthermore, in some cases, the role of the clinic consists of providing assistance at the pretrial stage or of explaining that court proceedings are not (or no longer) available.[41] However, a more formal acknowledgement of the important role that clinics play in providing legal information would be very helpful, particularly for those clinics that receive only limited support from their home university.

After nearly twenty years of existence in Poland, one may wonder what influence the clinics have exercised over the teaching and practice of law.

---

[37] Interviews with Fryderyk Zoll and Eleonora Zielińska.
[38] Asylum proceedings are considered administrative proceedings, which provides an important exception for both students and their clients.
[39] K. Furman-Łajszczak, *Ograniczenia pomocy świadczonej przez uniwersyteckie poradnie prawne* 13 (17) KLINIKA 15–19 (2012).
[40] Ustawa z dnia 5 sierpnia 2015 r. o nieodpłatnej pomocy prawnej oraz edukacji prawnej.
[41] Interview with Katarzyna Syroka-Marczewska.

HAS THE TEACHING OF LAW CHANGED?

Izabela Kraśnicka, in an article published in 2008,[42] described legal studies in Poland as theory-oriented and not providing students with any practical knowledge or skills. She also mentions the poor quality of lectures and tutorials. An even more negative picture may be found in a paper by Fryderyk Zoll, discussing the need to reform legal education in Poland. In it, he deplores the lack of a coherent concept of legal education, little coordination between university education and professional legal training, the lack of skills-oriented teaching, and the low motivation of academic staff (which partly explains the reliance on lectures and the reticence to embrace more interactive methods of teaching, which are more time- and effort-consuming).[43]

Clinics, as a reaction to these problems described, offer a promising teaching alternative. However, only a fraction of law students benefit from a clinical experience during their five years at university.[44] Although the presence of clinics in all law faculties is a big change in comparison with the beginning of the 1990s, the question remains whether CLE has altered how the law is taught in general. An overview of Polish clinical scholarship shows little reflection on the broader impact of clinical education on law schools in general, legal research, or teaching.[45] The major focus is on clinical methodology, rather narrowly construed, and the internal functioning of clinics, whereas any deeper reflection relating to legal philosophy or critical legal studies is absent.[46]

To assess the influence that the establishment of clinics has had on the teaching of law in Poland requires more research and goes beyond the scope of this chapter. It seems justified to assume that academics who have benefited from a clinical experience (as students or in particular as teachers) will teach differently, even if outside the clinical context. As there are no formal "clinical" professors in Poland, all clinicians also teach conventional legal subjects, such as criminal, civil, or family law. Maxim Tomoszek describes, in Chapter 4 of this volume, the influence of clinical experience on the teaching methods applied in traditional settings by the faculty members of the Olomouc law

---

[42] Krasnicka, *supra* note 7 at 50.
[43] F. Zoll, Przyszłość kształcenia prawników w Polsce, 6 PAŃSTWO I PRAWO 19–28 (2010). Zoll also provides a reform programme, partly based and inspired by his clinical experience. In particular, he advocates a greater focus on the methods of teaching than on its content and emphasis on developing the capacity for legal reasoning and analysis rather than knowledge of specific areas of law.
[44] Furman-Łajszczak, *supra* note 39 at 18.
[45] There are exceptions to this trend. For example, Fryderyk Zoll wrote a book analysing the potential application of the US methods of legal education, including clinical education, in Polish law schools JAKA SZKOŁA PRAWA? : CZY AMERYKAŃSKIE METODY NAUCZANIA PRAWA MOGĄ BYĆ PRZYDATNE W POLSCE? (Dom Wydawniczy ABC, Warsaw, 2004). F. Zoll also led the team which prepared the curriculum for the new national training programme for future judges and prosecutors, which is based on interactive methods of teaching. See Zoll, *supra* note 43 at 27.
[46] See Chapter 8 by Nora Markard and Chapter 3 by Marzia Barbera in this volume, which both analyse clinical experience in relation with more theoretical reflection on law and legal education.

school.[47] Similar processes are taking place in Polish law schools. In particular, the Polish clinical movement made a significant effort to develop clinical methodology adapted to local circumstances and to promote interactive teaching methods, such as moot courts or simulations. However, it is difficult to instil critical thinking and the sense of social responsibility among students, just as it is a great challenge to change the hierarchical and distant relations between faculty members and students that do not encourage dialogue and reflection.[48]

It should also be borne in mind that the context in which law is taught has changed in the past twenty years. In particular, clinics are not the only opportunity for students to gain practical experience. The market of legal services has developed significantly, providing many possibilities for students to do traineeships or even start working while still at university. This option may also be favoured by some students because it may involve remuneration and enhance their career prospects. Another important change is greater accessibility to the legal professions. Since 2005,[49] the entry exams for solicitor and barrister apprenticeships have been organized by the Ministry of Justice, and the number of candidates admitted each year has increased significantly. Accordingly, apprenticeship has become an attainable option for law graduates. It lasts three years and combines practical and theoretical training. Importantly, the apprentices may represent clients in court.

The existence of other possibilities to gain practical skills could point to the importance of the "nurture" element of clinical education. Some authors indicate that law graduates involved in clinical activities during their time at university often retain a commitment to public interest initiatives. However, this leads to the well-known chicken-or-egg causality dilemma. Does the clinical experience shape students' sensibility and attitudes, or do clinics attract students with a preexisting sense of social responsibility and commitment to social justice? Similarly, clinics will appeal to faculty members who enjoy teaching and like working with students, but it may not change teacher–student relations outside

---

[47] Tomoszek, *supra* note 20. In Olomouc the changes were considerable, relating not only to the methods, but also to the content of teaching, and led to the accreditation of a new curriculum very different from any previous legal curriculum used in the Czech Republic. See also Chapter 4 by Veronika Tomoszková and Maxim Tomoszek in this volume.

[48] It quite common for law school teachers to combine academic work with legal practice, which may be partly explained by low salaries in Polish universities. This may either enhance the quality of the teaching, if the teacher shares insights from his or her practice, but may also lead to a neglectful approach to academic duties.

[49] Michał Kłaczyński, a graduate of the Jagiellonian University, successfully challenged the refusal to enrol him as a bar apprentice. The Constitutional Court (judgment of February 18, 2004, P 21/02) agreed that the regulation which gave the bar associations unlimited control over access to the apprenticeship was incompatible with the constitutional freedom to choose one's occupation in life. The resulting amendments to the laws on legal professions (laws of June 30, 2005, and February 20, 2009) not only opened access to apprenticeship, but also introduced new possibilities of joining the bar for those who hold a PhD in law or have worked in a law firm.

the clinic. Nonetheless, clinics provide a possibility for like-minded students (and faculty members) to work together.

PRO BONO LAWYERS, FREE LEGAL AID, AND SOCIAL JUSTICE IN POLAND

Lawyers in communist societies tended to be rather "marginalized"[50] as their tasks were limited to the management of criminal and civil law cases. The democratic transition "resulted in the legal profession's inability, lack of competence, and/or reluctance to engage in rule of law, human rights, and public interest lawyering on behalf of the most vulnerable groups."[51] At the same time, Polish legal practitioners seem to have adapted pretty easily to the new capitalist reality which brought new possibilities of financial gain.

Polish legal clinics were established with a very strong commitment to helping the poor and disadvantaged members of society. Many founders underline their dual objective: educational and charitable.[52] The aim was to provide students with teaching of better quality and focused on learning practical skills while at the same time helping those who could not afford professional legal services. The idea for some was to "nurture" students, to instil in them social sensibility and the sense of responsibility for their fellow human beings. However, the question arises whether the focus of clinical teachers and students goes beyond the individual problem they help to solve to one of critically assessing the legal system and trying to change it.[53] The question of systemic change is much less present in the Polish manifestation of CLE than the question of developing individual human sensibility and social responsibility among young lawyers.[54]

The impact of clinical education on the practice of law (and social attitudes of legal practitioners) is something extremely difficult to measure. Potential research is further complicated by the fact that the development of the clinical movement coincided with European integration, the increase in academic mobility, and the development of NGOs. The role of clinics is further limited by the fact that students cannot represent clients in court proceedings.[55] In this sense, the clinical experience is only a kind of initiation into legal practice. At the same time, many lawyers who are or have been involved in the clinical movement are also engaged with projects

---

[50] Berbec-Rostas, Gutnikov, and Namysłowska-Gabrysiak, *supra* note 7 at 54–55.   [51] *Id.*
[52] M. Szewczyk, *The Concept of Students Legal Clinics*, 1 KLINIKA 19–23 (1999); F. Zoll, On the Clinical Method of Teaching Law, 1 KLINIKA 41–48 (1999); Furman-Łajszczak, *supra* note 39; Skrodzka, *supra* note 15.
[53] Wortham, *supra* note 7 at 657.
[54] In this context, a recently renewed agreement between the LCF and the Polish Ombudsman may be considered a positive step because it foresees that students may refer to the Ombudsman Office systemic problems they have identified while working in the clinic.
[55] It may explain why the clinics in Poland have not contributed to the development of strategic litigation. A successful project of strategic litigation has been developed in the framework of the Polish Helsinki Foundation by Prof. Wiktor Osiatyński and Dr. Adam Bodnar.

relating to *pro bono* lawyering and access to justice. The LCF has created the Pro Bono Centre which matches NGOs in need of legal assistance with law firms willing to help them. It also promotes the idea of *pro bono* lawyering, in particular through the yearly Pro Bono Lawyer competition.[56] The LCF was also involved, along with the Institute for Law and Society, in research on access to free legal aid in Poland and in lobbying for new legislation in this area.[57] More broadly, many clinicians promote a certain ethos of lawyering as a profession that comes with a strong social responsibility.

CONCLUSION

Even though the transplantation of university legal clinics in Central and Eastern Europe has not been free from difficulties, some failures, setbacks, and challenges, the overall experience is generally judged successful.[58] Clinics have become a permanent element of the educational landscape in the region. This success has many mothers and fathers, lawyers who effectively combined a commitment to social justice with academic competence and managerial skills. Understanding the principles underpinning the concept of CLE and the ability to adapt clinical education to local needs and limitations, as well as effective coordination within and across countries have been key enabling factors for the clinical movement to develop. Likewise, the support from senior scholars, law schools, and state authorities also played an important role.

Nevertheless, as the sustainability and overall acceptance of CLE as part of the law curriculum were, and sometimes remain, a challenge, most clinical literature focused on those very questions. Many publications recount the history of the clinics in the region (or a particular country) and the modalities of the clinics' everyday work. Of course, they allow us to identify good practices or even learn from others' mistakes. However, more reflection should follow on the relations between clinical education on the one hand and legal education and legal practice on the other. This expectation seems particularly legitimate in relation to countries, such as Poland, which have successfully overcome the sustainability phase. Nevertheless, in other countries of the region, the primary challenge to the effective implementation of clinical education is not their incorporation into law schools' curricula but the opposition of many senior scholars to the changes in content and style of teaching.[59]

After almost two decades of permanent existence, CLE in Central and Eastern Europe requires more reflection on its impact on the teaching of law in general, outside the clinical context, and on the practice of law. This calls for the use of

---

[56] www.centrumprobono.pl/en/ (last visited June 27, 2016).
[57] www.fupp.org.pl/poradnictwo-prawne-i-obywatelskie and www.inpris.pl/en/pomoc-prawna/ (both last visited June 27, 2016).
[58] Berbec-Rostas, Gutnikov, and Namysłowska-Gabrysiak, *supra* note 7 at 6.
[59] Aksamovic and Genty, *supra* note 7.

empirical research, which is not very widely accepted among legal scholars in the region.[60] Moreover, it will also require a shift in focus:

> [I]n my understanding, clinical legal education is not a goal in itself; it is just one of the steps on the road to achieve truly important goals on global scale, most importantly reforming legal education and achieving social justice for everyone. I think that now the focus within clinical legal education will shift from expansion to quality and effectively achieving these goals, (re-)opening questions such as "How can we improve non-clinical legal education by our clinical experience?" and "How can legal clinics have greater social impact?"[61]

---

[60] Tomoszek, *supra* note 20. [61] *Id.*

PART II

Where Are We Now and Where Are We Going?

Insights into the Second Wave of Clinical Legal Education in Europe (Mid-2000s to the Present)

PART IIA

National Perspectives on Clinical Legal Education in Europe

Exploring the Strength and Diversity of National Clinical Movements

3

The Emergence of an Italian Clinical Legal Education Movement

The University of Brescia Law Clinic

Marzia Barbera

INTRODUCTION

The Law Clinic at the University of Brescia, launched in 2009, was the first clinical programme ever established in Italy. It is a "live-client" clinic that adopts a "hybrid model." Given that, at present, the Italian university system does not recognize the position of "clinical professor" (i.e. an academic admitted to legal practice who may run a university law clinic), the clinic has implemented a programme whereby in-house and external activities are blended and supervision is jointly carried out by a faculty member and a lawyer (hired as a fixed-term adjunct professor) who represents clients in court.

Currently, there are eighteen faculty members at the Department of Legal Sciences and eleven lawyers (the majority of whom are members of the Brescia Bar Association) working side by side in the clinical programme. Together, they supervise clinic cases; give lectures on specialized topics; and organize seminars, meetings, and training courses for present and future clinicians. The cases taken on by the programme, which must meet the case selection requirements adopted by the clinic teachers committee,[1] may be submitted by nongovernmental organizations (NGOs) or by the lawyers themselves, selecting them from among the cases they handle on a *pro bono* basis or have been assigned through the public legal aid system.

The same hybrid model, with different characteristics, can be seen in the other Italian universities which have established clinical programmes.[2] The main difference is that the Brescia clinic has adopted a structure under which there is a single clinic programme with multiple clinics engaging multiple legal fields: Private Law, Criminal Law, Labour Law, Consumer Law, Family Law, International Law,

---

[1] Cases are chosen taking into account different factors: exemplarity, social relevance, educational value. Once the case has been selected and assigned, students working on the case take the obligation to comply with legal ethics' rules, including confidentiality rules.

[2] See Clelia Bartoli (ed.), *Legal Clinics in Europe: For a Commitment of Higher Education to Social Justice*, Diritto e Questioni Pubbliche, Special Issue (2016).

Migration and Refugee Law, Antidiscrimination Law, Administrative Law, Criminology, Mediation, Legal Theory, and Legal Method.[3]

The Legal Clinic programme is an elective course, offered across two semesters (Clinic I and Clinic II) and coordinated by two academics.[4] In the 2014–2015 academic year, the clinical handled fourteen different cases, with subjects ranging from discrimination against migrants in relation to disability benefits, to medical malpractice and repatriation of a refugee sentenced to death in his country. About ninety students participated in the two courses, making this the largest clinical programme in the country and one of the largest in Europe.

In 2015, the Department established a new Labour Law Clinic, aimed at bachelor-degree students who intend to become labour consultants for corporations.[5] The new clinic operates within a new legal framework (Law n. 27/2012), which makes it possible for students to carry out six of the eighteen-month traineeship required to become a licensed consultant during their last year at University. The Labour Clinic is seen as the best way to do this. The clinic carries out mainly transactional work (management of employment relations, contract drafting, providing assistance during collective bargaining sessions, mediation and conciliation of individual and collective disputes, providing start-up support to small businesses and cooperatives) while maintaining a social and community-oriented approach. Again, the model is a hybrid one whereby faculty members and professional labour consultants supervise the cases alongside faculty supervision.

In the near future, the Brescia Clinic will be launching a street law programme comprising a legal help desk run by students and clinical supervisors for local community members with the dual aim of providing listening support and a first review of cases that may eventually be transmitted to the Clinics.

EMERGENCE OF CLINICAL LEGAL EDUCATION

Genesis and Context

One way to tell the story of the Brescia Law Clinic is to look at it as an example of that experiential and reflective practice which constitutes one of the distinctive features of the clinical methodology. In fact, the Clinic was initially born out of the deep

---

[3] A similar model, where clinics give advice and assistance in many areas of law, can be found in the Czech experience (see Chapter 4 by Veronika Tomoszková and Maxim Tomoszek in this volume).

[4] The Clinic is open to students enrolled in the five-year master's degree course in Law who are in their third, fourth, or fifth, and to students enrolled in the three-year bachelor's degree course for Labour Consultants and Corporate Lawyers who are in their third year.

[5] Labour consultants give legal advice and provide solutions to businesses on every stage of the employment relationship, from recruitment to termination, give assistance in company reorganization and restructuring, and provide representation in conciliation of labour disputes and in individual and collective trade union disputes.

feeling of discontent among a group of faculty members who decried the state of legal education in Italy and the lack of appreciation for the social dimension of the law within the academy.

We felt that it was time to experiment with new methods of teaching and learning the law and, at the same time, that we had to make a contribution to the community in which we were embedded as researchers and teachers.

Almost by chance, we came across clinical legal education (CLE), and it seemed to be a good answer to both problems. We started studying it and mapping the best practices, paying special attention to the United States, where CLE had first been tried and tested.

At the beginning, we felt a sense of loneliness. We were aware that there were no clinics in any Italian university. But, at the same time, we felt we were like explorers, like pathfinders going through new territories, new lands to be conquered. In the Spring of 2009 we invited a group of clinicians from Yale Law School to give a series of workshops on the clinical methodology and on their specific experience to both faculty members and students. Professors Jim Silk, Bob Solomon, and Camille Carey came along, together with some of their brilliant clinical students, and gave us an exciting and inspiring account of what a clinic might look like. In October 2009, a small team of faculty members and students undertook a study trip on clinical teaching in the United States, trying to capture the essence of that model and figure out how to organize a clinical programme in Italy. The journey included trips to clinics at the law schools of Yale University, the University of Connecticut, New York University, and City University of New York. We owe a lot to the intellectual generosity and spirit of sharing of the clinicians we met. Many of them have reciprocated our visit, and they still keep on talking and working with us, together with other clinicians we have subsequently gotten to know. But already on the way back, we knew we had to find our own way, we had to reinvent the original model and adapt it to our experience and context.

By that time, the initial small team had been supplemented by a larger group of colleagues and had gained the institutional support of the Head of the Department and of the Headmaster of the Faculty, eager to innovate teaching methods but also to open new communication and interaction channels with local civil society. In the same semester, we started our Clinic's first class, with the support and *pro bono* collaboration of the local bar association, with some NGOs providing the first cases.

Drivers

It may be argued that the making of the Brescia Law Clinic was mainly driven by individual voluntarism and idiosyncratic institutional adaptation, but the fact that, in a very short time, other clinics were established in other Italian Universities and elsewhere in Europe suggests a different, more complex explanation.

Indeed, the emergence of CLE in Europe has manifold reasons, depending on the local cultural, political, and social contexts.

First, to talk of a current "clinical boom" certainly does not reflect the situation of the United Kingdom, where clinics have existed for decades and, although clearly influenced by the American clinical approaches, have grown differently, being more centred on pedagogical, vocational, and professional objectives.[6]

Second, there is nothing in the current development which looks like a regionwide strategy, driven by organizations like the Open Society Justice Initiative or the Ford Foundation, that in the 1990s led to the construction, in Central and Eastern Europe, of a network of legal clinics[7] as part and parcel of a bigger political program which concerned the transition to democratic systems and the (re)construction of an active civil society. This does not mean that the same organizations haven't supported, financially and otherwise, the most recent expansion of the clinical movement to Western Europe. But the best-known critique made of these earlier experiences, namely the fact that they were the offspring of a legal imperialism based on financial aid that often failed to survive the withdrawal of the donors' funding (Gardner, 1980; Kennedy, 2006; Bonilla, 2014), could hardly be applied to the present experiences.

If we consider the clinics more recently established in Western Europe (including the Italian ones), we have to conclude that they were mainly born from an indigenous cause; that is, as said before, a feeling of dissatisfaction with the cultural and political premises on which legal education is based, namely the formalism of legal studies and their separateness from objectives of social justice and commitment to public goods.[8]

Civil law systems are deeply influenced by legal formalism. Although formalism is today hugely criticized at the level of scholarship, in legal education and, as a result, in the work of practitioners, judges, and lawmakers, it still dominates the field. As such, formalism has shaped the process of constructing legal knowledge in its own image.

Indeed, in the past, there have been breaks with this tradition, which coincided with periods of social and political conflict. For example, in Italy, the 1970s were years when a struggle over the meaning of the law itself took place, a struggle that invested all fields of legal culture and all legal professions. The formula then used was that lawyers, judges, and practitioners had to be committed to an "*alternative use of the law,*" which was a way of saying that law had to be deconstructed and recreated as a tool for progressive change.

---

[6] See Chapter 13 by Lynn Welchman in this volume.

[7] See Chapter 1 by Philip Genty in this volume. This does not mean that Western European clinics have not also received financial support from US donors, such as the Open Society Foundations, but their role has been less influential.

[8] On this regard, the description of the development of the legal clinical movement in other civil law systems given in this book tells a very similar story (see Chapter 6 by Xavier Aurey, Chapter 8 by Nora Markard, and Chapter 10 by Anthony Valcke in this volume).

The Italian movement of the '70s, however, finds a greater parallel in the American critical legal studies (CLS) movement than in the current legal clinic movement. The CLS movement maintained that the function of the law was the reproduction and consolidation, never the criticism, of the existing social order. Clinics and their vocation to use the law as a means to achieve aims of social justice seem to adopt some of the CLS arguments, such as the denial of a purely technical nature of legal rule and the need to consider the political dimension of legal rules and judicial decisions. But in the clinical movement there remains a basic trust in the law as an instrument to achieve justice and equality, without having to drive all the way down the path of deconstructing the law.[9]

In the current European clinical movement and its rejection of the formalist tradition, we can see more the influence of a realist and instrumentalist approach to the law than a return to a deconstructive approach. The creative and flexible use of the law suggested by clinical methodology is seen as an antidote to what constitutes a specific feature of the formalist tradition; that is, the primacy of the text and the primacy of the knowledge of the text in legal education.

In Italy, attention to clinical methodology started from our questioning this cultural tradition. The reflective perspective of CLE takes leave not from the texts (i.e. from the "law on the books") but from the "law in action" and helps to rethink and reconceptualize legal norms, institutions, law-making processes, and the role of the different actors involved in these mechanisms.

The second reason that prompted Italian legal scholars to pursue clinical education was a conservative attitude with respect to the established social relations of power which characterizes large sectors of our legal culture. This attitude is presented as a neutral approach to the law. We wanted to reintroduce in legal education the idea of the law as an instrument of social change.

In fact, as noted earlier, the instrumentalist approach is not new in our experience. But, in the past decades, to use the law as a social weapon has mainly meant to bend the law to the logic of the market, to conceive the law as a product of the economy. Law and economics theories, which can be seen as another example of US "legal imperialism," have supplied a powerful and hegemonic model for conservative legal reforms in many fields. The clinical model provided a way to reintroduce into the legal discourse an alternative, transformative vision of the law.

Italian scholars were aware of the severe criticism made of clinical legal education by some eminent American legal scholars at the mid-1980s, by which time clinics had already lost their initial elements of radical political transformation and had settled at the "periphery" of legal education, often assuming the no more than comforting role of softening the system and making it more acceptable.[10] But

---

[9] See Luca Cruciani, *And Justice for All. Accesso alla giustizia e law clinics come beni comuni*, 30 RIVISTA CRITICA DI DIRITTO PRIVATO 307 (2012).
[10] Duncan Kenney, LEGAL EDUCATION AND THE REPRODUCTION OF HIERARCHY: A POLEMIC AGAINST THE SYSTEM (A Far Press, 1983).

it was precisely the peripheral, nonstructured nature of legal clinics which attracted their attention. They recalled that, in a fine essay on legal education, Mark Tushnet wrote that legal clinics deal with people, with unstructured legal experience, and with emotions, features that are all associated with the female sphere and which are a disturbing factor to traditional legal education and its academic followers.[11] It is perhaps not the case that the Italian clinical movement is a process mainly driven by female academics. On the other hand, legal clinics have been conceived by Italian scholars as "transformative commons," as a cultural and intellectual resource accessible to all members of society and, at the same time, as a site of the production of "commoning" – that is, the creation, enjoyment, and redistribution of shared resources and knowledge.[12]

Finally, the diffusion of legal clinics in Italian and other European universities can be seen as an example of how globalization reshapes and redefines legal education. In a globalized world, the transnational circulation of legal models influences every aspect of the law, including structures of legal expertise and education. The diffusion of these models is mainly realized through the connection among academic and professional élites operating in different legal systems and connected on the basis of a variety of inclinations: field of interests, ideology, methodological approaches, shared legal policies, and so on. Such networks do not operate in a formal or targeted manner but are the result of a series of migrations of student and scholars who take part in doctoral or LLM programs or are involved in academic or research project exchanges. They are then brought to review their training and their teaching in light of that experience and to transfer it into their legal system.[13] Through these fluid networks, different conceptions and approaches circulate from one system to another and influence the local legal educational and professional models.

REFORMING THE TEACHING AND PRACTICE OF LAW IN EUROPE

Goals and Methods

The implications of the cultural hegemony of formalism in education in terms of the hegemony of a certain model of teaching the law are various. The main competencies that we require our students to acquire are a knowledge and mastery of substantive, written law and of what judges and legal doctrine elaborate.

---

[11] Mark Tushnet, *Scenes from the Metropolitan Underground: A Critical Perspective on the Status of Clinical Education*, 52 GEO. WASH. L. REV. 272 (1984).

[12] Rosaria Marella Maria and Enrica Rigo, *Le cliniche legali, i beni comuni e la globalizzazione dei modelli di accesso alla giustizia e di lawyering*, 33 RIVISTA CRITICA DI DIRITTO PRIVATO 537 (2015).

[13] On this type of legal transplant, *see* Giacomo Capuzzo, *"In mani esperte": il ruolo della legal expertise nei sistemi transnazionali*, 32 RIVISTA CRITICA DI DIRITTO PRIVATO 497 (2014). More generally, on the role of epistemic communities in the creation of transnational legal regimes *see Knowledge, Power and International Policy Coordination*, INTERNATIONAL ORGANIZATION, Special Issue (1992).

Traditional academic classes are characterized by very little interaction between teachers and students. When students are particularly active, they ask questions, but they hardly ever discuss the legal issues at stake with their teachers. In Brescia, we wanted to develop alternative ways of teaching and learning, focusing not only on the knowledge of legal rules and tools of interpretation, but also on the development of other capabilities which are based on inductive or pragmatic mental operations – such as problem identification analysis and ends–means thinking.

The process of learning that takes place within legal clinics does not focus on cases decided by the courts and retrospectively analysed, but on real cases, handled while "in action." The experiential learning thus complements the learning "in the books," allowing the student to comprehend and even reach out and touch the economic, social, ideological, political, and institutional contexts in which the "objective" legal principles operate.[14] However, the pedagogical model at the heart of legal clinics also appears as a particularly fertile ground for an epistemological questioning and even renewal of legal research on "the law in action." Clinics afford us not only the opportunity to learn the law in practice, but also the possibility to better think of and understand the law.[15]

On the one hand, the law we can think of and understand through clinical practice is the law as described by American legal realists[16] for whom it was not desirable to embrace a concept of law since "[i]n one aspect law is as broad as life, and for some purposes one will have to follow life pretty far to get the bearings of the legal matters one is examining."[17] This explains why to conceptualize what the law is constitutes a secondary task in clinical methodology. The meaning of the law is only revealed by the practice of the law, where the order of abstract and objective principles give way to the disorder of reality, which appears confused, subjective, indefinite, contradictory.[18]

On the other hand, the current European clinical movement's discourse cannot be entirely assimilated to the sceptical view of judicial interpretation expressed by the traditional realist scholarship. By incorporating a public interest law perspective and choosing a justice-oriented clinical model, European clinicians have implicitly endorsed the neo-constitutionalist position.

"Neo-constitutionalism" is a term recently suggested in legal and political philosophy to describe the writings by legal and political philosophers such as Ronald Dworkin, Robert Alexy, Carlos Nino, and, in Italy, Luigi Ferrajoli and Gustavo Zagrebelsky. They all maintain an understanding of the notion of law which connects law and moral values as a consequence of the legal acknowledgement in

[14] Jerome Frank, *Why Not a Clinical-Lawyer School?*, 81 U. PA. L. REV. 907 (1933).
[15] Jeremy Perelman, *Penser la pratique, théoriser le droit en action: des cliniques juridiques et des nouvelles frontières épistémologiques du droit*, 72 REVUE INTERDISCIPLINAIRE D'ÉTUDES JURIDIQUES 133, 143 (2014).
[16] Diego Blázquez Martín, *Apuntes acerca de la educación jurídica clínica*, 3 REVISTA DE FILOSOFÍA, DERECHO Y POLÍTICA 43, 48 (2006).
[17] Karl Llewellyn, *A Realistic Jurisprudence -The Next Step*, 30 COLUM. L. REV. 431, 432 (1930).
[18] Perelman, *supra* note 15 at 317.

postwar constitutions of fundamental rights and principles that are axiological in nature because they express moral values such as equality, individual freedom, human dignity, solidarity, and so on.[19] This acknowledgement goes together with a set of procedures, practices, and devices aiming at promoting their legal implementation and granting their judicial protection. Legal clinics participate in this process of implementation of fundamental rights and principles by promoting an antiformalist method of interpreting law and hence of judicial application of the law. But they also reorient the path of legal education by shifting students' attention towards the structure of legal reasoning and towards the functions of weighing and balancing among eventually competing legal principles and hence, towards an "approximate" rather than an allegedly deductive nature of legal reasoning.

Beyond the Educational Goals

As mentioned earlier, behind the decision to establish a clinic at Brescia University, there were more than educational considerations. The transformative and flexible use of the law suggested by clinical methodology was a rejection of the view of the law as a closed normative system and a way of offering an answer to entrenched problems of social conflicts and social injustice in an era of declining effectiveness and scope of public legal aid.[20]

Over the past few years, the Brescia Clinic has amassed a significant experience of public interest litigation on social rights in areas such as employment, social security, the environment, and discrimination. But this move, beyond any optimistic and self-laudatory view, also has been a problematic one.

This practice has exposed the clinic to the opportunities but also to the tensions that are inherent in any mobilization of law – as a normative system and as discourse – in contexts and situations where the practice of the law seeks to promote social justice. It must be admitted that one of the reasons for the boom of legal clinics, not only in Italy but in all other Europe countries, is the retreat of the forms of political and other forms of social mobilization. Acting through the language of rights has often become a surrogate for acting through social action. This forces us, as clinicians, to ask ourselves what happens when recourse to the law and to the

---

[19] Tecla Mazzarese, Towards a Positivist Reading of Neo-constitutionalism, JURA GENTIUM (2008), www.juragentium.org/topics/rights/en/mazzares.htm (last visited September 8, 2016); Mauro Barberis, Diritto e morale: la discussione odierna, REVUS (2011), http://revus.revues.org/2108#text (last visited September 8, 2016).

[20] Presidential Decree May 30, 2002 n. 115 has extended legal aid to cover criminal, civil, administrative, and tax law; labour disputes; and so on. Nationals and stateless persons, foreigners with a valid residence permit, and also NGOs can benefit from it. However, the annual income threshold which qualifies a person for legal aid in civil, administrative, criminal, and tax disputes is quite low (currently €11,528.41). Another requirement which hampers the effectiveness of the system in civil and administrative disputes is that the claim must be based on "reason not manifestly ungrounded," which presupposes a sort of pretrial judgment by the local bar association and by the judge who exams the request.

courts is no longer a subsidiary or auxiliary weapon with respect to collective action and social conflict, but instead it becomes their substitute. I will come back to this point later in the conclusion.

From the very beginning, the focus of the Brescia Law Clinic did not remain solely attached to domestic concerns but looked also at the major human rights emergency going on at the moment in Europe: the unprecedented migration crisis, what Amnesty, in a report released in 2014, called "the human cost of Fortress Europe," denouncing how European Union (EU) migration policies and border control practices were preventing refugees from accessing asylum in the EU and putting their lives at risk in the course of increasingly perilous journeys.

In 2015 alone, more than 1 million migrants and asylum seekers reached the EU via the Mediterranean. More than 3,700 people died or went missing in the same period while making the journey. More than 130,000 have made the crossing since the start of 2016, while more than 410 have lost their lives in the attempt. Arrivals to Greece via Turkey across the Aegean Sea now far outstrip crossings via Libya to Italy. More than 80% of those taking the dangerous journey originate from countries beset by war, generalized violence, or with repressive governments, such as Syria, Eritrea, Somalia, Afghanistan, and Iraq.

The Brescia Law Clinic, in addition to assisting asylum and international protection seekers in the preparation and submission of applications to the local commission, has handled two major cases connected to these issues.

One case regards the so-called *left-to-die* migrant vessel. In May 2012, having set sail from Tripoli, the vessel – which was packed with 72 African migrants attempting to reach Europe – ran into trouble and was left floating with the currents for two weeks before washing back up on Libyan shores. Despite emergency calls being issued and the boat being located and identified by European coast guard officials, no rescue was ever attempted. All but nine of those on board died from thirst and starvation or in storms, including two babies. As the Council of Europe stressed in a Resolution on the case adopted on 24 April 2012, "[w]hat made this case different, beyond the tragedy of the lives lost, was that the boat's distress calls appear to have been ignored by a range of fishing vessels, a military helicopter and a large military vessel. Whereas many people have lost their lives in the Mediterranean Sea, the people involved in this boat tragedy could have been rescued if all those involved had complied with their obligations."[21] The Council found that, in doing so, "vessels under national and/or NATO command failed in their duty to rescue a boat in distress."

In 2014, the Brescia clinic submitted to the Italian General Attorney for the military forces a request to speed up the inquiry, which had been meandering along quite ineffectively for two years. The request has been ignored by the military magistrate so far, and the case is now going to be brought to the Strasbourg Court by

---

[21] Council of Europe, Resolution 1872 (2012) Final version, *Lives Lost in the Mediterranean Sea: Who Is Responsible?*

a group of human rights lawyers that includes the faculty who supervised the preliminary complaint in the Clinic.[22]

The second case regards the management of migrant flows by the Italian government in the Centre for Identification and Expulsion (CIE) located on the island of Lampedusa. In 2011, a ship had been intercepted by the coast guard and escorted to the closest harbour (Lampedusa). There, the migrants were disembarked and given first aid, transported to the CIE, deprived of their personal belongings, strip-searched, and detained in the shelter indefinitely, without a word on their legal status, without a mention of what would be the following steps or when they would be able to learn more of their situation. Because of overcrowding, migrants were ultimately forced to spend nights outside, sleeping on bare concrete pavements where they also ate the food handed out to them. After taking part in a demonstration against such conditions, one that culminated in arson, and with no possibility to resort to the judiciary, the claimant we represented was finally deported back to Tunis, with the charge of having taken part in the arson of the centre. Acting on his behalf, we submitted a complaint to the UN Committee Against Torture, maintaining the necessity to extend the notion of torture to such scenarios. The complaint has been declared admissible, and we are waiting now to discuss its merit.

The Weight and Value of Internationalization

Globalization has not only impacted the economic processes, it has also affected legal education, highlighting the need to train lawyers capable of adapting to and acting in different legal contexts, not so much with reference to knowledge of the law of each national legal system, but rather in terms of skills and working methods. This has resulted in an expanding transnational practice and a growing standardization of professional requirements.[23]

The internationalization of the legal profession, however, is not only a market-driven process. A growing number of issues are being increasingly regulated at supranational or transnational level, in particular, in certain "human rights sensitive" sectors such as immigration law, discrimination law, environmental law,

---

[22] The clinic is collaborating on this issue with Fédération internationale des ligues des droits de l'Homme (FIDH), an international human rights NGO federating 178 organizations from 120 countries. FIDH had filed complaints against the military forces of all the other countries participating in NATO operations in that area (France, UK, Spain, Belgium, USA, Canada, Malta) for failure of duty to rescue. Presently, on appeal, the French chambre de l'instruction has reviewed the decision of the first instance prosecutor not to proceed and has started a judicial inquiry which is still going on.

[23] See Robert Lutz, *Reforming Approaches to Educating Transnational Lawyers: Observations from America*, 61J. LEGAL EDUC. 449 (2012); more generally, see Jane Knight, *Internationalization Remodelled: Definition, Approaches, and Rationales*, 8 JOURNAL OF STUDIES IN INTERNATIONAL EDUCATION 5 (2004).

asylum and refugees law.[24] In spite of the differences between national legal systems, legal clinics have come to embrace a common goal of reforming academic curricula and reorienting the training of lawyers towards a public/social perspective. Under this perspective, clinics contribute to educate globally minded lawyers, bringing law students within the broader, transnational advocacy community.[25]

However, although we deem the international law–human rights cases described earlier as some of the most important cases addressed by our clinic, we feel that legal clinic action may risk minimalism. We fear that unless we coordinate litigation with advocacy and other political and social initiatives, we will reduce a problem of gigantic dimension to the solution provided in an individual case. This will make the legal action not part of a strategy to achieve broader systemic change but an impoverished surrogate of political and social mobilization.

We see these questions as crucial for the development of the European clinical movement. It is for these reasons that we support the idea of a coordinated action to be taken, together with NGOs and a network of professionals at local and European levels, to build up cross-border cooperation between clinicians not only on pedagogical issues but also on systemic political and social issues. What we should work out is a road map for creating human rights/social rights-oriented CLE programmes, which might include individual actions, group actions, proposals for law reform, policy and case support, reporting, and so on.

Cooperation in CLE

Networking between legal clinics and cooperation with civil society are important not only to link courtroom battles to political mobilization and advocacy, but also to support the process of consolidation and institutionalization of the CLE model and to create a common frame of reference (starting from the very definition of a legal clinic).

For this reason, from its origin, the Brescia Law Clinic has promoted and strongly supported a network of Italian legal clinics (*Rete delle cliniche legali*), with the aim of providing a structure through which to exchange experiences, organize training for teachers, encourage the creation of new clinical programmes, and overcome the institutional barriers and bureaucratic obstacles that hinder the development of the clinical movement. In 2011, we launched the first national conference on clinical education, and, since then, we have been participating in periodic meetings on the activities and projects of Italian clinics hosted by different clinics across the country. The scholars involved in the network are collaborating – both at the academic level and through cultural and scientific initiatives – in many different areas, from

---

[24] Deena Hurwitz, *Lawyering for Justice and the Inevitability of International Human Rights Clinics*, 28 YALE J. INT'L. L. 505 (2003); Arturo Carrillo, *Bringing International Law Home: The Innovative Role of Human Rights Clinics in the Transnational Legal Process*, 35 COLUM. HUM. R. L. REV. 527 (2004).

[25] *See* Frank Bloch and N.R. Madava Menon, *The Global Clinical Movement*, in THE GLOBAL CLINICAL MOVEMENT. EDUCATING LAWYERS FOR SOCIAL JUSTICE (Bloch ed., Oxford University Press, 2011), 267.

experimenting with educational innovations to research on clinical methodology and campaigns on sensitive issues.

Our clinic has also developed fruitful relationships with several EU (Valencia and Northumbria) and US (Yale, NYU, CUNY, UniCT, Berkeley, Irvine) clinics and regularly hosts visiting scholars from Europe, the United States, and South America. They lecture students, teach training courses, and participate in seminars and workshops on clinical methodology and educational matters. In particular, since 2011, an exchange agreement involving staff and students has been established with the School of Law of the University of Connecticut. We also collaborate with the *Clínica Jurídica per la Justícia Social* of the University of Valencia, with exchange programmes involving students and teachers.[26]

Members of the clinic routinely attend training events and international conferences on clinical education and legal ethics, such as those organized by the International Journal of Clinical Legal Education and the International Association of Legal Ethics. We are also part of the European Network for Clinical Legal Education (ENCLE) since its inception and of its board of directors, as well as of the Global Alliance for Justice education (GAJE), in whose Steering Committee I myself represent, together with Jose Garcia-Anon, clinics from the region of Western Europe.

Diffusion of CLE

After the first pioneering experiences at the universities of Brescia (2009) and Turin and Rome (2010), in the past five years, there has been a steady growth of legal clinics in other universities in Northern and Central Italy (Bergamo, Verona, Ferrara, Perugia, and Teramo). Legal clinic start-up projects also exist at the universities of Palermo, Bari, Sassari, Naples, and Milano.[27]

As said earlier, in Italy, as in other countries of Western Europe, the clinical movement, although clearly influenced by the American experience, has been propelled so far mainly by endogenous (academic and cultural) forces. However, these forces are also far from becoming mainstream. The general institutional framework of the University system has remained unchanged. This means that new legal clinics have to cope with a series of institutional, financial, and bureaucratic constraints. I will try to summarize the most important of these constrains in the Italian context and possible ways of gaining institutional footholds.

---

[26] In 2015, the programme included seminars, meetings, and workshops on cases concerning sexual and reproductive rights and discrimination against people with HIV on the one hand, and prisoners' rights and the condition of migrants in detention centres on the other. In 2016, a research on the role of empathy in clinical education, with a special focus on the experience of students involved in prisoner/inmates cases, was presented at the GAJE Conference held in Toronto by a team of researchers of the two universities.

[27] For more details, see Clelia Bartoli, *The Italian Legal Clinics Movements: Data and Prospects*, 22 INT'L. J. CLINICAL LEGAL EDUC. 213 (2015).

1. As noted earlier, at present, our university system does not recognize the position of "clinical professor." Teachers involved in the clinical programme cannot expect any official status, nor (very often) can they expect to receive any salary as clinicians. They merely add their clinical class (which is an elective) to others they are teaching.[28] Because we do not have the formal status of "clinician," the "in-house" model (embraced throughout US law schools) could not be implemented at the time when the first Italian clinics were established. This situation has not changed in the intervening time. One possibility would have been to rely on externships, but we wanted the clinic to be rooted in the university and, in the future, in the ordinary law school curricula.

That is why, as previously noted, in Brescia and in other universities, we opted to implement a hybrid clinic model. We were able to use the University's regulatory autonomy and establish a legal clinic course as an elective, offered in both semesters. Yet, formally, the clinic course belongs to the classes taught by the faculty member in charge of the coordination of the clinic. In other universities, clinics are offered as a laboratory or as a master course. In summary, across Italy, we are still in an experimental, insecure stage for the future of CLE.

The problem is how long can this hybrid model survive and be financially sustainable? We think not long. This is why it is of the utmost importance to carve out a stable role for legal clinics by inserting them into the ordinary curricula and incorporating legal clinics into the ordinary life of law schools. Such stabilization would eventually free legal clinics from the bureaucratic and financial constrains which have so far impaired their development, giving appropriate human and financial resources to clinical programmes. Moreover, stabilization would eventually lead to the recognition of a different professional skill (clinical teaching), having its own educational techniques and therefore deserving special training.

This goal does not necessarily imply that we shall replicate the dual professional track system which operates in the United States, often creating a hierarchy inside legal teaching and the academy. On the other hand, we need to issue a set of quality standards that a legal clinic should meet in order to be fully recognized as part of a university-validated system of legal clinics. Although we need to come out of the experimental stage, it may be advisable to preserve some aspects of it. For example, adopting a hybrid clinic model was a path-dependent choice due to the initial organizational and institutional constraints described earlier. However, these solutions have proved to have some qualities that encourage one to see the merits of keeping elements of this model by choice and not by necessity, as part of one possible new European clinic model.

[28] In the Italian university education system, each class of teaching must be approved by the Ministry of Education (MIUR) and classified under a bureaucratic heading, which are known as "scientific branches." This process gives qualified professors the opportunity of being officially in charge of the course. Because a new clinical teaching has not (yet) been approved by the Ministry, it consequently does not belong to any scientific branch.

2. The second type of factors that have affected the development of clinical education relate to the role of students and what they can actually do within a clinical programme. Under the Italian civil and criminal procedure code, only a qualified lawyer may take legal responsibility for individual representation, and only a qualified lawyer has rights of audience. This means that (1) students cannot speak before the court, although they (with the judge's permission) are allowed to attend the hearings; and that (2) all claims, briefs, appeals, and other acts must be approved and signed by the relevant responsible lawyer. This gives a remarkably directive character to our clinical teaching which, as things stand, is hardly modifiable.

However, at least in Italy, this situation may change following a recent reform concerning access to the legal profession (Presidential Decree n. 137/2012). The reform makes it possible for students in their last year of university to carry out part of the 18-month practical experience which must be completed before taking the national Bar exam. In this new status as "trainees," when working in a clinical programme, students will be allowed to speak before the lower courts and sign briefs. This development gives rise to new opportunities as well as new challenges. The risk is that clinics become mere precursor to professional training, but it is a risk worth taking since the new rules also offer a chance of empowering students and strengthening their role within legal clinics.

3. A third type of impairment is the absence or poor development of a literature on clinical education and for clinical education. Such literature is abundant in the United States, where it developed at the same time as the clinical movement, yet it is sporadic at best in most European countries, where there are just a few journals providing systematic reflection on clinical work, and the number of articles published that describe, criticize, or set normative standards relating to clinical work is quite small. Equally scarce is systematic and well-written material for the classroom, as well as skills training material for students. We need to fill this gap, which constitutes one of the most significant impediments to the development of an effective teaching enterprise for clinical education.

4. Finally, for clinics that are oriented towards public-interest ideals, it is important to produce a public impact. This means that it is necessary to assess which mechanisms among those inherent to access to justice-oriented strategies (lobbying, litigation, public policy initiatives, protest, public confrontation) are more effective, how they can interplay, and which fora (domestic or supranational, political, or courts) are the most suitable (according to the issue/subject one is confronted with). This approach is consistent with legal mobilization theory, which posits that rights advocacy encompasses more than what happens in the courtroom.[29] Law

---

[29] See Michael McCann, *How Does Law Matter for Social Movements?*, in HOW DOES LAW MATTER? (Bryant G. Garth, Austin Sarat eds., Northwestern University Press, 1998), 76; Michael McCann, RIGHTS AT WORK: PAY EQUITY REFORM AND THE POLITICS OF LEGAL MOBILIZATION (University of Chicago Press, 1994); Scott Cummings and Deborah Rhode, *Public Interest Litigation: Insights from Theory*

can be mobilized much earlier, before cases are taken to court, in advocacy, education, media, outreach, collaboration with NGOs, research, drafting legislation, lobbying, and other grassroots activities.

Future of CLE in Europe

There is a clear asymmetry between academic capital and economic resources when you compare European and American clinics, and this is sometimes reproduced in unequal exchanges among them. However, to overcome this asymmetry does not necessarily mean replicating the same model. A distinctive identity of European clinics is likely to be the natural output of a different input. This is true both whether we look at clinics as a tool of a new pedagogy or as a tool in a struggle for rights.

Starting from the pedagogical side of the question, in order to develop a sustainable and dynamic model of CLE, we need to take into account the specific structure of legal education in our respective countries, the typical profile of a professor of law, the resources available, and the successful or unsuccessful experiences clinics have had in the past. But we also need a common normative frame of reference. This can be provided, for example, by the Bologna Process, which aims at reviewing and homogenizing the different university systems of the Member States of the EU and beyond. Legal clinics sit perfectly with some of the objectives of the Bologna Process (enhancing high-quality legal knowledge education, overcoming the self-training system, opening the university to society, involving and empowering students, integrating basic skills and skills which cut across all fields), but, what is more important, they can be seen as a powerful catalyst for change in this process of modernization of our education systems.

If we look instead at the sociolegal function of clinics – improving the level of social justice and enhancing a human rights culture – again, a distinctive identity of European clinics is, we could say, in "the nature of things." Pursuing such objectives requires a specific knowledge of the problems to be addressed, of their origins as well as of the political, social, or economic obstacles that should be addressed in order to overcome them.

One of the distinctive features of European clinics is precisely the presence of this specific knowledge, which is necessarily context-based. By the same token, the legal and political solutions to the problems which must be addressed also will be based mainly on a specific political and legal context, although this does not mean that European clinics cannot receive consultancy from long-established non-European clinics or that it is not possible to import and adapt legal principles and rules coming

and Practice, 36 FORDHAM URB. L. J. 603 (2009); Austin Sarat and Stuart Scheingold, CAUSE LAWYERS AND SOCIAL MOVEMENTS (Stanford University Press, 2006).

from countries that have a different legal tradition or to resort to possible international solutions if there are no domestic legal answers.

Also in this case we have a common frame of reference, a shared culture of human rights which is normatively grounded in European higher law – the European Convention on Human Rights and the Charter of Fundamental Rights of the EU – and in the common values which are embodied in this supranational legal order.

CONCLUSION

Like any other example of legal transplant, the diffusion of CLE in the Italian context, and more generally in Europe, has involved a complex process of legal and cultural adaptation and complicated interactions of domestic and foreign actors. It has been suggested that differences in the diffusion process among different countries are due to the fact that the choices of domestic actors are constrained by the domestically available legal models and that at least some of the differences between core legal models (such as those between common law and civil law models) survive the transplantation.[30] As previously noted, however, drivers of differences also include institutional complementarities; linguistic, educational, or professional ties; and also being more or less part of the sphere of political and cultural influences of the exporting country.

Differences in the process of diffusion and adaptation of CLE across various European countries do not prevent us from talking of an emerging European model, one that has its own characteristics. In adapting to European soil, legal clinics are giving shape to an original form of hybridization which might eventually result in a mutually beneficial cross-fertilization of the two legal cultures and education models. This is actually becoming the most common mode of transplant generated by globalization, which, by producing the strong transnational mobility of people and knowledge, leads to a dynamic relationship between different, locally situated sources, traditions, and cultures.[31]

Can European legal clinics at the same time spearhead national and transnational legal activism and mobilize social movements, and are these two enterprises complementary or disjointed, harmonious or antagonistic?

Indeed, a theory and a practice that entrust the solution of problems of justice mainly to the state (in particular, to courts) and to the individualistic, adversarial logic of litigation may conflict with a pluralistic vision of society and with the flexible logic of social bargaining, as well as with the interests of collective social actors.

---

[30] See Holger Spamann, *Contemporary Legal Transplants: Legal Families and the Diffusion of (Corporate) Law*, Harvard Public Law Working Paper n. 09/33, 26 BYU L. REV. 1813 (2009).

[31] Rosaria Ferrarese Maria, DIRITTO SCONFINATO: INVENTIVA GIURIDICA E SPAZI NEL MONDO GLOBALE (Editori Laterza, 2006).

We also feel the danger of cultural elitism: public interest litigation is a technical tool that requires specialist skills to be mastered. And if it is mastered, it is mastered by few people. The number of actors is inevitably reduced. A social change becomes an affair of the few people who can participate in the conversation.

These concerns are not new. As it is well known, litigation as a strategy for social change has been systematically criticized in its ability to bring about social change. Such critiques have centred mainly on two basic claims. The first one is related to its effectiveness: litigation cannot in itself reform social institutions.[32] The second one is related to the concern that litigation strategies divert efforts from collective political struggle and disempower clients' communities.[33]

The impact of litigation in the struggle for social justice is, however, far from being considered a settled issue. This is particularly clear if we look at the work of law and social movement scholars theorizing, on grounds of empirical evidence, how litigation strategies matter for social change by raising public consciousness or stimulating movement activity.[34] As for the problem of interest representation, in a seminal article, Chayes had already suggested various techniques for inducing in the process the representation of affected groups and people that did not appear on their own initiative.[35] More recently, it has been argued that the current discussion has tended to underrate the potential of public law litigation because it has tended to misperceive its forms: "[m]uch criticism has been directed at a model of judge-centered, hierarchical, and rule-bound intervention that has ceased to correspond to trial court practice. In fact, trial judges and litigants have crafted more decentralized and indirect forms of intervention that rely on stakeholder negotiation, rolling-rule regimes, and transparency."[36]

Although no definite assessment of the efficacy of this "experimentalist" approach is offered by its supporters, exploring this "new public law approach" may create opportunities for a new learning of the law in action. It is for these reason that we believe that, in the coming years, one of our most important and exciting practical and research tasks will be to test the positions of both critics and supporters of public law interest litigation strategies.

---

[32] Gerald Rosenberg, THE HOLLOW HOPE: CAN COURTS BRING ABOUT SOCIAL CHANGE? (University of Chicago Press, 2008).

[33] Stuart Scheingold, THE POLITICS OF RIGHTS: LAWYERS, PUBLIC POLICY AND SOCIAL CHANGE (Yale University Press 1974).

[34] McCann, *supra* note 28. See also Venera Protopapa, *Shaping Equality for Migrants* (unpublished doctoral dissertation; University of Milano 2016).

[35] Abram Chayes. *The Role of the Judge in Public Law Litigation*, 89 HARV. L. REV. 1281 (1976).

[36] Charles Sabel and William Simon, *Destabilization Rights: How Public Law Litigation Succeeds*. 117 HARV. L. REV. 1015 (2004).

4

A New Dawn in the Czech Clinical Movement

The Clinical Programme at the Law School of Palacký University in Olomouc

Veronika Tomoszková and Maxim Tomoszek

INTRODUCTION

Palacký University in Olomouc, Faculty of Law, in the Czech Republic, represents one of the first successful attempts at integrating clinical legal education (CLE) into the law curriculum. The programme consists of various optional clinical classes but also includes compulsory skills classes, street-law, moot courts, other specialized skills courses, and a course on professional ethics.

The structure of the programme can be best described from the perspective of our students pursuing the five-year Master of Law degree. In their very first semester, students engage in the compulsory study skills course, which focuses on skills necessary for studying law using the problem-based learning method. In their second year, students experience street-law classes, teaching law at elementary school and high schools. In the third year, students undertake a compulsory legal skills course which walks them through the process of providing legal advice to a client in a simulated simple case, focusing on the development of students' lawyering skills.

By the third year, the students have access to virtually all of the clinical courses on offer. The clinical programme at Palacký consists of several self-standing clinical courses focusing on different areas of law and employing various methodologies. There are four separate live-client clinics:

1. The Student Law Office, which is a general legal advice clinic accepting cases from any area of law, except for areas covered by other live-client clinics; most of the time, students deal with civil law, family law, debt enforcement, personal bankruptcy, or housing.
2. The Administrative Law Clinic, where students most often provide advice on building law, planning law, administrative offences, or social security.
3. The Consumer Law Clinic, where students focus on validity of consumer contracts and liability of businesses.

4. The Small Business Clinic, where students cooperate with a university incubator to help get small businesses off the ground.

All live-client clinics work in a very similar way. Students meet with clients at the clinical office, gather information, and open a case-file. Over approximately one month, they prepare written legal advice – possibly accompanied with necessary legal documentation – for the client under the supervision of members of the faculty or practicing lawyers.[1] It is also important to mention that, at the beginning of the semester, students go for a weekend retreat workshop aimed at imparting skills and values deemed necessary for students to succeed in a live-client clinic.

There are also two clinics combining simulation and externship, which are carried out in cooperation with the office of the ombudsman, the Clinical of Ombudsman Practice and Clinic of Social Rights. In both, students take classes during the semester taught by lawyers from the office of ombudsman, where they work on simulated cases from the practice of the ombudsman. After such instruction, students undertake a forty-hour practical experience in the office of ombudsman.

There are, furthermore, several clinics operating without externship or clients and thus mostly relying on simulation or other practical methods of education, and these focus on specific areas of law, such as the Human Rights Clinic, the Patients' Rights Clinic, the Antidiscrimination Clinic, the Clinic of Refugees and Foreigners, the Environmental Law Clinic, the Construction Law Clinic, and the Laboratory of International Human Rights Law.

EMERGENCE OF CLE

The first legal clinic in Olomouc was established in 1996, and it was also the very first legal clinic established in Central and Eastern Europe. What factors led to this historical achievement for Palacký Law School?

Most of them were linked to the overall environment at the institution. The Palacký Law School was reestablished in 1991,[2] after the Velvet Revolution. Legal education during communism was obviously under strict control of the communist regime, so the newly established law school had an unprecedented opportunity to rid itself of communist influence and to orient itself internationally, drawing inspiration from foreign, especially US, law schools. This ambition was reflected in the goals envisioned by the academic senate of Palacký University, in its resolution reestablishing the Law School. The senate wanted the new law school to be modern, strictly separated from the communist party, based on Western

[1] Although majority of the members of the faculty are practicing lawyers, some of them are not, but all members of the faculty can supervise students in a live-client clinic.
[2] The University in Olomouc was established in 1573, but closed by the Austrian Emperor Franz Joseph I. in 1860. It was reestablished after World War II in 1946, but without a Law School, which was brought back into existence only in 1991.

democratic values, and embracing practical forms of education and strong international outlook, all this in order to educate a new generation of lawyers for a democratic society.[3]

Being such a young institution, the academic environment at Palacký Law School was far less conservative than other, older law schools in the Czech Republic (in Prague and Brno). Most professors were young or without significant experience in academia. The management of the law school was aware that they needed to distinguish Palacký Law School from other Czech law schools in order to be recognized and successful. Legal clinics and international outlook were ways to achieve this. US law professors were consulted in the process of designing the law school curriculum, and they regularly visited Palacký Law School to teach in the early 1990s. Establishing a legal clinic was a logical part of these efforts.[4] In the early 1990s, there were many opportunities for financial support connected to establishing legal clinics in Central and Eastern Europe.

The Palacký Law School, in cooperation with Hofstra Law School, especially professor Stefan H. Krieger, received a Ford Foundation grant to establish a housing clinic. Up to this point, the story goes like a fairy-tale. However, the clinic only lasted for one year, after which it was discontinued due to a variety of reasons – one of the important factors was the death of dean Liberda, who founded the Law School in 1991 and was a strong supporter of legal clinics, accompanied by subsequent trouble stabilizing the personal and institutional situation at the law school.[5] Between 1998 and 2003, Palacký Law School was several times at risk of losing accreditation and therefore being forced to shut down.

But there were other factors that caused the first legal clinic to fail. Although members of the faculty were generally supportive of legal clinics, or at least did not oppose them, most of them had no clinical experience and were not able to manage or supervise the legal clinic. A further important obstacle was the level of English-language proficiency at the Law School, which prevented many professors from visiting clinics in the United States and getting crucial personal experience. For these reasons, in the original project, a local attorney with a good level of English was contracted to supervise the clinic and carry out a study visit to US clinics. However, that attorney stopped supervising the clinic at the end of the project, and, with more pressing matters at hand, the law school did not allocate the necessary resources and energy to finding a new supervisor and keeping the clinic running.[6]

---

[3] E. Hrudníková, Jařabe, tady máš práci. Tak začala obnova právnické fakulty. Žurnál UP online. www.zurnal.upol.cz/pf/zprava/clanek/jarabe-tady-mas-praci-tak-zacala-obnova-pravnicke-fakulty/.
[4] For more detailed analysis of US support for European Clinical Legal Education see Chapter 1 by Genty in this volume.
[5] For details see S. H. Krieger, *The Stories Clinicians Tell*, in COMPLEX LAW TEACHING: KNOWLEDGE, SKILLS AND VALUES. (M. Tomoszek ed. VUP: Olomouc, 2013), 11–36; ##REKOSH, pp. 87–89, notes 98 and 102, AKSAMOVIC, D., GENTY, P., p. 432 ff.
[6] Compare with reasons for the decline of clinical legal education stated by Philip Genty in his chapter, p. 6.

This early failure of the clinical programme has been analysed by several authors who suggested additional reasons for this failure: for example, the Czech legal environment, which prohibited student practice; insufficient infrastructure at the law school; or the fact that the clinic was being run in almost the exact same manner as US clinics but without necessary adjustments reflecting differences within the Czech context and the specificities of Palacký Law School.[7]

Later development shows that, even though it was discontinued, the clinic was not a failure. It allowed other clinicians to learn from this experience, and it also established something we describe as the "institutional memory" of having a clinic, which consistently permeated the Law School in subsequent years and was one of the key motivations for reestablishing the clinical programme in Olomouc.

At first, the legal clinic was reintroduced in very limited form in 2001, by the newly elected young dean who was a student at the law school when the first clinic was running in 1996. The support of the dean for CLE resulted in a successful application for financial support from the European Social Fund and the Czech State Budget to develop practical forms of education at Palacký Law School. This project enabled, in 2006, the Law Faculty in Olomouc to restart the standardized live-client clinic, which since that time has become a stable part of the curriculum.

Looking more closely at the reestablishment of the live-client clinic in 2006, we can identify several important factors making this attempt significantly more successful. First, there was experience deriving from the previous attempt to establish a clinic. Second, there was already a simulation clinic (running in cooperation with a nongovernmental organization [NGO]) focusing on Public Interest Law, which later transformed into the live-client Administrative Law Clinic. Moreover, several members of the faculty had visited clinics outside of the Czech Republic (Poland, Serbia, the United States), which gave the team a very good idea of what types of clinics existed and how they were run. This allowed the team working on the reestablished clinic to design it in a way that seemed most suitable to the circumstances of Palacký Law School.

Due to the lack of a student representation rule, we decided to design the live-client clinic as a nonrepresentation, written advice–only clinic, based on the Polish model. In these clinics, students, under the supervision of practicing attorneys or academics, prepare a legal analysis of the client's case, including in some cases legal documents, and it is up to the client to act on her own. Even though this was a problematic issue from the point of view of US clinicians who helped to establish the first clinic in 1996 and also the Ford Foundation, it fit much better into the Czech environment. The need for representation of some clients was solved later through cooperation with the NGO Pro Bono Alliance, which is a clearinghouse that sources *pro bono* representation from the private sector.

---

[7] For details see KRIEGER, S. H. The Stories Clinicians Tell. in: TOMOSZEK, M. (ed.) Complex Law Teaching: Knowledge, Skills and Values. VUP: Olomouc, 2013, p. 11–36, ##REKOSH, pp. 87–89, notes 98 and 102, ##AKSAMOVIC, D., GENTY, P., p. 432 ff.

Another important factor that motivated the law school to restart the clinics was the opportunity to fund (at least initially) the clinical programme via a grant from the European Social Fund. The reputation of the Law School in Olomouc was damaged by the previous difficult years, so developing a clinical programme was a way to enhance its public image and to attract students.[8] Compared to law schools in Brno and Prague, Palacký Law School is situated in Olomouc, which is a significantly smaller city with fewer opportunities for students to work in law firms and legal institutions, and the same is true for members of the faculty. Legal clinics offer an important opportunity for students to get experience with the practice of law, whereas for teachers, whose only job is teaching at the law school, legal clinics are a valuable source of practical inspiration for their research and other academic activities.

From the institutional perspective, the factors helping to sustain the clinic were:

- establishment of an internal organizational unit – Centre for CLE – which guaranteed methodological and administrative support for clinical courses and also ensured continuity;
- involvement of faculty members as supervisors in clinics. In this way, the clinic was not dependant on an external supervisor whose decision to leave would mean shutting down the clinic;
- support of the dean of the law school, which in our case was at first based on liking the idea of the clinic and later on the realization of the benefits of the clinical programme for the law school, especially because clinics were significantly contributing to a positive public image of the law school,
- designing the clinic to meet the highest professional standards – creating an insurance policy, establishing a rigorous internal review procedure, ensuring personal data protection, and putting in place confidentiality policies,
- involving the clinical students beyond case work. In Olomouc, clinical students organize cultural, family, or sport events or work with charities. This creates a stronger bond between the law school and its students, who often come back after graduation, willing to be involved in the clinical courses as supervisors or in other roles;
- and last, but not least, creating a sustainable funding scheme, preferably with at least partial external contribution in the beginning (grants or donors).

For many students, their clinical experience is determinative with regard to their future job – if they enjoy the clinic, they are often motivated to go into private practice; if they find helping clients in clinic too time-consuming, difficult, or simply not interesting, they often pursue alternative career paths.

---

[8] According to unpublished survey conducted among the first-year students of Palacký Law School in 2015, approximately 10,5% of them chose the Palacký Law School over other Czech law schools because of the clinical programme and the overall practical focus of the curriculum.

As will be discussed in the next section, legal clinics were also reintroduced with the aim of improving the law school curriculum and learning outcomes and, to some extent, even undertaking the general reform of law teaching at Palacký Law School.

Since 2006, the clinical programme of Palacký Law School continues to develop. In 2006, we introduced six clinical courses. The main goal was to introduce live-client clinics (Student Law Office, Administrative Law Clinic) and to cover some of the most interesting and complicated areas of law in simulation clinics (Refugee Law Clinic, Human Rights Clinic, Small Business and NGO Clinic, Electronic Communications Clinic). It must be stressed that even the simulation clinics usually contain some real-life practical elements, such as drafting answers to legal questions posted on legal advice websites, visiting institutions, visiting court proceedings, and the like.

Based on the experience with these courses, it became very clear that legal clinics, both the live-client and simulation variety, are far better suited to teaching in complex multidisciplinary fields of legal practice with strong value elements, such as human rights, migration, discrimination, and health care, in comparison with traditional law teaching (lectures, seminars). This resulted in further development of the clinic by adding new clinical courses, such as the Consumer Protection Clinic, the Antidiscrimination Clinic, the Patient's Rights Clinic, the Environmental Law Clinic, the Social Rights Clinic, the Laboratory of International Human Rights, and others. Some of the clinical courses run continuously without interruption, some have been subsequently transformed, and some have even wholly replaced other preexisting courses. Recently, some of them shifted towards policy clinics, which seem increasingly popular, particularly in Western Europe.

The success of this second attempt was based on involving faculty members instead of external supervisors and also on modelling the new clinic on the Polish experience. A similar story could be told about all Czech law schools, where clinics have existed in various forms and at various points in time over the past twenty years or so. As of 2015, legal clinics featured at all four Czech law schools, and three of them (Olomouc, Pilsen, and Prague) offer live-client clinics. What makes Palacký Law School different is the existence of a complex system of skills development; clinics are accompanied by two compulsory skill courses, a street-law programme, moot courts, specialized skill courses, and a course on professional ethics.

REFORMING THE TEACHING AND PRACTICE OF LAW IN EUROPE

Goals and Methods

Traditionally, legal education in the Czech Republic is very theoretical in orientation.[9] This partially derives from the prominence of the so-called historical

---

[9] This is similar in other countries of continental Europe and is discussed in other chapters of this book, especially in Chapter 8 by N. Markard and Chapter 6 by X. Aurey.

law method or approach, whereby much emphasis is placed on legal history, which is understood as the basis for understanding the current law. Another reason for this theoretical orientation is the hangover from forty years of communist rule, which did not need well-educated, capable, and morally strong lawyers who would protect the rights of individuals and democratic values. Lawyers were understood as a threat to the regime, and therefore the legal professions and law schools were under strict control of the communist party, which careful selected ideologically "suitable" candidates.

The prevailing teaching methods at Czech law schools are still predominantly reliant on both lectures, usually absent any student involvement,[10] or seminars, where the degree of student interaction varies. In some classes, seminars are very similar to lectures. In others, students practise their theoretical knowledge on hypotheticals, present on various issues to their colleagues, or discuss problems among themselves and with the teacher. Although the majority of law school alumni work as attorneys, law schools pay little to no attention to the development of practical skills or key competences, which are essential for success in the profession.[11] The focus of legal education is on knowledge to make sure that graduates meet the qualification criteria for the regulated legal profession. However, legal regulation is changing at such a fast pace (in part due to the penetration of international and European law into the domestic legal system) that the value of possessing exhaustive substantive knowledge with respect to any given area of law has decreased significantly. Furthermore, with the increasing amount of legal regulation, it has become impossible for any single lawyer to comprehensively know all of the law in relation to any field, especially given the overlapping of several legal systems. Legal education should therefore focus on skills, which help lawyers to navigate in the variable legal environment; to grasp, identify, and interpret legal norms and thus provide durable outcomes. It is of no surprise that young lawyers often complain that law school did not prepare them for the practice of law and that they were required to learn much of the practical aspects of legal work from their supervisors and peers in the workplace.

To sum up, legal education in the Czech Republic has been largely theoretical in nature, delivered in lecture-style classes, with a strong separation between different areas of law and a lack of any ethical and social-justice dimension. This is slowly changing, especially thanks to internationalization, Europeanization, education reform, student demand, and, last, but not least, legal clinics. Legal clinics challenge the status quo – they allow students to apply the law in the context of individual cases and connect different areas of law, allowing them to understand the law from

---

[10] Lectures are still a prevailing method of law teaching in Germany and France; compare with Chapter 8 by N. Markard and Chapter 6 by X. Aurey.
[11] The relevance of skills for practice and their lack in law school curricula was confirmed by the empirical study conducted by the Law Faculty of Masaryk University in Brno in 2014 among alumni of Czech law schools: Znalosti a dovednosti absolventů právnických fakult v ČR, Brno, 20. 1. 2015.

a practical perspective. The passive approach[12] to legal education that is a core feature of the *status quo* is very efficiently challenged head-on by CLE. In addition to facilitating a deeper knowledge and understanding of the law, clinics also allow students to acquire practical experience and develop important lawyering skills. Students experience, first-hand, ethical issues and come to realize the social and ethical context of law and legal regulation. Through this process, students may come to identify and internalize values embedded in law and protected by it. It is also important to allow and encourage students to enjoy the feeling of contributing to social justice.

Our experience with CLE (live-client clinics as well as other models) shows that clinics enrich the law curriculum with contextual, interdisciplinary, and experiential elements. The cases we deal with in the clinics are not stripped bare from the social context out of which they arise. Students analyse cases themselves and are immersed in the facts and, through this, come to identify the legal problem which emerges from the social context. Real-life cases, in all their complexity, enable the future lawyers to learn humane lawyering through hands-on experience which helps them to "bring the whole self"[13] to the practice of law. The students experience the ownership and responsibility implicit in working on a client's case. To maximize the connection between students and clients, the Student Law Office at Palacký Law School provides free legal assistance to underrepresented members of the local community. The legal services are provided only in person (i.e. we do not accept cases via e-mail because we want our students to have the genuine experience of a personal contact with the client). This rule limits the range of our potential clients to those who are able to visit the office during our opening hours throughout the semester.

Furthermore, the clinics afford students the opportunity to see how different legal disciplines and branches relate to one another in a single case. In doctrinal courses, the cases used for teaching are usually compressed and the legal problem is presented from the perspective of a particular branch of law (civil law, criminal law, consumer law, etc.). The clinics allow for a holistic approach to the law that reveals and confronts, rather than conceals and avoids, complexity.

From the point of view of education reform, legal clinics are a very efficient method for improving learning outcomes and the achievement of educational goals throughout the curriculum. Palacký Law School made the strategic decision to involve teachers from various departments of the law school in clinical teaching. These are faculty members who also teach other classes, typically compulsory

---

[12] The theoretical approach to legal education is often criticized, even with identification of negative implications for legal practice. *See, e.g.,* David Kolaja, Vojtěch Cepl: O právnické fakultě UK a jejích třech dcerách, May 11, 2004, ejustice.cz (online), transcript of the interview with professor Vojtěch Cepl from radio show Česká justice from April 23, 2004, http://ejustice.cz/vojtech-cepl-o-pravnicke-fakulte-uk-jejich-trech-dcerach.

[13] Mike Robbins, Bring Your Whole Self to Work, http://mike-robbins.com/tedxberkeley/.

substantive courses. After experiencing the benefits of CLE, these teachers often embrace interactive teaching methods in their other classes, thus improving the overall quality of teaching at the law school.

In the Czech Republic, the Bologna Process and the creation of the European Higher Education Area brought on a sense of urgency with respect to efforts to reform legal education. Education was supposed to focus more strongly on skills and competences, rather than pure knowledge, as was demonstrated by various strategic documents on the European level, such as the Recommendation 2006/962/EC of the European Parliament and of the Council of 18 December 2006 on key competences for lifelong learning.[14] On the other hand, the Bologna Process in itself probably cannot be said to have induced the development of legal clinics, especially since it was not wholeheartedly accepted by all relevant stakeholders. For example, in the area of legal education, being very conservative, the Bologna model of three-year bachelor-degree and two-year follow-up master's degree has still not been implemented in the Czech Republic. Having said that, even though the Bologna Process's influence is rather minor, it can still be seen as an important piece of the puzzle, leading to an overall shift from theoretical to practical higher education that can be observed in many contexts in Europe and in the Czech Republic.

It is also perhaps interesting to note that at most Czech law schools, CLE was the first educational scheme to systematically address legal ethics, eventually leading to the creation of specialized courses. The importance of legal ethics for legal education was emphasized by a recent regulation of the Czech government that defines the framework teaching outcomes for different study areas. For the area of law, it states that the alumni of law schools should demonstrate in appropriate breadth and detail an understanding of the ethical aspects of the practice of law and the social responsibility of the legal profession.[15]

Also, by involving the students in *pro bono* legal work, legal clinics teach them about the importance of access to justice, and many alumni of legal clinics continue to provide *pro bono* services in their practice.

Beyond the Educational Goals

Traditionally, there has been no expectation in the Czech context for universities or law faculties to transcend educational goals and become involved with the problems afflicting the community in which they are based. Societal engagement among universities (the so-called *third mission*) started in Western Europe in the 1960s.[16] However, in Czechoslovakia, universities were used by the communist regime to

---

[14] Official Journal L 394 of December 30, 2006.
[15] See the Appendix, Part 22, of the Government Regulation No. 275/2016 Coll., on areas of higher education.
[16] Paul Benneworth and Michael Osborne. KNOWLEDGE ENGAGEMENT AND HIGHER EDUCATION IN EUROPE (Global University Network for Innovation, 2014) 220.

achieve its goals and to control society and thus enjoyed only very limited academic freedom.[17] As discussed earlier, this was especially true in relation to the study of law, which was of utmost importance for the regime because it prepared new judges and prosecutors. Therefore, the shift towards societal engagement could start only as late as the 1990s and is still in progress.

Legal clinics are very important for the development of social justice and community awareness within law schools. Scholars tend at times to live in an ivory tower, without connection to the society around them.[18] Legal clinics bring the engaging and troubling social justice issues right to the doorsteps of legal academics and law students.

Helping people in need with their everyday legal troubles is a core principle of CLE, which naturally makes both teachers and students think reflectively and critically about law and its effects on society, whether positive or negative. In this way, clinics help educate lawyers who will be equipped for future challenges, empathetic, socially aware, and who appreciate the responsibility of the legal profession and the broader role of lawyers in society. Even those legal clinics that do not work with real clients, which are based on simulation, analysis of the legislative process, or writing amicus briefs, still all contain social justice elements and contribute to improvement of the overall quality of life of every member of society. By reaching out to the community, law schools adopt a new role, and they contribute to improving the overall of negative public perception of lawyers. Based on the experience of Palacký Law School, public outreach is best achieved through street-law programmes, where students improve the legal awareness of vulnerable groups.

Legal clinics play an important role in strengthening access to justice. The Czech Republic has a relatively well-developed model of free legal aid provided by lawyers appointed by the Czech Bar Association or, in certain situations, by courts. An important role is also played by NGOs, especially where clients require multidisciplinary counselling (not only legal, but also psychological, social, financial, etc.). Even with this well-developed system of free legal aid, there are significant groups of people who have limited or no access to free legal aid with respect to many difficult situations and for whom legal clinics, due to their flexibility, represent the only opportunity to receive qualified legal aid.[19] In the Czech Republic, provision of free legal aid is usually linked to court proceedings. But there are many situations

---

[17] Hynek Baňouch, *Metody, motivy a cíle studia komunistického práva*, in KOMUNISTICKÉ PRÁVO V ČESKOSLOVENSKU. KAPITOLY Z DĚJIN BEZPRÁVÍ(Brno: MPO a MU, 2009), 274–77. www.komunistickepravo.cz/.

[18] In 2005, Michal Bobek identified the disconnectedness of legal education from practice and social reality as one of its main weaknesses; see M. Bobek, *Klepání na nebeskou bránu: O nereformovatelnosti studia práv v Čechách, Díl I.: Právní vzdělání a právní kultura*. 10 PRÁVNÍ ROZHLEDY Č. 365–70 (2005).

[19] Compare with different, but also significant roles of legal clinics in the existing system of legal aid as mentioned in Chapter 8 by N. Markard and Chapter 6 by X. Aurey in this volume.

where legal advice is needed outside the court process, or when it is too late to provide legal advice after court proceedings have commenced because the source of the problem is a mistake or negligence in the past that cannot be mended. Legal clinics at Palacký Law School provide legal advice outside of court proceedings. Usually, they serve around 100 clients during each semester, which for a city the size of Olomouc – with approximately 100,000 inhabitants – is a significant number.

However, legal clinics do not only cover gaps in the free legal aid system – they can also help to develop long-term solutions. First, legal clinics educate professionals who are sensitive to social justice issues and reflect this in their future practice. Legal clinics have also proved useful in identifying the problems of the current free legal aid system, and, through publicizing this information and participating in public debate, they may contribute to systemic changes.[20]

The Weight and Value of Internationalization

The curriculum of Palacký Law School contains compulsory classes dedicated to European law and international law that aim to equip students with basic knowledge and skills for working within European and international law. Since both European and international law are incorporated into the Czech legal system, it is essential to approach any legal problem with awareness of the possible European or international law implications.

From the perspective of legal clinics, the level of engagement with European and international law depends significantly on the focus of the clinic. In clinics dedicated to human rights issues (for example the Patients' Rights Clinic, the Antidiscrimination Clinic, the Human Rights Clinic) or areas of law where the influence of European or international law is very strong (the Refugee Law Clinic, the Consumer Law Clinic, the Environmental Law Clinic), the supranational context is a very important part of the educational goals.

While the clinics are not the forum in which students are supposed to acquire basic knowledge of European and international law or how they operate in the Czech legal system, in the clinical setting, students gain, in our opinion, more advanced knowledge and skills related to European and international law. They learn how to apply the theoretical knowledge about supranational law gained in their compulsory courses to complex real-life situations and cases and in the context of specific problems. These are skills that are essential for contemporary Czech lawyers across many practice areas. The Czech reality is that if a legal case

---

[20] See O., Drummond and G. McKeever, ACCESS TO JUSTICE THROUGH UNIVERSITY LAW CLINICS (Belfast: Ulster University Law School, 2015), 17 and 29; Margaret Martin Barry, *Accessing Justice: Are Pro Se Clinics a Reasonable Response to the Lack of Pro Bono Legal Services and Should Law School Clinics Conduct Them?* 67 FORDHAM L. REV. (1999), http://ssrn.com/abstract=2607328; Cath Sylvester, *Bridging the Gap? The Effect of Pro Bono Initiatives on Clinical Legal Education in the UK.* 3 INT'L. J. CLINICAL LEGAL EDUC. 29–40 (June 2003), http://journals.northumbria.ac.uk/index.php/ijcle/article/view/116.

does not contain an obvious supranational dimension, lawyers tend to solve it only through national law and do not see the bigger picture, sometimes because they lack relevant knowledge and skills. There are significant differences between generations, since the emphasis put on supranational law by the law schools' curricula significantly increased in past fifteen years. For these reasons, it can often be observed that district courts or administrative authorities at the local level avoid the supranational dimension of the cases they deal with, and that dimension often appears only on appeal or at the Supreme Court, Supreme Administrative Court, or Constitutional Court.

Legal clinics in European law schools provide a unique forum in which future lawyers can learn to see the whole picture of the cases they are working on, including their supranational dimension, and ensuring that this happens is one of the most important tasks that clinic supervisors must undertake. In this way, students also learn what it means to be part of the EU as well as of the international community and which instruments of law enforcement derive from this. Where there is an awareness of the supranational dimension of a given case, a lawyer is encouraged to view the national legal order more critically and may be more alert to opportunities to challenge national laws. Such awareness also creates the opportunity for strategic litigation, pursuing change that may transcend an individual case. If national legislation or practice is not in compliance with EU or international law, individual cases may work as vehicles for change on the macro level.

Cooperation in CLE

The success of CLE at the Palacký Law School is, to a significant degree, the outcome of intensive international cooperation which started right after the law school was founded in 1991. Regular visits by US law professors in early 1990s gradually resulted in the establishment of the first legal clinic. Discontinuation of the clinic in the late 1990s can be attributed to weakening of international links. The restart of the clinical programme in 2006 was enabled by strong cooperation with the Polish Foundation of Legal Clinics (FUPP). During the preparatory phase, the clinical team visited the Polish national clinical conference several times and gathered a great deal of inspiration and experience that enabled us to design the new clinical programme in a sustainable and efficient way.

Another very fruitful cooperation is unfolding with Northumbria School of Law in Newcastle, United Kingdom. There is an Erasmus exchange in place,[21] which allows for regular visits of teaching staff, mostly from clinical classes, to visit the award-winning and very well-developed clinical programme at Northumbria University. There is also a student exchange in place, where up to four students in

---

[21] It must be noted that there is a special subnetwork of law schools with clinical programmes within the Erasmus exchange network, which shows that clinical teachers are very active in seeking opportunities for international cooperation with other clinics.

each academic year can move from one university to another for the whole semester. The exchange is not specifically dedicated to legal clinics, but the students have the opportunity to participate in the clinical programme to the degree allowed by their language abilities and knowledge of appropriate legal regulation. The exchange also applies to PhD students, and one such student has already visited Palacký Law School, gathering data for research on legal clinics.

Palacký Law School regularly organizes or hosts international conferences on CLE and welcomes study visits from other universities intending to establish clinical programmes, including training sessions on how to start, run, and sustain a legal clinic. In each, there are several visits by clinical professors from different countries who offer courses or workshops for both students and teachers, but they are also encouraged to reflect on the clinical programme at Palacký and consult on possible improvements.

Diffusion of CLE

Internationalization within Czech education is strongly connected to the emergence of legal clinics. Since 1990, law school teachers began visiting foreign universities much more frequently than they had during the communist regime, and they became acquainted with modern teaching methods and best practices at prestigious global universities. Also, foreign teachers coming to the Czech Republic injected inspiration and introduced some novel teaching methods.

This can be illustrated by the statistical data accumulated by the Czech Ministry of education: in the academic year 1998/1999, there were 879 students going abroad, 243 foreign students coming to the Czech Republic, and 366 teachers going abroad. These figures are totals for all Czech universities. By the academic year 2007/2008, there were 5,587 students going abroad, 3,789 foreign students in the Czech Republic, and 1,942 teachers going abroad. In 2014, Palacký University alone recorded 1,782 students going abroad, 844 incoming foreign students, 693 teachers going abroad, and 615 incoming foreign teachers, counting only those visits lasting for more than four weeks for students and more than five days for teachers.

Before 1989, most of the exchanges took place within the countries of Comecon, so mostly the countries of the Soviet bloc, and only after 1989 did the exchanges start to focus more on the United States and countries of Western Europe. This increase in international exchanges has been largely thanks to the Erasmus programme. However, for development of legal clinics, the most significant issue was cooperation with US universities and teachers. This was significant for the first clinical programme established at Palacký Law School. However, the restart in 2006 drew strongly on the experience of Polish legal clinics, thanks to cooperation with FUPP and U.K. legal clinics. Another extremely important resource was the international clinical conferences, especially the International Journal of CLE (IJCLE) conference and the GAJE conference.

The model of a live-client legal clinic as applied at Palacký Law School since 2006 is based on the model and standards developed by FUPP. Although it has been significantly adjusted over the past ten years, the main features, such as providing a written legal advice document, nonrepresentation at court, and internal structure of the clinic, are still effective. Thanks to continuous communication with the European and global clinical community (especially at IJCLE, GAJE, and European Network for CLE [ENCLE] conferences), our clinical teachers are constantly gaining new inspiration and improving their teaching methodology.

One such source of inspiration was the "orientation week," which is held at some universities with clinical programmes to prepare students for their work in the clinic. At Palacký, it proved extremely useful to have a retreat, two-day, weekend workshop outside of the city where the students get training in skills, psychology, and legal analysis, but also go through team-building activities to develop a feeling of community and teamwork. This workshop runs in each semester, and there have already been more than ten of them.

Palacký Law School has also significantly contributed to establishing ENCLE. After a group of European clinicians decided in 2012 that they would like to establish ENCLE, legal research was commissioned comparing the regulation of NGOs in several countries, which demonstrated that that the Czech legal context was the most favourable; so ENCLE was registered as an association under Czech Law, with its seat in Olomouc.

Future of CLE in Europe

The most important goal at the moment for the clinical programme at Palacký is to increase the number of students who are affected by it. In the best-case scenario, we might introduce a requirement to undertake at least one clinical subject or externship in order to successfully complete law school. This will also require rethinking the role of legal clinics in the law school curriculum. Another goal is to react in the clinics to problems of the day. Let us provide some examples. With regard to the right to education in the Czech Republic, the central debate at the moment relates to inclusive education at elementary schools revolving around several long-existing problems. Based on the initiative of the students, this topic was the main focus of the Human Rights Clinic in the winter semester of 2016. Using the Freedom of Information Act,[22] the students gathered data about the inclusion of children with disabilities in physical education, analysed the compatibility of current by-legislation with the constitution, and researched the system of provision of educational support. In the Refugee Law Clinic, the students presented their perspective on migration during an international conference organized by Palacký Law School in October 2016.

---

[22] Law No. 106/1999 Coll., on free access to information, as amended by later legislation.

Another important task not only for the clinics in Olomouc, but also for all European clinics and perhaps clinics all over the world, is to analyse and research how clinics work and what they contribute to legal education, how they affect students and future lawyers. We can again draw inspiration from education in the area of medicine, where the idea of clinic-based education originates.[23] There is a solid amount of research based on empirical data showing the difference of outcomes between different teaching methods in medical education,[24] but no such data exist in relation to legal education. This does not mean that practical forms of legal education do not have merit. Some advantages of legal clinics over traditional education are clear, like the development of skills or values; however, we do not understand the effect of legal clinics fully. For example, there is no empirical evidence shedding light on the extent of skills development or comparing the results of clinics and traditional education with respect to knowledge transfer, not to mention other new trends like problem-based learning and so on. If such research existed, empirically demonstrating the merit of CLE, it would not only be an undisputable argument in favour of the further development of legal clinics, but it would improve the overall quality of legal education.

This type of research is only just getting under way, but it is necessary if we want to understand the real value of CLE and ensure that we are using legal clinics to their maximum potential. Many law schools gather data from clinical students via student evaluation forms, and some clinical programmes even use special tools to research the effects of clinics. From the experience of the Palacký clinics, the progress of students can be well-measured by using an adapted self-efficacy scale questionnaire.[25] When used at the beginning of the clinic and at the end, it allows us to compare changes in self-perceived mastery of different skills developed by the clinic. We have also used the life-line scheme to encourage students to reflect on their clinical experience, identifying how the clinic contributes to their professional and personal development later in life.

---

[23] See S. H. Krieger, *The Stories Clinicians Tell*, in COMPLEX LAW TEACHING: KNOWLEDGE, SKILLS AND VALUES (Tomoszek, M. ed., Olomouc: Palacký University, 2013) 11–36. www.pf.upol.cz/fileadmin/user_upload/PF/Centrum/Complex_Law_elektronicky-_upravena.pdf. Especially relevant in this regard is the part "Where do we go from here?" on page 30 and following.

[24] As an example, this article shows that lecture had a 16.8% rate of improvement, whereas using interactive software led to a 42.5% improvement. See Anuradha Subramanian, Matthew Timberlake, Harsha Mittakanti, Michael Lara, and Mary L Brandt. *Novel Educational Approach for Medical Students: Improved Retention Rates Using Interactive Medical Software Compared with Traditional Lecture-Based Format*, 69 (2) JOURNAL OF SURGICAL EDUCATION 253–56 (March–April 2012).

[25] For more information about general self-efficacy, see A. Luszczynska, U. Scholz, and R. Schwarzer, *The General Self-Efficacy Scale: Multicultural Validation Studies*. 139 (5) JOURNAL OF PSYCHOLOGY, 439–57 (2005); R. Schwarzer, J. Bäßler, P. Kwiatek, K. Schröder, and J. X. Zhang, *The Assessment of Optimistic Self-Beliefs: Comparison of the German, Spanish, and Chinese Versions of the General Self-Efficacy Scale*. 46 APPLIED PSYCHOLOGY 69–88 (1997); S. M. Maddox, J. E. Mercandante, S. Prentice-Dunn, B. Jacobs, and R. W. Rogers, *The Self-Efficacy Scale: Construction and Validation*. 51 PSYCHOLOGICAL REPORTS 663–71 (1982).

Finally, legal clinics also play an important role in the development of professional values, and, to gain insight into student's perspectives on this, we ask our students to include a reflection on the value elements of each case they work on at the end of their case reports. If similar tools were used in different clinics across Europe, their results could be compared to show overall shared trends but also differences. ENCLE actively seeks opportunities to create or initiate research proposals in this area, but none of them has been funded so far.

Notwithstanding the lack of empirical data, from the information that is available, it is clear that legal education in Europe has already changed thanks to the clinical movement. With hundreds of new clinics being established in Germany, France, Italy, and other countries of Western Europe, clinics are becoming a standard part of legal education rather than some extravagant experiment. More law teachers than ever realize that law is a living discipline affecting the everyday lives of people, and they are beginning to change the way they teach, not only by implementing CLE, but also transforming teaching methods in general. We can see examples of law schools using problem-based learning, the growth of moot court competitions, skills courses, street-law programmes, and other new approaches to legal education.

CONCLUSION

CLE provides answers to many challenges faced by the current higher education system. It delivers on ideas promoted by the Bologna Process or EU policy on key competences. Legal clinics benefit everyone involved: students are better prepared for their future jobs, law schools and teachers provide better education and build stronger ties to their communities, and the local community gets better access to free legal aid, with significant multiplication effect. For all these reasons, it would be only logical to include some form of CLE in every law school's curriculum and create a suitable legal framework for its operation. Some of the legal regulation problems that need to be addressed are privilege of confidentiality of legal clinics and law students and teachers working in them, as well as a student practice rule or involvement of legal clinics in legal aid schemes. If there would be a legal framework providing clinics with basic certainty in these issues, it would allow more intensive development of legal clinics and improve the quality of both educational outcomes and services provided to the community. In the United States, the so-called MacCrate report[26] and American Bar Association (ABA) standards for accreditation of law schools were very important factors in establishing legal clinics, to the point that clinics are now present at virtually every law school in the United States.

---

[26] American Bar Association, Legal Education and Professional Development – An Educational Continuum. Report of the Task Force on Law Schools and the Profession: Narrowing the Gap, www .americanbar.org/content/dam/aba/publications/misc/legal_education/2013_legal_education_and _professional_development_maccrate_report).authcheckdam.pdf

CLE is a proven method used in many countries worldwide for many years with tremendous results. Legal clinics have been recently mentioned by a UN document as an example of best practices in ensuring access to justice in criminal matters.[27] Legal clinics very persuasively show that legal education, which traditionally was perceived as boring, often using lectures for hundreds of students, can be also very interactive, practical, and fun and, at the same time, very efficient and useful. The idea of the legal clinic itself is very attractive and motivates many teachers to at least try to run a clinical course. At the same time, teaching a legal clinic requires a lot of methodological background, which makes all clinical teachers explore the methodology of legal education (and education in general) and improve their teaching methods. Most of them use advanced teaching methods in all of their courses (even substantive), not only in clinics. Legal clinics also contribute to the outreach of law schools and their connection to the local community, providing free legal aid and raising legal awareness in society. For all these reasons, there should be more encouragement for law schools and law teachers to establish clinics, either in the form of funding schemes or even as a required part of the curriculum.

---

[27] Resolution adopted by the General Assembly of the United Nations: United Nations Principles and Guidelines on Access to Legal Aid in Criminal Justice Systems, www.unodc.org/documents/justice-and-prison-reform/UN_principles_and_guidlines_on_access_to_legal_aid.pdf (last visited May 30, 2014) para. 61 (a), 71 (e), 72 (a) and (b).

5

Towards the Institutionalization of Legal Clinics in Spain

The Environmental Law Clinic at Rovira I Virgili University

Maria Marquès i Banqué

INTRODUCTION

Clinical legal education (CLE) has not yet been fully embraced in Spain; however, the numbers are growing with every passing year. A few public universities made up the first wave of legal clinics in the 2000s.[1] More recently, a second wave has emerged in public and private universities, although mostly in the latter.

As part of the first wave, the Environmental Law Clinic at Universitat Rovira i Virgili is a live-client clinic which was set up in 2005 on the initiative of a group of teachers and researchers specialized in environmental law at the Faculty of Legal Sciences. Universitat Rovira i Virgili is a public university based in the city of Tarragona, in the region of Catalonia, Spain. Since The Tarragona Centre for Environmental Law Studies (CEDAT) was established in 2007 at the same university to boost and carry out research, teaching, and knowledge transfer in this field, the Clinic is part of it and has become one of its flagships, considered one of the strengths of the master's degree in Environmental Law. Institutionally, the Environmental Law Clinic is also part of the Service-Learning Programme, established by the University Senate in February 2012 with the aim of institutionalizing service-learning throughout the whole university. Thus, the clinic is aligned to the social responsibility mission of the university.

Both undergraduate and postgraduate students are involved in the Clinic. For final-year undergraduate students, the Clinic is an opportunity of fulfilling the mandatory 135-hour work experience required to complete their law degrees. However, because the Clinic is a compulsory subject for the master's degree in Environmental Law, students involved in the clinic are mainly postgraduate with a high level of environmental awareness who already work in the field of environmental law or seek jobs in this field in either the public or the private sector. Supervisors are both academics and members of the legal profession, although academics are clearly in the majority since the Clinic forms part of their regular

---

[1] Universitat Rovira i Virgili, Universitat de Barcelona, Universitat Carlos III de Madrid, and Universitat de València.

teaching. In addition to cases in which students work under faculty supervision, CEDAT researchers occasionally work on other cases on a *pro bono* basis.

Clients are organizations or institutions with public or community interest aims (i.e. nongovernmental organizations [NGOs], foundations, public administration, etc.). The Clinic focuses mainly on providing legal advice on matters of environmental law and environmental justice. The main outcome of clinic projects is usually a legal report containing a legal analysis of the environmental problem and providing a legal strategy or specific recommendations to the client. Therefore, the Clinic is not a litigation clinic and does not work for individuals. Nevertheless, the Clinic does collaborate with *pro bono* environmental lawyers on cases with educational potential.[2]

Along with advising clients on environmental legal issues, the Clinic also acts as a policy clinic and, less frequently, as a mediation clinic. When working as a policy clinic, cases are focused on legislative and regulatory activities (rulemaking, legislative drafting, and policy development) at the request of government agencies and legislators. The Clinic also helps nonprofit organizations with environmental policy issues that they have neither the time nor resources to address. As a mediation and conciliation clinic, the Clinic deals with environmental conflicts by playing the role of a neutral third party or by providing to the parties a solution to their problem.

In its first decade (2005–2015), the Clinic has worked on domestic and international cases. Domestic cases were located in Catalonia (60%) and Spain (24%), while international cases were located in Latin American countries (16%). In terms of client profile, 76% were NGOs or other community organizations, while 24% were public authorities. Currently, the Clinic is entering a new challenging and inspiring stage due to the fact that, as of 2014, the master's degree in environmental law is taught online.

EMERGENCE OF CLE

Genesis and Context

The Environmental Law Clinic followed a previous successful initiative at the same university. In 2002, my criminal law colleagues at the Department of Public Law and I had the opportunity to develop a law clinic in the field of penitentiary law. It was run in collaboration with the Tarragona Penitentiary and was aimed at providing legal advice to inmates on a range of matters relating to their rights and life in prison, which are not subject to mandatory legal representation by a lawyer. Since it was the first law clinic at a Spanish university, and, at that time, my colleagues and I were not aware of the CLE movement, the context out of which that first Clinic emerged was

---

[2] "Educational potential" here means those cases affecting issues and contents specifically covered by the master's degree in environmental law. One example is the work undertaken by our students to support *pro bono* lawyers representing a community organization on a case relating to noise pollution caused by air traffic at Madrid's airport.

our personal concerns about the quality of legal education as well as our commitment to the social responsibility of our university. Actually, the Clinic was originally known as the "Law & Prison Initiative" rather than the "Penitentiary Law Clinic," as it was not until a year later that we fully learned that this type of initiative was internationally known as a "law clinic" or "legal clinic."[3] From that moment onwards, we have described the "Law & Prison Initiative" as a form of CLE.

In 2003, the Penitentiary Law Clinic received awards for teaching quality, both from the Universitat Rovira i Virgili and the Catalan government. These awards proved to be an incentive in two respects: first, we started to look for similar initiatives in other universities; and second, given the institutional context described later, it encouraged us to explore further clinic development opportunities within the Department of Public Law. While the first move led us to the global CLE movement, the second led us to the development of the Environmental Law Clinic.

Institutionally, the debate on the creation of an environmental law clinic took place at a time when the Faculty of Legal Sciences, founded in 1992, was developing a strategy of specialization aimed at achieving excellence in research and teaching while encouraging the promotion of its young tenure-track faculty. In the field of public law, environmental law was identified as a good option for specialization due to the existence of researchers already specialized in this area at the Department of Public Law, the high growth potential of this relatively new field of Law, and the possibility of fostering an approach to teaching and research within the Department involving different areas of Public Law, thereby challenging the traditional discrete subject approach taken up to then by Spanish law faculties.

This institutional context determined the nature and practice of the new clinic. From an educational point of view, the Environmental Law Clinic was considered part of a broader teaching quality strategy due to its ability to provide practical, skill-based training as well as to promote social justice. It was fully embedded into the curriculum of the master's degree programme in environmental law taught by the faculty. This represented a significant advance, since the Penitentiary Law Clinic, which ran until 2005, was a co-curricular activity. As a learning methodology, it was later fully consistent with the Bologna Process. In this regard, it is important to stress, however, that since our first clinic emerged prior to the full implementation of the Bologna Process at our university, we cannot properly say that our interest in CLE arose as a result of it, despite having retrospectively explained in other works how that first initiative met its goals.[4]

---

[3] Probably the first time we heard about legal clinics was at a seminar held at our university in 2001. The seminar focused on the teaching of environmental law, and a law teacher at the University of Puerto Rico mentioned the existence of legal clinics. However, we did not delve into this concept until 2003. It was then when we realized that the initiative undertaken in the field of penitentiary law fit the concept of CLE.

[4] Joan Baucells, Maria Marquès, and Carolina Morán, *La asignatura "Derecho Y Cárcel": Una Experiencia de "Clinical Legal Education" En El Ámbito Penitenciario*, in CINCO AÑOS DE PREMIOS CONSEJO SOCIAL URV A LA CALIDAD DOCENTE (Jordi Gavaldà ed., Universitat Rovira i Virgili 2006).

The profile of the teaching staff, mostly academic, determined at the time, and still determines, the type of service, case, and client provided and engaged by the clinic. As I pointed out earlier, the clinic focuses on legal advice to clients and works as policy clinic at the request of the public authorities. This allows an interesting link between teaching and research that benefits both students and teachers. The cross-functional approach to environmental law influences the selection of cases and how the clinic works. Regarding cases, those that offer a more comprehensive approach to environmental issues are selected. Regarding the way of working, a system of plenary sessions and co-supervision of each case is established.

In addition to the pursuit of excellence in education and research, a third concern lies at the heart of the Environmental Law Clinic: contributing towards the social responsibility of the university. In Spain, this concept is relatively new and still open to many interpretations. Therefore, it cannot be stated that, in 2005, the Clinic was the result of an institutional strategy aimed at social responsibility. However, what is certain is the existence at that time of a shared concern among teachers involved in the Clinic for social issues and the need to develop social commitment as an educational goal.

Presently, the objective of integrating social responsibility into academic teaching has taken a step forward at the Universitat Rovira i Virgili. The institutionalization of service-learning throughout the university is evidence of this. Legal clinics, as a form of service-learning in the field of law, have today attained an institutional dimension that continues to be deepened. I will return to this point later in the chapter.

Drivers

In order to achieve a better sense of why legal clinics are taking root in Spain, in preparation for this chapter, Spanish clinicians were invited to send me their insights. The content of this section relies on the kind responses received from some of the Spanish legal clinics belonging both to the first and second waves.[5]

The main finding is that the Bologna Process seems to be, almost universally, the primary catalyst for the emergence of CLE in Spain. The scope of this statement must, however, be clarified.

Unlike other countries, Spain lacks any real discussion (at least with any depth) on legal education. The role that law and lawyers play in a given model of society and the impact that legal education can have on the continuation or challenge of this model has never been the focus of much debate inside or outside faculties of law. The implementation of the Bologna Process has, in many respects, been a missed

---

[5] Universidad Carlos III de Madrid; Universidad de Alcalá; ICADE, Universidad Pontificia Comillas; Centro Universitario Villanueva; Universitat de València; and Universitat Rovira i Virgili (Business Law Clinic).

opportunity for addressing a deep reflection on the concept of "lawyer" and the meaning and scope of legal education in the twenty-first century.[6]

Thus, the reference to the Bologna Process by Spanish clinicians must be understood mainly as a teaching and learning quality issue. Legal clinics are seen mostly as one among a range of educational tools that happened to fit the new skill- and experiential-oriented learning model promoted by the Bologna Process. CLE is also considered to provide students with a good outlet for developing a final degree project, both at undergraduate and postgraduate levels.

This observation is not meant to suggest that those behind Spanish legal clinics do not have a personal concern with the social dimension of legal education. Skills-training is not seen as the only educational goal of CLE. Making students more ethically committed in law practice and aware of the social responsibilities of the legal profession is also a common objective of Spanish legal clinics. However, Spanish clinicians do not usually link this educational goal to the Bologna Process, which is by itself evidence of the lack of a deep institutional commitment towards the broader transformative potential of CLE in the context of Spanish legal education. A decade ago, those who were against the Bologna Process focused the debate on whether law faculties should teach practical skills at all, rather than engaging in a serious discussion about the full set of generic and specific legal skills and competencies that might potentially be included in law curriculum reform. One of the main concerns of those opposed to the reforms (and consequently also opposed to CLE) was that a skill-based legal education could lead to a generation of uncritical lawyers mostly concerned about the day-to-day application of law along with other generic practical issues such as teamwork, interviewing skills, or oral communication. Those academics opposing the Bologna reform, by focusing solely on its emphasis on these skills, did not pay enough attention to the fact that, along with such generic skills, the reform was targeted at developing specific legal competencies such as "an awareness of the role of law as a regulatory system of social and economic relations" or "the ability to distinguish between legal reasoning and arguments of ethical, political, economic and social nature," which are expressions of the concept of "lawyer" those in favour of clinical education were advocating for. As I then wrote elsewhere, at the end of the day, the power of educating lawyers with a critical, ethical, and social sense of the legal profession depends on us – law teachers – using the right teaching and learning methodologies.[7] As stressed later, the key is to secure the necessary institutional support to make this possible.

---

[6] Of the same opinion: Diego Blázquez Martín and José García Añón, *Las Clínicas Jurídicas Españolas En El Movimiento Clínico Global* in EL MOVIMIENTO GLOBAL DE CLÍNICAS JURÍDICAS. FORMANDO JURISTAS EN LA JUSTICIA SOCIAL (Frank Bloch ed., Tirant lo Blanch 2013), 15; José García Añón, *Transformaciones En La Docencia Y El Aprendizaje Del Derecho: ¿La Educación Jurídica Clínica Como Elemento Transformador?* 15 TEORÍA & DERECHO 12 (2014).

[7] Maria Marquès Banqué, *La Evaluación de Competencias En La Educación Superior: Retos E Instrumentos*) o REVISTA DE EDUCACIÓN Y DERECHO 47 (2009); Teresa Franquet Sugrañes and

Over the past few years, the opportunity to collaborate with law firms working on *pro bono* cases is emerging as a new incentive to create legal clinics. Some of the youngest Spanish legal clinics specifically refer to this point when asked for their reasons for joining the CLE movement. This can be explained by the increasing strength of the *pro bono* movement within the legal profession in Spain and the efforts made by some organizations to build bridges between socially engaged law firms, legal clinics, and individuals and communities in need of legal aid.[8]

Specialization in a particular field of law, opportunities to undertake community-based research, and institutional justifications such as the pursuit of excellence are also mentioned as justification for creating legal clinics, although to a lesser extent. One of the youngest legal clinics also refers to the existence of a service-learning programme in its university within which the clinic is framed, which points in the direction that I will develop in the next section.

Those law teachers wishing to but still not joining the clinical legal movement mention the lack of recognition by their faculties and universities. As every clinician knows, running a legal clinic requires time and resources. At a time in which law teachers are compelled to focus on research and the resources available are scarce, the creation of legal clinics cannot rely on the initiative of those personally committed to the idea of educating lawyers for social justice. Again, what is required is an institutional approach to expanding CLE.

REFORMING THE TEACHING AND PRACTICE OF LAW IN EUROPE

Goals and Methods

The Environmental Law Clinic is aimed at providing skill-based learning to students. Legal skills and generic skills are both educational goals of the Clinic. In the first group, we can find, among others, the ability to put theory into practice, the ability to provide legal advice and outline legal strategies to address a legal issue, and the ability to draft local legislation in the field of environmental law. Among generic skills, the Clinic particularly focuses on teamwork, problem-solving, communication skills, and concern for quality. This set of legal and generic skills are complemented by two additional key educational goals at our Clinic: instilling a cross-functional approach to environmental law and a deep commitment to environmental justice issues. Environmental justice here is understood as the fair distribution of costs and benefits in the management of natural resources.

The way in which the Clinic works is carefully planned to achieve these goals. The composition of the teaching team emphasizes the cross-functional approach.

Maria Marquès Banqué, Hitos En La Generación de Una Cultura de La Calidad Docente En Los Estudios de Derecho En España o REVISTA DE EDUCACIÓN Y DERECHO 101 (2009).

[8] One example is "Conexión Pro Bono," the clearinghouse created by Fundación LexNova-Thomson Reuters Aranzadi.

More than one supervisor is appointed to each case, each belonging to a different legal field and with different legal expertise. Supervisors meet regularly to coordinate their work and discuss the problems that arise at the clinic. All students are required to attend plenary sessions in which work-plan, ethical issues, and partial and final outcomes are discussed. Students are also required to attend training sessions on issues affecting their cases. Cases are assigned to students regardless of their personal preferences, with the aim of forcing them to develop greater commitment to ensuring quality of service.[9]

Though the Bologna Process has been a missed opportunity in the sense mentioned earlier, it must be acknowledged that it led all Spanish faculties of law to adopt a more skill-oriented and student-centred approach to learning. Given that the Bologna Process was not sufficiently funded by the Spanish government, the commitment of many law teachers, in spite of this, to improve legal education should be recognized and commended. Currently, many methods beyond traditional lectures are been used across Spain (problem based-learning, simulations, case-method, etc.), although, unfortunately, the lack of recognition by university authorities in terms of workload can put them at risk.

From the perspective of the Bologna Process, CLE is one among these "new" teaching and learning methodologies. Moreover, since the acquisition of legal and generic skills should be considered a progressive process, legal clinics do not necessarily constitute a better methodology but a chronologically "subsequent" methodology. In other words, live-client legal clinics are best suited for last-year undergraduate students and postgraduate students, once they have achieved substantive knowledge in the legal fields they will work in, whereas other methodologies such as problem-based learning, simulations, or case method can be used in an earlier stage. Despite the fact that, as described earlier, the clinical movement is taking root in Spain, legal clinics are far from being universally adopted. In this sense, it can be stated that the existing legal clinics challenge the status quo of legal education.

Although legal clinics are a great skill-oriented methodology, it is in the promotion of social justice where they really make a difference. The transformative potential of CLE in this field is internationally known and does not need further development here.[10] It is from this perspective that legal clinics really challenge the status quo of legal education in Spain. In this sense, my insights and concerns are those of my Spanish colleagues as well as of many clinicians around the world.[11] What I additionally seek to stress in the next section is that if we consider legal clinics

[9] Susana Borràs et al., *The Environmental Law Clinic: A New Experience in Legal Education in Spain*, in THE NEW LAW SCHOOL (Daniela Ikawa and Leah Wortham eds., Public Interest Law Institute & Jagiellonian University Press 2010).

[10] Due to the extensive literature on this topic, see Frank S. Bloch, ed., THE GLOBAL CLINICAL MOVEMENT. EDUCATING LAWYERS FOR SOCIAL JUSTICE (Oxford University Press 2011).

[11] From the Spanish perspective, see Diego Blázquez Martín, *Apuntes Acerca de La Educación Jurídica Clínica*, 3 Universitas. Revista de Filosofía, 43 DERECHO Y POLÍTICA (2006); José García Añón, *La*

as part of a broader institutional strategy, we can legitimately assert that they challenge the status quo not only of legal education but of higher education in general.

Beyond the Educational Goals

Historically, beyond the educational goals, one of the often-mentioned benefits of legal clinics is the delivery of legal aid to those who cannot afford it. This is not, however, how I see the social goal of our Clinic. The reasons are threefold: (1) in Spain, although increasingly in jeopardy, there is already a state-sponsored legal aid for individuals who cannot afford the cost of a lawyer; (2) the Environmental Law Clinic, as stressed earlier, does not take individuals as clients; and (3) since it is a Clinic based within a university, its social value must be explained within the framework of the university's social responsibility, rather than focusing on legal aid or advice provided.

University social responsibility, which refers to the civic role of higher education institutions, affects all missions of universities. Specifically, legal clinics find their place in the educational dimension of university social responsibility. One among several possible actions recommended to realize the social responsibility of higher education institutions is so-called *student integral education*. By integral education, what is meant here meant is education of the students not only as professionals but also as citizens who, with their level of culture, their specific knowledge and skills, and their critical and humanistic spirit, will be the basis of a more socially committed, sustainable, and fairer society.[12]

This definition allows me to refer to what I call the direct and the indirect impact of integral education. The direct impact refers to the development of a greater social commitment among students, which is an educational goal in itself. But there is also an indirect social impact, which, in my opinion, is the sociopolitical justification for institutionalizing a legal clinic at a public university. In short: given the current deep crisis of the Social State and its values, more than ever we need our graduates – those who, in the medium term, will be leading public and private institutions and organizations – to be aware of the social impact of their future profession and to understand the need for a strong Social State as a basic condition for the full exercise of rights and freedoms by all citizens.[13] Only by giving them the opportunity to work

---

Integración de La Educación Jurídica Clínica En El Proceso Formativo de Los Juristas, 12 REDU-REVISTA DE DOCENCIA UNIVERSITARIA 153 (2014).

[12] *See*, among others, Miquel Martínez, ed., APRENDIZAJE SERVICIO Y RESPONSABILIDAD SOCIAL DE LAS UNIVERSIDADES (MEC & Octaedro 2008); Gobierno de España-Ministerio de Educación, LA RESPONSABILIDAD SOCIAL DE LA UNIVERSIDAD Y EL DESARROLLO SOSTENIBLE (Ministerio de Educación 2011); François Vallaeys, Cristina de la Cruz, and Pedro Sasia, RESPONSABILIDAD SOCIAL UNIVERSITARIA. MANUAL DE PRIMEROS PASOS (McGraw Hill & BID 2009).

[13] Please note that I'm using the sociopolitical concept of "social state" instead of the economic concept of "welfare state."

with social problems and appreciate the idea of shared responsibility will our graduates indeed form the basis for a more socially committed, sustainable, and fairer society.[14] The idea that I seek here to emphasize is that this applies to all university students, not only to law students, since the achievement of social justice, which goes beyond the concept of access to justice, will depend on all of them in the near future. This particular sociopolitical approach to legal clinics as part of an overall approach to university social responsibility likely differs not only from the goals of typical law school education in Spain, but also from a law school–centred approach to CLE.

It is obvious that among the social benefits of a clinic is the legal service provided to the client. However, I consider this an important added value, but not an end in itself. A criticism that can be made of initiatives that have as their primary objective or as a secondary consequence the development of new collaborative-based strategies to address social needs, such as social innovation, community-based research, service-learning, and legal clinics, is that such initiatives may be premised on or may promote the idea that they can replace the State in providing services.[15] If we focus on the legal service provided instead of on the educational goals and their direct and indirect impact and benefits, we will be contributing to the weakening of the Social State rather than to its strengthening.

The Weight and Value of Internationalization

Three forms of internationalization can be found at the Environmental Law Clinic, each with different educational goals. A first form is substantive and is a consequence of the specialization of the clinic in the environmental field, in which there is an abundance of EU regulation. Even in cases that initially appear to be domestic, students must analyse the EU law applicable to the case and verify compliance by Spain with the relevant EU standards. This is an opportunity to deepen knowledge of EU law and its relationship with the legal systems of the Member States. In addition, the clinic has worked on cases in which, specifically, the legal report has focused on legal courses of action to be taken by the client and aimed at European institutions. However, we must recall that it is not a litigation

[14] As Xavier Aurey refers to in Chapter 6 this volume when writing about legal clinics in France, such an approach is criticized when seen as a way of forcing students to adhere to the social justice morality of law faculty and law school administrators. However, I could not be in more disagreement with this idea for two reasons: first, as Aurey points out, "behind this criticism lies the illusion that the traditional way of teaching of law is ideologically neutral." Second, I think that the key is to provide students with the opportunity to confront social reality while giving them the tools and freedom to develop critical thinking by themselves. The point is not whether legal clinics must be mandatory or not. What is really critical, in order to avoid any attempt of ideological manipulation, is that clinicians are ethically trained to play their role in such a sensitive learning environment.

[15] Again, Xavier Aurey shows the same concern: "it is important that the development of law clinics do not serve at the same time as deposits for the disinvestment of the State in this critical area of the access to the law."

clinic, so the legal report is aimed at analysing the problem, advising the client on the available legal strategies, and developing the legal arguments to be used before the European and Spanish institutions.

A second form of internationalization arises through our work on international cases. Work on international cases is an activity undertaken under the umbrella of the so-called *Internationalization at Home* (IaH) strategy, aimed at ensuring that all students will be prepared to work in a more internationalized and intercultural world, whether or not they have benefited from the opportunity to study abroad.[16] One among many strategies that universities can implement to address this overall goal is internationalizing the curriculum by incorporating a global perspective into it. International cases play this role at the Environmental Law Clinic, and the plenary sessions system, described earlier, assures that the benefits will extend to all students participating in the clinic, regardless of the case they directly work on.

The third form of internationalization is a consequence of the existence of students from different nationalities enrolled to earn a master's degree in Environmental Law. Over the past five years (2011–2016), 42% of students were international, with most of them coming from Latin American countries such as Argentina, Bolivia, Brasil, Chile, Colombia, Ecuador, Mexico, or Peru. Recently, students from European countries (France, Italy) have also joined the programme. Faculty delivering the courses are encouraged to take this as another opportunity of IaH.

Cooperation in CLE

Cooperation with other law schools (meaning working together on clinical projects) is still a pending issue. Joint development of projects, which is the form of cooperation that could have more direct benefit for students, faces two major difficulties. On the one hand, the specialization of our clinic in the environmental field limits the possibilities of cooperation with other European legal clinics. At the ENCLE meeting held in Olomouc in 2014, we proposed the creation of a specific working group for environmental law clinics in order to explore specific collaborations. However, among attendants there was only one representative of an environmental law clinic, and the initiative was unsuccessful. Since 2011, our strategy to seek this kind of cooperation between environmental law clinics was developed in the context of another organization, the IUCN Academy of Environmental Law (IUCNAEL), in which I serve as co-chair of the Teaching and Capacity Building Committee. In this context, we work to identify environmental law clinics in Europe and

---

[16] Much has been written about this topic. From the European perspective, see the context in which the debate arose in Paul Crowther et al., INTERNATIONALISATION AT HOME. A POSITION PAPER (European Association for International Education (EAIE) 2000), www.iau-aiu.net/sites/all/files /Internationalisation; Bernd Wächter, *An Introduction: Internationalisation at Home in Context*, 7 JOURNAL OF STUDIES IN INTERNATIONAL EDUCATION 5 (2003).

worldwide in order to promote forms of collaboration. However, the kind of direct cooperation to which we now refer has not yet occurred.

In addition to the possibility of sharing cases of transnational interest, in the context of IUCNAEL we also seek to promote a specific student exchange programme, either at the European or international level, aimed at promoting externship opportunities in environmental law clinics.

However, we must bear in mind that cooperation between law schools, either in the form of externships or joint cases, faces a major challenge: students need to know the domestic law applicable to the case. Even in the cases to which I have referred earlier, where the EU law plays a role, the case has to be resolved according to national law. For this reason, when we choose an international case, we take into account the nationality of our students. So far, students have been mostly Spanish or Latin American due to the fact that the master's degree in Environmental Law is taught in Spanish. More recently, students from European countries joined the master's programme, which for us is an opportunity to enhance cooperation with law schools and other organizations in Europe.

Clients afford another opportunity for cooperation with European and international organizations. When the Clinic has worked at the request of big European or international organizations (e.g. Engineers Without Borders or SEO/Birdlife), students have had the opportunity to encounter the international dimension of environmental issues and the concept of environmental justice and its relationship to social justice, which is especially relevant in our Clinic.

Diffusion of CLE

When the Penitentiary Law Clinic received the award for teaching excellence in 2003, as described earlier, we decided to look for similar experiences. This led us to the CLE movement, basically through the information available on the Internet and particularly on the website of PILI (now PILnet). When the Environmental Law Clinic was set up in 2005, we were already aware of the movement, although we had not yet had the opportunity to interact with other clinics. In 2005, I presented for the first time at an international conference the experience of the Penitentiary Law Clinic from the perspective of the Bologna Process. It was at the European Law Faculties Association (ELFA) Annual Conference, and there I had the opportunity to meet Lusine Hovhannisian, from PILI, whose work I already knew. She was the author of the first paper on legal clinics and the Bologna Process that I later read.[17] In 2006, my colleagues also presented for the first time the experience of the Environmental Law Clinic at a teaching conference in Spain, focusing on the educational goals and the quality of legal education.

---

[17] Lusine Hovhannisian, Clinical Legal Education and the Bologna Process (2006), PILI Papers 2, www.pilnet.org/component/docman/doc_download/25-clinical-legal-education-and-the-bologna-process.html.

In 2007, we organized the first international seminar on CLE in Spain, with the participation of two universities from Canada and Puerto Rico and the four Spanish universities that make up the first wave of legal clinics in Spain.[18] In the following years, we deepened knowledge of CLE in Spain by inviting Canadian and American colleagues to give seminars on legal clinics, and I personally had the opportunity to attend a Clinical Legal Education Organization (CLEO) Symposium in Newcastle upon Tyne (2009) and an Association of American Law Schools (AALS) Clinical Legal Education Conference in Baltimore (2010). Since then, the Environmental Law Clinic has been presented in many national and international conferences, including the Global Alliance for Justice Education (GAJE) Conference held in Valencia, Spain (2011); we have networked and shared experiences with other Spanish clinics; we have participated in the birth of ENCLE and attended almost all of its meetings; and, internationally, as mentioned earlier, I have had the opportunity to promote legal clinics in the context of IUCNAEL, where interest in this topic was already strong and shared with other colleagues.

This brief chronology shows the long-term, complex, and interdependent nature of the emergence of legal clinics at Universitat Rovira i Virgili and in Spain. At least in our case, it was not an externally driven process of "training-implementation-dissemination of results," but rather an experience of learning by doing, in which the exchange of experiences with other clinics, first Spanish, later European and international, was a key factor for development and improvement. While learning, we also contributed to the spread of legal clinics, participating in numerous conferences, providing training courses in Spain at the request of other universities, and contributing to the publication of practical guidelines.[19] This pattern of learning and disseminating was also followed by the three other Spanish universities belonging to the first "wave" of legal clinics in Spain.

From a pan-European perspective, prior to the existence of ENCLE, legal clinics had been discussed several times in the context of the aforementioned ELFA. There, we had the opportunity to learn about other initiatives, like the many legal clinics in Poland. In the past decade, however, ELFA has not established a working group or a specific strategy to boost CLE comparable to that existing, for instance, at AALS. Thus, opportunities to participate in spreading legal clinics at ELFA have been limited.

Future of CLE in Europe

In my opinion, the key to the future of CLE in Europe lies in its full institutionalization. In Spain, the first clinics emerged on the initiative of law teachers, without full

---

[18] Université du Québec à Montréal, University of Puerto Rico, Universidad Carlos III de Madrid, Universitat de Barcelona, Universitat de València, and Universitat Rovira i Virgili.

[19] Maria Marquès Banqué, *Formando Para El Pro Bono: El Diseño de Una Clínica Jurídica Universitaria*, in GUÍA PARA LA PRÁCTICA DEL VOLUNTARIADO JURÍDICO (Fundación Aranzadi Lex Nova 2015).

recognition by universities and faculties of law. However, legal clinics should be part of an institutional strategy.

Where institutionalization has not yet occurred, it may be that clinical teachers themselves will be required to promote it. If this is the scenario, it is important to stress that they must make a leap from personal beliefs and motivations to institutional reasoning and justifications. In doing so, it is important to bear in mind that institutionalization is not only about how to embed legal clinics into the law curriculum. It is much broader than this. The first question that requires an answer is why a university should be interested in establishing a legal clinic. This implies using the relevant institutional language. It must be explained how a legal clinic contributes to the missions of the university. Law teachers pushing for institutionalization need to know how legal clinics fit into the strategic plans of their university and must be able to explain what added value they have in relation to other actions that can be taken to achieve the same goals. And, in doing all this, they must consider legislation related to higher education institutions in their country and the European system of higher education.

Given the nature and goals of legal clinics, institutional justification refers both to teaching and social aspects. In terms of teaching methodology, as already pointed out, the common justification for all European universities is the Bologna Process. This is a process with its strengths, weaknesses, and implementation deficits but, at least theoretically, it establishes a framework within which legal clinics fit perfectly.

In the coming years, the focus should therefore be on social justification. Although the social value of legal clinics appears obvious to any clinician, using institutional language means framing legal clinics within the broader debate on university social responsibility, to which I referred earlier.

Unfortunately, and despite the relevant existing international initiatives, university social responsibility is not so consolidated in the higher education system as teaching, research, and knowledge transfer.[20] The explanation is twofold: first, its scope is an ideological question which is open to debate; second, international systems and tools aimed at measuring the quality of universities do not usually include social issues among their indicators. As brilliantly developed by Paul Benneworth and Michael Osborne, despite the existence of interesting initiatives and good practices across Europe, "European policy-makers have had difficulty finding ways to place university engagement with society at the heart of Higher

---

[20] Initiatives aimed at promoting civically engaged and socially responsible higher education institutions are numerous both at international and regional levels and involve many universities around the world. See a list of national and global initiatives on the Talloires Network's webpage (http://talloiresnetwork.tufts.edu/). The Talloires Network was created in 2005 with the aim of fostering the implementation of the Talloires Declaration on the Civic Roles and Social Responsibilities of Higher Education.

Education missions."[21] Social responsibility is therefore far from being a priority for universities competing to position themselves globally.

For this reason, legal clinics need to look beyond faculties of law and promote their institutionalization as part of a wider movement. Those seeking recognition by their universities should know which other initiatives, similar to legal clinics, are developed at their universities and whether there is an umbrella term for all of them that the university has already adopted or may embrace institutionally as a strategy for social responsibility, in addition to a strategy for teaching quality. In this task, I usually suggest framing legal clinics through the concept of service-learning, which is a movement increasingly widespread in Spanish and European universities.[22]

Legal clinics are one of the forms that service-learning can take in the field of law. The moment should be seized to take advantage of the increasingly widespread promotion of service-learning to ensure the proper recognition of the work of legal clinics. This is the approach that I had the opportunity to employ when I served as Vice-rector for Teaching and the European Higher Education Area at my university (2010–2014), and it has proved to be beneficial for all parties involved.[23]

It must be noted that institutionalization can lead to some changes in the practice of CLE. The most important, in my opinion, is the need to learn how to measure social impact in order to be accountable to the university and society. Consistent with what I articulated in section "Beyond Education Goals," measuring impact should focus on the social commitment of the students, rather than on the environment in which the clinic has intervened. Even though some clinicians may be reluctant to do so, it is important to bear in mind that such an approach has potential benefits. Thus, for example, it opens the possibility of exploring new funding opportunities in the field of philanthropy, which in Europe is a sector that is far less developed than in other countries with respect to universities. Nowadays,

---

[21] Paul Benneworth and Michael Osborne, *Knowledge Engagement and Higher Education in Europe*, in HIGHER EDUCATION IN THE WORLD 5: KNOWLEDGE, ENGAGEMENT AND HIGHER EDUCATION: CONTRIBUTING TO SOCIAL CHANGE (Global University Network for Innovation-GUNI 2014).

[22] Maria Marquès Banqué, *Clínicas Jurídicas Y Universidad Pública*, 11 REVISTA DE EDUCACIÓN Y DERECHO (2015). Considering legal clinics as a part of a wider movement poses some additional difficulties if we are to reach the kind of standardization of legal clinics that Nora Markard suggests in Chapter 8 of this volume. Although I totally agree with her that quality must be guaranteed, I would never push for some kind of official certificate, at least if it is expected to be granted by an external agency. Experience shows that legal clinics and other service-learning initiatives that can be found across universities can take many different forms. In my view, any process of institutionalization already embraces quality assurance since quality is at the heart of any of academic institution. Universities, when institutionalizing service-learning, need to establish their internal procedures to guarantee that anyone willing to be recognized as part of that institutional programme meets the minimum international standards that define service-learning and apply to any discipline. This balance between quality assurance and flexibility was one of my main concerns as Vice-Rector for Teaching when institutionalizing service-learning (and, therefore, legal clinics) at my university in 2012.

[23] Maria Marquès Banqué, *La Dimensión Docente de La Responsabilidad Social Universitaria: La Institucionalización Del Aprendizaje Servicio En La Universitat Rovira I Virgili*, I JORNADAS INTERNACIONALES SOBRE RESPONSABILIDAD SOCIAL UNIVERSITARIA (2014), www.urv.cat/media/upload// arxius/Aprenentatge Servei/MMarques- RSU – APS.pdf.

philanthropy – particularly venture philanthropy – is a highly professionalized sector that requires grantees to follow strict accountability measures.[24]

Returning to the Environmental Law Clinic, in the coming years, our focus will not be on institutionalization due to the fact that the clinic is already part of an institutional programme of service-learning. Our challenge is the transformation of part of our work online into the virtual environment. This will substantially change the way we work, but we hope that it will also give rise to new opportunities, cases, and clients, domestic and international.

CONCLUSION

The clinical movement has gone global due to the existence of a shared view of legal education among many law teachers around the world. What is meant – in words of Frank Bloch – by "socially relevant legal education" and its value is not discussed in this chapter,[25] but I share the approach so brilliantly developed over the past decades by so many colleagues abroad.

This chapter is rather aimed to emphasize what, in my view, should be analysed in more depth when exploring legal clinics from a Spanish and Western European perspective. I am convinced that we need to find our own way to justify the existence of legal clinics in our universities and higher education system(s). We need to develop our own discourse instead of taking the risk of replicating arguments that may not make sense in our context. Europeans must think of legal clinics as a strategy to be deployed in law schools with the aim of contributing to the development of "European values" oriented towards achieving social cohesion, rather thinking about clinics in terms of the adaptation of a foreign model in the teaching of law. The first legal clinic at Universitat Rovira i Virgili was established with no awareness of the US CLE movement and was not supported by any kind of foreign funding. I am convinced that, even in the absence of US models of CLE, we would be doing the same, just probably under a different name. It's a matter of active commitment to the social mission of the university, and the literature shows that, despite the lack of incentives for universities to institutionalize social engagement, there are good practices across Europe that evidence the social commitment of many academics in all fields and disciplines.[26]

Obviously, this is not to say that we don't have anything to learn from legal clinics abroad. To the contrary, we are lucky to join the movement at a time at which experts around the world are available to share their expertise and best practices.

---

[24] Again, from the European perspective, it is interesting to know about the work and publications of the European Venture Philanthropy Association (EVPA), such as the *Practical Guide to Measuring and Managing Impact*, that can be downloaded from its webpage: http://evpa.eu.com/.

[25] Frank S. Bloch, Introduction, in THE GLOBAL CLINICAL MOVEMENT. EDUCATING LAWYERS FOR SOCIAL JUSTICE (F. Bloch, ed., Oxford University Press, 2011).

[26] Benneworth and Osborne, *supra* note 12.

This has already contributed and will continue to contribute to the blossoming of legal clinics in Spain and Europe. However, the idea that I am particularly keen to stress here is that consolidation of legal clinics in our universities is not only about achieving a critical mass of law teachers sharing the concept and international goals of CLE and having been trained by experts to run a legal clinic. Consolidation requires full institutionalization.

And, in my view, there is still a lack of reflection on what institutionalization means. Institutionalization requires looking beyond faculties of law. Institutionalization is not only about how to embed legal clinics into the law curriculum; it is first about how legal clinics fit the missions of the university. Only through full and sincere institutionalization can legal clinics achieve adequate academic recognition, and recognition is a key factor to ensure and enhance that critical mass of law teachers that make possible social change in and beyond the classroom. It requires, therefore, a wider discussion about the institutional justifications and strategies that can lead to the consolidation of CLE in each university and country.

References

Baucells, J., Marquès, M., and Morán, C. La asignatura "Derecho Y Cárcel": Una Experiencia de "Clinical Legal Education" En El Ámbito Penitenciario, in Jordi Gavaldà (ed.), *Cinco años de premios Consejo Social URV a la calidad docente* (Universitat Rovira i Virgili, 2006).

Benneworth, P., and Osborne, M. Knowledge Engagement and Higher Education in Europe, in *Higher Education in the World 5: Knowledge, Engagement and Higher Education: Contributing to Social Change* (Global University Network for Innovation-GUNI 2014).

Blázquez, Martín D. Apuntes Acerca de La Educación Jurídica Clínica' 3 Universitas. *Revista de Filosofía, Derecho y Política* 43 (2006) 43–60.

Blázquez, Martín D., and García Añón, J. Las Clínicas Jurídicas Españolas En El Movimiento Clínico Global, in Frank Bloch (ed.), *El movimiento global de clínicas jurídicas. Formando juristas en la justicia social* (Tirant lo Blanch, 2013).

Bloch, F. S. Introduction, in F. Bloch (ed.), *The Global Clinical Movement. Educating Lawyers for Social Justice* (Oxford University Press, 2011).

Bloch, F. S. (ed.). *The Global Clinical Movement. Educating Lawyers for Social Justice* (Oxford University Press, 2011).

Borràs, S., et al, The Environmental Law Clinic: A New Experience in Legal Education in Spain, in Daniela Ikawa and Leah Wortham (eds.), *The New Law School* (Public Interest Law Institute & Jagiellonian University Press, 2010).

Crowther, P., et al. *Internationalisation at Home. A Position Paper* (European Association for International Education [EAIE], 2000); www.iau–aiu.net/sites/all/files/Internationalisation at Home. a Position Paper.pdf

Franquet Sugrañes, T., and Marquès Banqué, M. Hitos En La Generación de Una Cultura de La Calidad Docente En Los Estudios de Derecho En España, o *Revista de Educación y Derecho* 0 (2009), 101.

García Añón, J. La Integración de La Educación Jurídica Clínica En El Proceso Formativo de Los Juristas, 12 *REDU-Revista de Docencia Universitaria* (2014), 153.

García Añón, J. *Transformaciones En La Docencia Y El Aprendizaje Del Derecho: ¿La Educación Jurídica Clínica Como Elemento Transformador?* 15 Teoría & Derecho (2014), 12.
Gobierno de España-Ministerio de. *La Responsabilidad Social de La Universidad Y El Desarrollo Sostenible* (Ministerio de Educación, 2011).
Hovhannisian, L. Clinical Legal Education and the Bologna Process (2006), PILI Papers 2, www.pilnet.org/component/docman/doc_download/25-clinical-legal-education-and-the-bologna-process.html.
Marquès Banqué, M. La Evaluación de Competencias En La Educación Superior: Retos E Instrumentos, o *Revista de Educación y Derecho* (2009), 47.
Marquès Banqué, M. La Dimensión Docente de La Responsabilidad Social Universitaria: La Institucionalización Del Aprendizaje Servicio En La Universitat Rovira I Virgili, *I Jornadas Internacionales sobre Responsabilidad Social Universitaria* (2014), www.urv.cat/media/upload//arxius/Aprenentatge Servei/MMARQUES-RSU - APS.pdf.
Marquès Banqué, M. Clínicas Jurídicas Y Universidad Pública, 11 *Revista de Educación y Derecho* (2015).
Marquès Banqué, M. Formando Para El Pro Bono: El Diseño de Una Clínica Jurídica Universitaria, in *Guía para la práctica del voluntariado jurídico* (Fundación Aranzadi Lex Nova, 2015).
Martínez, M. (ed.). *Aprendizaje Servicio Y Responsabilidad Social de Las Universidades* (MEC & Octaedro, 2008).
Vallaeys, F., de la Cruz, C., and Sasia, P. *Responsabilidad Social Universitaria. Manual de Primeros Pasos* (McGraw Hill & BID, 2009).
Wächter, B. An Introduction: Internationalisation at Home in Context, 7 *Journal of Studies in International Education* (2003), 5.

6

Law Clinics in France through the Prism of the Fundamental Rights Law Clinic, University of Caen Normandy

Xavier Aurey

INTRODUCTION

In the nascent landscape of clinical legal education (CLE) in France, the Fundamental Rights Law Clinic (CJDF[1]) was one of the first legal clinics to be set up and was certainly the first focused on human rights. As of 2016, there are around fifteen law clinics in France, most of them established during the past three years. The CJDF was born in fall 2009, at the University of Caen, Normandy, from an initiative launched a year earlier. After a pilot project (2009–2010) which aimed at testing procedures, the clinic sent a report to the French Constitutional Council in May 2011 relating to the constitutionality of certain provisions of the law concerning immigration, integration, and nationality. Since then, students have worked on various issues ranging from the laws surrounding homelessness (2012), to the status of the Assembly of French nationals living abroad (2013), the rights and freedoms of persons living in homes for the aged (2014), economic and social rights in Western Sahara (2015), and visitation rights in prison (2016). Working in collaboration with nongovernmental organizations (NGOs) and public institutions, the CJDF can be defined as a support clinic.[2] Students are thus not in direct contact with an individual litigant, unlike in live-client clinics.

As a training and research body, the Clinic helps to connect the university with broader society by affording students the possibility to disseminate and implement skills and knowledge acquired in university courses and research activities. From the tripartite relationship among students, faculty, and practitioners emerges an added value for teaching and research in fundamental rights and more widely for the field of human rights. The Clinic thus acts as a practical and theoretical forum about the possibilities and impact of the law as a tool to improve social practices.

The Clinic and its members are also working on the development of CLE in the Francophone world. Francophonie is indeed usually left aside by the major

---

[1] Clinique Juridique des Droits Fondamentaux, www.unicaen.fr/recherche/mrsh/crdfed/clinique.
[2] For other support clinics, see also Chapter 8 by Nora Markard and Chapter 12 by Renáta Uitz and Eszter Polgári.

foundations interested in the subject. While a real enthusiasm for law clinics currently exists, whether in Europe or in North and Sub-Saharan Africa, there is a severe lack of documentation and tools in the French language. In 2013, the Clinic thus organized an international symposium, and its proceedings have recently been published.[3] The following year, we also organized a training-workshop on CLE for the Francophone world in partnership with the NGO PILnet. We hosted teachers and lawyers from nearly ten countries. That same year, in 2014, the clinic had the honour of welcoming, for a semester, Sandra Babcock, professor at Cornell University, United States, thanks to the prestigious Tocqueville-Fulbright Chair. With her expertise on international human rights law clinics, Sandra Babcock has been an invaluable resource for both the students and the supervisors of our clinic. Finally, the CJDF is one of the founding members of the Network of Francophone law clinics, officially launched at a symposium at Sciences-Po Paris in February 2016.

EMERGENCE OF CLE

Genesis and Context

When the project to create the Fundamental Rights Law Clinic was launched in 2008, CLE was still unrecognized, even almost unknown in France. Indeed, the term "law clinic" appears for the first time in France in a 1927 book,[4] and only three papers were published on clinics in the intervening time, respectively in 2005,[5] 2006,[6] and 2007.[7] In 2008, I was a PhD candidate in international law and an assistant lecturer in law. I was reflecting deeply on my own teaching method. It is important to understand that, in France, as in many countries, most university teachers are simply dropped in front of students without any prior training or any follow-up. A victim of inertia, I was reproducing an extremely theoretical model of education that Christophe Jamin called a "doctrinal model,"[8] without ever having spared thought about its purpose, its qualities, or its defects.

[3] Xavier Aurey and Marie-Joëlle Redor-Fichot (dir.), LES CLINIQUES JURIDIQUES (Presses universitaires de Caen 2015).
[4] J. Bonnecase, PRÉCIS DE PRATIQUE JUDICIAIRE ET EXTRA-JUDICIAIRE. ELÉMENTS DE CLINIQUE JURIDIQUE (Sirey 1927) ; voir également, J. Bonnecase, Clinique juridique et facultés de droit. L'Institut clinique de jurisprudence, in REVUE GÉNÉRALE DU DROIT, DE LA LÉGISLATION ET DE LA JURISPRUDENCE (Paris 1931).
[5] N. Olszak, La professionnalisation des études de droit. Pour le développement d'un enseignement clinique (au-delà de la création d'une filière "hospitalo-universitaire" en matière juridique), 18 RECUEIL DALLOZ 1172–73 mai (2005).
[6] S. Hennette-Vauchez and D. Roman, Pour un enseignement clinique du droit, 218–19 LES PETITES AFFICHES 5–6 (2006).
[7] E. Millard, Sur un argument d'analogie entre l'activité universitaire des juristes et des médecins, in DROITS ET LIBERTÉS EN QUESTION, BILLETS D'HUMEUR EN L'HONNEUR DE DANIÈLE LOCHAK, LGDJ (LGDJ 2007), 343–52.
[8] Christophe Jamin, Ouverture et réalisme dans la formation des juristes en France, 2015 GAZETTE DU PALAIS 242.

These reflections therefore led me to read French papers about academic teaching methods in general, but also the aforementioned contributions. The one written by Stephanie Hennette-Vauchez and Diane Roman[9] has particularly motivated my desire to learn more about the law clinics they described, mainly relying on North American examples. Moreover, as I searched, I discovered a wide collection of English-language legal teaching literature – in contrast to the vacuum in France on the same topic. From the beginning, this law clinic project has been thus designed around the educational innovation it represented for the legal curriculum at the University of Caen. The clinic was first built as a teaching tool before becoming a tool for social justice.[10]

The theme of fundamental rights emerged because of the direct link with the Fundamental Rights Research Centre (CRDFED).[11] In addition to being an educational project, the clinic has also been conceived as a research project.[12] This project aimed at developing within the University of Caen, specifically within the CRDFED, a centre of expertise in the field of "clinical research" and "clinical education" in fundamental rights. As originally conceived, clinical activity in law schools, especially in the United States, has a dual educational and social vocation. These educational enterprises are dedicated to training students through provision of legal services to disadvantaged populations. However, law clinics generally do not support or encourage the ascription of scientific value to this exercise.

With this in mind, the CRDFED team wanted the Fundamental Rights Law Clinic to embrace all the missions of a university and, above all, those of a research centre. The CRDFED therefore associates, within the clinic, a research and a teaching component, complementing one other. In addition and in parallel to teaching, clinical legal research should be understood as research activity that aims at improving legal knowledge (be that of a particular right or a legal mechanism) through the study of specific cases. This same approach can be found in clinical medical research and clinical trials, except that it is not possible for the lawyer to test her models *in vivo*. Far from being opposed to "fundamental research," clinical research was to be a meeting place between academia and legal practice. It is also important to note that there is currently within the French legal academic community no appreciation of "the qualitative contribution of professional practice to scientific research."[13] It is in this sense that clinical research has a particular role to play. To valorize research is to give it a value other than it already has

---

[9] Hennette-Vauchez and Roman, *supra* note 7.
[10] *A contrario*, see Chapter 11 by Eva Brems and Stijn Smet in this volume.
[11] Centre de Recherche sur les Droits Fondamentaux et les Evolutions du Droit.
[12] Xavier Aurey, Projet de recherche : Clinique juridique des droits fondamentaux , Université de Caen Basse-Normandie, www.unicaen.fr/recherche/mrsh/sites/default/files/public/crdfed/ProjetdeRecherche.pdf.
[13] Eric Millard, Sur un argument d'analogie entre l'activité universitaire des juristes et des médecins, in DROITS ET LIBERTÉS EN QUESTION, BILLETS D'HUMEUR EN L'HONNEUR DE DANIÈLE LOCHAK, LGDJ (LGDJ 2007), 352.

ontologically. Its basic objectives aim at enhancing both the expertise of academic researchers (their knowledge and know-how) and the results of their research. In itself, the activity of the Clinic thus consists in a social valorization of scientific activity corresponding to the "development and dissemination, from research works, practical solutions or applications intended to improve a situation or to solve a social problem (at large)."[14] It thus participates in a social innovation process by aiming at the conversion of new knowledge into social benefits. This structure also serves as a theoretical forum for reflection about the possibilities and the impact of the law as a tool to improve social practices. For example, a clinic project on the rights and freedoms of persons living in homes for the aged (2014) was included in a broader research project, in partnership with sociologists and psychologists, and funded by the Regional Council.

One of the interesting outcomes of this research-led approach is that, each year, one to three students who have participated in the clinical programme choose to pursue their research through a PhD. Indeed, even if the clinical work is essentially considered as a practical way of teaching law, it can also reveal the importance of strong legal research and motivate students to pursue academic careers. Aware of the potential practical impact of their work, these young researchers would furthermore be able to help reduce the gap between universities and civil society.

Drivers

It is recognized that the action of some US foundations has been a key factor in the development of law clinics in the United States, in Africa,[15] in Asia,[16] and in Eastern Europe.[17] Within an academic system that still tends to work with a view to self-preservation, the action of these foundations has served as an impulse to change the legal curriculum. However, Western Europe remained, at least historically, somewhat beyond the gaze of US foundations. Lacking this influx of external energy, reflections on clinical legal education only emerged in France in the mid-2000s. Several factors explain this recent interest of French academia in university law clinics. The 2000s were indeed significant for law schools. Both the reforms resulting

---

[14] Conseil de la science et de la technologie du Québec, La valorisation de la recherche universitaire, Clarification conceptuelle (février 2005), 9; www.cst.gouv.qc.ca/IMG/pdf/Valorisation_Rech_Univ.pdf.

[15] See David McQuoid-Mason, et al., *Clinical Legal Education in Africa: Legal Education and Community Service*, in THE GLOBAL CLINICAL MOVEMENT: EDUCATING LAWYERS FOR SOCIAL JUSTICE (Frank S. Bloch ed., Oxford University Press 2010).

[16] See Bruce Lasky and M. R. K. Prasad, *The Clinical Movement in Southeast Asia and India: A Comparative Perspective and Lessons to Be Learned*, in THE GLOBAL CLINICAL MOVEMENT: EDUCATING LAWYERS FOR SOCIAL JUSTICE (Frank S. Bloch ed., Oxford University Press 2010).

[17] See Chapter 12 by Renáta Uitz and Eszter Polgári in this volume. *See also* Mariana Berbec-Rostas, Arkady Gutnikov, and Barbara Namyslowska-Gabrysiak, *Clinical Legal Education in Central and Eastern Europe*, in THE GLOBAL CLINICAL MOVEMENT: EDUCATING LAWYERS FOR SOCIAL JUSTICE (Frank S. Bloch ed., Oxford University Press, 2010), 53–68.

from the Bologna Process and the emergence of national and international academic competition in the market for legal education came together to shake up a teaching model that was rooted in a secular tradition.[18] It is therefore difficult to see the growing interest in CLE as mere coincidence.

In 1999, the European ministers of higher education adopted the Bologna Declaration, in which they affirmed their willingness to pursue convergence among the European university systems in order to create a European Higher Education Area. Diego Blázquez-Martín affirms that, in Spain, this Bologna Process "offers the opportunity to make decisions that should have been made twenty-five or thirty years ago, to make legal education and law more effective and to create progressive tools for social and cultural change after a long and repressive dictatorship."[19] In France, law schools have experienced this process somewhat passively rather than proactively, using it to rethink and transform their practices. In the first years following the Declaration, adjustments were made to the legal curriculum without major changes. The impact of the Bologna Process was more formal than it was substantive.

However, among the three main objectives of the Bologna Process – international competitiveness, mobility, and employability – two found a special resonance in the French context, thus opening a space for the emergence of law clinics. Two developments perceived as potentially dangerous by faculty confronted law schools in the mid-2000s. The first was the willingness and ability of non–university education providers to award law degrees – ushering in a level of national competition previously unknown. The second came in the form of criticism from sectors of the legal profession, starting with barristers, about the limited focus on professionalization within academic curriculum – thus affecting the employability of students.

To slightly simplify, the French higher education system is made up of two factions. On one side, there are the public general and nonselective universities, and, on the other side, specialized schools – public or private (known in France as *Grandes Ecoles*). At one time, only the first group of institutions were permitted to grant a law degree, authorizing its holder to take the entrance exam that acts as the gateway to professional schools for lawyers. Facing repeated requests from business schools and Sciences Po Paris to change this situation, the vast majority of law school deans signed, in 2004, an opinion column calling on the government not to allow these nonacademic institutions to grant law degrees.[20] Two main fears were behind this reaction: first, losing the best students in favour of selective and fee-paying private schools, and, second and incidentally, the prospect of only being able to

---

[18] As highlighted by Yves Gaudemet, today's universities are the heirs of reforms from the nineteenth century; see Yves Gaudemet, Les facultés de droit dans la réforme universitaire , 3 REVUE DU DROIT PUBLIC, 680 (2008).

[19] Diego Blázquez-Martín, *The Bologna Process and the Future of Clinical Education in Europe: A View from Spain* , in THE GLOBAL CLINICAL MOVEMENT (Frank S. Bloch, dir., Oxford University Press, 2012), 132.

[20] Rudolf Von Jhering and Olivier Jouanjan, LA LUTTE POUR LE DROIT, (Dalloz 1872/2006), 2579.

maintain research centres in some major universities, while others would be relegated to nonresearch colleges.[21] In response to this discontent, a first decision was published by the government in 2004 reminding institutions that the "national master degree in law is granted [only] by universities authorized to do so."[22]

However, the respite was short when facing what some have called a "logical and inevitable evolution," according to which "legal education becomes a competitive market."[23] The first step towards liberalization within the market was taken in 2007, when the government added to the lists of qualifications recognized as "equivalent to the maîtrise de droit [LL.B] for the exercise of the profession of lawyer ... 9. Judicial and Legal Careers [specification] and economic law [specification] from the degree granted by the Institute of Political Studies in Paris."[24] Various academic players challenged this eruption of Sciences Po Paris onto the academic scene of legal studies in court, but the Conseil d'Etat considered that the government, through this reform, had not committed any manifest error of assessment, nor did this lead to a breach of the principle of equality among students.[25] As Myriam Ait Aoudia recalled, "the breakdown is historic," and the law schools then wondered how to "counter the rise of an unprecedented competition in law degrees."[26]

At the same time, legal professionals, mostly lawyers, complained that university students "are often poorly or not prepared to implement logical reasoning and overall legal strategies."[27] They blamed the law curriculum for being too theoretical.[28] In the French system, where there are professional law schools following initial training at university (i.e. regional lawyer schools, a national school of magistrates, and notary professional training centres), universities are accused of not delivering a professional degree and not preparing students for the specific practice of the job.[29]

By rightly or wrongly questioning the relevance of the academic legal teaching model, these two developments created a space where CLE could thrive. The various clinical projects that were born in France since 2007 aimed at

---

[21] Id. [22] Arrêté du 8 décembre 2004 relatif au diplôme national de master en droit.
[23] Didier Truchet, Les facultés de droit et le marché de l'enseignement du droit, RECUEIL DALLOZ (2005), 2892.
[24] Arrêté du 21 mars 2007 modifiant l'arrêté du 25 novembre 1998 fixant la liste des titres ou diplômes reconnus comme équivalents à la maîtrise en droit pour l'exercice de la profession d'avocat, art. 1er.
[25] Conseil d'Etat, 28 juillet 2008, *Syndicat autonome du personnel enseignant des sciences juridiques, politiques, économiques et de gestion des universités et al.*
[26] Myriam Aït-Aoudia, Le droit dans la concurrence. Mobilisations universitaires contre la création de diplômes de droit à Sciences Po Paris, 83(1)DROIT ET SOCIÉTÉ 99–116 (2013).
[27] Christophe Bigot, Réflexions d'un avocat sur la professionnalisation des études de droit, RECUEIL DALLOZ (2005), 1724.
[28] Hervé Croze, Les écoles de droit, RECUEIL DALLOZ (2004), 3003.
[29] Thierry Wickers, Pierre-Yves Gautier, La formation d'un jeune juriste au XXIe siècle, 2013 GAZETTE DU PALAIS 22 (2013); Rachel Vanneuville, La formation contemporaine des avocats : aiguillon d'une recomposition de l'enseignement du droit en France?, 83 DROIT ET SOCIÉTÉ 67–82 (2013).

developing, at the very minimum, "a training combining theory and practice [leading to] a better understanding of concepts."[30] This moment also invited law schools and academics to rethink the role of universities as a social player, anchored in the surrounding community. Thus, in Bordeaux for example, it has been highlighted that "the clinic's activities promote the development of a social awareness within the university."[31] This combination of two traditional elements of law clinics – "learning by doing" and social justice – has characterized the clinical movement in France. Beyond these core aspects, some, like Nanterre or Sciences Po, want moreover to "encourage critical self-reflection on the ethical, normative, ideological and institutional dimensions of this practice"[32] by the establishment of specific training modules related to clinical activity.

REFORMING THE TEACHING AND PRACTICE OF LAW IN EUROPE

Goals and Methods

As in many other countries, legal education in France is mainly dogmatic in the sense that the law is taught to students according to a coherent and systematized vision.[33] This approach to legal matters as a stand-alone system leads to the presentation of legal interpretation to students as though it were detached from any outside influence, from any sociopolitical context. Such a vision is part and parcel of a positivist tradition that views the study and interpretation of law as a value-neutral legal science.[34] In response, one of the first advocates of law clinics, Jerome Frank, uses the distinction made by Roscoe Pound between law in the books and law in action[35] to position law clinics as a beachhead for a general reform of legal studies.[36] He founded his theory on a radical questioning of the doctrinal model,[37] noting cynically that studying legal decisions in books comes to

---

[30] Jeremy Pereleman, *La clinique de l'École de droit de Sciences Po*, in LES CLINIQUES JURIDIQUES (Xavier Aurey and Marie-Joëlle Redor-Fichot (dir.), Presses universitaires de Caen 2015), 209.

[31] Marie Lamarche and Cécile Castaing, *Clinique du droit de l'université de Bordeaux*, in LES CLINIQUES JURIDIQUES (Xavier Aurey and Marie-Joëlle Redor-Fichot (dir.), Presses universitaires de Caen, 2015), 193.

[32] Pereleman, *supra* note 31, at 209.

[33] Cf. Christophe Jamin, *Le rôle créateur de la pratique dans la formation des juristes. Table ronde* (François Terré et al. eds.), 108 GAZETTE DU PALAIS (2013).

[34] Cf. notamment Alexandre Viala, *Le positivisme juridique : Kelsen et l'héritage kantien*, 67 REVUE INTERDISCIPLINAIRE D'ÉTUDES JURIDIQUES 95–117 (2011).

[35] R. Pound, *Law in Books and Law in Action*, 44 AM. L. REV. 15 (1910).

[36] J. Frank, *Why Not a Clinical Lawyer School*, 81 UNIV. PA L. REV. 907 (1933); J. Frank, *What Constitutes a Good Legal Education?* 19 A.B.A. J. 723 (1933); J. Frank *A Plea for Lawyers-Schools*, 56 YALE L. J. 1303 (1947). For an analysis, see K. R. Kruse, *Getting Real about Legal Realism, New Legal Realism and Clinical Legal Education*, 56 N. Y. LAW SCHOOL L. REV. 295–320 (2012); N. Duxbury, *Jerome Frank and the Legacy of Legal Realism*, 18 J. L. SOC. 175 (1991).

[37] Jamin, *supra* note 9.

the same thing as training dog breeders without allowing them to see anything but stuffed dogs.[38]

However, if the lecture-in-an-amphitheatre model of legal education remains a firm favourite, especially during the first three years of legal education, it is not so much due to a kind of prestige or secular tradition, but because it is the most economical method to teach a large number of students.[39] The lack of change in French universities is thus not only an issue of will and priority in the allocation of resources within universities, but also a more general issue of the resources invested in public higher education.

That being said, the possibility of law clinics questioning and perhaps reforming the traditional legal teaching model should not be ruled out. To the contrary, like many other clinics, the educational contribution of the Fundamental Rights Law Clinic consists of three interrelated focus areas; namely, those of the professionalization of legal studies, the link between theory and practice, and critical reflection on law. As noted earlier, many legal professionals blame law schools for not training their students adequately for legal practice, particularly to perform the role of an attorney. In view of this criticism of the nonprofessionalizing character of legal curriculum, we must recall, as noted by Philippe Brun, that "the first vocation of law schools is not to meet the 'expectations' of a profession, as important as [that] is ... but to fulfil its public service mission, which is to ensure quality education to students preparing for various legal professions."[40]

At the same time, we must acknowledge that French law schools have for a long time underestimated the qualitative contribution of legal practice to legal education. More than a science, discourse on law is functional insofar as it consists of a "set of means, conscious processes by which man tends to a certain end, seeks to achieve a certain result."[41] Where science is conceived as pure knowledge (that is to say, independent of its potential applications), the same cannot be said of law and legal knowledge. In thinking on legal education, a parallel with medical school and the art of medicine comes up regularly.[42] Just as the medical student who learns to put into practice the theoretical training received, the law student must also receive the means to conceive the link between legal theory and practice. Understood in this way, the professionalization of the legal curriculum does not reject theory; rather, it is inspired by it. According to this line of thought, law clinics are one of the best tools

---

[38] Frank, *supra* note 37, at 912. Cf. A. Benjamin Spencer, *The Law School Critique in Historical Perspective*, 69 WASH. & LEE L. REV. 1949–2063 (2012).

[39] Hervé Croze, Qu'est-ce qu'enseigner le droit?, RECUEIL DALLOZ (2004), 1315.

[40] Philippe Brun, *Les Facultés de droit sont au service des usagers de l'enseignement supérieur*, 318 GAZETTE DU PALAIS 13 (2012) (réponse à T. Wickers, *Remettre la faculté de droit au service de la profession d'avocat*, 290 GAZETTE DU PALAIS 13 (16 Oct. 2012), J1275.

[41] CNRTL, TLFi, "art."

[42] Hervé Croze, *Recherche juridique et professionnalisation des études de droit Pour une filière hospitalo-universitaire en matière juridique*, RECUEIL DALLOZ (2005), 908 ; Stéphanie Hennette-Vauchez and Diane Roman, *Pour un enseignement clinique du droit*, 219 LPA 3 (2006).

to guide students towards the implementation of knowledge. They are all the more interesting when they enable a critical feedback on the practice.

As emphasized by Christophe Jamin, clinics are "places where we learn that the law is not only dominated by principles, that these principles are unstable and often contradictory, that legal reasoning often lacks consistency, that the arguments are almost all reversible."[43] Clinical students will thus have experienced the law in action, an experience that they then have the opportunity to go back over with their teachers and classmates. This dialogue within the university is fundamental in building the identity of students as lawyers. It perhaps reduces the level of disenchantment experienced by students in confrontation with the actual practice of law. At the same time, it invites them to continue to examine their own practice throughout their careers.

Beyond the Educational Goals

Through direct contact with the reality of the law, beyond merely the study of laws and court decisions, CLE questions both the place of social and political issues in the training of students, but also the role of universities as sociopolitical players.[44] However, if it is fundamental to reinstate universities, and especially law schools, in the social context, one must not forget that their primary mission remains to teach law to students. In this sense, a law clinic is neither an NGO nor a state's decentralized legal aid provider. On this last point, it is important that the development of law clinics does not result in the disinvestment of the government from this critical area of state responsibility.

In France, law clinics are working in parallel with a state-funded legal aid system that, on the whole, operates pretty well for its beneficiaries.[45] This system helps people with limited resources to benefit from a total or partial payment of legal fees and court costs by the state.[46] It is available for both French nationals and non-nationals lawfully and habitually resident in France and for asylum seekers. "Illegal"

---

[43] Jamin, *supra* note 9.

[44] We can think of the movement on the social responsibility of universities; cf. Robert M. Hollister, et al., *The Talloires Network: A Global Network of Engaged Universities*, 16 (4) JOURNAL OF HIGHER EDUCATION OUTREACH AND ENGAGEMENT 81 (2012); J.-F. Balaudé, La responsabilité sociale des universités: une vision de l'université, *Educpro.fr* (6 mars 2013), www.letudiant.fr/educpros/opinions/la-responsabilite-sociale-des-universites-une-vision-de-l-universite.html.

[45] Cf. Jules-Marc Baudel, L'accès à la justice : la situation en France,58 (2) REVUE INTERNATIONALE DE DROIT COMPARÉ 477–91 (2006); Édouard Lamaze, *Quelle effectivité du droit à l'assistance d'un avocat? L'aide juridictionnelle en question* , 9 SEMAINE JURIDIQUE 406–07 (2012). Recent reforms of legal aid, however, pose questions, with lawyers accusing the government of not sufficiently remunerate the supported actions. Cf. Jean-Charles Marrigues, Réforme de l'AJ : déception, incompréhension, colère ... Les mots (maux) ne manquent pas , 275–76 LA GAZETTE DU PALAIS 9–11 (2015); Conseil National des Barreaux, Les propositions de réforme de l'aide juridictionnelle "ne sont (pas) acceptables," 39 JCP G 1704 (2015).

[46] Loi n° 91-647 du 10 juillet 1991 relative à l'aide juridique.

immigrants can also benefit under some conditions.[47] Furthermore, since 1998, there are "houses of justice and law" operating under the authority of the public prosecutor and the president of the High Court,[48] and offering free and confidential legal consultations. There are currently nearly 140 houses of justice and law throughout the French territory.

However, NGOs do not have access to this kind of legal aid and generally do not have sufficient resources to work on all the legal issues they face. As a clinic supporting civil society organizations, the CJDF is part of a capacity-building process for these organizations. Like other clinics, it thus contributes towards a rethinking of the place of universities in their surrounding community. Should universities only teach knowledge and skills through a value-neutral method? Or can we imagine that they might also – or should[49] – be conceived of as social players with a social justice mission?

This promotion of social justice is fundamental and at the foundation of the clinical movement in the United States and in other countries, but it is at the same time increasingly criticized.[50] In a recent paper,[51] Julie D. Lawton reproached American law schools for imposing *pro bono* activities on students and for requiring students "to adhere to the social justice morality of law faculty and law school administrators."[52] She does not question the need for social justice in the United States, but she believes that student engagement in this sense is a moral choice that should not be imposed.

But behind this criticism lies the illusion that the traditional way of teaching law would be ideologically neutral. However, it is not. A product of a history and a culture, every legal system conveys an ideology. Teaching law in a way that we think neutral is also to impose this ideology. Like students, teachers must "stop considering law as a single technique, that is to say, as a single arrangement of categories and rules and agree to see, in addition, the manifestation of a cultural phenomenon."[53] Thinking of law clinics as a vector of social justice within law schools can rather be seen as a rebalancing of approaches in legal education, one fostering a critical detachment from the dominant ideology.

---

[47] *Id.*, art. 3.
[48] Loi n° 98–1163 du 18 décembre 1998 relative à l'accès au droit et à la résolution amiable des conflits, art. 21. Today in Code de l'organisation judiciaire, art. R-131-1 à R-131-11.
[49] Paul Benneworth and Michael Osborne, *Knowledge Engagement and Higher Education in Europe*, 5 HIGHER EDUCATION IN THE WORLD 219–31 (2014).
[50] Cf., *e.g.*, Praveen Kosuri, *Losing My Religion: The Place of Social Justice in Clinical Legal Education*, 32 (2) B. C. J. L. & SOC. JUST. 338 (2012).
[51] Julie D. Lawton, *The Imposition of Social Justice Morality in Legal Education*, 4 (1) INDIANA JOURNAL OF LAW AND SOCIAL EQUALITY 57–75 (2016).
[52] *Id.*, at 58.
[53] Pierre Legrand, *Notes inspirées par une gêne persistante à l'égard de la fascination exercée par l'habitude, l'autorité, la loi et l'Etat dans les facultés de droit françaises*, RTD CIV. (1998), 299.

The Weight and Value of Internationalization

Working on human rights, the Law Clinic of Caen regularly deals with questions of European and international law. Three examples seem relevant in order to comprehend the clinical action in this field. In their report sent to the Constitutional Council in the context of the review of the bill on immigration, integration, and nationality (May 2011), the students based their research on the case law of the European Court of Human Rights and on the provisions of the Citizens' Rights Directive[54] to ask the Council to suppress a provision which was de facto limiting the access of irregular migrants to emergency help. They also reviewed the decisions of the Court of Justice of the European Union to ask the Council to enforce by law a ban on penalizing the illegal stay of a migrants as provided for under the Returns Directive,[55] as interpreted by the Court. Even while the Constitutional Council has not surpassed the relevant provision, the students were able to realize directly the potential impact of international standards on national laws and practices. They were also required to juggle between different normative corpuses whose legal scope differs in accordance with their authors.

The following year, they collaborated with FNASAT[56] to prepare a priority question of constitutionality in relation to some articles of the law relating to homelessness.[57] Beyond direct compliance with the Constitution, the students were interested in the compatibility of the provisions of this law with the European Convention of Human Rights (ECHR) and the International Covenant on Civil and Political Rights (ICCPR). In their 124-page report, they demonstrated that the restrictions imposed by the law on the lifestyle of these people were disproportionate with respect to the "right to respect a minority lifestyle" as derived from Article 8 of the ECHR by the Strasbourg Court[58] and the right of freedom of movement and to choose one's residence within a state as protected by Article 2 of Protocol No. 4 and Article 12 of the ICCPR. Based on this work, FNASAT supported a priority question of constitutionality referred to the Constitutional Council in July 2012. In its decision, the Council found that certain provisions of the 1969 Law were unconstitutional, but without taking into account the students' main arguments. Subsequently, FNASAT has also used this report to support an

---

[54] EU, European Parliament and Council, 29 April 2004, *Directive 2004/38/EC on the right of citizens of the Union and their family members to move and reside freely within the territory of the Member States*.
[55] EU, European Parliament and Council, 16 December 2008, *Directive 2008/115/EC on common standards and procedures in Member States for returning illegally staying third-country nationals*.
[56] Fédération nationale des associations solidaires d'action avec les Tsiganes et les Gens du voyage.
[57] France, Law No. 69-3 of January 3, 1969, relating to the exercise of ambulatory activities and to the regime applicable to persons circulating in France without a fixed domicile or residence.
[58] Cf. J.-P. Marguénaud, *La lente émergence d'un droit européen au respect des modes de vie minoritaires*, RTD CIV. (2001), 448; D. Fiorina, *Mode de vie : la consécration du droit à la différence*, DALLOZ (2002), 2758; F. Benoit-Rohmer, *La Cour de Strasbourg et la protection de l'intérêt minoritaire : une avancée décisive sur le plan des principes?*, RTDH (2001), 1004.

individual complaint before the Human Rights Committee that condemned France on the basis of a violation of Article 12 of the Covenant.[59]

Finally, in 2014–2015, the students worked with a range of different NGOs to write a "shadow report" for the Committee on Economic, Social, and Cultural Rights in the context of the examination of the Kingdom of Morocco's fourth periodic report about the implementation of the International Covenant on Economic, Social, and Cultural Rights. In this report, the students focused on the issue of respect of human rights in the territory of Western Sahara. In its concluding observations,[60] the Committee went in the same direction as the Clinic's report, especially on issues about the Sahrawi's self-determination and about their participation in the use and exploitation of the territory's natural resources. In general, the Committee asked Morocco to "provide in its next periodic report, detailed information on the enjoyment by the Saharawi of all rights enshrined in the Covenant."[61]

Through these works, the students were confronted by the reality of international and European law and with the realization that its implementation by states differs from the relevant internal standards. They understand that "there are few significant legal or social problems today that are purely domestic"[62] and thus that "there is almost no area of national law that cannot be challenged in the light of a possible conflict with" supranational law.[63] As Bernard Duhaime emphasizes, "the clinical approach also allows them demystify international law,"[64] it illustrates that the implementation of the law is not the exclusive preserve of "often remote and inaccessible institutions."[65] Using international and supranational legal standards as part of their work, clinical students give such standards a concrete materiality and make them accessible both for their partners and for themselves. They also realize the leverage effect that these standards may have, obliging states to defend themselves and to justify themselves beyond their own borders.

At the same time, they understand that, beyond the traditional legal system, the work of NGOs and of civil society is essential to maximize the effects of international norms. This work on supplementary reports enables the students discover another facet of legal work, one that exists in parallel to litigation and is no less important.

---

[59] CDH, March 28, 2014, *Claude Ory c. France*, Communication n°1960/2010, U.N. Doc. CCPR/C/110/D/1960/2010.

[60] CDESC, October 8, 2015, *Concluding observations on the fourth periodic report of Morocco*, U.N. Doc. E/C.12/MAR/CO/4.

[61] *Id.*, at § 8.

[62] John Edward Sexton, *The Global Law School Program at New York University*, 46 J. LEGAL EDUC. 329 (1996), at 331.

[63] Miguel Poiares Maduro, *Legal Education and the Europeanisation and Globalisation of Law*, 4 CROATIAN YEARBOOK OF EUROPEAN LAW & POLICY (2008).

[64] Bernard Duhaime, *La pertinence de l'approche clinique pour enseigner le droit international des droits de la personne*, in LES CLINIQUES JURIDIQUES (Xavier Aurey, Marie-Joëlle Redor-Fichot, dir., Presses universitaires de Caen,2015), 129.

[65] *Id.*

Cooperation in CLE

Having defined itself primarily as a support clinic for civil society organizations, the Fundamental Rights Law Clinic collaborates with different partners for each of its projects. However, the clinic has not yet had the opportunity to work with other law clinics on a common project. Clinical work with NGOs on a particular issue is quite different from the type of work undertaken by live-client clinics. Individuals come to consult these latter clinics to better understand their rights in relation to a particular legal issue, whereas NGOs most often come to a support clinic with a specific purpose in mind, in connection with an action they are undertaking or wish to undertake. The clinic's expertise becomes part of the NGO's strategy, a strategy that must necessarily be taken into account by the students. Beyond the objective, the temporality of such a clinical project is also different. The engagement with an individual beneficiary usually lasts two to three weeks whereas an NGO project will take several months. Beyond a certain ability to listen and to undertake research and analysis common to both types of clinics, students must also learn how to organize and manage a calendar and to work with the external partner, including responding effectively to his or her requests for modification of their work. They are thus in regular contact with one or more members of the NGO in a relationship of exchange – that is to say, not in a relationship of subordination, as would be the case, for example, during an internship. The difference is important because it necessarily induces an active positioning of the student, promoting the development of professional autonomy.

Other clinical collaborations happen at the level of the supervisory team and consist of a process of mutual exchanges of experience and of dissemination of the concept of CLE. Because of the relative youth of clinical programmes in France, it seems indeed essential to take advantage of other experiences in order to question and improve our own teaching practice.

Diffusion of CLE

From the beginning, members of the Fundamental Rights Law Clinic wished to work in collaboration with other players invested in CLE, whether in France or elsewhere. We wanted to benefit from the experience of more senior clinicians and to create synergy between emerging projects in the area. To create the clinic in Caen, I turned to Francophone Canada, and I have been fortunate to benefit from Québec's expertise, particularly through the advice of Bernard Duhaime, former director and founder of the University of Quebec at Montreal (UQAM)'s International Clinic of Human Rights.

With regard to a clinical teaching method often accused of being only the expression of an American academic model, the support of a teacher involved in a legal system in part inherited from his French ancestors was a significant asset for the launch of the project. A second powerful experience for the clinic was to host Sandra Babcock, Clinical Professor at Cornell Law School, on a Tocqueville-Fulbright Chair in 2014. Direct sharing of experience is a key asset that cannot be replaced by any reading, as interesting and relevant as it might be.

We wanted to strengthen this face-to-face sharing of experience by organizing or participating in CLE training-of-trainers events. With the support of the NGO PILnet, we thus welcomed in Caen, in March 2014, four expert trainers from Spain, the United States, and Canada and twenty participants from about ten different countries. From this training, several legal clinics were born and have consolidated in France, Belgium, and Morocco. With PILnet and the Regional Commission for Human Rights in Casablanca, we renewed this initiative during the Second World Forum on Human Rights, held in Marrakech in November 2014. During these two workshops, we employed clinical teaching techniques, encouraging participants to learn and test their relevance as learning methods.

Regarding participation in networks, because of its history, France has the opportunity to be at the crossroads of two important cultural spaces, Europe and Francophonie. It was therefore important for us to come within the scope of both spaces. As soon as we could, we partnered with the European network for CLE (ENCLE). Furthermore, noting the gaps in the Francophonie in this field, we wanted to bring together initiatives in the form of a new Francophone network. The idea germinated during the symposium on law clinics that I organized in Caen in December 2013. Many of the participants wished to continue this conversation by formally creating a network. Officially launched at Sciences Po Paris in February 2016, the Network of Francophone Law Clinics[66] aims to develop expertise in French on CLE. We want to share the experiences of all clinics, to create a permanent link between those created in Francophone countries during recent years, and to foster the creation of new law clinics by providing tools, connections, and helpful resources. Those participating in the network often hail from beyond France, including teachers and students from countries as diverse as Belgium, Canada, Switzerland, Morocco, Lebanon, or Togo.

Future of CLE in Europe

In Europe, we have to distinguish between countries that have received financial and technical support from American foundations involved in the promotion of law clinics and from other countries. For the former, among which are many countries in eastern and southern Europe, law clinic programmes are generally well established (as in Poland or the Czech Republic) or have not survived the reduced financial and human support (we especially think of Macedonia and Russia). For other countries, including France, the situation is different, and clinical programmes must first find

[66] www.cliniques-juridiques.org.

their place and a modicum of institutional recognition. With a few exceptions – Bordeaux and Sciences Po Paris – French law clinics were first developed as volunteer projects on the initiative of students or teachers. The example of Caen is illustrative of the uncertain reality of law clinics in France.

Launched in October 2009, the clinic was formally integrated into a master's degree programme in September 2012. This integration was quite a struggle, and the clinic is only included as a small option. Indeed, this first step towards recognizing the educational contribution of the clinic is insufficient to take full account of the investment of both supervisors and students. On the student side, the credits associated with participation in the clinic do not reflect the work done and can sometimes be a source of discouragement, or at least of a shift in priorities with regards to other courses. Despite this slight handicap, the clinic still attracts students, a proof of the interest it arouses. On the teacher side, the fifteen hours of service associated with a Master 2 option are quickly swallowed up, and supervisors therefore remain involved as volunteers. This point is the more problematic of the two, threatening over the medium term the sustainability of any clinical project. After two or three years in this regime, it is difficult to condemn the trainer who stands back to find the time to better prepare his other courses and to do research. At the same time, it is also unjust to condemn the university, already juggling with extremely tight budgets, for not providing more hours to clinical teaching or even permitting part-time or full-time staff.

One of the major challenges for the clinical movement in Europe will thus be to find ways to support the institutionalization of law clinics in universities. A reflection on this point will be necessary in each country but also at the European level. Various examples can serve as a basis for discussion, including Poland and its Clinics Foundation.[67]

CONCLUSION

Present in France for less than ten years, CLE is gradually gaining momentum. This enthusiasm for law clinics should not be seen as a passing fad or an Americanization of the curriculum, but as a response to criticism faced by universities, especially law schools, for many years. These criticisms about the lack of professionalization in education or the disconnection of teaching with the reality of the law have opened a space for reflection and action in which many teachers and students have rushed to adapt the concept of the law clinic to the French context. The movement is growing slowly, with now nearly a dozen law clinics operating in France, most of them created less than three years ago.

If it wants to be sustainable, this French movement must be rooted in the very foundations of the global movement for CLE that are both educational innovation

---

[67] Fundacja Uniwersyteckich Poradni Prawnych, www.fupp.org.pl/.

and social commitment. With respect to educational innovation, it is fundamental to stress the triptych of professionalization, theory/practical relationship, and critical approach to law. Law clinics are thus not intended to replace other forms of education, but to bring significant added value to traditional training while serving as a stimulus for their own evolution. With respect to social engagement, law clinics are part of a movement for the social responsibility of universities. They allow for a rethinking of the place of these institutions within the local communities in which they are embedded, but also more widely in the international arena. Collaborations and exchanges at the various levels, either with NGOs, individuals, public partners, or other academic structures, are fundamental both to strengthen clinical programmes and the training of students. Students take advantage of all experiences, and they learn how to incorporate other cultures and practices as constitutive elements of their future careers. Through their clinical experience, students are undoubtedly fit to meet the legal and social issues of today and tomorrow.

PART IIB

The Europeanization of Clinical Legal Education

How Clinical Legal Education Is Being Adapted for European Law and European Issues

7

On the Front Line of the Migrant Crisis

The Human Rights and Migration Law Clinic (HRMLC) of Turin

Ulrich Stege and Maurizio Veglio

INTRODUCTION

The Human Rights and Migration Law Clinic of Turin (HRMLC) attempts to bridge the gap between classroom education and the reality of professional practice. The HRLMC emphasizes the sensitization of students as future professionals to the problems of social justice and seeks to foster in them a sense of social responsibility. It has two primary objectives: first, to encourage students throughout their clinical experience to envisage how legal institutions and practices can be reformed and reorganized to provide the best service, and second, to provide much-needed *pro bono* legal assistance to underrepresented individuals and organizations within the Turin area, complementing the already existing support provided by local organizations working for the benefit of migrants.

Each HRMLC cycle lasts for one academic year and is implemented with the support of various partner institutions. The HRMLC was established in 2011 by the International University College of Turin (IUC)[1] in cooperation with the Departments of Law of the Universities of Turin and Eastern Piedmont in Alessandria. It is open to the international student body of the IUC master's degree programmes. In addition, the clinical programme involves undergraduate law students from the Universities of Turin and Eastern Piedmont. It thus engages a group of select Italian and international students (approximately twenty-five students per academic year) who are highly qualified and motivated. In addition, the programme enhances the cooperation between these institutions by using the synergies of their different activities, competencies, and structures for the benefit of the students and the local migrant community. The three institutional partners play a key role for the clinic management by connecting the clinical programme to the actual curriculum of the universities, selecting the clinical students, defining the clinical priorities, supervising the clinical activities, and determining and supporting the areas of research.

---

[1] For more details about the IUC, *se:* www.iuctorino.it.

Another strategic partner is the Associazione per gli Studi Giuridici sull'Immigrazione (ASGI),[2] which has proven expertise in the field of asylum and migration law in Italy. ASGI and its associated and specialized lawyers play a key role in the clinic by advising, supporting, and supervising the clinical activities at all stages. In addition, the HRMLC has signed cooperation agreements with local and international actors working in the field of asylum and migration.[3]

The HRMLC combines a classroom component (first trimester) with practical activities (second and third trimesters). It is focused on establishing independent thinking and seeks to give students the possibility of experiencing the gaps between the law on the books and its implementation in practice, especially in the context of human rights and migration law practice. The activities range from *pro bono* legal advice (to migrants and refugees) to strategic litigation (e.g. providing support with respect to claims to the European Court of Human Rights in Strasbourg), research, and advocacy activities (such as work regarding the detention conditions for migrants in Turin's centre for identification and expulsion[4] or involvement in the monitoring of case law on deportation, detention, and return of migrants[5]).

EMERGENCE OF CLINICAL LEGAL EDUCATION

Genesis and Context

The HRMLC was established in 2011 as the first law clinic in the Piedmont region and one of the first law clinics in Italy. It is the product of a unique combination of (1) institutional factors, (2) personal experiences, and (3) the local context.

Institutional Factors

The main institution behind the HRMLC's establishment was the IUC, which was established under the guidance of Professor Ugo Mattei[6] in 2006, for the interdisciplinary and comparative study of law, economics, and finance, in response to the perceived lack of a transnational set of normative principles capable of directing economic processes.

---

[2] ASGI is an Italian network of legal experts working in the area of asylum and migration. For more details, *see* www.asgi.it.

[3] For more about the HRMLC and its partners, *see* www.iuctorino.it/studies/clinical-education/legal-clinics/.

[4] For more details, *see* www.iuctorino.it/cie-research-project/; *see also* the published report: Stege et al, *Betwixt and Between: Turin's CIE. A Human Rights Investigation into Turin's Immigration Detention Centre*, International University College of Turin, IPEL Report Series (2012), www.iuctorino.it/wp-content/uploads/CIE_09_2012FV.pdf.

[5] Together with other universities and legal clinics in Italy, see the website of the observatory: www.lexilium.it.

[6] Prof. Ugo Mattei is founder and academic coordinator of the IUC. He is also Law Professor at the University of Turin (Italy) and at the UC Hasting College of Law (California, USA).

The IUC's programme specifically seeks to engage students and young scholars from all over the world – with special emphasis on the periphery, or "global south" – with leading figures in economics, law, and the humanities. In the past years, 301 students (some 60% women) from sixty-four countries[7] have made up the IUC's interdisciplinary community that is collectively oriented towards the institutional commitment to search for a more sustainable and equitable Earth for future generations.

In all its programmes and researches, the IUC emphasizes the relationship between theory and practice, favouring actual experience and empirical findings over black letter law. Accordingly, each course of the IUC master's programmes explores law in action, investigating the myriad of legal and nonlegal factors which influence the social, legal, political, and economic arrangements in society, while practical teaching components are designed to prepare students for the rigorous demands of public or private practice as well as to synthesize their theoretical understanding with actual experience.

Given this emphasis and character of the IUC, developing a proper CLE programme was an obvious decision from the very beginning. In a spirit of social activism, the creation of the HRMLC was thus motivated by the desire to evolve from traditional forms of legal education and to create an academic tool for systematic social change.

Another institutional aspect must be highlighted. Throughout its joint master's programmes, the IUC was already closely cooperating with the Universities of Turin[8] and of Eastern Piedmont (Alessandria)[9] (prior to the establishment of the clinic). It was thus also natural to continue this cooperation in the establishment of the clinical legal education (CLE) programme. This initiative was also timely because the desire to create an effective and innovative CLE programme was also shared by the law departments of both partner universities, which wished to incorporate inside the classical law faculty curriculum a "law-in-action programme." While the attractiveness for the law schools might have played a role, the main motivation was, again, the awareness that current legal systems require new legal professionals who should be trained differently and must be able to critically analyse the law in action.

The University of Turin, under the lead of Professor Gianmaria Ajani as director of the law department at that time and facilitated by the team of Professors Claudio Sarzotti and Cecilia Blengino, piloted their first attempts to create a law clinic in 2010/2011.[10] The effort resulted in cooperation among the three universities and the establishment of the HRMLC in 2011 as a joint project, coordinated and mainly financed by the master's programmes of the IUC, open to students from the three

---

[7] For more details, see www.iuctorino.it/301-master-students-from-2008-to-2017/.
[8] For more details, see www.giurisprudenza.unito.it/do/home.pl.
[9] For more details, see www.digspes.uniupo.it.
[10] A Clinical Conference was organized in March 2011 at the University of Turin by Prof. Sarzotti, with the help of a former clinical student from Poland, Mr. Jacek Kowalewksi, who connected the team of Sarzotti with the Polish and international CLE movement.

institutions, and with the support from lecturers of all three institutions.[11] From the very beginning, the students participating in the HRMLC received academic credits from their universities for their clinical involvement.

Being part of the joint master's programmes offered by the IUC and its partners,[12] the HRMLC has been mainly financed by the budget available for those programmes,[13] namely grants from public donors (like the Piedmont Region) and private donors (like the Compania di San Paolo). In addition, the IUC received and receives project-based funding (at times made available directly to the HRMLC and its projects) from institutions like the European Commission or private funders like the Open Society Foundation.[14]

Interestingly, the HRMLC is very probably the only CLE programme in Italy where an individual (Ulrich Stege) is engaged (on a full-time basis) with a specific mandate to create, run, and coordinate a CLE programme and all related projects.[15] This shows not only the specific commitment by the IUC, but also manifests the fact that the CLE programme director is also part of the academic coordination team of the IUC and its related master's programmes. It shows also the specificity that the IUC, a small private master's and research institute, has in relation to public universities and their CLE programmes. In public universities, academic staff plays a crucial role in the management of the different CLE programmes, but they are often not at all, or only to a limited extent, mandated to manage the clinical activities as part of their academic activities. This leads to an obvious sustainability issue as long as clinical activities are not recognized as effective means to develop an academic career.

However, even the "IUC model" does not prevent sustainability issues as it is closely linked to the master's programmes that the IUC and its partner are offering. As soon as these master's programmes – as regrettably happened in the past years – come under financial pressure, the future of the CLE programme is also at stake.

Experiences
Given this institutional backing, both authors were thus in the very lucky position of benefiting from a fertile ground for the development of the HRMLC. The institutions involved pushed for its creation and welcomed, in a very open

---

[11] In addition to the HRMLC, which continues to be a joint project among the three institutions, the law department of the University of Turin has developed over the last three years four other clinical activities: two Prison and Rights Clinics ("Carcere e diritti I & II"), the Family and Minors Rights clinic ("Famiglie, minori e diritti"), and the clinic on Disability Rights ("Clinica legale della disabilità e della vulnerabilità"). For more details, see http://clinichelegali.campusnet.unito.it/do/home.pl.
[12] Find more about the master's degrees offered by the IUC and its partners at www.iuctorino.it/studies/.
[13] The funds are mainly used to sustain the engagement of the CLE programme director (the legal practitioner), who intervenes in the preparation, coordination, and supervision of the clinical activities and the clinical programme seminar series.
[14] For more information about the IUC, see www.iuctorino.it/.
[15] In addition, out of his mandate, Ulrich Stege also coordinates the clinical programmes at the University of Turin.

way, the particular spirit and character of the CLE programme. Therefore both authors were able to take advantage of a series of factors that facilitated the design and that explain the unique features of the HRMLC.

First, the international student body of the IUC itself supported the creation of the CLE programme. IUC students often experienced law clinics (e.g. in China, Latin America, India, Eastern Europe, etc.) in their undergraduate studies before coming to Turin. It was thus also a group of eight international IUC students who gave their important input to the creation of the HRMLC in its pilot phase in 2010/2011. Building upon the particular character of the IUC, rooted in comparative studies, one of the authors (Ulrich Stege) who was mandated by the IUC to coordinate the creation of an active CLE programme together with these students visited and analysed different models of CLE programmes (e.g. clinical programmes in Poland, Spain, the United States, Italy). The IUC CLE programme was then designed on the basis of influences, methods, and models from other more experienced clinical programme.[16] Fundamental was the organization of the workshop, mainly managed by these students in March 2011, on "Fostering Social Responsibility through a Practice-Oriented Legal Education," which was the first seminar on CLE in Turin and which brought together international, national, and local actors active in the fields of asylum, migration, and legal education.

Another crucial aspect was the fact that both authors, as the main designers and personal drivers behind the HRMLC project, have from the very beginning been extremely attracted by the CLE method. Motivated by the interesting combination of CLE programmes and professional capacity building with social justice activism, they saw enormous potential in CLE programmes. As legal practitioners active in the field of human rights, migration, and asylum law at local and international levels, both authors also realized in their daily practice the obvious need for such legal education programmes.

Local Context
The HRMLC was also a response to the situation of migrants and refugees in Italy, particularly in Turin. Since the turn of this century, Italy has become a veritable country of immigration. Before 2000, cities like Turin counted only about 2% of foreigners among the total population. In just ten to fifteen years, the number of non-Italians "exploded" to more than 15% by the end of 2015.[17] In addition, since the Arab Spring in 2011, thousands of refugees are reaching the Italian coasts every year and are then distributed across numerous hosting facilities throughout the entire country. All this created, in a very short time, the need for quick legal, social, and political responses, for which authorities were not entirely prepared. In addition, Italy lacked

---

[16] The HRMLC, for example, got inspiration for its work on the migration detention center in Turin from the CLE programme of the University of Valencia; see www.uv.es/clinica/clinica/clinicas.html.
[17] See www.tuttitalia.it/piemonte/72-torino/statistiche/cittadini-stranieri-2016/.

and still lacks well-prepared professionals capable of dealing with such situations, and this issue is a significant deficit of targeted educational programmes.

In this context, the HRMLC has thus been established with a clear focus on allowing clinical students to experience, first-hand, the striking consequences of global crisis in the hope of fostering a new generation of well-trained and socially committed legal professionals who might envisage how legal institutions and practices can be reformed and reorganized in order to better respond to the actual need of migrants and refugees.

Drivers

The HRMLC was among a handful of pioneers of CLE in Italy. The other main drivers of the CLE movement in Italy were the Universities of Florence (the Altro Diritto association), Brescia, and Roma Tre.

Although not called a law clinic and structurally and physically situated outside (but nevertheless very close to) the Law Faculty of the University of Florence, the first Italian clinical programme, in which law students provided *pro bono* legal assistance to prisoners, was established by the association Altro Diritto in Florence.[18]

The first university hosting an active CLE programme within the confines of the university curriculum in Italy was the University of Brescia. Its innovative law clinic (discussed by Marzia Barbera in Chapter 3 of this volume) commenced in 2009 and incorporates a multidisciplinary approach involving civil law, criminal law, labour law, international and European Union (EU) law, comparative law, family law, consumer protection law, antidiscrimination law, and immigration law. Clinical students work under lawyers' supervision to interview clients and to draft legal statements relevant to the client's proceedings.[19]

In 2011, the University of Roma Tre started its CLE programme focusing on migration and asylum law. It is the first and so far only law clinic in Italy structured as an in-house clinic, and it runs a university legal assistance office (*sportello*) that supports and empowers migrants and asylum seekers by providing them with legal advice. In addition to the work undertaken at the legal assistance office, students provide support to strategic litigation initiatives and are involved in the monitoring of case law on deportation, detention, and the return of migrants.[20] The University of Roma Tre also runs a Children's Rights Clinic, a law clinic related to the rights of savers involved in banking arbitration, and a law clinic which focuses on human rights guarantees in the fight against terrorism.[21]

---

[18] For more details, *see* www.altrodiritto.unifi.it/.
[19] For more details, *see* www.clinicalegale.jus.unibs.it/.
[20] The Osservatorio sul Giudice di Pace is a nationwide project in which also other legal clinics participate. For more detail, *see* the website of the observatory www.lexilium.it.
[21] For more details, *see* http://clinicalegale.giur.uniroma3.it.

In addition to these first CLE programmes in Italy, other CLE programmes have followed in the past few years or are in the process of getting started.[22] Examples are found in the Universities of Turin,[23] Perugia,[24] Teramo,[25] Verona,[26] Bergamo,[27] and Palermo.[28]

Furthermore, with guidance from the University of Brescia, an initiative has been commenced with the aim of linking Italian law schools and clinicians that run clinical programmes or are interested in establishing them. The aim is to create a national association for the promotion of CLE in Italy whose main goals would be providing a platform to share experiences, organize trainings for clinicians, support the creation of new clinical programmes, and emphasize the social justice mission of CLE. While still an informal network, the Italian CLE movement has organized, since 2011, one or two national conferences/training workshops every year in order to exchange experiences and to gather wider knowledge and acceptance.[29]

Given these recent developments, it can be concluded that we are certainly observing the rise of a CLE movement in Italy. As in many other continental European countries, the main driver is the inadequacy of the traditional model of legal education. This has two elements.

First, the separation of legal training into a theoretical/doctrinal part (university education) and a practical part (an apprenticeship phase regulated by bar associations or judges' schools) has hindered the development of more practical and skills-oriented training at universities. In particular, bar associations are still adamantly arguing that they are in the better position to prepare future lawyers for practice. This argument has recently been thrust to the fore in Italian discussions around legal education. Since changes to the law regulating the legal profession were introduced in 2012,[30] law students may now commence their practical traineeships during their

---

[22] For more details, see Clelia Bartoli, *The Italian Legal Clinics Movements: Data and Prospects*, 22 (2) IJCLE 213 (2015).

[23] For more details, see http://clinichelegali.campusnet.unito.it/do/home.pl.

[24] Students are providing, together with the Association ANTIGONE, legal advice to prisoners; see http://giurisprudenza.unipg.it/index.php/ricerca/sportello-per-i-diritti.

[25] For more details, see www.unite.it/UniTE/Engine/RAServePG.php/P/190601UTE2850.

[26] For more details, see www.dsg.univr.it/dol/?ent=oi&codiceCs=G52&codins=4S003071&cs=274&discr=&discrCd=&lang=it&aa=2014/2015.

[27] For more details, see www.unibg.it/sites/default/files/bando/progetto_di_ricerca_-_codice_2_0.pdf.

[28] For more details, see http://dirittiefrontiere.blogspot.it/2015/03/una-clinica-legale-per-i-diritti-umani.html.

[29] Such as the conference "Law in Action: cliniche legali e accesso alla giustizia" organized in April 2015 in Turin (www.giurisprudenza.unito.it/do/documenti.pl/Show?_id=ucpr;sort=DEFAULT;search=;hits=1909); the conference "Diffusione dell'insegnamento clinico in Italia e in Europa: radici teoriche e dimensioni pratiche" held in October 2015 in Naples (https://www.unina.it/documents/11897/8949349/insegnamento+clinico/c426f0a8-38da-4539-b527-1a5c4d90fc3c); or the conference on "Le cliniche legali multidisciplinari quale strumento per facilitare l'accesso alla giustizia per persone vulnerabili e per creare legami intragenerazionali" organized in Bergamo (www.unibg.it/sites/default/files/news_e_appuntamenti/locandina_cliniche_legali_30_05_16.pdf).

[30] For more details, see the Law No. 247 adopted on December 31, 2012: www.professionegiustizia.it/guide/Legge_Professione_Forense_-_Legge_31_dicembre_2012,_n_247.php?cap=4.

university studies.[31] The Italian CLE community, although it cannot take credit for this reform, has strongly supported and drawn attention to it in order to encourage the development CLE programmes in the law departments of Italian universities.

Second, both law students and a new generation of law teachers are dissatisfied with the way law is traditionally taught and how they are prepared (or rather not prepared) for their professional legal careers. As soon as students enter the job market, they face enormous competition in Italy due to the high number of legal professionals.[32] CLE is perceived as an interesting and innovative alternative, offering the potential to bridge the gap between law in the books and law in action, to get students engaged and involved, and to make law and the law school experience more appealing and meaningful. In addition, clinical students feel themselves – and are increasingly perceived as – better prepared for the practice of law and their future professional life. Finally, CLE is also a way for law schools to fulfil their social justice mission, which forms part of the third mission of universities.[33]

Furthermore, Italy is experiencing a revitalization of the notion of *pro bono* legal services related to public interest and social justice, particularly within the corporate legal bar.[34] Time will tell if the increasing range of *pro bono* public interest law projects will serve as a catalyst for CLE development in Italy, and vice versa – a familiar path in many other countries.

Interestingly, and perhaps distinctive of CLE more broadly in Europe, almost all the different CLE programmes in Italy have developed their own best-fit model. Even though similarities are there, we cannot define an "Italian" clinical model. Different models have been developed accommodating and, to an extent, also "respecting" the preexisting legal education structures. For example, as in most Western continental European countries, students in Italy are not allowed to provide direct legal advice and to represent clients. The different CLE programmes in Italy were required therefore to find alternative ways to bring students closer to legal practice (for example, by using students to provide legal information, by getting students involved in practical legal research and advocacy projects, by providing support to lawyers or nongovernmental organizations (NGOs) offering *pro bono* legal advice to vulnerable people, etc.). However, since a national framework for CLE does not exist (as is the case in Poland – see Chapter 2 by Katarzyna Ważyńska-Finck in this volume), the design and development of any given CLE programme is still very much dependent on contextual circumstances such as the willingness of the law departments of

---

[31] *See* Art. 41 para. 6, lett. *d*), Law No. 247, of 31.12.2012.
[32] Italy has the highest total number of lawyers in Europe (about four times more than France), *see* www.ccbe.eu/fileadmin/user_upload/NTCdocument/2012_table_of_lawyer1_1356088494.pdf.
[33] See the comments from Enrica Rigo (at the end of the page) on the link of CLE and the new law on the regulation of the legal profession and on the Universities' third mission and CLE: http://clinicalegale.giur.uniroma3.it/?page_id=27.
[34] A good example for that is the Ninth PILnet European Pro Bono Forum, which was organized for the first time in Italy (Rome) in 2015; *see* www.pilnet.org.

universities, the personal capacity and motivation of the clinical teachers, the cooperation (or noncooperation) of the local legal profession and NGOs, and more.

REFORMING THE TEACHING AND PRACTICE OF LAW IN EUROPE

Goals and Methods

Over the past several years, EU law has become one of the fundamental legal sources for many areas of law in Europe. This means that today it is essential for legal professionals to have a strong and practical knowledge of EU law, just as they are required to have a firm grasp on domestic legal sources.

Despite this, EU law teaching in Italy is similar to many other European countries insofar as it is insufficiently and abstractly covered/dealt with in undergraduate legal education.[35] Even where basic EU law classes are included among the fundamental subjects and even where EU law forms a part of each substantive law subject impacted by it, its teaching remains – as is also true for most of Italian legal education – based on an abstract transfer of theoretical knowledge related to general concepts, black letter law, doctrines, and high court decisions.[36] The educational goals of EU law courses are often very generic and mainly aiming at providing a general "understanding of the European Union's legal system, the development of the European integration process and its impact on national systems."[37]

The only exceptions can be found in isolated teaching projects (like moot courts, summer schools, EU decision-making workshops,[38] etc.), which only in rare instances form part of the law school curriculum.

If we speak specifically of migration and asylum law teaching, the picture is even more troubling as legal education programmes in this field are nonexistent in most of the current law school curriculums in Italy. Furthermore, even though Italian migration and asylum law has its main roots in EU law and international human rights law, asylum and migration are rarely touched upon in regular EU law teaching courses.

In addition, teaching methodologies deployed by law schools in Italy are often unable to enhance the capacities and skills of future professionals, nor do they encourage a critical reflection on law and its practice. Until now, Italian law school classes have been mainly characterized by traditional front of class lectures delivered for a large number of students, with little interaction and almost no time for discussion. Interactive teaching methods are rarely used. One clinical student

---

[35] See Chapter 9 by Alberto Alemanno and Lamin Khadar, and Chapter 10 by Anthony Valcke, in this volume.
[36] See Chapter 3 by Marzia Barbera, in this volume.
[37] See, as an example the educational goals of the EU law course ("Diritto dell'U.E.") of the University of Turin, www.giurisprudenza.unito.it/do/corsi.pl.
[38] As an example, see the EU Model project, www.eumodeltorino.org/index.php?c=about.

summarized the methodological problem of law schools in the following words: "In the legal clinic, the teacher helps you to reflect, in classical courses, the teacher tells you what to think!"[39]

Given this general framework, the IUC wanted to explore new ways of teaching and thus established, together with its partner institutions, the HRMLC as one of the first practical courses on migration and asylum law in Italy. The HRMLC is pursuing the following objectives:

- To provide students with (1) a window into the true operation of migration and asylum law, (2) an opportunity to understand for themselves and to empirically test the influence that EU law and international human rights law have on Italian migration and asylum law practice, (3) a hands-on learning experience and exposure to real-world legal problems, and (4) an opportunity to interact with international and local organizations and professionals.
- To offer in general (1) a contribution from qualified, motivated, and supervised students towards improving access to justice for migrants/asylum seekers and (2) support to research activities and advocacy in the field of migration and asylum in its social, cultural, and economic dimensions.

As mentioned already, the HRMLC combines a classroom component with practical activities. The course work (i.e. the first two months) provides clinical students with the necessary theoretical background for the clinical activities in the areas of "International, European and Italian Asylum and Migration Law" and of "Human Rights." In addition, capacity-building workshops on "Interview Skills" and "Legal Research and Writing" aim at broadening skills for the practical activities. All elements of the course work encourage a multidisciplinary and practical view through active teaching methods.[40] This course work is furthermore accompanied by a Clinical Seminar Series where professionals are invited to provide insights from legal practice in the field of human rights, asylum, and migration.

After this preparatory phase, practical activities[41] become the key focus of the clinical programme. For a period of four to five months, the clinical students are engaged in a defined practical legal activity. As a significant example, in the Refugee Law Clinic of the HRMLC students work on real asylum law cases.

---

[39] Which tells much about the "reproduction of hierarchy," as Duncan Kennedy describes it; see Duncan Kennedy, LEGAL EDUCATION AND THE REPRODUCTION OF HIERARCHY. A POLEMIC AGAINST THE SYSTEM (New York University Press, 2004).

[40] Since 2014, the workshop on Interview Skills is co-organized with the help of psychologists specializing in ethnopsychology and anthropology.

[41] For more details about practical activities offered by the HRMLC, see www.iuctorino.it/studies/clinical-education/.

In particular, clinical students – supervised by specialized lawyers – engage in (1) meeting asylum seekers, (2) scrutinizing the applicants' stories, (3) searching for all relevant case law and country of origin information, (4) preparing legal memos containing the background story and an analysis of all relevant legal issues, and (5) providing asylum seekers with theoretical and practical information about their hearing.

Aware of the need to broaden the competencies and abilities of students, the HRMLC enhanced its multidisciplinary approach in 2015 by beginning cooperation with Turin University's Department of Anthropology. Supervised anthropology students support clinical students in interviewing asylum seekers and researching relevant country of origin information. The hope is that this will improve mutual understanding (between students and asylum seeker) and provide decision-makers with a more thorough view of the case.[42]

In addition, the Refugee Law Clinic is now also operating the entire year round (i.e. also in periods outside the traditional academic year). Former clinical students/ young lawyers continue to provide legal assistance to asylum seekers as an outside curriculum activity, with a view to become tutors of new clinical students.

The Refugee Law Clinic activity of the HRMLC is a good paradigm illustrating how the CLE programme challenges the traditional legal education model. First, the students are provided with a much deeper knowledge of asylum law consequent upon their exposure to the real life of asylum law as they "learn by doing." In addition, they are delving into and reflecting upon practical challenges, something which often even practicing lawyers – confronted with time constraints – may struggle to do. Within the clinical setting, the students get individual feedback from peers, from specialized lawyers, and from the associated psychologist/anthropologist. Learning from nonlegal professionals helps law students to reconsider well-established legal conceptions, fostering in them the necessary competencies to become better and more aware professionals.

Furthermore, the HRMLC engages students in general supervision/reflection sessions. These are crucial moments when students share their experience and reflect on how legal institutions and practices operate and how they could be reformed to better meet the needs of asylum seekers, refugees, and migrants.

Beyond the Educational Goals

By establishing CLE programmes such as the HRMLC, the coordinators find themselves confronted by a dilemma. It is obvious that a university programme should have a clear educational goal. But, in addition, creating a CLE programme goes often hand

---

[42] In cooperation with the team of Prof. Roberto Beneduce and Prof. Simona Taliani of the Department on Culture, Politics and Society ("Dipartimento Cultura, Politica e Società") of the University of Turin; see www.didattica-cps.unito.it/do/docenti.pl/Show?_id=rbeneduc.

in hand[43] with a social justice mission, and it is not always easy to find the right balance between both of these major objectives.

A preliminary question arises: What does a "social justice mission" actually mean?[44] Even though essential to CLE discourse, it is hard to find a clear definition to this notion. At the last Global Alliance for Justice Education (GAJE) conference in Turkey, in 2015, during the session on "Keeping the Focus on Social Justice in Our Clinics in an Environment of Competing Priorities,"[45] Catherine Klein, Paula Galowitz, Marzia Barbera, and one of the authors (Ulrich Stege) referred to a pluralistic approach, focusing on a process rather than on a strict definition. According to them, a CLE programme with a social justice mission should share some broad components, such as aiming (1) to provide support to people/communities falling outside of the institutional system of support; (2) to build among students a sensitivity to social problems, promoting the role of lawyers as "social actors"; (3) to promote systemic change; and (4) to understand the law as a social policy tool.

From the very beginning, these components have been fundamental for the HRMLC, with a particular focus on local settings. Again, the activity of the Refugee Law Clinic of the HRMLC can serve as an example. The students are involved in a phase of the asylum procedure when legal assistance – even though foreseen by the law – is almost always absent. Providing such a service helps to tackle a systemic problem and empowers a new generation of responsible lawyers. However, it might well be that the circumstances change and the clinical intervention should shift to different activities.

This example clarifies that the social justice mission is a process, in constant need of assessment and reshaping. Sometimes, this process can even be implemented within the clinical activity itself. The HRMLC, for example, commenced a legal empowerment project together with the International Labour Organization (ILO; Geneva) and the International Training Center of the ILO (ITC-ILO; Turin) in 2016 aiming to inform asylum seekers about their rights on access to work and social protection.[46] Before being able to design the proper legal information tool, a group

---

[43] Such as also proposed by the definition of Clinical Legal Education provided by ENCLE; see: http://encle.org/about-encle/definition-of-a-legal-clinic. The need for a social justice mission in CLE programmes is, however, also subject of a debate. As examples of this debate, see Praveen Kosuri, *Losing My Religion: The Place of Social Justice in Clinical Legal Education*, 32 B.C.J.L. & Soc. Just. 331 (2012), http://lawdigitalcommons.bc.edu/jlsj/vol32/iss2/6; *or see* Stephen Wizner, Is Social Justice Still Relevant? (2012). Faculty Scholarship Series. Paper 4987, http://digitalcommons.law.yale.edu/fss_papers/4987.

[44] See Frank S. Bloch, *Introduction*, in The Global Clinical Movement – Educating Lawyers For Social Justice (Oxford University Press, 2011), at xxiv; *see also* Jane H. Aiken and Stephen Wizner, *Teaching and Doing: The Role of Law School Clinics in Enhancing Access to Justice*, 73 Fordham L. Rev.997–1011 (2004), http://scholarship.law.georgetown.edu/facpub/303/.

[45] For more details, see www.gaje.org/8th-worldwide-conference/session-abstracts/?id=4953.

[46] For more information on the project, see www.social-protection.org/gimi/gess/ShowProject.action?id=3045.

of five clinical students started investigating the actual informational needs of migrants.

This project (and similar such projects) proved to be as interesting from the social justice point of view as from the educational point of view. In fact, such projects allow students to gain a better understanding of certain areas of law (here, the international, European, and national legal frameworks on access to work and to social protection for asylum seekers), train professional capacities (such as interviewing skills or legal research and writing skills), and provide students with a unique view about the systematic deficits of the asylum seeker' hosting system Italy.

It is worth finally mentioning that the social justice mission of CLE has recently gained additional importance in Italy. Since 2015, the so-called third mission[47] (*terza missione*) of universities has been analysed and assessed by the National Agency for the evaluation of universities and research centers (ANVUR).[48] Within this context, CLE programmes can play a key role in fostering the third mission of universities.[49]

Apart from the highly innovative educational aspects of law clinics, which render them significantly different and therefore typically more attractive to students as compared to traditional law teaching (e.g. by minimizing the traditional academic hierarchy and by putting the student at the centre of the learning process, by creating moments of contact with the law in action, by encouraging critical thinking and autonomy mastery in addition to teamwork skills, etc.), it seems, however, that HRMLC students are mainly attracted by the social justice aspect of the programme. Experiencing the ability to provide legal support to persons in need creates a strong motivation and a sense of purpose, pushing students further. In fact, the HRMLC benefitted from the strong interest of clinical student alumni to create an extracurricular part of the law clinic that now allows them to continue their clinical experience even outside the university settings but with the same spirit and support.

The Weight and Value of Internationalization

The impact of internationalization on the HRMLC and its educational import can be observed at many levels.

First, there is the international student body of the IUC,[50] which lends a unique quality to the HRMLC. Delving into asylum law, teaming-up or working together

---

[47] Which contends that universities should carry out their classical mission of education and research, and also embrace the "third mission" of encouraging societal impact; for more details, see the green paper on Fostering and Measuring Third Mission in Higher Education Institutions, http://e3mproject.eu/Green%20paper-p.pdf.

[48] Evaluation plan of ANVUR; www.anvur.org/index.php?option=com_content&view=article&id=875&Itemid=628&lang=it.

[49] See Rigo, *supra* note 33; *see also* Maria Rosaria Marella and Enrica Rigo, Cliniche legali, Commons e giustizia sociale (2015), www.euronomade.info/?p=5524.

[50] See, e.g., the IUC class of 2017: www.iuctorino.it/studies/master-clef/class-of-2017/.

with students from basically all continents of the world helps to widen perspectives and to challenge presumptions and prejudices, a mission intrinsic to CLE.[51]

As noted earlier, asylum and migration law in Italy is strongly influenced by EU law and international/European human rights law. The European and international legal frameworks therefore need to be integrated into and dispersed throughout the different activities of the HRMLC.

One good example is the strategic litigation work undertaken by the HRMLC.[52] Clinical students have been supporting a law firm engaging a strategic litigation before the European Court of Human Rights (2015) and the UN Human Rights Committee (2016) concerning migration and refugee law issues.

Another example is the report of the HRMLC to the European Commission on the inefficiencies and shortcomings of the domestic reception system of asylum seekers in Italy, highlighting the troublesome transposition of EU directive 2013/33/EU, which lays down standards for the reception of applicants for international protection.

In both examples, clinical students are actually analysing local asylum and migration problems through the lenses of international and EU law. This kind of activity confronts students, as future legal professionals, with international legal praxis and provides them with practical understanding of how to access and strategically make use of international and European complaint mechanisms.

Cooperation in CLE

The HRMLC has developed a wide range of institutional, individual, and project-based collaborations with other universities, CLE programmes, NGOs, and individuals from Italy, Europe, and abroad, mainly related to specific activities or to the exchange of clinical students.

In Italy, together with other national CLE programmes led by the CLE programme of the University of Roma Tre, the HRMLC is part of the Monitoring Centre on deportation case law (Osservatorio della giurisprudenza dei Giudici di Pace).[53] Within this project, clinical students are involved in a research activity regarding the judicial review of migrants' rights, with particular attention paid to the jurisprudence of judges of peace (JPs) on the expulsion, detention, and return of migrants. The aim of the project is to ensure due publicity and assessment with respect to these decisions.

At the European level, the HRMLC has participated, together with the EU Law Clinic of the Kent University Brussels, in the European project "My Mobility

---

[51] Since the beginning, 136 students from thirty-five different countries (e.g., Albania, Australia, Belorussia, Bolivia, Brazil, Canada, China, Egypt, Ethiopia, France, Gambia, Germania, Ghana, Greece, Haiti, India, Italy, Jordan, Lebanon, Lithuania, Nigeria, Pakistan, Puerto-Rico, Palestine, Panama, Romania, Rwanda, Russia, Sierra Leone, Slovakia, Sweden, Tanzania, Tunisia, UK, and Ukraine) participated at the HRMLC.

[52] For more details about practical activities offered by the HRMLC, see www.iuctorino.it/studies/clinical-education/.

[53] For more detail, see the observatory's website: www.lexilium.it.

Mentor – An Experiment for Workers from Bulgaria and Romania Going to Other EU Member States."[54] This project was funded by the European Commission (DG Employment, Social Affairs and Inclusion) and aimed at getting students involved in providing Bulgarian and Romanian workers moving to Belgium, Italy, and the UK with legal information related to their EU free movement rights.

Recently, the HRMLC commenced another collaboration at the European level with the European Council on Refugees and Exiles (ECRE),[55] by virtue of which students are producing summaries of asylum cases for the European database on asylum case law (EDAL).[56]

At the international level, the aforementioned collaboration among the HRMLC, the ILO (Geneva), and the ITC-ILO (Turin) aiming at providing legal information to asylum seekers related to access to work and social protection will be further developed in 2017 by getting other CLE programmes in Europe involved.

As funding is a fundamental issue, the HRMLC was furthermore involved in a number of European project proposals together with other CLE programmes in Europe. Even if these project proposals were not often successful, these joint efforts help to develop new ideas and are therefore extremely beneficial to further improve and innovate CLE teaching and practice.

Among other advantages, national and European experiences help students to connect with other institutions and partner organizations. A direct consequence of this has been that students from the HRMLC have gotten involved (independently and outside the school curriculum) in projects being run by other institutions (for instance, a former student from the HRMLC is now volunteering with the EU law clinic at the Kent University in Brussels).

Diffusion of CLE

One of the decisive events leading to the creation of the HRMLC was the GAJE/International Journal of Clinical Legal Education (IJCLE) conference organized at the University of Valencia in July 2011, which one of the authors (Ulrich Stege) attended. As a unique gathering of clinicians from all over the world, the conference was a crucial contributing factor to the creation of the HRMLC in a number of respects. Through powerful testimonies from different parts of the world, the conference illustrated the global reach, shared social justice mission, and emergence of CLE as a worldwide movement. It created the necessary motivation, inspiration, network, and capacity to engage fruitfully in CLE. Since then, both authors have become increasingly committed to GAJE, having attended all subsequent conferences (in New Delhi, India, in 2013; and in Eskisehir, Turkey, in 2015).

---

[54] For more details, *see* the project's website: http://mymobilitymentor.ning.com.
[55] For more detail about ECRE, *see* www.ecre.org.
[56] For more detail about EDAL, *see* www.asylumlawdatabase.eu/en.

Other important inputs for the creation and development of the HRMLC came from other experiences with CLE. During the first years of the HRMLC, the authors were able to visit clinical programmes at the University of Warsaw (Poland), University of Brescia (Italy), University of Roma Tre (Italy), University of Valencia (Spain), University of Bordeaux (France), the Humboldt University Berlin (Germany), Columbia University (New York, USA), Fordham University (New York, USA), New York University (NYU; New York, USA), and more.

Convinced of the advantages of CLE and the important contribution law clinics can make to legal education, the IUC and one of the authors (Ulrich Stege) in particular are among the central promoters of CLE in Italy and Europe. After the creation of its own CLE programme, the IUC has assisted a range of universities in effectively promoting this new style of legal education within their respective institutions.[57] In addition, the IUC was a founding member and one of the driving institutions[58] behind the establishment of the European Network for Clinical Legal Education (ENCLE),[59] which is gaining increasing acceptance and acknowledgement in Europe. Finally, the IUC has been involved in the recent steps towards the formalization of an Italian network of law clinics.

In addition to these efforts of the IUC, both authors have attended and co-organized many conferences, workshops, and trainings on CLE in Italy, Europe, and outside Europe. They also served as CLE trainers at workshops in Turin and Brescia, Italy (2014/2015/2016/2017); in Brussels, Belgium (organized by ENCLE in 2014); in Eskisehir, Turkey (organized by GAJE in 2015); in Weinarten, Germany (organized by the German Refugee Law Clinic Network in 2015, 2016); in Rabat, Morocco (organized by the UNHCR in 2016); in Tunis, Tunisia (organized by the NGO Terre d'Asile Tunisia in 2016); and in Lebanon (organized by the European Research Institute in 2017).

Future of CLE in Europe

The demand for this publication, as well as the recent work of Clelia Bartoli[60] and the creation of ENCLE, demonstrate that CLE is earning a reputation and taking

---

[57] IUC supports CLE projects in Italy (e.g. at the Universities of Palermo or Trieste), but also outside Italy (e.g. in Morocco or Tunesia). In addition, the IUC in the person of Ulrich Stege is also supporting the German Refugee Law Clinic Network in its efforts to set national standards for Refugee Law Clinic programmes.

[58] The idea of the creation of ENCLE emerged in a conversation between European clinicians at the GAJE conference in Valencia in 2011. The ENCLE's first meeting was then funded and organized by the IUC and took place within IUC facilities in Turin on June 1-2, 2012. Since then, Ulrich serves as Executive Secretary of ENCLE, and the IUC was involved in the organization of almost all ENCLE meetings, training workshops, and conferences.

[59] For further details, *see* www.encle.eu.

[60] Clelia Bartoli, Legal Clinics in Europe: For a Commitment of Higher Education in Social Justice, Diritto & Questioni Pubbliche, Special Issue (2016), www.dirittoequestionipubbliche.org/page/2016_nSE_Legal-clinics-in-Europe/index.htm.

root in legal education throughout Europe, most notably in the European West. Countries like France, Italy, and Germany, that resisted the clinical movement for years, have become important players and drivers for the CLE movement in Europe.

Still, we cannot yet maintain that clinical programmes enjoy full acknowledgement and acceptance throughout Europe. Even if CLE is spreading, there are only a limited number of pioneering universities (with the notable exceptions of the United Kingdom and Poland, where CLE is already significantly widespread) that run CLE projects. In addition, we are still talking about a very small number of students who are able to secure one of the rare places available within CLE programmes across Europe. Moreover, many CLE programmes face sustainability problems[61] or are fighting for broader acceptance within law school curricula, and, in that sense, their future might be problematic.

We believe, however, that the CLE movement in Europe will have a successful future, especially if, in upcoming years, it can tackle the following challenges:

1. CLE programmes should be stabilized and increased, and, with this, there should be an increase in the number of students who can participate.
2. Universities should find adequate academic structures and resources to keep and to encourage the engagement of faculty who run a CLE programme. Academic recognition, but also regular and specific funding for clinical programmes, will be fundamental.
3. The CLE network and community in Europe should be strengthened, which would allow further sharing of ideas and resources and an expansion of collaborative capacity-building and research.
4. The awareness of CLE at the European level should be enhanced because there is the potential that, particularly, the EU could be interested in a widespread CLE movement given its established and highly developed supranational legal system.

For all these challenges, it might be important that the European CLE movement intensifies its effort in the coming years by (1) constantly monitoring the status quo of CLE in Europe; (2) agreeing on some minimum standards, which would help to gain European recognition of CLE; (3) fostering joint clinical projects and exchange programmes which transport knowledge and share experiences more effectively; (4) running training workshops for new clinicians; and (5) creating stable funding schemes and academic structures for CLE teachers.

CONCLUSION

The experience of the HRMLC, together with many other innovative CLE programmes across Europe, sheds light on the power, the potential, and the success of

---

[61] An example of this is the closed clinical programme at the University of Maastricht after more than twenty years of successful activity.

this particular form of legal education. It proves to be an adequate tool to disseminate competencies and values among young professionals who should then be able to confront the increasingly globalized world and, at the same time, provide qualified and socially relevant support for communities in need. Even if significant empirical data on the added value of CLE programmes are still missing, feedback from students, clients, lawyers, and clinical partners, together with the professional success stories of former clinical students, should give anyone working in the field of CLE the motivation to continue.

Each of these programmes shows furthermore the complexity of CLE enterprises. Not only do they have to tackle strong reservations and often outright hostility and opposition (e.g. from within traditional educational structures, public authorities, bar associations, etc.), they additionally have to overcome many logistical obstacles (e.g. infrastructure, funding, time constraints, etc.). The history of CLE in Europe (especially looking at Eastern Europe) suggests that it is equally as essential to invest in efforts to establish new CLE programmes as it is to secure sufficient power, resources, and support and maintain them in their daily practice.

We strongly believe that the benefits of CLE for students, clients, lawyers, universities, and society at large clearly outweigh the difficulties and efforts that are presented in establishing and maintaining CLE programmes. It is therefore paramount to devote the proper time to analyse, evaluate, and demonstrate them. Within the European CLE movement, we can (and have already) certainly build upon the large experience with CLE in other regions of the world. Nevertheless, given the particularities of the European context, we should intensify our individual and collective efforts towards innovative European CLE models.

And, last but not least (actually, most importantly), comes the immense privilege and responsibility of working with young, motivated students, a dazzling mix of gratification and fun!

8

The Refugee Rights Movement and the Birth of Clinical Legal Education in Germany

Humboldt Law Clinic Human and Fundamental Rights, Berlin, and Refugee Law Clinic, Hamburg

Nora Markard

INTRODUCTION

Clinical legal education (CLE) is evidently on the rise in Germany. Students, in particular, have claimed the format, starting self-organized clinics around the country to support the quickly growing number of refugees and to complement the German legal aid system. Their interest in practical legal work can also be read as an intervention into a largely academic university education that precedes a two-year legal apprenticeship. This ties in with top-down efforts to promote more practice-oriented legal education; yet universities are still somewhat hesitant in supporting these initiatives with the resources they require and integrating them into the wider curriculum.

The first German legal clinic (identifying itself as a clinic) was founded in Gießen in 2007.[1] The Berlin-based Humboldt Law Clinic Grund- und Menschenrechte (Fundamental and Human Rights, HLCMR)[2] followed in 2010. It is designed to support local nongovernmental organizations (NGOs) and attorneys with expertise on human rights issues and with advice on litigation strategies. It takes on longer term projects with structural reach, worked out with partner NGOs to "bring human rights home" – be it in the form of a template for a test case, a legal memo, an amicus brief, or a database. Since 2010, a Consumer Law Clinic and an Internet Law Clinic have joined; the Human Rights Clinic, though, is unique in that it is also open to Gender Studies students – a strong asset in antidiscrimination work, although finding a common language can also be challenging.

---

[1] Some other projects involving law students giving free legal advice existed before; e.g., a project at the University of Bremen providing legal advice to prisoners; see C. M. Graebsch, *Rechtsberatung für Gefangene in Bremen: Clinical Legal Education seit mehr als 30 Jahren'* in PRAKTISCHE JURISPRUDENZ, CLINICAL LEGAL EDUCATION UND ANWALTSORIENTIERUNG IM STUDIUM (S Barton, S Hähnchen and F Jost eds., Dr Kovac 2011), 147.

[2] *See* http://hlcmr.de, all links last accessed March 30, 2016.

For each one-year cycle, around twenty students are selected based on anonymized curriculum vitae (CV) and letters of motivation. In the introductory seminar, the projects are assigned to teams of two and serve as examples in exercises, as the students discover the human rights system and acquire basic litigation skills. During the term break, they intern with the respective partner NGO or cooperating attorney; law students can get credit for the internship. During the second term, the students revise and finalize their written piece. Over the years, the HLCMR has supported an NGO in bringing a parallel report on the rights of intersex children in Germany to the Committee Against Torture, participated in an amicus brief in the *Kiobel* case, secured health insurance for a visually impaired client, brought a complaint over production standards in the transnational cotton industry to a national contact point for the Organization for Economic Cooperation and Development (OECD), and developed guidelines on legal mechanisms against Internet hate speech. It publishes a Working Paper Series[3] and a blog.[4]

The Refugee Law Clinic Hamburg (RLC Hamburg),[5] founded in 2014/15, started as part of the student clinic movement, but has been integrated into the law school. Its structure is similar to that of the HLCMR, adapted to its live-client orientation: an introductory seminar provides the legal basics and prepares the students for client interaction, including through diversity training and trauma workshops. After an internship with an attorney, an in-depth seminar offers exercises in advice work, while students start assisting the active advice teams. Once their training is completed, students start working as legal advisers. Bi-weekly supervision is ensured by two specialized attorneys, including during term break. Peer meetings serve to discuss difficult situations or stress among the advisors. Weekly advice work commenced in the fall of 2015 in two refugee support facilities located near first-reception centres; a third location was added in July 2016.

EMERGENCE OF CLE

Genesis and Context

In Germany, as in France and Italy,[6] legal education is structured into a university phase and a practical phase. Students enter law school right after high school and generally take their First State Exam after four years of study, an additional year being taken up by prep courses and the actual exams. The Second State Exam (necessary to take the bar or become a judge) is preceded by the *Referendariat*, a two-

---

[3] See http://hlcmr.de/publikationen. [4] See www.grundundmenschenrechtsblog.de.
[5] See http://uhh.de/rlc.
[6] See Chapter 6 by Xavier Aurey and Chapter 7 by Stege and Veglio on law clinics in France and Italy, in this volume.

year series of traineeships for a civil judge, a public prosecutor, or criminal judge, the administration, and an attorney, accompanied by classes. Three months in a freely chosen institution – including NGOs or intergovernmental organizations (IGOs) – can also be completed abroad. Both State Exams are very demanding and comprehensive and can only be repeated once. About 10–40% of the students fail, only about 10–20% obtain the coveted distinction or *Prädikat*,[7] and many simply drop out of law school.[8] Students who sign up for the First State Exam within the first four years of their studies can repeat the exam to improve their grade, and a failure in the first "free shot" (*Freischuss* or *Freiversuch*) does not formally count – a major incentive for taking the exam early.

This consecutive two-part structure has survived a number of reform projects in the 1970s and 1980s. As a result, university studies have remained largely academic in nature.[9] Students receive a broad but also quite detailed overview over the legal field. They are trained to solve mock cases – often modelled on lead cases, but with perfectly streamlined facts involving flat characters such as applicant A and neighbour N – by writing advisory opinions on the legal issues in a highly formalized style. In-depth engagement with specialized topics is reserved for the last year of studies and counts towards the final exam grade. While all students learn about the intersections of German law with international and European Union (EU) law, they will usually not develop a proper understanding of human rights unless they specialized in the area of international and European law. The only glimpse of actual legal practice most students get during these five years of studies are three months of mandatory internships under the supervision of a qualified lawyer (although some work in law firms on the side).

The Bologna Process has been partly resisted by German law schools, especially in relation to the bachelor's/master's degree structure, as law schools wish to retain the traditional State Exam.[10] The push towards more practice-oriented education,[11] on the other hand, has met with a more positive response. Universities have introduced mandatory skill-building courses on legal rhetoric, contract drafting,

[7] The numbers vary tremendously among the *Länder*, as education is a matter for the federal states.
[8] About 26% leave law school without a degree; this includes those who failed the First State Exam twice. U. Heublein, J. Richter, R. Schmelzer and D. Sommer, *Die Entwicklung der Schwund- und Studienabbruchquoten an den deutschen Hochschulen. Statistische Berechnungen auf der Basis des Absolventenjahrgangs 2010*, 3 IS: FORUM HOCHSCHULE 30–31, 50 (2012).
[9] For a more in-depth analysis, see, Wissenschaftsrat, Prospects of Legal Scholarship in Germany: Current Situation, Analyses, Recommendations (2013), www.wissenschaftsrat.de/download/archiv/2558-12_engl.pdf.
[10] For a more proactive approach, see A. Bücker and W. A. Woodruff, *The Bologna Process and German Legal Education: Developing Professional Competence through Clinical Experiences*, 9 (5) GERMAN LAW JOURNAL 575–617, at 609ff (2008); see also L. S. Terry, *Living with the Bologna Process: Recommendations to the German Legal Education Community from a US Perspective*, 7 (11) GERMAN LAW JOURNAL 863–905 (2006).
[11] See, e.g., European Commission, Supporting growth and jobs – an agenda for the modernisation of Europe's higher education systems, COM/2011/0567 final, 20 Sept. 2011; EHEA Yerevan Communiqué, 14–15 May 2015, www.ehea.info/Uploads/SubmittedFiles/5_2015/112705.pdf.

and more; moot court competition have also become more popular.[12] In its 2012 recommendations, the German Science Council highlighted the role of legal clinics in this respect.[13] The development towards integrating practice element into legal education has, however, been slow, and few of the skill-building courses are geared towards public interest careers.

Humboldt Law Clinic, Berlin

Against this background, Professor Susanne Baer and her team of student assistants and graduate students at the Chair for Public Law and Gender Studies – which then included the author – looked for ways to integrate public interest concerns into university studies while also finding ways to transfer academic knowledge into practice.

Susanne Baer, now a Federal Constitutional Court Judge, was then already involved in a number of policy advice projects.[14] Both she and her team members were in close contact with NGOs working on social justice and human rights issues and knew of their frequent lack of time and financial resources for in-depth legal research to support their work, not to mention the fact that their staff usually did not include lawyers.[15] At the same time, we knew of the frustration of many students who had chosen law school in order to help change the world and who found themselves trapped by exam requirements, textbooks, flashcards, and prep courses without a glimpse of how they might ever be able to use all of this detailed but largely theoretical knowledge for the public interest work they yearned to get into.

We had already explored different options, including summer schools, open online courses, or a clinic, when we were contacted by Liza Zamd, a US-trained lawyer, who was then a Robert Bosch Fellow at the European Centre for Constitutional and Human Rights (ECCHR) in Berlin, and Jacqui Zalcberg, an Australian human rights attorney, was also based in Berlin. Pairing our local expertise, network, and knowledge of the curricular requirements with their international background and practical experience seemed like a perfect opportunity.

The HLCMR adopted the two-semester structure developed by the Refugee Law Clinic Gießen (RLC Gießen), but decided against a live-client clinic. We felt that our areas of specialty lent themselves more to long-term projects, but we were also unsure about insurance and concerned about the intensity of the necessary supervision. German law professors generally teach nine hours per week (i.e. four to five

---

[12] For an overview of practice-oriented formats, see S. Barton, S. Hähnchen, and F. Jost, eds, PRAKTISCHE JURISPRUDENZ, CLINICAL LEGAL EDUCATION UND ANWALTSORIENTIERUNG IM STUDIUM (Dr Kovac 2011).
[13] Wissenschaftsrat, supra note 8, at 59–60.
[14] E.g., www.genderkompetenz.info/, and a cooperation with the Berlin Anti-Discrimination Office: https://www.berlin.de/lb/ads/main-side-english/.
[15] In its approach, the HLCMR is comparable to the SOAS International Human Rights Clinic, which, however, has a more international orientation; see Chapter 13 by Lynn Welchman in this volume.

classes), clinical professorships do not exist (although a few clinics have been granted honorary professorships for practitioners), and German universities – largely public in nature – have very limited funds for additional staff, certainly not for longer periods of time. We therefore decided to work with NGOs and attorneys and to support their individual advice work with more substantial pieces of research and expertise, which did not require a lot of ad-hoc meetings and decisions under pressure of deadlines.

The institutional constraints also meant that the clinical training had to be integrated into the regular curriculum as much as possible. The human rights training was therefore designed as a skill-building course, and the internships can be taken for credit; only the in-depth seminar had to be tacked on as a no-credit class (Gender Studies students can get credit for both classes). A certificate, awarded in a ceremony at the start of the new year, acknowledges the extra work. The first cycle started in the winter term of 2010/11, taught in English; the Clinic now primarily works in German.

The University quickly came to see the Clinic as a flagship teaching project and included it in its funding application to the Quality Pact for Teaching, a €2bn federal funding programme, now in its second five-year phase.[16] This secured the HLCMR staff resources over the course of five years, allowing it to expand into the areas of Consumer Law and Internet Law; the grant was recently renewed. The Clinic certainly fit well into the funding line, focusing on the transition from university into practice.[17] Another positive factor for the University's engagement may have been that the Clinic aims at educating well-rounded students, thereby promoting the Humboldtian ideal of higher education, which strives to form well-rounded, enlightened citizens of the world.[18] It is less likely that competitive aspects played a large role, as Humboldt University's very good reputation and its highly attractive location already secure an excellent student body,[19] and competition between universities is otherwise very much geared towards research.[20]

Refugee Law Clinic Hamburg

Unlike the HLCMR, the RLC Hamburg is a student-initiated project; here, too, access to justice was a central motive, as I will explain later. When it started in the late summer of 2014, there was already what one could call a refugee law clinic

---

[16] Funding phases: 2011–15, 2016–20. See www.qualitaetspakt-lehre.de/en/1294.php.
[17] See www.qualitaetspakt-lehre.de/de/1334.php.
[18] See, e.g., R. D. Anderson, EUROPEAN UNIVERSITIES FROM THE ENLIGHTENMENT TO 1914 (Oxford University Press 2004), chap. 4.
[19] German high schools award grades from 1–6, with 1 being the best grade. Law students at Humboldt University have a grade point average of at least 1.7: https://www.hu-berlin.de/de/studium/beratung/merk/grundstaendig (winter term 2015/16).
[20] See, in particular, the federal Excellence Initiative, which seeks to promote top-level research by funding graduate schools, clusters of excellence, and institutional strategies: www.dfg.de/en/research_funding/programmes/excellence_initiative/index.html.

movement; by now, about 20 refugee law clinics exist across Germany,[21] many in the form of registered associations (eingetragener Verein, e.V.) founded by students.

Refugee and migration law are not part of the regular curriculum and have traditionally been a special interest of very few professors, such that many refugee law clinics have to rely on lecturing contracts with specialized practitioners who often also supervise the advice work. This field may become more established as increasing numbers of PhDs are being written in this area – a trend that will certainly increase against the background of the current political and practical importance of the topic. Two quickly growing networks have supported this development. Founded in 2007, the Network Migration Law[22] now counts around 180 academics and practitioners at different levels of seniority and from several countries and disciplines who stay in touch via a mailing list and meet for an annual conference as well as a workshop. The Forced Migration Studies Network (Netzwerk Flüchtlingsforschung),[23] founded in 2013, brings together researchers from different disciplines to promote forced migration studies in Germany, including through a popular blog,[24] and has secured research funding from the German Research Foundation (DFG).[25]

Having worked on refugee law for more than ten years, I agreed to support the establishment of a refugee law clinic. However, assistant professors like myself (or Junior Professors, as they are called in German) teach between four and six hours a week on a nonrenewable six-year contract and are expected to write a post-doc monograph (Habilitation) on the side; most are without staff. Additional resources were therefore essential.

On the basis of a concept paper, the faculty agreed to fund a graduate clinic coordinator for 20 hours per week, as well as a teaching contract for an attorney supervising the advice work for three years, and to match my sponsorship of the clinic founders as student assistants. Both Katharina Leithoff and Fiona Schönbohm have been working relentlessly for the project, way beyond the paid hours, and it was a particular stroke of luck that in Helene Heuser we found a coordinator who is not only qualified with the German bar, but who also has three years of on-the-ground experience with organizational and refugee advice work. It is also thanks to her and attorney Heiko Habbe's hands-on approach to teaching that the author received the Hamburg Teaching Award 2015 for the Clinic's teaching team in July 2016.[26]

Additional funding was needed for our talk series and intensive workshops with selected experts, as well as for supervising attorneys during term break. It was important to us that our own *pro bono* engagement did not require additional *pro bono* hours from attorneys at the expense of other clients. However, third-party funds are usually either geared towards research or are designed as start-up funds for

---

[21] See http://rlc-network.org/#members; several of these also include students from other disciplines.
[22] See www.netzwerk-migrationsrecht.akademie-rs.de.   [23] See www.fluechtlingsforschung.net.
[24] See www.fluechtlingsforschung.net/blog.   [25] See www.fluechtlingsforschung.net/grundlagen.
[26] See https://www.uni-hamburg.de/campuscenter/lehrpreis.html.

teaching innovations; an application for a one-year teaching grant[27] was rejected in 2015 on the basis that clinics have become so common that they are no longer innovative. Instead, we obtained funding from Hamburg Universitätskolleg,[28] have received a donation from the Thalia Theater, and have been sponsored by two corporate law firms, Freshfields Bruckhaus Deringer LLP and CMS Hasche Sigle LLP (which has recently set up a foundation for legal clinics).

The faculty also supported the Clinic in extending the period for the "free shot" (Freischuss) by one semester for students who have been involved in the Clinic's work for at least a year (mirroring the recognition for moot courts). In cooperation with Hamburg's Department of Justice and the Hamburg Judicial Examination Office, we drafted the first amendment of this kind in Germany,[29] to be passed over the summer.

Drivers

Soon after the Humboldt Law Clinic was founded in 2010, a number of practice projects started springing up in different locations across Germany, and, over the past few years, fully fledged clinics have started sprouting all over the country. One major factor behind this development was a change in the legal situation. Until 2008, it was illegal for anyone not a member of the bar[30] to provide legal advice without a licence, even for free.[31] This licensing requirement was first introduced by the 1935 Act for the Prevention of Abuse in the Field of Legal Advice.[32] In 1933, Jewish attorneys had been excluded from the bar;[33] pursuant to the new Act's Regulations, Jews were also unable to procure such a licence, preventing them from exercising their profession outside the bar. Despite its despicable background, the Act was retained after the war (changing names in 1965 to the Legal Advice Act[34]) as a tool to protect consumers against unqualified legal advice – and to protect the members of the bar against unwanted competition. Apart from advice to family members or neighbours, the 2008 Legal Services Act[35] for the first time permitted the provision free legal services by or under the supervision of a qualified lawyer. This supervision requires the necessary introductory and further training as well as active participation if and as far as this is necessary in the individual instance. This has

[27] See https://www.stifterverband.org/lehrfellowships.
[28] See https://tp27.universitaetskolleg.uni-hamburg.de/; see also www.qualitaetspakt-lehre.de/de/1422.php.
[29] Section 26 of the Hamburg Legal Education Act – Juristenausbildungsgesetz Hamburg, www.landesrecht-hamburg.de.
[30] Notaries and accountants were also allowed to provide legal advice.
[31] Rechtsberatungsgesetz. It was not, however, illegal for licensed attorneys to provide advice for free.
[32] Gesetz zur Verhütung von Mißbräuchen auf dem Gebiete der Rechtsberatung.
[33] Gesetz über die Zulassung zur Rechtsanwaltschaft; many, however, were spared by the Frontkämpferprivileg, i.e., were privileged due to their active participation at the front in the First World War.
[34] Rechtsberatungsgesetz.   [35] Rechtsdienstleistungsgesetz.

finally opened the door to the possibility of law students giving legal advice, provided they are properly trained and supervised by qualified legal staff.

A second factor that has catalysed CLE development in Germany is the refugee protests preceding the so-called refugee crisis. Many in civil society sided with the refugees who marched from Würzburg to Berlin and started a protest camp on Berlin's Oranienplatz against restrictions to their freedom of movement or with those who had made their way from Lampedusa to a church asylum in Hamburg's St Pauli in protest of the Dublin system.[36] When the arrival numbers peaked in 2015, so did civil society support; many who were not normally politically active started volunteering in soup kitchens, sorting through tons of donated clothes, offering language classes or activities for children, or supporting individual refugee families in reception centres nearby in their daily lives and bureaucratic struggles.[37]

As more and more students got involved in this type of support work, they also got more interested in the legal issues and in finding ways to use their evolving legal expertise to support refugees. Moreover, it was obvious that, due to the sharp increase in arrival numbers over the course of 2014 and 2015, the need for legal advice by far exceeded the available capacities, both of attorneys and of support organizations, and would continue to do so.[38]

Many students started clinical projects on their own, founding associations and training themselves with the help of local attorneys, often supported by but only loosely attached to the law faculties. As a result, very few of the refugee law clinics in Germany are fully institutionalized and supervised by academic staff, although several of them have over time managed to obtain university or faculty support in

---

[36] See, e.g., Joint press statement by the Landesflüchtlingsräte and Pro Asyl, "Flüchtlingsprotestmarsch von Würzburg nach Berlin", September 6, 2012, www.fluechtlingsrat-berlin.de/print_pe2.php?post_id=611; Chronologie der Flüchtlingsproteste in Berlin, rbb-online, October 4, 2014, www.rbb-online.de/politik/thema/fluechtlinge/hintergrund/Chronologie-Fluechtlingsproteste-Oranienplatz-Brandenburger-Tor.html; M. Anjahid, "Die geheimen Verhandlungen zwischen Senat und den Flüchtlingen", Der Tagesspiegel, September 29, 2014, www.tagesspiegel.de/berlin/bezirke/friedrichshain-kreuzberg/fluechtlingsprotest-am-oranienplatz-in-berlin-die-geheimen-verhandlungen-zwischen-senat-und-den-fluechtlingen/10762246.html; Pro Asyl, "International vernetzt, lokal eingebunden: Flüchtlingsproteste gehen weiter", February 2, 2015, https://www.proasyl.de/news/international-vernetzt-lokal-eingebunden-fluechtlingsproteste-gehen-weiter/; "Protestmarsch nach St.-Pauli-Spiel", taz.de, October 26, 2013, www.taz.de/Solidaritaet-mit-Fluechtlingen/!5056299/; "Wir interessieren nicht mehr", taz.de, May 29, 2016, www.taz.de/Lampedusa-Fluechtlinge-im-Abseits/!5304876/.

[37] See the study by S. Karakayali and O. Kleist, Strukturen und Motive der ehrenamtlichen Flüchtlingsarbeit (EFA) in Deutschland (2015), www.bim.hu-berlin.de/media/2015-05-16_EFA-Forschungsbericht_Endfassung.pdf; reported in S. Karakayali and O. Kleist, *Volunteers and Asylum Seekers*, 51 FORCED MIGRATION REVIEW 65–67 (2016). At the same time, attacks against asylum-seeker homes multiplied, and a recent poll showed a sharp increase in xenophobic and racist views; see M. Broomfield, *Majority of Germans Think Islam Does Not "Belong" in Their Country*, THE INDEPENDENT, May 13, 2016, www.independent.co.uk/news/world/europe/refugee-crisis-germany-islam-does-not-belong-in-country-a7027361.html.

[38] In responding to a quickly growing need, the RLC movement in Germany resembles the Turin Human Rights and Migration Law Clinic (HRMLC), founded in 2011 against the background of the Arab Spring.

the form of teaching contracts for practitioners (e.g. in Augsburg, Frankfurt/M., Hamburg, Munich, and Regensburg).[39] This was also the case for Humboldt University's RLC Berlin, which is now also cooperating with the HLCMR. However, as of summer 2016, it will officially join the Humboldt Law Clinics and be taught by an honorary professor (*Honorarprofessor*) from the judiciary, sponsored by the law school.

REFORMING THE TEACHING AND PRACTICE OF LAW IN EUROPE

Goals and Methods

The educational goal of a German law school is to produce a legal professional who is able to work in any type of legal career and any legal field; the profession of a judge serves as the standard. As explained earlier, legal education is therefore both broad and detailed. Interdisciplinary or more theoretical courses, so-called foundational matters (*Grundlagenfächer*), are part of the curriculum; this includes classes in legal sociology, legal philosophy, legal history, and legal theory. However, these approaches are rarely, if ever, picked up by the regular classes. Here, students are trained to learn the state of the art in each particular matter, which involves being able to reproduce doctrinal controversies, with a strong focus on the "prevailing view" (*herrschende Meinung*), with which students are ultimately encouraged to agree. The internationalization and Europeanization of the domestic legal order is a topic mostly confined to one class, typically taught in the second or third semester, and rarely plays a part in the other classes.

Most courses are held as lectures; in the first-year courses, up to 500 or even 600 law students share an auditorium. While professors may encourage student participation, these large formats make it very difficult to spark in-depth debates. More analysis-oriented, creative debates are also discouraged by the fact that lectures are supposed to cover the matter of the course in its entirety and students have little time to read up for class, with a lot of class hours per week and often working on the side. Smaller tutorials run by graduate students teach mock cases to prepare students for their written exams, which consist of writing a legal advice memo on such a mock case. Most law students do not take a smaller in-depth, text-based seminar until their last year of law school. Students have to take at least one skill-building course, which is typically taught by practitioners, and complete a three-month internship. While it thus includes some practice-oriented elements, this type of curriculum and learning environment does little to promote the development of a well-rounded person with a critical mind.

The HLCMR and the RLC Hamburg therefore strive to integrate substantive learning about the respective areas of law and skill-development for advice, policy,

---

[39] See L. Hilb and L. vom Felde, *Refugee Law Clinics in Deutschland – ein studentisches Modell für die Veränderung der juristischen Ausbildung?*, 49 (2) KRITISCHE JUSTIZ 220–32, at 225, 230–31 (2016).

and litigation work in those areas and to encourage both critical thinking and strategic argumentation. For example, the Clinics challenge students to critically assess the limits of human rights, to address global and local power differentials underlying legal structures and the role of gender, race, ethnicity, and so on in the ability to mobilize rights and to shape their meaning. They also challenge students to reflect on their own position, often from a privileged background, in the complex power field of law generally and human rights, antidiscrimination, and refugee law more specifically. Students are required to study by themselves for class by way of comprehensive research assignments. Different types of in-class exercises, often in small groups, as well as antidiscrimination and diversity trainings help them begin to understand the challenges awaiting them in practice. Avoiding hierarchy in our teaching practice encourages in-depth discussions and interactive learning.

Working with "their" NGO or an asylum attorney during the internship then provides the students with an impression of the real-world context of their "case" or of actual legal advice work. It puts them in touch with experienced practitioners who will share with them how they got to where they are now, what skills are necessary, the ethics of what to do and what not to do, how to act strategically in a highly political field, and how both failure and success can be useful for the "good cause."

In working on their piece of writing in the second semester, the HLCMR students learn to remain committed to one topic over a longer period of time and to cater to both high academic standards and to the expectations of the intended user. This requires intense supervision, and we often involve external experts to secure optimal quality. For the RLC Hamburg students, assisting the active legal advice teams in their second semester makes them realize how big the step is from learning about doing something to actually doing it. The in-depth exercise course as well as regular peer consulting meetings support them in developing their capacity to professionally interact with clients and – crucially – to assess the limits of their own ability to provide sound legal advice.

Beyond the Educational Goals

The educational goals feed into the wider goals of the HLCMR. The idea is to familiarize students with human rights early on and to give them the tools to use them in different settings, with a critical spirit. Students are encouraged to both understand law in its context and to "think outside the box" in terms of what is legally feasible; to develop new ways of using the law, of reshaping its meaning, of supporting silenced voices in making themselves heard; and perhaps even embrace, if not solicit, failure which can be used to scandalize the legal status quo. These skills can be used by attorneys and NGO workers as well as administrative officers, and they will make for better-informed judgments.

Moreover, the HLCMR's clinical projects seek to explore new avenues to assert the rights of those excluded by legal or societal structures or targeted by discrimination. With its partner NGOs or attorneys, the HLCMR identifies cutting-edge projects requiring in-depth research and legal argumentation, where the partner either lacks the formal legal training or is too busy to do this, producing advice, guidelines, or legal memoranda of immediate use to their constituencies or clients in pending cases. The Clinic thus provides its partners with in-depth expertise, enabling them to integrate these insights into their day-to-day work.

In the field of human rights and refugee law, clients are often without the necessary means to pay for legal advice – especially in situations where, due to the underdevelopment of the field, it is quite uncertain whether they will win and, if so, in what instance and thus after how many years. In the area of asylum law, the sheer number of clients, the frequent lack of supporting evidence – requiring additional background research – and the extremely short deadlines make it even more difficult for the limited number of attorneys to serve the rapidly growing client base. In the pretrial stage, indigent claimants in Berlin can obtain legal aid in the form of *Beratungshilfe* (i.e. support for legal advice) upon contribution of 15€ on their part, and attorneys are obligated to provide advice to such clients. In Hamburg, legal aid is not available in the pretrial stage, and public legal services[40] and local *pro bono* advice structures are as overburdened. In the trial stage, *Prozesskostenhilfe* (i.e. legal aid) is available, but it is dependent on the likelihood of winning the case, as determined by the court that is seized with the claim.[41] In risky cases without precedent, this can be a major obstacle. Moreover, legal aid is rather minimal and does not begin to cover the in-depth research and strategic consultation necessary to explore new avenues in legal argument.

The HLCMR seeks to fill this gap to a certain extent by supplying attorneys and NGOs advising such clients with *pro bono* expertise and strategic advice.[42] The RLC Hamburg seeks to relieve some of the pressure on existing advice structures and attorneys by providing high-quality legal advice to applicants in the pretrial stage. Both the HLCMR and the RLC Hamburg hope that, in the long run, some Clinic students will later choose to enter these fields professionally, thus broadening the base of qualified practitioners.

Complementing legal aid is also important because of a lack of a *pro bono* culture among German law firms,[43] although many activist attorneys take on individual cases *pro bono* and take it upon themselves to cross-finance these cases somehow. Multinational law firms often do encourage their German branches to take on *pro bono* work, but their narrow focus on corporate law often makes it difficult for them to pursue high-impact projects that promote the public interest or the rights of particularly vulnerable client groups. Thus, proboneo offers *pro*

---

[40] *Öffentliche Rechtsauskunft*, www.hamburg.de/oera/.
[41] Sections 114–127 of the Civil Procedure Act (*Zivilprozessordnung*), https://www.gesetze-im-internet.de /englisch_zpo/englisch_zpo.html#p0420.
[42] In that way, the HLCMR operates similarly as the Caen Fundamental Rights Law Clinic (CJDF).
[43] Pro Bono Deutschland e.V. seeks to change this: www.pro-bono-deutschland.org/en/.

bono legal advice in the following areas: legal forms for organizations, legal aspects of online presence, tax law, social franchising, labour law, data protection law, and trademark and copyright law (an open category also exists).[44] Individual big law firms advise community projects on corporate law or contracts, or do their taxes for them.[45] Given the intricacy of the problems that human rights clinics or refugee law clinics deal with, they have often struggled to include corporate lawyers in their work or found that setting up and maintaining this involvement is too time-consuming relative to its output.[46] Examples of more low-level involvement include the RLC Gießen, which has corporate lawyers accompany students in their advice work,[47] and the RLC Hamburg, which has organized a training whereby corporate lawyers give presentations on asylum law in reception centres.[48] Several firms instead (or in addition) prefer to sponsor clinics financially.[49]

The Weight and Value of Internationalization

Given the strong influence of EU and international law on German asylum law, the RLC Hamburg teaches refugee law in the multilevel system as a matter of course. The HLCMR has a strong focus on regional and international human rights law and heavily relies on the 2006 Equal Treatment Act,[50] which transposes EU antidiscrimination directives. The HLCMR seeks to "bring human rights home" by using these instruments for domestic cases, but also to use international forums to promote domestic human rights and antidiscrimination work.

For example, in the most recent cycle, HLCMR students cooperating with the ECCHR explored how business and human rights principles can be incorporated into German torts law in relation to precarious working conditions in subcontracting corporations supplying foreign "freelance" workers for the German meat industry. In the very first cycle, it supported the German NGO Intersexuelle Menschen e.V. in submitting a parallel report to Germany's state report to the Committee Against Torture, arguing that routinely subjecting small children with ambiguous genitals to medically unnecessary surgery constituted inhuman and

---

[44] This offer is supported by a number of corporate law firms; proboneo also offers *pro bono* support in areas other than law; e.g., on finance and communication. See, https://www.proboneo.de/recht/.
[45] See, e.g., www.freshfields.com/de/germany/what_we_do/clients_sectors/Pro_bono/.
[46] The Marburg Business Law Clinic is successfully cooperating with corporate lawyers, see F. Möslein and C. Rennig, *Die Business Law Clinic an der Philipps-Universität Marburg*, 3 GERMAN JOURNAL OF LEGAL EDUCATION 173–79, at 177 (2016).
[47] Freshfields Bruckhaus Deringer LLP.
[48] Latham & Watkins LLP, training session conducted in the Fall of 2015; staff attorneys can use *pro bono* hours for this.
[49] The HLCMR received kick-off funding from several corporate law firms and has been continuously sponsored and supported by Freshfields Bruckhaus Deringer LLP. See http://hlcmr.de/kooperationen/. The RLC Hamburg is also funded by two corporate law firms, see above.
[50] *Allgemeines Gleichbehandlungsgesetz*, AGG.

degrading treatment or torture.[51] The Committee sided with this argument and issued recommendations that were instrumental in the domestic advocacy process, which culminated in the recommendations of the German Ethics Council to immediately cease such practices and to stop requiring the choice of an either male or female gender at birth.[52] The German legislature has recently acted upon the second recommendation.[53] In 2012/13, a follow-up HLCMR project investigated Germany's duty to pay damages to intersex children who had been subjected to genital surgery.[54]

This integrated approach takes into account the degree to which our legal order has become internationalized and is influenced by EU law. For a contemporary lawyer, it is indispensable to be familiar with the relevant instruments at these levels, to be able to put them to effect in domestic settings, and to be able to mobilize their enforcement structures where domestic remedies prove fruitless or where this is strategically advisable.

Cooperation in CLE

Both the HLCMR and the RLC Hamburg have ties with other clinics in Germany. Thus, the HLCMR has sought in-house cooperation with its sister Humboldt Law Clinic on Cyber Law (on protection from hate speech on the Internet) as well as the student-founded RLC Berlin (on the rights of refugee children and undocumented migrants). Moreover, it hosted an interdisciplinary conference on the German authorities' failure to adequately deal with the series of racist murders of the Nationalsozialistischer Untergrund (NSU).[55] The RLC Hamburg is in close contact with other refugee law clinics to develop best practices and help new clinics get on their feet. This exchange has been sponsored since 2015 by the Catholic Academy of Stuttgart, which hosts the biggest migration law conference in Germany and has supported the Network Migration Law from its inception.[56]

Exchange at the European level is also becoming an increasing priority. In the HLCMR's first year, Jacqui Zalcberg represented it at the Global Public Interest Law Network's (PILnet) European Pro Bono Forum.[57] Since then, both clinics have

---

[51] See www2.ohchr.org/english/bodies/cat/docs/ngos/IMF_Germany_CAT47.pdf; the Caen Fundamental Rights Law Clinic (CJDF) has also used this type of instrument.
[52] Deutscher Ethikrat, Intersexuality.OPINION (2012), www.ethikrat.org/files/opinion-intersexuality.pdf. On the process, see www.ethikrat.org/themen/medizin-und-pflege/intersexualitaet.
[53] Section 22(3) of the Civil Status Act (*Personenstandsgesetz*, PStG).
[54] F. Bruchhäuser and T. Richarz, Zwischen Norm und Geschlecht – Erste Entwürfe möglicher nationaler Entschädigungs- und Schadensersatzansprüche untersexueller Menschen gegen die Bundesrepublik Deutschland, HLCMR Working Paper No. 5 (2014), http://hlcmr.de/publikationen/.
[55] See http://hlcmr.de/nsu-tagung/.
[56] Akademie der Diözese Rottenburg-Stuttgart, www.akademie-rs.de; *Hohenheimer Tage zum Migrationsrecht*.
[57] See www.pilnet.org/component/docman/doc_download/3-2010-european-pro-bono-forum.html.

joined the European Network for Clinical Legal Education (ENCLE) and have been attending the Network's annual conferences on CLE. For the RLC Hamburg, such travels have become much more feasible since third-party funding has started coming in, as faculty support only covers staff cost.

The HLCMR has also sought exchange early on with the Turin Human Rights and Migration Law Clinic (featured in this volume) as well as a legal clinic at the University of Valencia. In January of 2016, the three Humboldt Law Clinics hosted an international conference on interdisciplinary CLE[58] with speakers from the Universities of Turin, Warsaw, Queen Mary (London), and Osijek (Croatia). In June 2016, a conference on strategic litigation and CLE brought together speakers from European and international NGOs, such as the European Roma Rights Centre (ERRC), the Socio-Economic Rights Institute of South Africa (SERI), the Electronic Frontiers Foundation (EFF), and the American Civil Liberties Union (ACLU); a preconference workshop with ERRC legal director Adam Weiss explored possible applications in the work of the HLCMR.

The RLC Hamburg has established contact with the HEC/NYU's EU Clinic in Paris (also featured in this volume) and the European University Institute's Law in Action project on human rights in Florence. To expand these ties, it developed a tandem project with the HEC/NYU Clinic to develop best practice standard in exchange with clinicians from around Europe; as mentioned earlier, however, this application did not receive funding.[59] The author has also co-taught a refugee law summer school with José Fischel de Andrade of Milan and has explored ways to cooperate with the Association for Juridical Studies on Immigration (ASGI).

The HLCMR has also established ties beyond Europe. Thus, the Clinic is collaborating with the DePaul College of Law (Chicago) in a Summer School on Law and Critical Social Justice held at Humboldt University, Berlin.[60] It also developed plans for a Human Rights Summer School with the Universidad de Costa Rica; this project, however, failed to receive funding as well.[61]

Diffusion of CLE

Personal clinical experience in other legal systems has played a role in developing some of the legal clinics in Germany. However, much of the recent developments in the area of CLE in Germany have taken place rather autonomously, as adaptation to the local institutional and educational context is crucial to a clinic's chance of success.

---

[58] Learning from Real Cases: Law Clinics as an Interdisciplinary Teaching Concept, http://hlcmr.de/event/lernen-an-echten-fa%CC%88llen-law-clinics-als-fachu%CC%88bergreifendes-lehrkonzept/.
[59] This was part of the application for a *Lehrfellowship*, see *supra* note 14.
[60] See http://law.depaul.edu/academics/study-abroad/berlin-germany/Pages/default.aspx.
[61] See https://www.daad.de/hochschulen/programme-weltweit/sommerschulen/ausland/de/23469-sommerschulen-im-ausland/.

Thus, some of the co-founders of the Humboldt Law Clinic were relatively strongly influenced by personal experiences with the US university system. Professor Susanne Baer holds an LL.M. from the University of Michigan Law School, where she has been a William W. Cook Global Law Professor since 2010. Clinic co-initiators Liza Zamd and Jacqui Zalcberg were educated in the United States and in Australia and had both worked with a law clinic at Columbia Law School. I myself was more influenced by my internship with the AIRE Centre in London,[62] which demonstrated to me how quickly students can be put to work on complicated legal matters if they are properly trained and closely supervised.

Despite these influences, and despite contacts with the Turin Law Clinic,[63] the HLCMR (and later the RLC Hamburg) reached out to a German clinic for guidance, the RLC Gießen. This domestic orientation has much to do with the structure of German legal education, where clinical professorships do not exist and where students take a lot of classes each semester, thus limiting the time they can devote to any one project. This meant that we could not simply copy the very labour- and time-intensive US model. Instead, we had to find a way to make CLE work in our specific context by way of adaptation, integrating it as far as possible into existing curricular formats and finding ways for students to provide high-quality legal advice while being able to fulfil their other curricular demands (including a high number of class hours per week).

Eastern European clinics appear to have had similar experiences, copying US models and then – much more successfully – developing their own.[64] However, this experience appears not to be well-known in Germany, where CLE is seen as a uniquely American format. As mentioned, though, the HLCMR and the RLC Hamburg have sought to become more involved in the ongoing exchange at the European and international levels as they have found such participation very rewarding in light of the wealth of experience accumulated by more long-standing legal clinics around Europe. This includes, for example, advanced engagement with legal ethics or the existence of minimum standards for live-client clinics.

The HLCMR's two conferences on CLE, mentioned earlier, have been serving to deepen this experience by exchanging views on the issues of interdisciplinarity and strategic litigation. In the latter area especially, there is still much room for development in Germany, and legal clinics are in the process of figuring out what "strategic litigation" might mean in their areas of practice and how best to support such efforts. The conference brought together speakers from European and international NGOs such as the ERRC, SERI, the EFF and ACLU in order to clarify the

---

[62] See www.airecentre.org/pages/internships.html.
[63] See Chapter 7 by Ulrich Stege and Maurizio Veglio on the Human Rights and Migration Law Clinic (HLCMR), in this volume.
[64] See E. Rekosh, *Constructing Public Interest Law: Transnational Collaboration and Exchange in Central and Eastern Europe*, 13 UCLA J. INT'L L. & FOREIGN AFF. 55–96 (2008). *See also* Chapter 4 by Veronika Tomoszková and Maxim Tomoszek on the Czech experience, in this volume.

concept and its use; a preconference workshop with ERRC legal director Adam Weiss explored possible applications in the work of the HLCMR. A follow-up event could involve clinicians from around Europe to further develop how clinics best get involved and how they could cooperate on high-level cases of European scope (e.g. through joint amicus briefs).

Future of CLE in Europe

The Humboldt Law Clinic expanded very early on, in 2012. The five-year public grant from the Quality Pact for Teaching, mentioned earlier, enabled us to branch out from human and fundamental rights into the areas of consumer law and Internet law, each supervised by another colleague. The grant was recently renewed, securing funding for the three clinics for another five years. As mentioned, the RLC Berlin will also be integrated into the Humboldt Law Clinic as of Fall 2016. The HLCMR recently celebrated its fifth anniversary with the launch of a blog,[65] and, as it consolidates its work, it is quite possible that additional colleagues will join its ranks with their own projects. The fact that the project was able to successfully multiply at the same faculty demonstrates that its educational model is not field-specific but can easily be adapted to other fields of law.

In the area of refugee law clinics in Germany especially, there appears to be a growing awareness that institutionalization is an important factor in quality management. As more legal clinics are founded by students around Germany, universities are increasingly confronted with requests to accommodate such projects and may become more willing to do so as projects turn out to be successful.

The problem remains that institutional funding is limited. German universities usually do not have extra funds for staff that can be mobilized at the drop of a hat. This means that, in most cases, third-party funding, whether public or private, remains essential for CLE. Humboldt University has twice secured five-year funding from the Quality Pact for Teaching for practice-related projects, from which the Humboldt Law Clinics are supported. The University of Hamburg mainly uses its Quality Pact Teaching funds for projects on entering university; therefore, funding for the RLC Hamburg is comparatively limited and requires annual applications. In the area of refugees, the obvious and alarming need for qualified support has recently led to some short-term funding for civil society projects in late 2015 and early 2016;[66] however, while the calls for applications explicitly mention refugee law clinics, their design often reveals that CLE is still poorly understood at an institutional level. The HLCMR has also participated in a number of applications for

---

[65] *See* www.grundundmenschenrechtsblog.de.
[66] *See* Bundeszentrale für Politische Bildung, "Zuwendungen für Modellprojekte zum Thema Flucht und Asyl", www.bpb.de/system/files/dokument_pdf/Ausschreibung_o.pdf. Deutscher Akademischer Austauschdienst, "Welcome – Studierende engagieren sich für Flüchtlinge", https://www.daad.de /hochschulen/ausschreibungen/projekte/de/11342-foerderprogramme-finden/?s=1&projektid=57253339.

funding at the EU level in collaboration with other legal clinics. But all of these funding possibilities are short-term and usually nonrenewable; they therefore do not address the long-term funding needs for CLE projects.

Longer term funding opportunities for teaching projects may therefore continue to develop both at the domestic and the European levels. It is heartening that support for CLE seems to be growing. Thus, the German president visited the RLC Gießen in 2015. The Minister of State to the Federal Chancellor and Federal Government Commissioner for Migrants, Refugees, and Integration, Aydan Özoğuz, has recently accepted patronage of three refugee law clinics, including the RLC Hamburg, and has invited them to the Chancellery in Berlin in July 2016. Thus, raising the profile of CLE may help to raise awareness for the need for long-term public funding.

In the area of standardization, some of the German refugee law clinics are pushing for quality standards or even some kind of certificate to protect the "brand" against poorly supervised projects that can create problems for the entire field. However, given that some refugee law clinics are association-based (i.e. organized by student associations) while others are institutionalized, there is also push-back against such efforts.

At the European level, the potential for standardization of CLE appears equally limited due to the large differences among the educational systems. Instead, best practices also seem like a more feasible project as they can be adapted to the individual domestic, institutional, and professional context. Thus, German refugee law clinics are actively networking to discuss best practices among each other. The Humboldt Law Clinic for Human and Fundamental Rights is equally interested in developing best practice standards and has hosted two international conferences to that effect. Here, a European exchange will also be fruitful.

CONCLUSION

CLE in Germany is clearly on the rise. Legal advice projects have been around for a while, but the first clinic by that name wasn't founded until 2007. Both the RLC Gießen and the Humboldt Law Clinic, which followed in 2010, were top-down projects developed by teaching staff. Since then, students have actively claimed the format and started to establish legal clinics all over Germany, including the RLC Hamburg. This movement was catalysed by the developing refugee crisis, as students became involved in supporting refugees and beginning to ask for ways to use their legal skills to do so. But it can also be read as a reaction to a legal education format most students find dry and unconnected to current, real-life problems – and one that tends to marginalize or exclude legal fields relevant to public interest work, such as refugee law or antidiscrimination law.

However, legal clinics have a number of handicaps to deal with. First, it can be difficult to integrate them into the law faculties; this is in part due to the fact that public interest law fields are underrepresented in the legal curriculum and therefore are seen as specialization at the professorial level where legal clinics would be hosted. Student associations only loosely connected to universities constitute an alternative, but raise concerns over quality management. Second, institutionalizing legal clinics requires staff resources, which are difficult to provide for law faculties. Third, third-party public funding is rare, and both public and private funding is usually short-term, often designed only to support the kick-off phase of projects. Many legal clinics therefore struggle to establish a long-term perspective.

Both the HLCMR and the RLC Hamburg have chosen to fully integrate the clinics into the legal curriculum and have managed to obtain institutional funding for a number of years. This has allowed them to develop not only sustainable structures for quality management, but also ways to transform legal education from within, integrating practice and public interest concerns into the traditional teaching formats. Moreover, fundamental rights, antidiscrimination, and refugee law are strongly influenced by international and EU law, fostering an in-depth engagement with law as a multilevel system and with legal pathways on these different levels. Deepening exchange at the European level will help to develop best practice standards that can be adapted to each individual clinical format.

Both projects have shown that the benefits of CLE clearly outweigh the difficulties, both for students and their clients, but also for the universities and society at large. Both clinics fill gaps where legal advice is otherwise not readily available, supporting NGOs in their human rights and antidiscrimination work and complementing the work of overstretched asylum attorneys and support centres in the area of refugee law. They thus support access to justice for clients with insufficient resources or in precarious situations, complementing a legal aid system that makes it difficult to challenge the status quo. They also enable students to actively shape their legal studies, transform their learning institutions, and become legal professionals with expertise in areas of public interest law who also understand the sociopolitical implications of their work.

9

The EU Public Interest Clinic and the Case for EU Law Clinics

A. Alemanno and L. Khadar

INTRODUCTION

The European Union (EU) Clinic is the result of a partnership between New York University School of Law and HEC Paris (Ecole des Hautes Etudes Commerciales de Paris). By building upon the American law clinic model and adapting it to the specificities of the unique European constitutional and institutional system, it is the first clinic devoted to experimenting with the various channels of participatory democracy existing within the EU. Through detailed legal and policy research, the EU Clinic aims to promote democratic, transparent, and accountable EU institutions by serving the advocacy needs of civil society organizations involved in the EU policy process.

The Clinic brings together selected law students from both NYU Law School (second and third years) and HEC Paris (master's degree second-year students) and involves them in working directly for nongovernmental organizations (NGOs) operating in the EU policy field. Through hands-on participation in legislative and administrative proceedings and a weekly seminar that focuses on the institutional structures and substantive standards of EU decision-making, students have the opportunity to gain skills in collaborative problem-solving, effective communication of legal issues and strategies, working with nonlegal experts, and relationship building. The students are supported by the Clinic faculty alongside a range of experienced academics and practitioners who work with the Clinic on a *pro bono* basis to advance the goals of the client NGOs.

In spite of the significant variation among substantive areas of EU law and policy, the course teaches a core set of skills, including statutory interpretation, policy analysis, advocacy techniques, and understanding the political context of regulation.[1] A particular emphasis is placed on the ability to influence the policy process

---

[1] The course focuses on European Union law and in 2016 covered the following topics: EU institutional framework and its major actors; constitutional principles and EU legislative acts; legislative-making, rule-making and treaty-making powers; the effects of EU law in the national legal systems; overview of EU judicial architecture and main EU legal remedies; the internal market and the power to harmonize; free movement of goods; competition law; free movement of persons and EU citizenship; and transatlantic regulatory cooperation: the case of TTIP.

through a detailed analysis of the major avenues for participation open to both business and civil society actors. Participation in the legislative and policy process is presented as an increasingly valuable tool for advocacy in the modern regulatory state. In the framework of the fieldwork (i.e. practical) components, students work in teams, and selected projects cover all major policy stages: drafting petitions or legislative proposals, submitting comments, recommending changes to the legislative or regulatory process, engaging with executive oversight, and participating in litigation as amicus or counsel. In addition to policy analysis and administrative law skills, fieldwork provides rich opportunities for students to meet and interact with a real-life client as well as with panoply of actors populating the EU policy space. Targeted actors include the European Commission, the European Parliament, and the European Ombudsman, as well as national actors.

The EU Clinic provides students with a unique opportunity to play an active role in future and ongoing policy processes and advocacy campaigns concerning important issues facing the EU, its twenty-eight Member States, and its 500 million inhabitants. In so doing, students help NGOs give voice to the often-underrepresented public interest in the complex supranational EU policy process.

EMERGENCE OF CLINICAL LEGAL EDUCATION

Genesis and Context

Personal
The idea to establish a legal clinic providing advice and assistance in EU law dates back to the days when one of the authors (Alberto Alemanno) worked as a *référendaire* at the Court of Justice of the European Union (CJEU). In his five-year stint, he was involved in dozens of cases ranging from free movement, citizenship, and consumer law to state aid, antitrust, and tax law. Two major features of EU litigation struck him at the time. First, the significant gap in time between the emergence of the factual situation at the centre of the dispute and the moment in which the case finally reached the court.[2] What is debated in Brussels today (e.g. whistle-blower protection or the new EU privacy shield) will only reach the EU Courts in five to ten years' time. Second, he was surprised by the underrepresentation of the interests of civil society in EU litigation. Only in a handful of cases did he witness the involvement of civil society organizations, either as plaintiff or as a third party intervening. While the former phenomenon (gap in time), by contributing to a growing detachment between policy action and academy research, questions/reduces academic relevance for society, the latter (civil society underrepresentation) explains the

---

[2] While in the case of preliminary reference, this gap is virtually nonexistent (due to the incidental nature of this proceedings), virtually all other legal remedies available before the EU Courts witnessed a significant temporal gap between the origin of the dispute and the actual dispute.

limited concern of EU legal academia for public interest representation.[3] Upon entering academia full time, Alberto experimented (largely unaware of clinical legal education) with some embryonic forms of experiential learning aimed at sensitizing students to (1) the need to become cognizant of major EU policy developments and (2) the importance of serving the public interest in the EU. To attain these objectives and prove that an EU lawyer today requires a sense of both reality and purpose to succeed, he encouraged his EU law students to identify ongoing EU policy files of interest at the beginning of the course. They were then required to prepare observations to be submitted to the relevant institutions, generally the EU Commission in the framework of public consultations.

After reiterating this exercise a few times over a couple of years, Alberto had a felicitous encounter at a conference organized at NYU Abu Dhabi. On that occasion he met Richard Revesz, at the time Dean of NYU School of Law, who, after showing great interest in Alberto's embryonic clinical efforts at HEC Paris, discussed his project to establish a Europe-based legal clinic open to NYU law students who were spending a semester studying abroad.

Institutional

This project later materialized in the establishment of the NYU Law Abroad programme, which forms part of a broader set of curricular enhancements emphasizing focused study in the third year of law school.[4] This programme gives NYU Law students[5] the opportunity to spend the Spring semester immersed in the law and legal culture of another part of the world through an academic programme designed and administered by the Law School. The programme is designed to help students develop global fluency – sensitivity to different legal cultures and contexts –linguistic ability, and the flexibility to work effectively across jurisdictions. The aim is to provide substantial exposure to the local legal system and distinct regional issues. In addition to traditional courses and seminars, each site offers a transactional course designed to give students direct exposure to the legal aspects of doing business in the relevant region. Moreover, a key feature of NYU Law Abroad is the offering –in both the Buenos Aires and Paris sites – of clinics that provide opportunities to participate in local policy debates.[6] The *EU Public Interest Clinic* is therefore the flagship programme of NYU Law at its new, and only European, campus. HEC Paris, the leading business school in Europe and partner in this programme, is in turn seeking

---

[3] See Olivier De Schutter, *Public Interest Litigation Before the European Court of Justice*, 13 MJ 9–34 (2006).

[4] See Press Release: NYU Law Announces Ambitious New Study-Abroad Program as Part of Curricular Enhancements Emphasizing Focused Study in Third Year, www.law.nyu.edu/news/nyu_law_announces_study-abroad_program_curricular_enhancements_third_year

[5] The programme is designed primarily for third-year NYU Law students; exceptions will be considered for other students on a case-by-case basis.

[6] At all of the sites, the classroom experience is complemented by study tours in the region and opportunities for language training.

through this Clinic to reinvent its corporate-focused approach to law and bring a public policy approach to the way it teaches European affairs.

Educational

The initial source of inspiration of the EU Public Interest Clinic in Paris is the well-established New York-based Regulatory Policy Clinic created and directed by NYU Law Dean Emeritus Richard Revesz and Michael Livermore. This clinic is sponsored by the Institute for Policy Integrity at the Law School, a think tank that works to improve the quality of government decision-making through advocacy in the fields of administrative law, economics, and public policy. The Clinic focuses on practice before federal agencies and courts to help students develop a set of core administrative lawyering skills. It consists of two major components: a seminar and a fieldwork element. While the course is designed to teach students how to conduct effective advocacy before administrative agencies and courts on a wide range of issues, from environmental protection to public safety, the fieldwork enables students to learn, while working with Policy Integrity's legal advocates and economic scholars, how to tackle cutting-edge regulatory matters.

Legal and Sociopolitical

The EU Clinic does not only share a common format with the Regulatory Policy Clinic at NYU, but it also embraces a similar understanding of social justice. The idea being that, in a world characterized by a systemic unbalance in the representation of interests in the policy process, it is imperative to counter undue influence by giving voice to the voiceless. As discussed later, this is a predominantly process-based understanding of social justice, with the goal being to make sure that all interests have a seat at the table. The privileged approach to attain this objective is by promoting a better understanding of the participatory and analytical tools available to all – and not only few – stakeholders. Civil society organizations should stop demonizing those tools and start learning how to actually use them.[7]

As is often the case, it was a serendipitous mix of encounters between like-minded individuals and a growing sense urgency with respect to the need for legal education reform that led to the establishment of the EU Clinic. What sets apart the genesis of the clinic is its inherently transnational/global dimension: while the involvement of EU students was instrumental to the attainment of the declared goals pursued by the EU-based legal clinic (to provide global legal fluency to US students), the very same EU students (and their institution) benefited from the reform of the US legal curriculum for third-year NYU law students. If the establishment of a legal clinic overseas was perceived as providing a possible solution to the problems debated within US legal curriculum reform, it also provided a unique opportunity for an EU

---

[7] Richard L. Revesz and Michael A. Livermore, RETAKING RATIONALITY (Oxford University Press 2010).

institution, such as HEC Paris, to embrace and experiment with a unique form of transnational clinic made up of students educated in either the United States or in various EU countries. This fits nicely with its international vocation and readiness to experiment with new cutting-edge teaching methods. In its three years of operation, the EU Clinic has already proved to be a source of attraction for the HEC Paris LLM programme. Moreover, the public interest vocation instilled by the clinic is already translating into deeper curriculum reforms aimed at providing greater perspectives to the students. Using both academic literature and fieldwork as jumping-off points, the new curriculum is focusing on developing a rounded approach to lawyering that includes consideration of the legal, policy, economic, and political issues that shape policies as well as administrative decisions.

Drivers

Clinics focusing predominantly on EU law are rare. However, in the past five years or so, a handful of clinics have emerged in Europe (including the EU Public Interest Clinic) dealing largely with EU law and serving both individuals and organizations. These include clinics such as the EU and International Migration Law Clinic at International University College in Turin (IUC Clinic) or the EU Fundamental Rights Clinic at the University of Kent at Brussels (Kent at Brussels Clinic), both of which are represented in this book (Chapters 7 and 10, respectively). The Kent at Brussels Clinic is a joint initiative with the European Citizen Action Service (ECAS) and its mission is "to help EU citizens and their family members who cannot afford the services of a lawyer in resolving any problems they may encounter when moving around the EU and assist them in enforcing their European rights."[8] This mission is carried out by LLM students on an EU Migration Law course in collaboration with qualified lawyers and citizens' rights advisors. Meanwhile, the IUC Clinic is a joint initiative between the University of Turin and the University of Eastern Piedmont in Alessandria and aims to "sensitiz[e] students as future professionals to the problems of social justice and to foster a sense of social responsibility ... provide research and the much-needed pro bono legal assistance to under-represented individuals and organizations within Turin, complementing the already existing support provided by local organizations working locally for the benefit of migrants."[9]

The clinic engages students from all three institutions in a wide range of activities, from directly assisting (alongside trained Italian lawyers) local migrants to access their EU law and European Court of Human Rights (ECHR) rights (typically in the context of residence security) within the Italian legal system, strategic litigation campaigns targeting the European supranational courts, or research into detention centre practices and their compliance with European human rights law.

---

[8] See http://blogs.kent.ac.uk/eu-rights-clinic/about-us/ (November 25, 2015).
[9] See www.iuctorino.it/content/clinical-program-0 (November 25, 2015).

It is perhaps too early to describe the emergence of such EU law–oriented clinics as a "trend," nevertheless, we might engage in some provisional reflection on why such clinics might be emerging now. Clearly, the emergence of the EU legal and institutional order has had profound effects on Europe and all of its inhabitants. The supranational EU governance structure, and in particular its major institutions, have become immensely powerful and now play a huge role in shaping the everyday experience of living in Europe, from regulating the currency we use and what we buy, eat, and drink to influencing how we travel and who we vote for in national elections.[10] Whether you are an Italian engineer moving to Poland for work or study, a Slovenian business owner trying to sell services in Spain, a French consumer buying products over the Internet from a Slovak online shop, or even simply a tourist from the United States flying around Europe on holiday, engaging with EU law will likely be both unavoidable and indispensable. Moreover, there is now a vast array of rights available under EU law, covering everything from free movement and data protection to consumer protection and voting.

However, studies consistently show that people in the EU face considerable obstacles in accessing their EU law rights and protections.[11] Many EU citizens, residents, and tourists are unaware of their rights or do not know how to advocate for them. Recent European commission studies[12] suggest that more than a quarter of polled EU citizens living outside of their home country (in a second EU Member State) experienced problems accessing their rights. Meanwhile, according to the 2013 Eurobarometer survey on EU citizenship,[13] 43% of respondents did not feel well informed about their EU law rights, and 20% did not feel informed at all. We might say that a gap has opened up between both the law and the institutions that produce it on the one hand and the citizens who experience it and are subject to it on the other. This gap is first of all geographical: the institutions in Brussels, Luxembourg, and Strasbourg are removed from citizens in Warsaw, Budapest, Lisbon, and Dublin, and – as epitomized by the authors of the Paris and Brussels terrorist attacks – very often from the very same citizens living in the capitals hosting the EU institutions. Yet, simultaneously, this gap is also characterized by knowledge and power discrepancies: the people of Europe have limited direct influence over EU policy and limited knowledge and understanding about the ways in which EU law and policy directly impact them. The EU has over time taken several measures to narrow these structural gaps, from the introduction of electoral rights for mobile Union citizens[14] to the establishment of the office of the European Ombudsman,[15] the fundamental right of access to EU documents,[16] the European Citizens'

---

[10] See, e.g., D. Keleman, *Eurolegalism*, in THE TRANSFORMATION OF LAW AND REGULATION IN THE EUROPEAN UNION (Harvard University Press 2011).
[11] Studies to be added.
[12] See http://ec.europa.eu/justice/citizen/files/2013eucitizenshipreport_en.pdf.
[13] See http://ec.europa.eu/public_opinion/flash/fl_365_en.pdf.   [14] Article 20 TFEU.
[15] Articles 20, 24, and 228 TFEU.   [16] Article 42 of the Charter of Fundamental Rights.

Initiative,[17] and the right to petition the Parliament[18] or even the possibility to participate in Commission consultations,[19] which have become mandatory since the Lisbon Treaty entered into force in 2009. However, awareness of these mechanisms among the average European is surprisingly modest, and use of them is predominantly the preserve of a clued-up, Brussels-based, European Europhile elite.

At the same time, a skills gap has also opened up. EU law has undoubtedly changed the practice of domestic law in several respects, requiring many national lawyers to have some understanding of EU law. Although empirical data are controversial,[20] it is safe to argue that more than half of Member States' legislations currently in force are no longer decided in their respective capitals but come out of the Brussels-based decision-making pipeline. Moreover, as the competence of the EU legislator has expanded (or has been stretched),[21] the scope of EU law has grown, too, far beyond the traditional core of the internal market, competition policy, and international trade. EU law now touches upon inter alia fundamental rights, family law, environmental law, consumer protection, labour law, intellectual property, and, in the area of freedom, security, and justice, it touches upon border checks, migration, and asylum, as well as civil, criminal, and police cooperation.[22] The ensuing penetration of EU law results in growing complexity; answering questions such as "what is the scope of EU law in X field," "how does EU law apply to X person," or "does the EU have competence to legislate in relation to X" is an increasingly complicated task. To be a good EU lawyer, one requires not only in-depth knowledge of the sophisticated EU constitutional and administrative architecture and policy process but also of the multiple domestic legal and social contexts in which EU law is (constantly being) applied. This substantive complexity is likely exacerbated by a practical complexity caused by the sheer volume of EU law: the net amount of EU legislation adopted (i.e. adopted legislation minus repealed legislation) rose from 715 instruments in 1997 to 1,614 in 2009,[23] while the number of new cases brought before the Courts of Justice of the European Union has been steadily rising from 445 new cases in 1997 to 713 in 2015,[24] not to mention the thousands of domestic cases litigated each year that in some way touch upon EU law.

[17] Article 11 (4) TUE. [18] Articles 20 and 227 TFEU. [19] Article 11 (3) TUE.
[20] Estimates suggest that, depending on how you measure, anywhere between 15% and 50% of domestic laws may now bear some trace of EU influence. See, e.g., Vaughne Miller, How Much Legislation Comes from Europe?, House of Commons Library, Research Paper 10/62 (13 October 2010), 24–40.
[21] See, e.g., A. Prechal, *Competence Creep and General Principles of Law*, 3 (1) REVIEW OF EUROPEAN AND ADMINISTRATIVE LAW 5–22 (2010).
[22] Miguel Poiares Maduro, *Legal Education and the Europeanisation and Globalisation of Law* [editorial note], 4 CROATIAN YEARBOOK OF EUROPEAN LAW & POLICY Croatian Y.B.E (2008); Aalt Willem Heringa, *European Legal Education or Legal Education in Europe* [editorial], 18 (3)MAASTRICHT JOURNAL OF EUROPEAN AND COMPARATIVE LAW 221–22 (2011).
[23] Miller, *supra* note 20, at 15.
[24] Court of Justice of the EU, Annual Report, 2015, http://curia.europa.eu/jcms/upload/docs/application/pdf/2016-04/en_ap_jur15_provisoire2.pdf.

However, as will be discussed in more detail later, teaching and practice of EU law have failed to keep pace, and while there may be some lawyers who understand particular fragments of EU law, there will be few who have sufficient grounding in EU law to see the forest from the trees.[25]

Against this background context, it is not difficult to understand the almost salvific appeal of EU law clinics. Clinical legal education (CLE) has been taking root in Europe since the mid 1990s[26] but has historically been oriented towards the national legal systems and domestic educational and social concerns. Give the increasingly deep penetration of European law into domestic legal systems and legal education in the recent decades, it was surely only a matter of time before CLE embraced European law and (pan) European structures, issues, and causes. What CLE brings to EU law is threefold: first, albeit on a small scale, CLE is a way to realize and put to the test the plethora of rights and participatory mechanisms that European institutions have furnished on Europeans in the preceding decades; second, CLE is way to involve European academics and students in emerging European issues and causes related to migration, for example, the democratic deficit surrounding EU institutions, or data and privacy protection; third, CLE has provided a teaching methodology that enables teachers of EU law to not only illustrate but also experience, for the benefit of students, the complexities of EU law (e.g. the institutional structure and processes and interaction with domestic law) and the particulars (e.g. multijurisdictionally/multilingualism) of the practice of EU law.

REFORMING THE TEACHING AND PRACTICE OF LAW IN EUROPE

Goals and Methods

EU Law Teaching and Training: The Status Quo
The very first point that should be made about EU law *teaching* (i.e. the academic stage of legal education) and *training* (i.e. the induction period or vocational/professional stage of legal education) is that there is no standardized system for EU law teaching and training *across the EU*. Each Member State within the EU has its own legal system and traditions when it comes to legal education, training, and licensing (i.e. meeting the respective bar requirements).[27] There is no "federal" (EU-level) oversight or centralized body (such as the American Bar Association [ABA])

---

[25] For a critique and presentation of an alternative model of legal education in Europe, *see* Nicole Kornet, Future-Minded Legal Education in Europe: The European Law School, MEPLI Working Paper Series 2013-10.

[26] Mariana Berbec-Rostas, Arkady Gutnikov, and Barbara Namyslowska-Gabrysiak, *Clinical Legal Education in Central and Eastern Europe: Selected Case Studies*, in THE GLOBAL CLINICAL MOVEMENT: EDUCATING LAWYERS FOR SOCIAL JUSTICE (Frank S. Bloch ed., Oxford University Press 2010).

[27] Julian Lonbay, *The Education, Licensing, and Training of Lawyers in the European Union, Part I: Cross-Border Practice in the Member States*. 77 (4) THE BAR EXAMINER 6 (2008).

with authority to regulate the legal education systems and professions of Europe. Indeed, the EU itself has limited competence,[28] within EU treaties, to harmonize the content of legal education across the Union, and so Member States are free to determine the entry routes into their respective legal professions.[29] Jean Monnet is alleged to have said: "If I were to start again, I would start with education."[30]

The European Law Faculties Association (ELFA), founded in 1995, has emerged as a liaison between EU institutions and Europe's many law faculties and, to an extent, taken up the task of coordinating reform and promoting convergence within legal education in Europe. Similarly, the Council of Bars and Law Societies of Europe (CCBE), founded in 1960, has stepped in as a liaison between the EU and Europe's national bars and law societies to make a concerted push towards achieving common standards in legal training in Europe (and in relation to EU law in particular). However, achieving common positions has reportedly proved very difficult.[31] Ultimately, both of these organizations remain relatively weak.

The second issue to note about EU law teaching and training is that there is very little comparative literature pertaining to these topics.[32] Perhaps, as has been suggested, EU law scholars are not inclined to self-reflexive scholarship, writing frequently about the nature of their object (EU law) but not about the nature of their trade (teaching, thinking, and writing about EU law).[33] Moreover, as mentioned, the postacademic stage of legal education falls to the relevant domestic bar or law society and is beyond the gaze of the university-based (EU law) scholar.[34] This state of affairs is regrettable because it means that some of what follows proceeds more on the basis

---

[28] Although limited, it has convincingly been argued that the competence of the EU in the area of education is broader than generally assumed. *See, e.g.*, S. Garben, *The Bologna Process: From a European Law Perspective*, EUI Working Paper, 2008/12 ; K. Grimonprez, *The European Dimension in Citizenship Education: Unused Potential of Article 165 TFEU*, 39(1) E.L.REV. 3–26 (2014) (arguing that Article 165 TFEU provides a sound legal basis for focused EU action to prepare the majority of pupils who remain at home for an active, informed, critical, and responsible EU citizenship, a prerequisite for democracy).

[29] For a critical analysis of the Bologna Process, *see, e.g.*, Garben, *supra* note 28.

[30] *See*, on this point, A. Corbett, UNIVERSITIES AND THE EUROPE OF KNOWLEDGE: IDEAS, INSTITUTIONS AND POLICY ENTREPRENEURSHIP IN EUROPEAN UNION HIGHER EDUCATION POLICY (Basingstoke: Palgrave Macmillan, 2005), xi (questioning whether he actually said so and adding that "but it is an aphorism which makes sense, wherever it comes from").

[31] Lonbay, *supra* note 27, at 26; Jonathan Goldsmith, Sieglinde Gamsjäger, and Alonso Hernández-Pinzón Garcia. *Training of Lawyers in the European Union*, in THE TRAINING OF LEGAL PRACTITIONERS: TEACHING EU LAW AND JUDGECRAFT. Compilation of briefing notes, Workshop on Judicial Training, Thursday, 28 November 2013, 161.

[32] Although, *see* S. Baroncelli, R. Farneti, I. Horga, and S. Vanhoonacker, TEACHING AND LEARNING THE EUROPEAN UNION: INNOVATION AND CHANGE IN PROFESSIONAL EDUCATION (Amsterdam: Springer Netherlands 2014), 9.

[33] Bruno De Witte, *European Union Law: A Unified Academic Discipline?* (2008),1; and Poiares, *supra* note 22. For a similar critique when it comes to European legal research, see R. van Gestel and H.-W. Micklitz, *Why Methods Matter in European Legal Scholarship*, 20 (3) EUROPEAN LAW JOURNAL 292–316 (2014).

[34] Richard J. Wilson, *Practical Training in Law in the Netherlands: Big Law Model or Clinical Model, and the Call of Public Interest Law*, 8 (1) UTRECHT LAW REVIEW 174 (2012).

of anecdote rather than substantial evidence. Having said that, it would not perhaps be fallacious to suggest that, barring a number of notable exceptions,[35] on the whole, across Europe, EU law *teaching* (certainly at bachelor's degree level) is predominantly doctrinal (i.e. involving a rehearsal of key case law, treaty provisions, and legal principles and norms), historical, and institutional (i.e. entailing an overview of the development of the EU institutions and the evolution of the EU legal order), and, much like all law teaching across Europe,[36] textbook-based, lecture-based, and written exam–based.[37] This admittedly rather anecdotal belief is, however, supported by a 2014 study carried out by the CCBE ("Study on the State of Play of Lawyers' Training in EU Law"), covering all twenty-eight EU Member States, which revealed that many survey respondents across the EU felt that "academic training in EU law is too much about theory and too little about its practical effect on legal cases."[38] Moreover, a recent broad survey of teaching methods in European studies (including EU legal studies) across twenty-seven Member States (plus Iceland, Turkey, and Norway) found that almost 60% of respondents never relied on fieldwork as a teaching methodology and almost 50% never relied on simulations, while almost 70% often made use of textbooks and PowerPoint presentations.[39]

Even at the master's degree level, where young EU lawyers may specialize in labour law or social rights, competition, tax, Union citizenship, the internal market, external relations, litigation, and so on, the situation will not change drastically. While there are certainly exceptions and examples of EU law teaching and academic work that is interdisciplinary in nature and focuses on the social and political context of EU law, these have not generally resulted in any revolution within core *EU law teaching methodology* or in an enhanced focus on the practical application of EU law.[40] Teaching remains, on the whole, based on textbooks, lectures or seminars, and written exams. It remains so also among leading LLM programmes in EU Law across the continents, such as those offered by the College of Europe, King's College, or the Université Libre de Bruxelles. You would have to search far and wide to find an EU law teaching module that encourages young EU lawyers to

[35] See, in general, A. W. Heringa and B. Akkermans, eds., EDUCATING EUROPEAN LAWYERS (Ius Commune: European and Comparative Law Series 2011); *see also* Chapter 10 by Anthony Valcke in this volume, discussing the teaching of EU law through MOOCs, moot courts, and case studies.
[36] Andras Jakab, *Dilemmas of Legal Education: A Comparative Overview*, 57 J LEGAL EDUC. 257 (2007).
[37] See, e.g., Richard Ball and Christian Dadomo, UKCLE Law Subject Survey: European Union Law (2010), 89, 104 (unpublished, http://eprints.uwe.ac.uk/14747), This survey related to EU law teaching in the UK and found that such teaching (at least at universities) was primarily conservative and doctrinal. However, anecdotal evidence suggests that this would be even more so for continental Europe, which is traditionally far more conservative in its approach to legal education.
[38] EIPA Luxembourg, CCBE, "Study on the State of Play of Lawyers' Training in EU Law," 18.
[39] S. Baroncelli, F. Fonti, and G. Stevancevic, *Mapping Innovative Teaching Methods and Tools in European Studies: Results from a Comprehensive Study*, in TEACHING AND LEARNING THE EUROPEAN UNION: INNOVATION AND CHANGE IN PROFESSIONAL EDUCATION (S. Baroncelli, R. Farneti, I. Horga, and S. Vanhoonacker, eds. Amsterdam: Springer Netherlands 2014), 103–05.
[40] See, e.g., the European Law Journal or the PhD and LLM programs of the European University Institute or the LLM program of the College of Europe (amongst others).

engage practically in *doing EU law*.[41] Even trying to locate a module that encourages young EU lawyers to go beyond the development of doctrine through CJEU case law and EU legislation and think about how EU law operates in practice (beyond the institutional context), its material impact (or lack thereof) on real persons, would still not be straightforward. Indeed, although it has been commented that EU law scholars as a community take a pragmatic and instrumental view of the law, this stance does not seem to have translated into EU law teaching, which remains largely conservative in approach and passive in delivery.[42]

When it comes to EU law professional *training*, the exposure of the average young trainee lawyer does not improve. The 2014 CCBE study mentioned earlier revealed that, of the twenty-eight EU Member States, *only thirteen* provide any form of explicit EU law training during the vocational stage of their legal studies.[43] Typically, this training, which is not always compulsory, is very short (with an average duration of just two days), is lecture-based, and is principally concerned with the EU institutions.[44] In the remainder of the EU Member States, the overwhelming trend seems to be to rely on the academic stage of legal education to cover EU law.

Arguably, some young EU lawyers do receive practical training in EU law during the apprenticeship phase of their professional legal education. Indeed, apprenticeships are a common feature of virtually all European legal systems. However, it might be argued that this late exposure to the EU legal system occurs when the lawyer has already shaped his legal understanding and therefore will no longer be able to fully appreciate this further dimension. By then, the young lawyer is already accustomed to his own national legal system that she or he will forever perceive as the default legal order against which other laws and systems should be assessed. As a result, any nondomestic sources will be perceived as foreign, other, and "less normal" than those populating his legal order.[45]

This is a position supported by the CCBE and the European Commission, both of which are increasingly calling for legal educators to produce law graduates who are practice-ready, well-endowed with core legal *skills* (as opposed to solely *knowledge*). Leaving things to the apprenticeship stage is problematic for a number of reasons: first, it will compound the tendency towards fragmentation (young French lawyers learn EU law in French from older French lawyers etc.); second, it means that there will be an inbuilt tendency towards conservatism in EU law training;[46] and, finally, as the majority of lawyers across the EU work in small firm contexts, there will in

---

[41] Note that there is a vast gap between applying EU law to concrete situations in theory as in a written exam and applying it in fact to a real situation.
[42] H. Schepel, *Professorenrecht? Le champ du droit privé européen*, 26 CRITIQUE INTERNATIONALE 147–58, at 152 (2005) (as referred to in De Witte, *supra* note 33, at 4).
[43] EIPA Luxembourg, CCBE, *supra* note 38, at 8.   [44] *Id.*, at 32.
[45] Jaakko Husa, *Turning the Curriculum Upside Down: Comparative Law as an Educational Tool for Constructing the Pluralistic Legal Mind*, 10 (7) GERMAN LAW JOURNAL 913–26 (2009).
[46] EIPA Luxembourg, CCBE, *supra* note 38, at 16.

many cases simply be insufficient institutional know-how to effectively train for the complex and increasingly pluralistic nature of EU law practice.

Another potential issue with leaving practical EU law training to the apprenticeship stage is the increasingly dominant role, throughout Europe, played by "Big Law" (large multinational commercial law firms)[47] in determining the content and scope of legal training during and prior to the apprenticeship stage. In the United Kingdom, consortiums of large law firms, each taking on up to 100 trainee lawyers a year, have recently come together to develop their own "accelerated" legal practice course (the accelerated LPC, which one of the authors – Lamin Khadar – graduated from) that all of their recruits are required to undertake.[48] Similarly, in the Netherlands, fourteen large firms came together to create the Law Firm School in 2009 to provide vocational training to their recruits.[49] These training programmes have been devised to provide, in tandem with the apprenticeship period they are linked to, an extensive socialization period for young commercial lawyers. The sponsoring firms also seek to make the vocational stage of legal education (for their recruits) more relevant to commercial law practice. While these programmes certainly add value in so far as they may provide for a more convergent approach to EU law training, the problem is that, so far as such training programmes and apprenticeships *are* concerned with EU law, their focus may (as on the accelerated LPC and at the Law Firm School) be limited to certain aspects of EU law (e.g. competition), paying no attention to the social justice or public interest aspects of EU law and their relevance to the young apprentices as future EU lawyers (or future lawyers within the EU).[50] Given the sizable number of top young lawyers inevitably trained through Big Law apprenticeship schemes, this is not a negligible concern.[51] Indeed, a 2015 CCBE report similarly pondered whether similar collaborative efforts at teaching EU law existed in the context of "criminal law, fundamental rights and for the legal services required by ordinary citizens."[52] The selective, elitist nature of these forms of legal training combined with their corporate focus seem to largely neglect the broad

[47] "Big Law" refers to the enormous, multinational law firms – "firms that have globalized in every sense of the word – and the economic power they exert in every country in which they operate. These law firms manage the legal aspects of gigantic corporate mergers and acquisitions; they litigate and arbitrate before domestic and international bodies for stakes involving billions of dollars." See Richard J. Wilson, *Practical Training in Law in the Netherlands: Big Law Model or Clinical Model, and the Call of Public Interest Law*, 8 (1) UTRECHT LAW REVIEW 179 (2012).
[48] I.e., Freshfields Bruckhaus Deringer, Herbert Smith Freehills, Hogan Lovells, Norton Rose or Slaughter and May, see www.bpp.com/accelerated-lpc (November 25, 2015).
[49] Wilson, *supra* note 47, at 178–79. See also http://thelawfirmschool.nl/ (November 25, 2015).
[50] We should note that the BBP law school does run a law clinic, although it has no focus on EU law, see www.bpp.com/bpp-university/pro-bono/advice (November 25, 2015).
[51] Of the approximately 15,000 law graduates in the UK in 2014, 5,000 went on to undertake training contracts (apprenticeships for solicitors). More than one-third of those will have secured jobs at the top twenty (Big Law) law firms. See The Law Society, Trends in the Solicitors' Profession: Annual Statistics Report 2014, http://www.lawsociety.org.uk/support-services/research-trends/annual-statistical-report-2014/ .
[52] EIPA Luxembourg, CCBE, *supra* note 38, at 19.

societal commitments that should drive the activity of all lawyers, in particular those who wield the most influence.

EU law clinics challenge the above-described status quo in a number of key respects. While all EU clinics will typically contain a textbook- and lecture-based component (a seminar on EU law or relevant aspects of it), they complement this with a fieldwork component that will expose students to the reality of the law. The student may be confronted with a Swedish woman and her Cameroonian husband seeking to build a life in France, or a Syrian refugee in Germany seeking to be reunited with his family who are stuck an asylum seeker reception centre in Lampedusa, or even with a human rights NGO looking to learn more about how it can make better use of EU law in its advocacy to reform EU asylum law. In these moments, the students is dropped into the deep end and forced to come to terms with the complexities of EU legal practice. How does the Citizens' Rights Directive[53] or the Family Reunification Directive[54] apply in X country to Y family? To what extent can the Dublin Regulation[55] be relied on and operationalized in X judicial or institutional context? What position have the institutions taken with respect to X, and how do national authorities practically deal with Y? In addition to being forced to tackle head-on such tricky questions, the students will come to see not only how EU law can directly impact the lives of real persons, but also how their expertise may improve those lives. It would be almost impossible for the student to get this kind of experience on the average EU law course that you might find in universities and training institutions across Europe today.

At the EU Public Interest Clinic in particular, we seek to promote the active learning of EU law rooted in practical experience and the real life of the law. We do this by having our student teams (of two to three students) work directly for NGO clients seeking to make use of EU law in some respect in their advocacy work. For example, our students, working for NGO clients, have prepared complaints to the European Ombudsman on issues such as judicial transparency at the CJEU or secrecy in the context of infringement proceedings. They have drafted directives on whistle-blower protection and alcohol marketing regulation. They have written legal memos on biodiversity and the Common Agricultural Policy, and on freedom of panorama under European copyright law. This work has required them to master both the fundamentals of EU law (the Treaties; the principles of conferral, subsidiarity, and proportionality) and become experts in specialized fields (EU copyright law, EU agricultural law, and EU transparency law). In addition however, they

[53] Directive 2004/38/EC of the European Parliament and of the Council of April 29, 2004, on the right of citizens of the Union and their family members to move and reside freely within the territory of the Member States, OJ L 158, 30.4.2004.
[54] Council Directive 2003/86/EC of September 22, 2003, on the right to family reunification. OJ L 251, 03/10/2003 P. 0012–0018.
[55] Council Regulation (EC) No. 343/2003 of February 18, 2003, establishing the criteria and mechanisms for determining the Member State responsible for examining an asylum application lodged in one of the Member States by a third-country national, OJ L 50 of 25.2.2003.

are required to come to terms with how EU law works in practice; the real weight and value of the law in any given context. It is hard to see how this level of exposure to the law would be achievable in a university setting outside the context of a clinic. Beyond these benefits to teaching and training, however, EU clinics also attain a higher ethical objective: they sensitize students to public interest values and prove to them that they can effectively pursue such values in their professional lives.

Transcending Educational Goals

The extent to which teaching and practice across the continent emphasizes or embraces questions of access to justice has not been academically explored and so, again, we must proceed on the basis of anecdote. Certainly, you can find courses on Union citizenship, EU asylum law, and EU labour law that take a keen interest in EU law from a social and political perspective.[56] Such courses, sometimes decedents in one way or another of the critical and realist legal traditions, seek to place EU law in its social and political context.[57] However, identifying courses with such an orientation at the bachelor's degree level will not be easy, and, more significantly, such courses will rarely bring students into direct and experiential confrontation with the political, social, and raw, real-life existence of the law.

When it comes to the practice of EU law, again, you can find notable examples of legal practice oriented towards access to justice. For example, for those who cannot afford a lawyer, there are a handful of individuals across Europe officially tasked by the EU to provide free-of-charge EU law advice (albeit that this is limited to information, advice, and problem-solving; i.e. not case management). More than 100,000 queries are received every year by the dedicated staff working for the various EU-wide free EU law advice providers (i.e. Europe Direct, SOLVIT, Your Europe Advice, and the Europeans Citizens Action Service). However, the number of cases and enquiries received is on the rise every year while staffing levels are stagnating or even decreasing.[58] Even at a generous rate of handling 200,000 queries per year, only 0.04% of the EU population is being serviced. At the national level, of course you have many sole practitioners and small and medium-sized law firms that engage in providing paid advice (sometimes funded or subsidized by legal aid) on issues such as freedom of movement, pensions, welfare benefits, consumer protection, human rights, and other issues where EU law plays a significant role. However, EU law–

---

[56] Here we think of EU scholars such Francis Synder, Christian Joerges, Michelle Everson, Jo Shaw, Catherine Barnard, and Claire Kilpatrick. *See also* Charlotte O'Brien, *European Union Law*, in INTEGRATING SOCIO-LEGAL STUDIES INTO THE LAW CURRICULUM (C. Hunter, ed., Palgrave Macmillan 2012),184.

[57] *See, e.g.*, the "law in context" approach developed by Francis Snyder, in NEW DIRECTIONS IN EUROPEAN COMMUNITY LAW (London: Weidenfeld & Nicolson, 1990), 3; and F. Snyder, *The Effectiveness of European Community Law: Institutions, Processes, Tools and Techniques*, 56 MODERN L. REV.19–56 (1993).

[58] *See* http://ec.europa.eu/civil_service/about/figures/index_en.htm.

related advice would often not be covered by legal aid in many European jurisdictions,[59] and so the situation for those persons in need of EU law advice (or who might benefit from such advice) but lacking the financial resources to afford a lawyer remains bleak.

CLE seeks to challenge this status quo. So far as teaching is concerned, many EU clinics (and certainly those discussed in this chapter) have a large focus on access to justice.[60] Whether that means working with low-income families trying to take advantage of their EU free movement rights (as in the case of the EU Rights Clinic), asylum seekers and refugees (the IUC Clinic), or civil society organizations (the EU Public Interest Clinic), these clinics all seek to extend EU law advice to those individuals or organizations who might ordinarily struggle to take advantage of paid EU law advice for one reason or another.

The EU Clinic in particular combines a focus on access to justice with a focus on participatory democracy and civic engagement. The EU Clinic takes inspiration from a model of public interest law that was first pioneered by Ralph Nader in the 1960s and 1970s. These public interest lawyers saw themselves as "citizen representatives" (or citizen lobbyists), taking aim at the Kafkaesque inaccessibility and opaqueness of various US governmental bureaucracies and the corporations they were mandated to regulate. The goal was to open up these agencies by enhancing public awareness and promoting the engagement of citizen groups and organizations (e.g. consumer groups) in the decision-making process via lobbying and litigation. The EU Clinic takes this tried and tested brand of public interest lawyering and applies it to the EU institutional and policy context. As already discussed, consequent upon the growing sophistication and complexity of the EU machinery, its attendant intangibility for the average EU citizen, the increasing role played by the EU institutions in regulating various aspects of the daily lives of Europeans, and the expansion of well-financed lobbying activity within the EU policy process (there are an estimated 25,000 lobbyists in Brussels), the EU citizenry are in desperate need of their own "citizen representatives." To this end, there are a growing number of NGOs representing various important social issues operating within the EU policy context (as many as 300 are based in Brussels alone). However, NGOs often lack the skills and resources to effectively advocate for the interests of their European constituents. Too often, policymaking resembles a David and Goliath contest, in which corporate interests hire Goliath and the public interest lies in the hands of David.

Against this background context, the EU Clinic seeks to expand access to justice by working for NGOs that aim to hold the EU institutions to account and provide a countervailing force to undue business influence by representing diffuse public interests. These NGOs may have limited financial resources, or they may simply

---

[59] See, e.g., Chapter 10 by Anthony Valcke in this volume, discussing legal aid in the UK.
[60] See the results of the survey on legal clinical education across Europe by ##Clelia Bartoli, Legal Clinics in Europe: For a Commitment of Higher Education to Social Justice, Special Issue DIRITTO E QUESTIONI PUBBLICHE 52–53 (2016) (showing the various areas of intervention and the major clients).

deprioritize spending on legal services; thus, by providing such services for free, the Clinic hopes to enhance their advocacy capacity and thus their ability to represent the public interest. We take leave from the institutional context rather than from a particular issue-based vision of social justice and thus engage in various policy areas ranging from public health and the environment to consumer protection, as well as in more horizontal issues such as institutional openness and judicial transparency.

We maintain a process-oriented vision of justice which consists in enhancing mechanisms and channels of democratic participation while promoting good legal practices which may ultimately not only encourage active citizen engagement among our students but also promote an active citizenry more broadly. To this end, we rely upon a growing network of *pro bono* consultants who share our values and are willing to share their expertise and experience with our students. In these respects, the EU Clinic transcends the aims of "typical" EU law teaching quite significantly.

The Weight and Value of Internationalization

During project selection, the EU Clinic heavily weights the possibility in any given project for direct engagement with the EU institutions. We believe that through interaction with bodies at the supranational level, our students can better equip themselves to be effective lawyers in Europe (in whichever capacity they ultimately practice). As noted earlier, our students have submitted complaints to the European Ombudsman, they have written to and presented for Members of the European Parliament (MEPs) and Commission officials, and drafted shadow briefs for the CJEU. Through their experiences in the Clinic, our students learn first-hand how the EU legislative process works and the relative roles and relations between the EU institutions. They learn where pressure should be exerted and at what point in order to make effective use of the policy process for advocacy purposes. At a more practical level, they learn how to write an email to an EU official, draft a blog post entry, and adapt their legal jargon to a generally legally illiterate NGO client.

This kind of training prepares them for professional roles within the institutions equally as it prepares them for roles at NGOs or within private practice. In our opinion, legal practice in Europe today necessitates some degree of awareness of and understating about the role and impact of supranational law and institutions, and, due to the complexity of the supranational legal field, a lecture- and textbook-based course will likely prove insufficient. This is due to the simple fact that, consequent upon the nature of EU law and policy, the difference between knowledge and practice is particularly significant. In practice, EU law will be applied differently across the Union, in spite of the conceptual claims of uniformity of application and effect. Even more critically, the EU policy process is marked by inequality of influence (both among the institutions and between civil society and private interests) in spite of what one might read in a textbook chapter on the EU's institutional make-up. In practice, there may be all manner of obstacles (financial, evidentiary, administrative) between an individual and their EU law rights, in spite of what you might read about the citizenship provisions in the Treaties.

Through exposure to the real life of supranational law and the institutions that produce and interpret it, our students will be better lawyers, endowed with core competencies related to research, advocacy, and document production. Ultimately, unlike many lawyers, they will have no reason to fear supranational sources and processes when they next encounter them in their professional lives. By gaining some familiarity and fluency with these sources, they might instead use them creatively to the benefit of their clients and, possibly, of society as a whole.

Cooperation and Diffusion in CLE

The EU Public Interest Clinic has a number of different models of collaboration which will likely benefit the students in their long-term professional practice and may also have wider benefits related to civic participation in the context of EU democracy. Under the first model, we are collaborating with our NGO clients. The relationship between the client and the Clinic goes beyond one of simple service delivery. In many respects, we are working together with one another to pursue common goals well beyond the individual assignment. A clear example would be our work with Transparency International (drafting a directive on whistle blowing protection) and Access Info Europe (perusing a complaint with the Ombudsman regarding judicial transparency), where the partnership continues well after the formal completion of the Clinic project (i.e. when the students leave the Clinic). This ethos of ongoing partnership is emphasized during the students' time in the Clinic. They are encouraged to maintain regular communication with their client contacts (both via email and Skype), and they also meet in person at least once during the three-month term of the Clinic. Sometimes, they rely on the work performed by their predecessors in the Clinic and question their choices.

In addition to this client–provider interaction, the Clinic relies on *pro bono* collaboration with academics and practitioners of EU law. Each Clinic project has both a lead scientific advisor (LSA) and an on-call clinic fellow. The LSAs are typically leading, established, or junior academics or seasoned practitioners in a relevant field, while the fellows will be PhD students or post-docs with relevant legal or policy knowledge. The *pro bono* actors work closely with the students, providing feedback on numerous occasions on the student work and also discussing questions of legal strategy and how to handle client relationships. They do so both offline (by visiting the Clinic) and online (via Skype calls). In this way, the Clinic incorporates – and modernizes – elements of the legal apprenticeship model found across much of Europe into the classroom.

We are hopeful that in partnering with clients and other legal actors on a voluntary basis the Clinic will help to spread a culture of *pro bono* work and sensitize various actors in the EU legal field to providing and receiving *pro bono* legal services. After all, we believe that, for lawyers, the provision of such services is a professional duty and, in the context of the EU (i.e. characterized by contested democratic legitimacy and accountability), it also becomes a civic duty.[61]

Beyond these two models of collaboration (client–provider and peer-to-peer interaction), the Clinic also benefits from and embraces collaboration both in its origins and in its broader practice. In this manner, we simultaneously benefit from and contribute towards the diffusion of CLE. It is clear from existing literature that CLE is experiencing somewhat of a "global movement" that has resulted from significant investment into the practice by US funders such as USAID, the Ford Foundation, the Open Society Foundations, and the ABA.[62] These organizations have invested time, expertise, and money into growing a culture of clinical teaching in North and South America, Southern Africa, and Central and Eastern Europe. The fallout of this investment appears to be a gradual diffusion of clinical teaching across the globe, and Europe (in particular Eastern Europe) is no exception. Certainly, the EU Public Interest Clinic bears the hallmarks of this process both in its origins and in its practice. In terms of origins, as discussed earlier, the Clinic would not have emerged without the input of NYU Law School, whose experience with CLE dates back to the early US clinical movement which really took institutional shape in the 1960s and 1970s.[63] Moreover, in terms of inspiration, we have been deeply inspired by clinical colleagues from both the United States[64] and Europe. In particular, we have learned a great deal from our fellow EU law clinics in Brussels and Turin, not to mention the broader European clinic movement (through the attendance of training events and conferences organized by the International Journal of Clinical Legal Education and the European Network for Clinical Legal Education), and, as previously discussed, the NYU Regulatory Policy Clinic.

In terms of our practice we, in turn, have operated as a vessel for the spread of clinical practice. We have, through our projects, worked with colleagues and students based at universities (such as KU Leuven, Oxford, Louvain-la-Neuve, Utrecht, Liverpool) that do not yet (or did not at the time) have institutionalized clinics. For instance, we have worked with students at the European University Institute (EUI) in Florence on a project with Access Info Europe. We relied on the

---

[61] According to the results of the survey on legal clinical education across Europe by Bartoli, the vast majority of European-based legal clinics do not perceive EU law as important for their own work. See Bartoli, *supra* note 60, at 59.

[62] See, generally, Frank S. Bloch, ed. THE GLOBAL CLINICAL MOVEMENT: EDUCATING LAWYERS FOR SOCIAL JUSTICE (Oxford University Press 2010); Edwin Rekosh. *Constructing Public Interest Law: Transnational Collaboration and Exchange in Central and Eastern Europe*, 13 UCLA J. INT'L L. & FOREIGN AFF. (2008); Richard J. Wilson, *Training for Justice: The Global Reach of Clinical Legal Education*, 22 PENN STATE INT'L. L. REV. (2004); Margaret Martin Barry, Jon C. Dubin, and Peter A. Joy. *Clinical Education for This Millennium: The Third Wave*, 7 CLINICAL L. REV. (2000).

[63] See Steven H. Leleiko, *The Clinic and NYU.* 24 (4) J. LEGAL EDUC. 429–61 (1972).

[64] At our NYU sister clinics and also at UCLA where one of the authors spent some time on a Fulbright exchange.

multilingual and multijurisdictional offerings of the EUI law school to make access to document requests across the EU part of a wider strategic litigation campaign related to judicial transparency. We also collaborated with colleagues at the University of Liverpool who specialized in EU health law and policy to draft an EU directive on alcohol marketing. These are but a handful of examples, but certainly we see ourselves as ambassadors for CLE, especially in the context of EU law, and aim to spread the practice where we can.

Future of CLE in Europe

The EU Public Interest Clinic has evolved considerably since its inception in 2014. While it has remained faithful to its original objectives, its methodology, format, and actors have grown more sophisticated. The quality of the clinical educational process has improved. Through a process of trial and error, we have not only adjusted the CLE method to our contingencies, but also strived to make it generalizable beyond our own clinical realities.[65] To ease and enhance the supervisory tasks required in clinical education, we have not only expanded the network of *pro bono* advisors involved in the individual projects, but also pioneered the use of behavioural-based insights to maintain motivation and prompt students' self-guidance.[66] The ideal result of self-directed learning in a clinical context is that students take ownership over and pride in their Clinic projects and also, to an extent, over their learning process. In order to achieve this, we have strived to maximize student choice, but also pay close attention to "choice architecture."[67] Behavioural sciences tell us that while a degree of choice can be constructive for motivation, providing too many options may be overwhelming for individuals and result in poor matching between preferences and the choices made. A solution (employed by the Clinic) is to offer fixed menus of options for students and provide information about what each choice would entail. It is only by playing with mechanisms such as framing and defaults that we are able to steer students towards the most desirable learning paths. While they can always opt out of our pre-framed indications, they tend to follow our indications and stick to them.

As shown by the charts here, both the number of projects and variety of matters have grown exponentially over a short period of time.

---

[65] EU Public Interest Clinic, Annual Report 2014, Annual Report 2015, and Annual Report 2016 (on file with the author but soon available on the dedicated webpage of the EU Clinic).
[66] Annual Report 2015, 8–9.
[67] R. H. Thaler and C. R. Sunstein, NUDGE: IMPROVING DECISIONS ABOUT HEALTH, WEALTH, AND HAPPINESS (New Haven: Yale University Press 2008); A. Dan, PREDICTABLY IRRATIONAL: THE HIDDEN FORCES THAT SHAPE OUR DECISIONS (New York: Harper Collins 2008); S. D. Levitt and S. J. Dubner, FREAKONOMICS: A ROGUE ECONOMIST EXPLORES THE HIDDEN SIDE OF EVERYTHING (New York: William Morrow 2005); D. Kahneman, THINKING, FAST AND SLOW (New York: Farrar, Straus and Giroux 2011); M. H. Bazerman and A. E. Tenbrunsel, BLIND SPOTS: WHY WE FAIL TO DO WHAT'S RIGHT AND WNAT TO DO ABOUT IT (Princeton: Princeton University Press 2011).

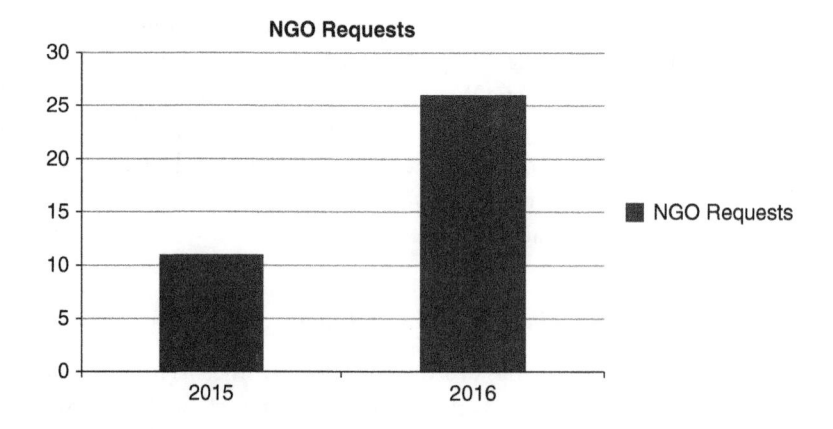

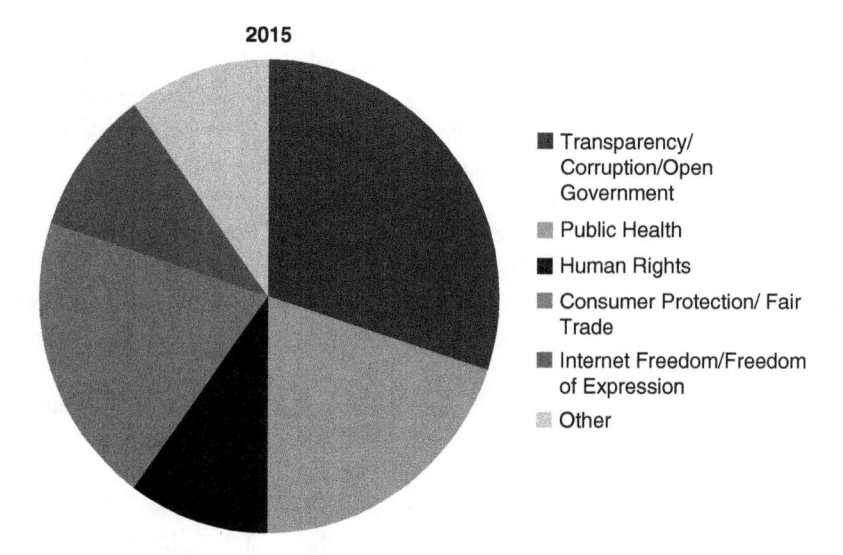

NGO Requests

[Bar chart: 2015 ≈ 11; 2016 = 26]

2015

[Pie chart with legend:
- Transparency/Corruption/Open Government
- Public Health
- Human Rights
- Consumer Protection/Fair Trade
- Internet Freedom/Freedom of Expression
- Other]

Number of NGO requests for assistance by the Clinic, substantive fields of NGO requests received by the Clinic, substantive fields of projects selected by the Clinic

Another major evolution of the clinic has to do with the number of clinic students enrolled. This number was not only halved, but also rendered more balanced in relation to the representation of its EU and US audiences.

As the EU Clinic is reaching maturity, both from a methodological and institutional perspective, our aim is to embed this clinical programme into a broader, nonacademic civil society organization capable of transforming the programme into a transnational clinic operating at both national and EU levels. When examined from afar (and possibly not through the clinician's eyes), the clinical programme developed

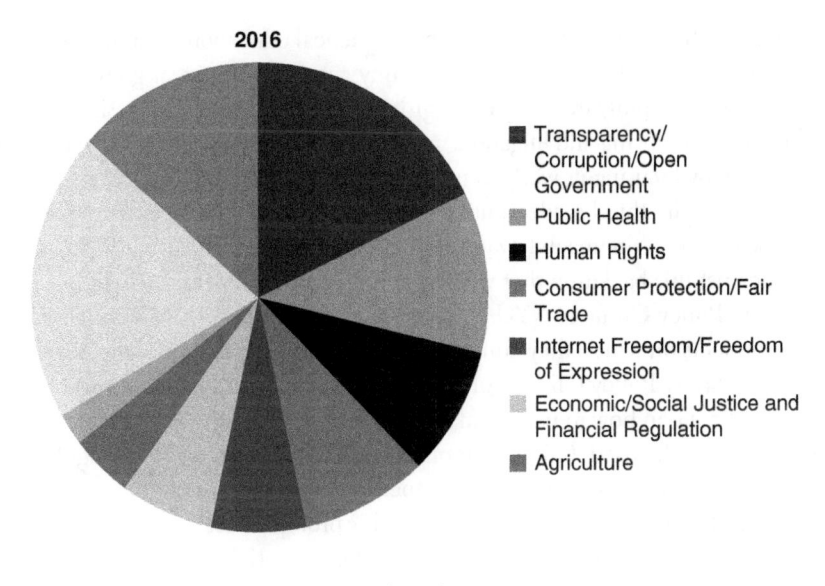

2016

- Transparency/Corruption/Open Government
- Public Health
- Human Rights
- Consumer Protection/Fair Trade
- Internet Freedom/Freedom of Expression
- Economic/Social Justice and Financial Regulation
- Agriculture

(cont.)

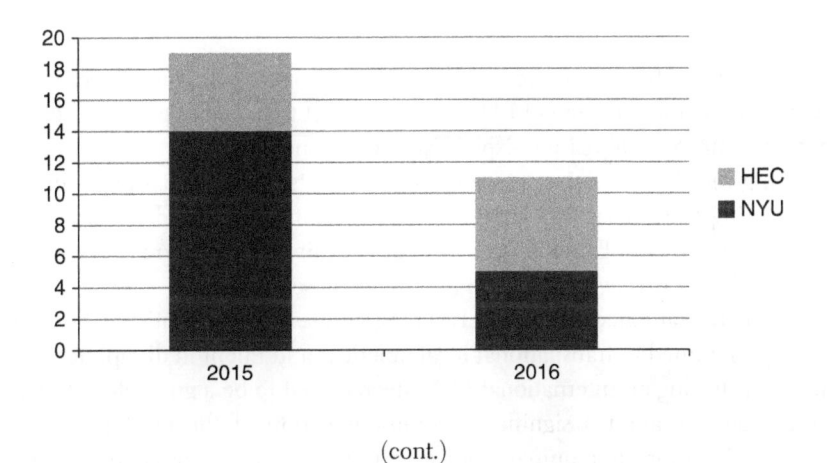

(cont.)

2015	2016
Public Health (2) Transparency/ Corruption/Open Government (1) Consumer Protection (1) Internet Freedom (1)	Transparency/ Corruption/Open Government (3) Environment and Agriculture (1)

in Paris fulfils the need for a better and more practical education of European lawyers – and especially public interest lawyers, a tiny category with great growth potential within the EU. Rapidly evolving EU legislation is offering ever-increasing space for public interest lobbying and litigation, and our clinic operates within and contributes to this space by focusing its work on increased participation and transparency. When contextualized in this broader public space, the EU Clinic seems to provide a prototype for a new approach towards legal and advocacy skill-sharing.

It is against this backdrop that we aim at enhancing cooperation with our fellow Regulatory Policy Clinic at NYU to have the two structures actively collaborate on similar projects on which they could work in parallel. For example, the New York–based Regulatory Policy Clinic worked in the second semester of 2013 and the first semester of 2014 on how to use social media for petitions for rule-making, while the Paris-based EU-focused Clinic elaborated improvements to be brought to the European Citizens' Initiative based on experiences of direct or participative democracy at the State level in the United States. This prompted teams on the two sides of the Atlantic to have fruitful discussions on the potential role and danger of the Internet in participatory processes.

CONCLUSION

Amid the successful experiences gained by a few, pioneering clinics, the case for the establishment and diffusion of EU law clinics is set to become more evident in the years to come. Several reasons explain and justify such a fate.

First, given the increasing awareness of the limits of traditional legal education and training to craft lawyers with a beyond-the-nation-state understanding of the daily legal realities of Europe, the spread of EU clinical education may enable the law schools and the legal profession to remedy those failures.

Second, the saturated market of LLM programmes no longer satisfies the demand for lawyers trained in transnational legal practices and fluent in disciplines beyond the law. If having an international LLM degree used to be a guarantee of employability, today – amid a significant commodification of the legal masters' programmes[68] – more is required from a young, entry-level lawyer to impress the hiring partners. More than ten years ago, this led the European Legal Faculties Association to encourage European legal education institutions to take "a number of additional and more courageous steps" towards curriculum reform.[69] In particular, the proposal put forward was to focus bachelor's degree education on national law

---

[68] Poiares, *supra* note 22, at vi (citing more than 100 European law schools offering some form of LLM open to foreign students).

[69] ELFA, For a European Space of Legal Education, 2002. Unpublished statement of the European Law Faculties Association concerning the Bologna-Declaration of the European Ministers of Education of 1999; The ELFA Board, 31 May 2002, http://www.eua.be/eua/jsp/en/upload/Position_paper_ELFA.1074529456361.pdf.

and the master's level on European and international education. While this two-degree model (bachelor's and master's) seems to satisfy the market demand for a dual legal education (national and international), postponing the study of EU law to the master's level risks being short-sighted. For the reasons mentioned earlier, EU and national are so intertwined in modern legal reality that any effort at distinguishing between them appears artificially and methodologically disputable. Mainstreaming clinical education into the bachelor's programme could offer a solution to a more Europeanized curriculum. But given the Americanization of legal education prompted by the panoply of LLM programmes,[70] clinical education may also provide, as illustrated by the EU Clinic and several other clinics studied in this volume, a differentiating factor in an increasingly competitive environment – an almost magic formula to educate "practice-ready lawyers" for today's European legal profession.

Third, the unprecedented problems faced by the EU in recent years, ranging from the economic slowdown to the migrant crisis, have shown the urgent need to mobilize a greater number of lawyers to address the urgent needs of both EU and non-EU populations. Many law students and young and senior lawyers come to the law out of a deep interest in contributing to and improving social justice. Although this aspiration to make a difference persists after graduation, the realities of the profession often define success at the expense of the satisfaction of personal and societal aspirations. We submit that this is often the case because European law students typically lack sufficient exposure and access to real-life public interest jobs. Legal clinics may provide a first-hand exposure to new pathways of financially viable legal professions (in NGOs, foundations, etc.) and instil a public interest vocation in young law graduates. As illustrated on the occasion of the EU migrant crisis, innovative forms of cooperation between EU law clinics and *pro bono* practices across Europe may – through an iterative process – set new professional standards in public interest law. Those tragic emergencies provide an unmissable opportunity for the legal profession to address the pressing problems of our time, problems that neither the state nor the market seem capable of solving. Clinical education may provide a unique chance for the EU legal profession to prove to be "a set of leaders with legitimacy in the eyes of the citizenry."[71]

Last, but not least, CLE may also provide an answer to another systemic problem that, although less salient in public opinion, Europe faces today. This is the unequal representation of interests in the EU policy process. As illustrated by the EU Public Interest Clinic, CLE might offer a unique opportunity to counter such an unbalanced situation by providing assistance to NGOs active in EU policymaking while offering a unique experiential learning opportunity to law students. This exposure to the world of advocacy on behalf of nonprofit organizations may shape lawyers ready to continue serving on a *pro bono* those organizations once in private practice.

---

[70] Poiares, *supra* note 22, at vi. [71] US Supreme Court, *Grutter v. Bollinger*, 539 US 306 (2003).

The EU Public Interest Clinic – together with its fellow EU clinics – fills a gap in the academic, legal, and public policy landscapes within the EU, joining practical lawyering and public advocacy skills; excellent academic institutions, practitioners, and community members; and pressing problems within the European sphere. In so doing, EU law clinical education does not only confirm CLE's traditional dual nature (educational and societal) and dual beneficiary (students and client organizations) but also contributes to building a more equal European society.

When measured against its socioeconomic potential (in reshaping legal education while contributing to social justice), one might expect EU legal clinical education to enjoy not only wider recognition but also greater institutional support, both from EU institutions and its Member States.

This chapter demonstrates how EU law clinical education might offer a promising and privileged springboard to build a case for clinical education across Europe.

10

The EU Rights Clinic at the University of Kent in Brussels

EU Free Movement Law in Action

Anthony Valcke

INTRODUCTION

The European Union (EU) Rights Clinic is the first law clinic that works exclusively in the field of EU law and the first law clinic to be set up in Belgium. The Clinic provides live-client advice on the free movement of persons. It can be categorized as a "hybrid" law clinic given that it is a joint project of the University of Kent in Brussels[1] and the European Citizen Action Service (ECAS),[2] a nongovernmental organization (NGO) based in Brussels. The EU Rights Clinic was launched in January 2013 to coincide with the European Year of Citizens and offers assistance to EU citizens and their family members who encounter problems when exercising their right of free movement under EU law. The Clinic has the twin aim of giving clients a chance of resolving their case when they cannot otherwise access legal advice and giving clients an opportunity to contribute to improvements in European policy and legislation by using their personal experience as the basis for evidence-based advocacy.

The EU Rights Clinic is a live-client clinic staffed by postgraduate students enrolled in the EU Migration Law course at the University of Kent, who provide free assistance to the Clinic's clients under the supervision of a visiting lecturer who is also a qualified lawyer. The Clinic is also supported by volunteers PhD students and volunteer case workers drawn from civil society groups in Brussels, as well as volunteer legal researchers and translators who are based throughout the EU and work remotely. The Clinic has drawn on the invaluable pro bono assistance of lawyers from Brussels-based law firms, most notably Freshfields.[3] ECAS provides administrative support as well as the use of its facilities for clinic meetings.

---

[1] Further information about the University of Kent's Brussels School of International Studies can be found at https://www.kent.ac.uk/brussels/.
[2] ECAS is a Brussels-based nongovernmental organization whose mission includes the defence of the rights of free movement of people and promotes a more inclusive European citizenship. Further information on ECAS's mission and activities can be found on its website www.ecas.org.
[3] Details of the firm's *pro bono* activities can be found at www.freshfields.com/en/global/who_we_are /Pro_bono_global/.

As its name implies, the EU Rights Clinic is a specialized law clinic that focuses on the EU rules relating to the free movement of persons. The case work it handles is therefore linked to situations involving individuals who face problems in exercising their EU right of free movement, which represents somewhat of a niche area within the field of immigration law. In its first three years of operation, the Clinic received more than 370 individual requests for assistance[4] and provided concrete advice in sixty-two cases. The EU Rights Clinic was devised as a transnational law clinic that handles cases throughout Europe. As a result, it has taken up cases involving EU citizens facing problems in Belgium, Cyprus, France, Germany, Spain, Sweden, and the UK and has assisted NGOs based in Belgium and Spain. Some of its cases have been reported in the press, including its assistance to ECAS in obtaining access to documents relating to the UK's professed opt-out from the EU Charter of Fundamental Rights,[5] lodging complaints to the EU institutions regarding excessive delays experienced by citizens crossing the border between Spain and Gibraltar,[6] and its assistance to EU citizens fighting their expulsion from Belgium.[7]

EMERGENCE OF CLE AT THE UNIVERSITY OF KENT IN BRUSSELS

The catalyst for the creation of the EU Rights Clinic was primarily personal. After working several years in the field of competition law, the author decided on a career change that led him to start work in the field of international development. Initially working as legal advisor on a human rights vetting programme in connection with the reform of Liberia's armed forces,[8] a vacancy with the American Bar Association offered him the opportunity to direct the organization's USAID-funded rule of law reform programme in Liberia.[9] Part of the programme involved the establishment of a legal aid clinic at the University of Liberia, and this instilled the idea to establish a law clinic upon the author's return to Belgium. A vacancy subsequently opened up

---

[4] One hundred eighty-seven of these consisted in requests for information which were referred to other services that provide legal information. One hundred one requests related to the same complaint in respect of delays at the border between Spain and Gibraltar.

[5] *See also*, European Ombudsman, Ombudsman Welcomes the Commission's Disclosure of Documents on UK Opt-Out from Charter of Fundamental Rights, Press release 5/2013, March 4, 2013, www.ombudsman.europa.eu/en/press/release.faces/en/49424/html.bookmark.

[6] *See also*, UK Threatens Legal Action over Gibraltar, EURACTIV (Brussels, August 13, 2013), www.euractiv.com/section/justice-home-affairs/news/uk-threatens-legal-action-over-gibraltar/.

[7] *See also*, Belgium Says Europeans Not Welcome If They Don't Take on Work, Euronews (Lyon, March 11, 2016), www.euronews.com/2016/03/11/belgium-says-jobless-europeans-not-welcome/.

[8] For background, *see*, International Crisis Group, Liberia: Uneven Progress in Security Sector Reform, Africa Report N°148, January 13, 2009, www.crisisgroup.org/en/regions/africa/west-africa/liberia/148-liberia-uneven-progress-in-security-sector-reform.aspx.

[9] *See* American Bar Association's Rule of Law Initiative website for the former Liberia programme, www.americanbar.org/advocacy/rule_of_law/where_we_work/africa/liberia/programs.html; *see also* American Bar Association Rule of Law Initiative, Support for a Human Rights Culture in Liberia – Final Report, on the USAID website, https://dec.usaid.gov/dec/GetDoc.axd?ctID=ODVhZjk4NWQtM2YyMi00YjRmLTk xNjktZTcxMjM2NDBmY2Uy&pID=NTYw&attchmnt=VHJ1ZQ==&rID=MzUwMzUy.

at the University of Kent in Brussels to resume teaching EU migration law, which provided the opportunity to bring this idea to life.

Having been involved as an adviser on free movement issues for ECAS since 2005, the author had kept up to date with developments in this field of law. The creation of a law clinic specialized in EU free movement cases can also trace its origins to legal and political developments in this field. Institutional factors linked to the University of Kent's commitment to clinical legal education (CLE) and its strong European links have also played a determining role in the establishment of the EU Rights Clinic, as has the invaluable support provided by its civil society partner, ECAS.

Legal Context: The "Implementation Gap" in EU Free Movement Law

The EU Rights Clinic was born out of a desire to teach EU free movement law from a practical perspective, with the aim of exploring and addressing the so-called "implementation gap."[10] This refers to the state of disconnect between the legislative framework as it is intended to work in theory and the way the rules are applied in practice by the EU Member States. The EU rules on the free movement of persons provide a particularly poignant example of such an implementation gap.

In 2006, a new EU directive relating to the free movement of people came into force.[11] It is the key legal instrument that regulates the free movement of persons within the EU. Adopted in 2004, it aimed to consolidate the existing different EU legal instruments on residence rights, reflect developments in the case law on EU citizenship, simplify visa and residence formalities, and improve the rights of family members. However, the implementation of this directive by the Member States has been far from satisfactory, and the Commission has deplored the fact that not a single Member State had been able to transpose the Directive correctly.[12]

---

[10] The term "implementation gap" has been coined by the European Commission and refers to the divide "between the EU legal framework and the way it is implemented and applied in practice"; Commission, *The Single Market through the Eyes of the People: A Snapshot of Citizens' and Businesses' Views and Concerns*, Press release IP/11/1074, September 26, 2011. See also Mario Monti, A New Strategy for the Single Market – At the Service of Europe's Economy and Society: Report to the President of the European Commission José Manuel Barroso (May 9, 2010), 38–39; Sir David Edwards et al., MIND THE GAP: TOWARDS A BETTER ENFORCEMENT OF EUROPEAN CITIZENS' RIGHTS OF FREE MOVEMENT, 2nd ed. (ECAS 2013), 8–11; Simona Millio, FROM POLICY TO IMPLEMENTATION IN THE EUROPEAN UNION: THE CHALLENGE OF A MULTI-LEVEL GOVERNANCE SYSTEM (I. B. Tauris 2010), 3–21.

[11] Directive 2004/38/EC of the European Parliament and of the Council of April 29, 2004, on the right of citizens of the Union and their family members to move and reside freely within the territory of the Member States, amending Regulation (EEC) No 1612/68 and repealing Directives 64/221/EEC, 68/360/EEC, 72/194/EEC, 73/148/EEC, 75/34/EEC, 75/35/EEC, 90/364/EEC, 90/365/EEC, and 93/96/EEC [2004] OJ L 158/77.

[12] Commission, *Report from the Commission to the European Parliament and the Council on the Application of Directive 2004/38/EC on the Right of Citizens of the Union and Their Family Members to Move and Reside Freely within the Territory of the Member States*, COM(2008) 840 final, 1.

Problems have not been limited to transposition: namely, the adoption of national enabling legislation by the Member States. The application of the rules on the ground has also generated all sorts of problems for citizens who move around the EU. The Commission's triennial EU citizenship reports have consistently referred to difficulties relating to the practical application of the directive,[13] and its public consultation on EU citizenship conducted in 2013 found that more than 25% of citizens had reported having encountered problems when moving within the EU.[14] Moreover, the Commission's own problem-solving networks, such as Your Europe Advice and SOLVIT, consistently report a relatively high proportion of cases relating to misapplication of the rules on the free movement of persons.[15] These findings all tend to confirm the existence of an implementation gap that affects the EU rules on free movement and, from an educational perspective, provide numerous opportunities and material to study EU law in action.

Sociopolitical Context: Free Movement under Threat

Paradoxically, although free movement is regarded as the most cherished right of EU citizens,[16] the free movement of persons has also become a politically sensitive issue in recent times.[17] The combination of EU enlargement, the ongoing economic crisis, disenchantment with mainstream politics, and the current refugee crisis have led to calls not only from populist politicians[18] but also from elected governments[19]

---

[13] See, e.g., Commission, *Report from the Commission to the European Parliament, the Council and the European Economic and Social Committee under Article 25 TFEU: On Progress towards Effective EU Citizenship 2007–2010*, COM(2010) 602 final 7, in which it revealed that it had initiated "63 infringement proceedings ... against Member States in the area of free movement and residence of EU citizens"; Commission, *Report from the Commission to the European Parliament, the Council and the European Economic and Social Committee under Article 25 TFEU: On Progress towards Effective EU Citizenship 2011–2013*, COM(2013) 270 final 4–5.

[14] Commission, *The EU Citizens' Agenda: Europeans Have Their Say* (2012) 8.

[15] See, e.g., Commission, *Report from the Commission to the European Parliament, the Council and the European Economic and Social Committee: EU Citizenship Report 2013 – EU Citizens: Your Rights, Your Future*, COM(2013) 269 final 11, which notes that 21% of Your Europe Advice enquiries and 13% of SOLVIT complaints related to free movement and residence rights in 2012; *see further*, Commission, Single Market Scoreboard (Your Europe Advice and SOLVIT governance tools), ec.europa.eu/internal_market/scoreboard/performance_by_governance_tool/.

[16] Standard Eurobarometer 79, *Public Opinion in the European Union*, Spring 2013, 33; Commission, *European Commission Upholds Free Movement of People*, Press release MEMO/13/1041, November 25, 2013; Eurobarometer 83, Report on European Citizenship, Spring 2015, 4.

[17] *Editorial Comments: Free Movement of Persons: Salvaging the Dream and Explaining the Nightmare* 51 COMMON MARKET LAW REVIEW 729–39 (2014). For a discussion of the political controversies generated by the EU free movement rules, *see* Christina Boswell and Andrew Geddes, MIGRATION AND MOBILITY IN THE EUROPEAN UNION (Palgrave Macmillan 2010), 190–195.

[18] *Europe's Far-Right Parties Seek Swiss-Style Immigration Curbs*, FINANCIAL TIMES (London, February 14, 2014).

[19] In April 2013, the Ministers of four EU Member States – the UK, Austria, Germany, and the Netherlands – wrote to the Irish Presidency of the European Council on the matter of free movement of persons within the Union. The letter specifically criticized the existing legal framework of Directive

for a rethink of one of the cornerstones of the EU's Single Market. Free movement was one of the key issues that determined the outcome of the UK's referendum on EU membership in favour of "Brexit,"[20] driven by the belief that the UK would be better able to control immigration if it were outside the EU.[21]

These developments have already had an impact on the implementation of the rules at national level.[22] Moreover, this adverse political climate has not gone unnoticed by the Judges in Luxembourg.[23] The recent rulings in *Dano*,[24] *Alimanovic*,[25] and *Garcia-Nieto*,[26] as well as the Commission's unsuccessful infringement proceedings against the UK,[27] would suggest a hardening of the Court of Justice's case law in respect of the free movement rights not only as regards economically inactive citizens[28] but also formerly employed workers.[29] These judgments are

---

2004/38 (n 11) as regards expulsions and re-entry bans. It also concerned the issue of "benefits tourism," namely the abuse of national welfare systems by EU citizens who move around the EU, and raised concerns of fraud, including marriages of convenience. The measures proposed by the quartet included curtailing the right of newly arrived migrants to claim benefits and introducing bans on re-entry for those found to be abusing or defrauding the system: docs.dpaq.de/3604-130415_letter_to _presidency_final_1_2.pdf. The letter was subsequently followed by a personal call by David Cameron to impose further restrictions on the free movement of persons; see *Free Movement within Europe Needs To Be Less Free*, FINANCIAL TIMES (November 26, 2013).

[20] John Curtice, The Two Poles of the Referendum Debate: Immigration and the Economy (*What the UK Thinks*, January 28, 2016), whatukthinks.org/eu/analysis/the-two-poles-of-the-referendum-debate-immigration-and-the-economy/; Sara B. Hobolt, *The Brexit Vote: A Divided Nation, a Divided Continent*, 23 JOURNAL OF EUROPEAN PUBLIC POLICY 1259–77, 1262–63 (2016).

[21] Lord Ashcroft, How the United Kingdom Voted on Thursday ... and Why (Lord Ashcroft Polls, June 24, 2016), lordashcroftpolls.com/2016/06/how-the-united-kingdom-voted-and-why/; Paul Whitely and Harold Clarke, Brexit: Why Did Older Voters Choose to Leave the EU? (*The Conversation*, June 25, 2016) https://theconversation.com/why-did-older-voters-choose-brexit-its-a-matter-of-identity-61636; Asa Bennett, *Did Britain Really Vote Brexit to Cut Immigration?* (DAILY TELEGRAPH, June 29, 2016); *Explaining the Brexit Vote* (THE ECONOMIST, July 16, 2016).

[22] Jo Shaw, *Between Law and Political Truth? Member State Preferences, EU Free Movement Rules and National Immigration Law* 17 CAMBRIDGE YEARBOOK OF EUROPEAN LEGAL STUDIES 247–86 (2015).

[23] Steve Peers, Benefit Tourism by EU Citizens: The CJEU Just Says No (EU LAW ANALYSIS, November 11, 2014) eulawanalysis.blogspot.be/2014/11/benefit-tourism-by-eu-citizens-cjeu.html; Géraldine Renaudière, Free Movement and Social Benefits for Economically Inactive EU Citizens: The Dano Judgment in Historical Context (EU LAW ANALYSIS, November 12, 2014), eulawanalysis.blogspot.co.uk/2014/11/free-movement-and-social-benefits-for.html.

[24] Case C-333/13 *Dano* [2014] ECLI:EU:C:2014:2358 (judgment of November 11, 2014).

[25] Case C-67/14 *Alimanovic* [2015] ECLI:EU:C:2015:597 (judgment of September 15, 2015).

[26] Case C-299/14 *Garcia-Nieto* [2016] ECLI:EU:C:2016:114 (judgment of February 25, 2016).

[27] Case C-308–14 *Commission v UK* [2016] ECLI:EU:C:2016:436 (judgment of June 14, 2016).

[28] Daniel Thym, *The Elusive Limits of Solidarity: Residence Rights of and Social Benefits for Economically Inactive Union Citizens*' 52 COMMON MARKET LAW REVIEW 17–50 (2015); Herwig Verschueren, *Preventing "Benefit Tourism" in the EU: A Narrow or Broad Interpretation of the Possibilities Offered by the ECJ in Dano?* 52 COMMON MARKET LAW REVIEW 363–90 (2015).

[29] Steve Peers, EU Citizens' Access to Benefits: The CJEU Clarifies the Position of Former Workers (EU LAW ANALYSIS, September 15, 2015), eulawanalysis.blogspot.co.uk/2015/09/eu-citizens-access-to-benefits-cjeu.html; Sion Kramer, Had They Only Worked One Month Longer! An Analysis of the Alimanovic Case [2015] C-67/14 (EUROPEAN LAW, September 29, 2015), europeanlawblog.eu /?tag=c-6714-alimanovic; Maria Haag, C-67/14 Alimanovic: The Not So Fundamental Status of Union Citizenship? (DURHAM EUROPEAN LAW INSTITUTE LAW BLOG, September 29, 2015), https://

the latest in a string of cases where the Court has been granting greater latitude to Member States to restrict the ability of EU citizens to enjoy equal treatment, thereby heralding a retrograde phase in the development of free movement in the EU.[30]

There is a further risk that Member States take advantage of these rulings to impose new restrictions on the free movement of citizens.[31] Some may even feel emboldened to do so as a result of ambiguous statements made by European Commissioners about what the free movement of people should entail in practice.[32] Moreover, those Member States that are sympathetic to the UK's previous calls to restrict the free movement of persons[33] may be tempted to revive the deal that was proposed by the Council prior to the UK's referendum[34] and accordingly amend the EU legal framework as a way to placate British postreferendum demands[35] to control the flow of EU migrants into the UK and thereby ensure that the UK can remain a part of the Single Market.[36] As a result, there is a real potential risk of further degradation in how EU citizens experience free movement on the ground.

delilawblog.wordpress.com/2015/09/29/maria-haag-c%E2%80%916714-alimanovic-the-not-so-fundamental-status-of-union-citizenship/.

[30] See, to this effect, Eleanor Spaventa, *Earned Citizenship: Understanding Union Citizenship through Its Scope*, in EU CITIZENSHIP AND FEDERALISM: THE ROLE OF RIGHTS (Dimitry Kochenov, ed., Cambridge University Press 2017).

[31] See, to this effect, Michael Blauberger and Susanne Schmidt, *Welfare migration? Free Movement of EU Citizens and Access to Social Benefits* 1 RESEARCH AND POLITICS 1–7 (2014).

[32] In March 2015, Commission Vice-President Timmermans declared that "access to the labour market does not mean automatic access to social security systems. We will need to work with that with a number of Member states in the years to come": Commission Press Release, *Transcript of Speech of First Vice-President Timmermans to Policy Network, London: A Fresh Start*, Speech 15-4571, March 6, 2015. Such a statement is difficult to reconcile with Article 7 of Regulation (EU) No 492/2011 of the European Parliament and of the Council of April 5, 2011, on freedom of movement for workers within the Union [2011] OJ L141/1, which guarantees migrant workers access to all social and tax advantages enjoyed by national workers, or even with the Court's case law such as Joined Cases C-22/08 and C-23/08 *Vatsouras and Koupatantze* [2009] ECR I-4585, para 32. A month later, the Commissioner for Employment, Social Affairs, Skills and Labour Mobility, Marianne Thyssen, asserted that "we need to ensure that the rules reflect the changes in the economy and society and, as I said before, that they are seen as being fair by citizens and political leaders": Commission Press Release, *Intervention of Commissioner Marianne Thyssen at 3rd Labour Mobility Congress*, Speech 15-4841 (April 23, 2015). This appears to be echoing calls made by politicians in the UK for "fair movement not free movement"; see, e.g., Nick Clegg to Call for Tighter Controls on Immigration from New EU States, THE GUARDIAN (August 4, 2014), www.theguardian.com/uk-news/2014/aug/04/nick-clegg-tighter-controls-immigration-new-eu-states.

[33] For background, see *supra* note 19.

[34] See Letter by President Donald Tusk to the Members of the European Council on his proposal for a new settlement for the United Kingdom within the European Union, February 2, 2016, www.consilium.europa.eu/en/press/press-releases/2016/02/02-letter-tusk-proposal-new-settlement-uk/. For a discussion, see Steve Peers, The Final UK Renegotiation Deal: Immigration Issues (EU LAW ANALYSIS, February 20, 2016), eulawanalysis.blogspot.it/2016/02/the-final-uk-renegotiation-deal.html.

[35] May on Collision Course with Conservative Backbenchers over Hard Brexit (THE GUARDIAN, October 2, 2016).

[36] Rather than Offer Clarity, Brexit Has Sown Confusion in Europe (THE GUARDIAN, August 21, 2016); Ministers Press for Interim EU Deal to Avoid Article 50 "Cliff Edge" (THE GUARDIAN, November 6, 2016).

Institutional Factors: Leveraging Kent's Experience in CLE

The EU Rights Clinic has been fortunate to be able to draw upon the assistance and experience of the Kent Law Clinic. The University of Kent has pioneered the development of CLE in the UK: it was one of the first universities to establish a law clinic in the UK and the first to integrate clinical legal practice into the curriculum of its law degree.

The award-winning Kent Law Clinic[37] was originally established in 1973. After a hiatus during the 1980s, the clinic relaunched in 1992 and now provides full-service legal advice to the local community in the county of Kent in South East England. Run by practicing solicitors who are members of the academic staff of the Kent Law School, the clinic provides advice and representation in employment, housing, welfare benefits, immigration and asylum, contract, family, policing, and public access to land cases.

The Kent Law Clinic was established with two aims in mind: to provide a legal service to local people who need but cannot afford to pay for such a service and to enhance the education of students at Kent Law School.

The commitment to providing a public service lies at the heart of the Kent Law Clinic. A large number of students, academics, and solicitors and barristers in private practice locally have maintained the determination for many years to work together in providing a free legal service. It is a voluntary and collective endeavour that rests on a shared view that, in a modern, civilized society, every person should be able to obtain access to legal assistance in order to defend and improve their quality of life.

The Kent Law Clinic also exists to enrich the legal education of students by enabling them to work on live cases. The focus, in educational terms, is on improving their knowledge and understanding of the law and on developing their critical faculties. Participation in the Kent Law Clinic is intended to expose students to the impact of law outside the university. This forms part of the educational process through which Kent Law School aspires to deepen the learning and broaden the minds of its students and of all who work in the Clinic.

Although the Kent Law Clinic has served as a model for the EU Rights Clinic, there are some notable differences between the two clinics owing to the latter's highly specialized nature and its organizational structure. For example, the modest size of the University of Kent's campus in Brussels meant that establishing an integrated in-house clinic was not feasible and therefore an external partner needed to be found. Fortunately, the search for an external partner was relatively swiftly concluded when ECAS offered to physically host the clinic within its premises. ECAS was a natural fit, given its extensive track record in helping EU citizens in exercising their right of free movement and in-depth knowledge of the problems

---

[37] The clinic has received numerous awards recognizing and celebrating its work, which are detailed on its website, https://www.kent.ac.uk/law/clinic.

associated with its implementation.[38] The EU Rights Clinic can therefore be classified as a "hybrid" law clinic[39] in which students work in an NGO that is external to the law school but under direct case supervision of a law school clinician.

On a final point, it should not be forgotten that the creation of the first law clinic in the heart of Europe owes much to the University of Kent being the UK's only university to have a campus in Brussels.[40] The university's long-running participation in a range of European programmes undoubtedly facilitated its successful application for initial funding of the teaching costs relating to the EU Rights Clinic under the Jean Monnet programme.[41] This financial support was able to mitigate in part the typical budgetary constraints which any university faces when contemplating setting up a new clinical education programme. In addition, the costs relating to the clinical case work – including case work supervision, facilities, and administrative support – was assumed by ECAS, the joint partner in setting up the EU Rights Clinic. These costs are partly funded by an operating grant under the Europe for Citizens programme.[42]

REFORMING THE TEACHING AND PRACTICE OF EU LAW

It would be difficult to suggest that the teaching of EU law is exclusively concerned with theoretical instruction that relies on traditional methods of lecturing and assessment. In recent years, many imaginative courses have been developed that teach EU law through case studies,[43] moot courts,[44] or even massive open online courses (MOOCs).[45] The related discipline of European studies also provides an example of the growing use of simulation and role-play in teaching how the EU

---

[38] *See further*, ECAS's website, ecas.org/focus-areas/eu-rights/.
[39] Here we use the term "hybrid clinic: as used by the Clinical Legal Education Association," HANDBOOK FOR NEW CLINICAL TEACHERS (CLEA 2015) 10. On the different clinic models, see also Kevin Kerrigan and Victoria Murray, A STUDENT GUIDE TO CLINICAL LEGAL EDUCATION AND PRO BONO (Palgrave McMillan 2011), 1–2.
[40] The Brussels School of International Studies brings together the disciplines of politics, international relations, law, and economics; *see further*, https://www.kent.ac.uk/brussels/.
[41] Jean Monnet European Module "Teaching EU Migration Law Through Clinical Legal Education," project file number 2012-2874, https://eacea.ec.europa.eu/JeanMonnetDirectory/#/project-details-screen/fileNo=528460-LLP-1-2012-1-UK-AJM-MO. Funding was obtained for three years beginning with the 2012/13 academic year. Since then, the University of Kent has borne all teaching costs related to the EU Rights Clinic.
[42] *See further*, https://eacea.ec.europa.eu/europe-for-citizens/funding/operating-grants_en.
[43] For example, the EUI's course "Competition Law and Economics through Case Studies," https://competitioncourses.wordpress.com/competition-law-and-economics-through-case-studies/.
[44] For examples of how moot court competitions are integrated into the curriculum, see the courses developed Europa Institut at Universität Basel, https://europa.unibas.ch/en/studies/ma-european-studies/european-law-moot-court/ and University of Turku, https://nettiopsu.utu.fi/opas/teaching/course.htm?id=9894.
[45] Joris Larik, EU Law and MOOCs: A Marriage Waiting to Happen (EUROPEAN LAW BLOG, May 21, 2013), europeanlawblog.eu/?p=1765; A. Alemanno, Understanding Europe: Why It Matters and What It Can Offer You, online, Coursera, 2014 to present.

works.[46] Nonetheless, we would not be amiss to suppose these more interactive approaches to teaching EU law still represent a minority.[47] Indeed, this is a criticism that can be levelled at the teaching of law in general, as Xavier Aurey suggests in Chapter 6 of this volume. In any event, teaching EU law through CLE does remain somewhat of a rarity, as Alberto Alemanno and Lamin Khadar discuss in their joint contribution in Chapter 9 of this volume. In this respect, the EU Rights Clinic can be considered a pioneer by virtue of being the first law clinic to focus exclusively on EU law. While there are several universities in Brussels and beyond offering specialized postgraduate degrees in EU law, Kent is the only university at present that offers CLE options to those pursuing a specialization in EU law.

Goals and Methods of the EU Rights Clinic: EU Free Movement Law in Action

The EU Rights Clinic module aims to provide students with the opportunity to study EU free movement law in action, thereby exposing students to how one of the cornerstone policies of the EU works in practice. The goals of the module are (1) to provide students with a thorough knowledge of EU free movement law, (2) to develop practical skills in client interviewing and counselling skills, and (3) to enable the students to put that knowledge and skills into practice by assisting citizens who face practical difficulties in exercising their EU free movement rights through the medium of clinical case work.

The EU Rights Clinic module is offered to postgraduate students enrolled on the LLM and MA in International Migration programmes at the University of Kent's campus in Brussels. It is aimed at students who are interested in undertaking a highly specialized course in EU law while at the same time developing practical skills and gaining practical work experience. Teaching is conducted in English, in line with interactive adult education techniques and following a Content and Language Integrated Learning[48] methodology. Around eight to twelve students take part every academic year.

The module is composed of two components spread over two terms of the academic year, following a similar set-up to the Human Rights and Migration Law Clinic in Turin.[49] The first theoretical component comprises forty-eight hours of

---

[46] See, e.g., Christian Kaunert, *The European Union Simulation: From Problem-Based Learning (PBL) to Student Interest* 8 EUROPEAN POLITICAL SCIENCE 254–65 (2009); Marco Brunazzo and Pierpaolo Settembri, *Teaching the European Union: A Simulation of Council's Negotiations* 14 EUROPEAN POLITICAL SCIENCE 1–14 (2015).

[47] See, to that effect, CCBE/EIPA, Study on the State of Play of Lawyers' Training in EU Law (2014) 18, which suggests that "there is scope for more to be done to encourage a greater understanding of the practical application and use of EU law" and found that many survey participants "mention[ed] that academic training in EU law is too much about theory and too little about its practical effect on legal cases and files."

[48] For further details on CLIL, please refer to https://ec.europa.eu/languages/language-teaching/content-and-language-integrated-learning_en.htm.

[49] *See further* Chapter 7 by Ulrich Stege and Maurizio Veglio in this volume.

classroom-based teaching spread over twelve weeks of the autumn term (October–December) and a second clinical component comprising at least forty-eight hours of case work plus thirty-four hours of case work discussion time in the spring term (January–April). Students are encouraged to continue working in the clinic on a volunteer basis in the last term of the academic year (May–June).

The theoretical component of the module aims to introduce students to the law governing free movement of EU citizens and their family members within the European Union. The objectives of the first component are to provide students with a thorough knowledge of EU rules on free movement law. It also gives insights into related issues such as fundamental rights and equal treatment, and the existence and scope of formal and informal legal redress mechanisms through which citizens can enforce their rights and freedoms in the EU. The first component is taught using a combination of lectures, group discussions, and group research work. In addition, students are provided an opportunity to develop their practical skills in researching and advising using role-play exercises to simulate advocacy efforts before the EU institutions. There are approximately 200 study hours for this component. The final assessment involves coursework in the form of a fact pattern drawn from a real-life case handled by the clinic. Upon successful completion of the first component, students gain ten ECTS credits towards their postgraduate degree.

The theoretical component of the course differs from traditional courses on EU law in that it also examines the implementation gap that exists between the theoretical legal framework and how the free movement rules are applied and experienced in practice. This requires going beyond the EU legal instrument by examining the implementation of the rules at the national level. Students are therefore invited to examine the conformity of national implementing measures by comparing and contrasting how certain key concepts of the free movement rules have been implemented in the Member States. The aim is to allow students to develop a capacity for identifying instances of noncompliance in how the EU rules are implemented at the national level. Such a skill is useful not only when undertaking individual case work, but it is also usefully deployed to engage in evidence-based advocacy.

Furthermore, the course not only aims to provide students with a knowledge of the legal instruments that govern free movement, but it also seeks to allow students to gain an appreciation of the practical obstacles which citizens encounter and to critically review the justifications advanced by Member States for their existence. As a result, the course also seeks to incorporate empirical research on free movement.[50] The aim is to ensure that students can use such sources to develop argumentation skills that go beyond invoking EU legal instruments and citing case

---

[50] See, e.g., Ettore Recchi, MOBILE EUROPE; THE THEORY AND PRACTICE OF FREE MOVEMENT IN THE EU (Palgrave McMillan 2015); Anthony Valcke, *Who Does Not Belong Here Anymore? A Statistical Snapshot of Member States' Practices* in Herwig Verschueren, ed., *Residence, Employment and Social Rights of Mobile Persons* (Intersentia, 2016), pp 111–128.

law, which has taken on additional importance in light of recent developments in the case law of the EU Court of Justice.[51]

The clinical component then follows during the twelve weeks of the second term of the academic year. This voluntary component of the course aims to enable students to apply their knowledge in a practical context by working on real-life cases of the EU Rights Clinic under the supervision of a qualified lawyer and PhD student volunteers. It therefore allows students to provide practical assistance to real-life clients who face problems in exercising their right to free movement. This component seeks to develop further research, advocacy, and counselling skills of the students.

Students are assigned cases based on requests for assistance received by the EU Rights Clinic predominantly by email, as well as cases passed on by its NGO partner ECAS. Each student will typically handle between one and four cases during the clinical component, depending on their complexity and the nature of the assistance required. Students are encouraged to pick their own cases and are expected to work on their case assignments in their own time (around four hours on average per week). In the weekly meetings of the EU Rights Clinic, students are invited to update the group on their progress, reflect on case work strategy, and more generally discuss their clinical experiences. This second component is not formally assessed, although it is hoped that this will change in the future.

The students are also actively encouraged to engage in volunteering projects with other Brussels-based organizations active in the field of migration. Due to the students' interest in migration issues in general, the clinic's students have conducted awareness-raising workshops for asylum seekers and refugees[52] hosted by the Bon integration centre.[53] More recently, the students also have volunteered with the Citizen's Platform for Refugee Support[54] to assist with the administration of the group's activities.[55]

---

[51] *See further*, Niamh Nic Shuibnhe and Marsela Maci, *Proving Public Interest: The Growing Impact of Evidence in Free Movement Case Law*, 50 COMMON MARKET LAW REVIEW 965–1006 (2013); Keith Puttick, *EEA Workers' Free Movement and Social Rights after Dano and St Prix: Is a Pandora's Box of New Economic Integration and "Contribution" Requirements Opening?* 37 JOURNAL OF SOCIAL WELFARE AND FAMILY LAW 253–73 (2015).

[52] The workshop covered issues such as work permits for asylum seekers, residence formalities in Belgium, and other practical issues. The event was organized by the students and they also drafted the presentation materials.

[53] The Bon Integration Center is the Brussels agency for integration. It offers information on integration programmes for asylum seekers, refugees, and newcomers as well as advice about living, working, and life in Brussels in addition to language classes; *see* bon.be/en.

[54] The Citizen's Platform for Refugee Support was formed in the wake of the ongoing refugee crisis and aims to provide concrete help to asylum seekers, refugees, and other migrants; *see* www.bxlrefugees.be/en/.

[55] Students volunteered to operate the welcome desk at the organization's premises, to help organize the "buddy" programme which aims to partner migrants with member of the local community where they live, and to assist with the "after" programme which helps recognized refugees to find housing, among other practical matters.

On a final note, it should be mentioned that another, albeit less obvious, goal in setting up the EU Rights Clinic has been to demonstrate to aspiring lawyers wishing to practice in the field of EU law that they should not see such a career choice as being limited to advising on commercial issues. While a career in the EU departments of major international law firms does usually mean focusing on the competition, state aid, or public procurement rules, there are many smaller firms and sole practitioners who also specialize in EU law, most notably those active in the field of immigration law. The EU Rights Clinic therefore seeks to illustrate how lawyers wishing to specialize in EU law can do so while also pursuing social justice.[56]

Beyond the Educational Goals: Encouraging Volunteerism and Promoting Access to Justice

The EU Rights Clinic also has wider aims that go beyond the confines of legal education in respect of the benefits which it hopefully procures for participating students and the promotion of volunteering as a means of learning. The clinic also seeks to enhance access to justice by providing a legal service to the public.

In the long run, it is hoped that students will benefit from their participation in a number of ways. First, it is anticipated that they will gain a greater appreciation of their own rights as citizens within the EU and of the practical problems that remain in exercising these rights. Second, the clinic seeks to inspire students to consider pursuing a career as immigration lawyers or advisors on migration issues. Third, they will have developed practical skills that will be useful to them throughout their careers, regardless of whether they choose to pursue a career in migration law or not, since interviewing and counselling skills are useful for a multitude of occupations. Fourth, through their clinical case work, the students will have acquired valuable work experience that will give them a competitive advantage over other students who have engaged in similar postgraduate study.[57] Finally, their participation will provide them with a point of entry into civil society, which may generate future employment prospects.

The EU Rights Clinic also aims to contribute towards a greater recognition of the role that volunteering can play as part of lifelong learning, in line with the European Parliament's resolution on volunteering.[58] As noted earlier, the clinic encourages students to volunteer with organizations that support migrants in Brussels as a way to enhance the integration of students into the Belgian social fabric by working for the benefit of the community where they live and study. The clinic therefore aims to

---

[56] For a discussion of what social justice entails, *see further* Chapter 7 by Ulrich Stege and Maurizio Veglio in this volume.

[57] *See further*, Heidi Maurer and Jocelyn Mawdsley, *Students' Skills, Employability and the Teaching of European Studies: Challenges and Opportunities*, 13 EUROPEAN POLITICAL SCIENCE 32–42 (2014).

[58] European Parliament resolution of April 22, 2008 on the role of volunteering in contributing to economic and social cohesion, 2007/2149(INI).

expose students to the benefits of volunteering and encourage their continued participation in volunteer work as part of their lifelong learning process.

As regards enhancing access to justice, the module seeks to play a role in addressing some of the problems noted by the European Commission in its Citizenship Report 2010.[59] The Commission deplored the continued existence of national obstacles to the exercise of the EU free movement rules law resulting from divergent and incorrect national implementing measures and cumbersome administrative procedures.[60] One of the goals in establishing the EU Rights Clinic has therefore been to provide a service that can help citizens to overcome those obstacles.

In addition, the ongoing economic crisis has had an impact on the ability of EU citizens and their family members to obtain legal advice and representation when their free movement rights are infringed. The austerity cuts imposed in several Member States have resulted in the slashing of legal aid budgets. The most extreme example of this has been in the UK, where it is no longer possible for EU citizens and their family members to obtain legal aid in order to bring proceedings before the first-level court in cases relating to residence rights or social security claims following changes to legal aid introduced by the Legal Aid, Sentencing, and Punishment of Offenders Act 2012.[61] Legal aid has also been cut in Germany, Ireland, and Portugal according the EU's Fundamental Rights Agency,[62] as well as in Belgium.[63] In light of these budgetary cuts, the availability of legal aid in residence cases has been reduced – if not completely withdrawn – in several EU Member States and has created a situation where there are unmet needs for legal advice in EU free movement cases. It was therefore anticipated that the EU Rights Clinic's case work would be able to cater to some of these unmet legal needs, even if on a modest scale. This also helps to explain why the clinic has a transnational perspective and has taken on cases in several EU jurisdictions.[64]

Moreover, it was felt necessary to ensure that the assistance contemplated by the EU Rights Clinic should not duplicate existing services. At present, there is no EU-

---

[59] Commission, *EU Citizenship Report 2010 – Dismantling the Obstacles to EU Citizens' Rights*, COM (2010) 603 final.
[60] *Id.*, 14–15.
[61] The Legal Aid, Sentencing and Punishment of Offenders Act 2012, s 9. This provides that legal aid is available only for civil legal services listed in Schedule 1, Part 1. Appeals against decisions issued in respect of residence rights or social security claims are not included with the effect that they are not eligible for legal aid. For a discussion, see Sheona York, *The End of Legal Aid in Immigration – A Barrier to Access to Justice for Migrants and a Decline in the Rule of Law* 27 JOURNAL OF IMMIGRATION, ASYLUM AND NATIONALITY LAW 106–38 (2013).
[62] Fundamental Rights Agency, "Fundamental rights: key legal and policy developments in 2013" (2014) 39; Fundamental Rights Agency, "Fundamental rights: challenges and achievements in 2012" (2013) 243.
[63] The issue of consistently reduced funding for legal aid lawyers was raised in 2012 by the Council of Bars and Law Societies in Europe in a letter addressed to the Belgian Minister of Justice, www.ccbe.eu/fileadmin/user_upload/NTCdocument/030712_Ministre_de_l2_1341318815.pdf.
[64] For examples of cases handled by the EU Rights Clinic, see https://blogs.kent.ac.uk/eu-rights-clinic/case-studies/.

wide problem-solving service giving tailored advice to EU citizens on free movement issues which is also able to represent them before the national courts. Indeed, the Commission's existing networks are limited to the provision of information, advice, and problem-solving.[65] In the absence of an EU-wide service going beyond advice that can provide representation in court cases, it was therefore concluded that the creation of the EU Rights Clinic would complement existing avenues of advice and assistance.

There is also another public service aspect to the case work of the EU Rights Clinic. In addition to helping EU citizens overcome obstacles to exercising their free movement rights, the clinic's case work is also used to engage in evidence-based advocacy. This may take the form of a complaint requesting the Commission to launch an investigation into the practices of the Member State where similar cases may reveal systematic problems in the application of the rules by the Member States.[66] At the same time, such a complaint may be backed up with a petition addressed to the European Parliament to ensure it can monitor the situation.[67] It may also take the form of a briefing paper advocating for improvements to the legal and policy frameworks at the EU level.[68] Finally, the clinic also publishes the documents it has received through requests for public access to documents and briefings on their contents.[69]

The Weight and Value of Internationalization

The specialized nature of the EU Rights Clinic means that the clinic extensively engages with EU law.[70] Given that EU law does not operate in a vacuum, the clinic also engages with the national legal frameworks that implement the EU free

---

[65] Europe Direct only provides general information on the EU; see europa.eu/contact/. Your Europe Advice provides personalized advice but it cannot intervene directly on behalf of users of the service; see europa.eu/youreurope/advice/eligibility_en.htm. SOLVIT has a limited mandate to solve problems with public administrations; see Commission, *Recommendation of 17 September 2013 on the Principles Governing SOLVIT*, C(2013) 5869 final.

[66] A complaint lodged by the EU Rights Clinic on behalf of Spanish NGO Abusos Urbanisticos NO in respect of discrimination by the Spanish authorities led the Commission to initiate infringement procedures under Article 258 TFEU against Spain; see infringement cases 2015/4119 and 2014/4330 |ex CHAP(2013) [1295] "certains traits de l'obligation de déclaration informative sur avoirs sis à l'étranger (Modelo 720)."

[67] See, e.g., Petition 0566/2013 by the EU Rights Clinic and Abusos Urbanísticos NO, on new Spanish legislation which mandates the reporting of assets and rights held abroad. The EU Rights Clinic presented the substance of the complaint at a meeting of the European Parliament's Committee on Petitions on November 11, 2014, see PETI OJ(2014)236.

[68] See, e.g., EU Rights Clinic, Seven Strategies to Improve the Free Movement of Persons, www.righttomove.eu/.

[69] These are subsequently made available on the EU Rights Clinic's blog, https://blogs.kent.ac.uk/eu-rights-clinic/resources/.

[70] For other examples of highly specialized law clinics, see the contributions to this volume by Maria Marquès i Banqué on the Environmental Law Clinic (Chapter 5) and Juan Pérez-León (Chapter 14) on the International Human Rights Clinic.

movement rules in the EU Member States. On occasion, it has also engaged with the legal orders of the states that comprise the European Economic Area, most notably Norway. As part of the first component of the course, students are taught how to search and locate EU legal sources and trace national implementing measures, most notably using the Internet. One of the advantages and convenience of studying EU law is that most source material is available online. Given the pervasiveness of EU law in so many fields of law, it goes without saying that being able to research EU sources and their national implementation is a necessary skill for both academic study and legal practice.

This is evident when looking at immigration policy. Historically, the control of borders has been an intrinsic aspect of a state's territorial sovereignty,[71] which enables a state to prevent interference with "the territorial integrity of the state."[72] Seen from this perspective, the freedom of movement represents "a substantial and important departure from international law,"[73] where the obligation of states to admit non-nationals into the national territory is limited to humanitarian situations.[74]

EU law has progressively encroached on the field of national immigration policy. The right of free movement has evolved over time, following consecutive amendments of the founding Treaty establishing the European Economic Community.[75] Initially, the right of free movement was limited to EU nationals who were moving to another country as economically active persons.[76] The creation of EU citizenship by the Maastricht Treaty[77] engendered a general right of free movement for all EU citizens and their family members.[78] These developments could be characterized as a "negative" form of European integration in that they have demanded compliance with EU law in a way which "reduces the range of national policy choices and

---

[71] Mark Salter, RIGHTS OF PASSAGE. THE PASSPORT IN INTERNATIONAL RELATIONS (Lynne Reiner 2003), 12–123 and 128–29.
[72] Charter of the United Nations, June 26, 1945, 1 UNTS xvi, art 2(4); *see further* Brian Opeskin, Richard Perruchoud, and Jillyanne Redpath-Cross, eds., FOUNDATIONS OF INTERNATIONAL MIGRATION LAW (Cambridge University Press 2012), 123–26.
[73] Elspeth Guild, THE LEGAL ELEMENTS OF EUROPEAN IDENTITY: EU CITIZENSHIP AND EU MIGRATION LAW (Kluwer 2004), 86.
[74] Universal Declaration of Human Rights, December 10, 1948, UNGA Res 217 A(III), arts 13–14; Convention relating to the Status of Refugees, July 28, 1951, 189 UNTS 150, arts 31–33. *See further* Alice Edwards, *Human Rights, Refugees, and the Right "To Enjoy" Asylum*, 17 INTERNATIONAL JOURNAL OF REFUGEE LAW 293–330, 302 (2005).
[75] Treaty establishing the European Economic Community, March 25, 1957, 298 UNTS 11. For a detailed examination of the development of the free movement of persons, see Sioffra O'Leary, THE EVOLVING CONCEPT OF COMMUNITY CITIZENSHIP. FROM THE FREE MOVEMENT OF PERSONS TO UNION CITIZENSHIP (Kluwer 1996).
[76] The free movement of workers was provided by Articles 48–51 EEC, now Articles 45–48 TFEU.
[77] Treaty on European Union [1992] OJ C 191/1 (hereafter the Maastricht Treaty). Article G(C) inserted new Articles 8 and 8a–8e into the EEC Treaty, which was renamed the Treaty Establishing the European Community.
[78] EC Treaty [1992] OJ C 224/6, Article 8a EC.

represents a fundamental loss of political control."[79] The EU's action in this field limits the discretion of the Member States to control access of non-nationals to their territory and therefore creates tensions between EU free movement rules and national legislation seeking to regulate immigration.[80]

It is therefore important for students to acknowledge this conflict between national immigration policy and European integration in order to understand whether a specific instance of noncompliance by a Member State is unintentional or results from wilful conduct[81] that is undertaken as part of a Member State's intentional strategy. The reason is that this has an impact on case work strategy. Knowing whether a Member State is intentionally departing from its EU obligations will determine what corrective strategy may be effectively deployed to bring an errant Member State back into line.

Cooperation in CLE

The EU Rights Clinic is a member of ENCLE[82] and LawWorks.[83] The Clinic has actively sought to partner with other clinics advising on migration or social security issues. For example, in 2013 it partnered with the IUC Turin's Human Rights and Migration Law Clinic[84] on a project led by ECAS which sought to mentor EU citizens moving from Bulgaria and Romania to Belgium, Italy, and the UK.[85] More recently, it has partnered with the EUI's Law in Action project to undertake a survey of health care rights in selected EU countries in order to identify the conditions under which EU citizens and their family members may access health care in those countries.[86] The survey results were then disseminated to the Immigration Law

---

[79] Maarten Vink, *Negative and Positive Integration in European Immigration Policies*, 6 (13) EUROPEAN INTEGRATION ONLINE PAPERS, 2 (2002), eiop.or.at/eiop/pdf/2002-013.pdf.

[80] Robin White, *Conflicting Competences: Free Movement Rules and Immigration Laws*, 29 EUROPEAN LAW REVIEW 385–96 (2004); Steve Peers, *Free Movement, Immigration Control and Constitutional Conflict*, 5 EUROPEAN CONSTITUTIONAL LAW REVIEW 173–96 (2009); Jo Shaw and Nina Miller, *When Legal Worlds Collide: An Exploration of What Happens When EU Free Movement Law Meets UK Immigration Law*, 38 EUROPEAN LAW REVIEW 137–66 (2012).

[81] Samuel Krislov, Claus-Dieter Ehlermann, and Joseph Weiler, *The Political Organs and the Decision-Making Process in the United States and the European Community*, in INTEGRATION THROUGH LAW, VOLUME 1: METHODS, TOOLS AND INSTITUTIONS BOOK: POLITICAL ORGANS, INTEGRATION TECHNIQUES AND JUDICIAL PROCESS (Mauro Cappelletti, Monica Seccombe, Joseph Weiler, eds., de Gruyter 1986), 3–112, 63–4; Zürn Michael Zürn, *Introduction: Law and Compliance at Different Levels*, in LAW AND GOVERNANCE IN POSTNATIONAL EUROPE (Michael Zürn and Christian Joerges, eds., Cambridge University Press 2007), 1–39, 9; and Christian Joerges, *Compliance Research in Legal Perspectives*, *Id.*, at 218–61, 228.

[82] ENCLE is a European network of persons committed to achieving justice through education; *see* encle.org/.

[83] LawWorks is a charity working in England and Wales to connect volunteer lawyers with people in need of legal advice but who are not eligible for legal aid and cannot afford to pay and with the not-for-profit organizations that support them; *see* https://www.lawworks.org.uk/.

[84] See Chapter 7 by Ulrich Stege and Maurizio Veglio in this volume.

[85] For further details of the "My Mobility Mentor" project, *see* mymobilitymentor.ning.com/.

[86] *See* https://blogs.eui.eu/lawinaction/projects/.

Practitioners Association[87] in order to provide information to legal practitioners as to how EU citizens may be able to retain their home health care entitlements when they move to the UK. At present, the UK Home Office refuses to recognize that EU citizens who do not work and rely on the UK's national health service are able to meet the condition for comprehensive sickness insurance[88] under the free movement directive.[89]

The EU Rights Clinic also aims to foster greater links with civil society organizations. As already discussed, the clinic itself is the product of a partnership between ECAS and the University of Kent. Since 2014, the EU Rights Clinic has worked with Europe4People[90] to operate a help desk for EU citizens facing expulsion from Belgium, which now provides regular case work referrals to the clinic. We have also collaborated with the UK's Law Centres Network[91] on mentoring migrants[92] with Crossroads Göteborg[93] concerning the

---

[87] The Immigration Law Practitioners' Association is a membership organization established in 1984 by a group of leading immigration law practitioners in the UK; see further www.ilpa.org.uk/.

[88] According to the UK administrative guidance, access to the UK's National Health Service does not meet this condition; see Home Office, "Guidance on European Economic Area (EEA) national qualified persons" (2015) 41–46. The policy reason is that reliance on the NHS creates a burden on the UK's social assistance system; see W (China) v X (China) [2006] EWCA Civ 1494 (November 9, 2006). This is despite the fact that, as a matter of UK law, any person ordinarily resident in the UK is entitled to NHS treatment. The UK operates a universal residency-based health care system which is free at the point of use for persons who are ordinarily resident in the UK. Under section 1(3) of the National Health Service Act 2006, treatment on the NHS is free for all residents of the UK. Moreover, the NHS (Charges to Overseas Visitors) Regulations 2011 exempts certain categories of EEA nationals (including workers, students, and pensioners) who are temporarily in the UK from the payment of overseas charges for treatment provided by the NHS. The Court of Appeal had upheld the legitimacy of this policy. As a result, EEA nationals who legitimately rely on the NHS for their health care needs while residing in the UK will effectively be penalized if they seek to obtain recognition of their residence rights by the UK authorities; see *Ahmad v Secretary of State for the Home Department* [2014] EWCA Civ 988 (July 16, 2014). The issue is currently the subject of ongoing infringement proceedings by the Commission, which has issued a reasoned opinion against the UK; see Commission, *Free Movement: Commission Asks the UK to Uphold EU Citizens' Rights*, Press release IP/12/417, April 26, 2012. For further discussion, see Anthony Valcke, *Five Years of the Citizens Directive – Part 2*, 25 JOURNAL OF IMMIGRATION, ASYLUM AND NATIONALITY LAW 331–57, 342–45 (2011); Sylvia de Mars, *Economically Inactive EU Migrants and the United Kingdom's National Health Service: Unreasonable Burdens without Real Links?* 39 EUROPEAN LAW REVIEW 770–89 (2014).

[89] EU citizens who do not work and reside in another Member State are required to hold comprehensive sickness insurance for themselves and their family members by virtue of Article 7 of Directive 2004/38 (n 11).

[90] Europe4People is a network of civil society organizations, legal practitioners, policy-makers, trade unionists, and individual citizens who work to defend and promote the right to free movement of EU citizens, particularly those facing expulsion from Belgium; see further, www.europe4people.org/en/about-us/.

[91] This cooperation was in the context of "My Mobility Mentor" (see supra note 75).

[92] Law Centres offer legal advice, case work, and representation to individuals and groups in the UK; see www.lawcentres.org.uk/.

[93] Crossroads Göteborg is a project of the Swedish faith-based organization Stads Missionen that aims to fight against the economic and social exclusion of EU citizens and non-EU nationals; see further www.stadsmissionen.org/category/crossroads/.

misapplication of the free movement rules in Sweden and with several Brussels-based NGOs[94] concerning the expulsion of EU citizens from Belgium. The EU Rights Clinic has also organized an informal network of organizations and clinics working on free movement issues in order to exchange information and refer cases.[95]

The value of such partnerships for students lies in them being exposed to the benefits of collaborative working. First, it demonstrates how the impact of advocacy work at EU level can be enhanced when multiple organizations come together to formulate joint complaints. Second, such collaboration serves to illustrate how organizations with different mandates can rally around an issue of common concern and effect changes in law and policy at national and European levels by pooling their resources.

Diffusion of CLE

In establishing the EU Rights Clinic, the Kent Law Clinic has naturally served as a major source of inspiration and assistance. In addition, the author was also able to draw on US perspectives as a result of his own experiences working on a rule of law project in postconflict Liberia.[96] These insights were instrumental in taking the decision to create a hybrid law clinic.[97]

Since its inception, the EU Rights Clinic has sought to play an active role in the promotion of CLE. The clinic has previously hosted a number of related events, including presenting its work to a delegation of students from Tilburg University, which has since gone on to set up a law clinic.[98] In 2014, it hosted a training workshop jointly organized by ENCLE and the Open Society Justice Initiative and assisted in the delivery of a training session dedicated to migration law.[99]

The EU Rights Clinic has also been given the opportunity to discuss various aspects of its clinical activities in a variety of for a, including the University of Zagreb,[100] the Croatian National Foundation for Civil Society Development,[101]

---

[94] The Italian trade union INCA CGIL, the Belgian trade union FGTB/ABVV, and Bruxelles Laïque. For the factual and legal background to the complaint, *see further* www.osservatorioinca.org/index.php?p=text&cmd=details&tbl=sezioni_record&cat_id=12&id=922.
[95] *See further* https://blogs.kent.ac.uk/eu-rights-clinic/about-us/our-network/.
[96] *See supra* note 8 and accompanying text.   [97] *See supra* note 33 and accompanying text.
[98] *See further,* https://www.tilburguniversity.edu/nl/samenwerken/universiteitsfonds/law-clinic/.
[99] *See further,* www.pilnet.org/public-interest-law-news/pilnet-listings/archive/view/listid-1-pilnet-listings/mailid-420-conferences-encle-human-rights-training-for-clinical-law-professors-supervisors.html.
[100] Zagreb University's annual law conference, "What Is the Evidence that Legal Clinics Are Expanding Access to Justice on National, Regional and International Level?" (Dubrovnik, May 31, 2013).
[101] Croatian National Foundation for Civil Society Development conference, "Triple A for Citizens – Access to Information, Advice & Active Help" (Zadar, July 3–5, 2013).

the Dutch immigration lawyers' association,[102] the European University Institute,[103] and the Université Libre de Bruxelles.[104]

Future of CLE in Europe

In terms of the EU Rights Clinic's own future development, a number of developments can be anticipated. First, it is anticipated that the clinic will engage in cooperation with Belgian universities active in the field of migration. This is particularly the case as regards the Ghent clinic, in view of its desire to develop a live-client refugee law clinic,[105] and the Université Libre de Bruxelles's equality rights clinic, which works on immigration and asylum law issues.[106] In addition, we hope to establish a partnership with the Université of Liège's centre for migration studies[107] that will be able to undertake sociological research in respect of the Clinic's client base to investigate their motivations for migrating to Belgium. Second, it is hoped that the Clinic's workload can be increased. At present, various options are being explored, including a targeted effort to recruit additional volunteers among Brussels-based law students and lawyers. Third, it is hoped that, in the longer term, the Clinic can work to develop a network of student and faculty exchange between clinics active in migration law in order to share best practices and develop common training materials.

However, as with many other clinics, the problem remains that institutional funding is limited. The original funding obtained by the EU Rights Clinic through the Jean Monnet programme was a one-off grant and cannot be renewed. The clinic is fortunate that the University of Kent has decided to continue funding the teaching components of the course. However, in order to expand its activities, the clinic would need to take on an additional clinician, which is not currently possible. As a result, the ability to raise funds is likely to become a key determinant in whether the clinic is able to expand. As a result, the long-term sustainability of the EU Rights Clinic still remains to be secured. This is one of the reasons for giving consideration to bringing in a further university as a partner of the Clinic. At the time of writing, discussions are under way with Vesalius College in Brussels to integrate a clinic education component into the curriculum for its undergraduate degree in International and European Law.[108]

---

[102] Specialistenvereniging migratierecht advocaten, annual conference (June 27, 2014).
[103] European University Institute Human Rights Working Group, "Law in Action Project Speaker Series on Strategic Litigation and Clinical Legal Education" (Fiesole, October 12, 2014).
[104] Université Libre de Bruxelles Centre de Philosophie du Droit "Perelman", internal seminar (January 20, 2015).
[105] See further, Chapter 11 by Eva Brems and Stijn Smet in this volume.
[106] See further, www.philodroit.be/-ELC-?lang=en.
[107] Centre d'Etudes de l'Ethnicité et des Migrations; see further, labos.ulg.ac.be/cedem/en/.
[108] See further, www.vesalius.edu/academics/international-european-law/ba-international-european-law/.

In respect of the future of CLE, it is likely that differences in clinical structures, fields of interest, and national legal education will prevent a drive towards standardization of CLE at both the European and national levels. Indeed, such standardization could even be considered to hamper the creativity and diversity of law clinics in Europe. Instead, as clinics in Europe become more established and experienced, it is hoped that, through the ENCLE network, European law clinics can play a more active role in disseminating best practices, sharing teaching resources, and facilitating the establishment of new clinics.

Furthermore, securing formal recognition of the value of CLE by the EU institutions and the European and national bar associations would be a first step towards the possibility of procuring long-term funding for law clinics in Europe, which is necessary to sustain the future and growth of CLE in Europe. Such recognition would pave the way for encouraging further access by law clinics to existing sources of EU funding, such as the Erasmus+,[109] Justice,[110] and Rights, Equality, and Citizenship[111] programmes.

CONCLUSION

The EU Rights Clinic represents an example of a law clinic that has drawn its inspiration from successful and well-established models from abroad, most notably the Kent Law Clinic. Like its elder sister, the EU Rights Clinic shares the twin aims of providing a public service to those who cannot otherwise obtain legal assistance while also providing an opportunity for students to experience and reflect on how law works in real life.

In order to cater to its specific mission and aims, the EU Rights Clinic has used different foreign clinical models – live-client clinic, hybrid clinic – and tailored them to suit the specific national context and substantive area of law in which it operates. The EU Rights Clinic is also testament to the fact that many of the newer clinics established in the past few years have adopted a specialized focus in terms of their legal subject matter and the nature of the services that they provide. As a result, the Clinic bears witness to the diversity and creativity of CLE in European universities.

The EU Rights Clinic remains one of the few clinics specializing in EU law. CLE in EU law therefore remains a novelty whose full potential is yet to be fully achieved. EU law offers many opportunities for the emergence of specialized law clinics.

---

[109] Regulation (EU) No 1288/2013 of the European Parliament and of the Council of December 11, 2013, establishing "Erasmus+": the Union programme for education, training, youth and sport [2013] OJ L 347/50.

[110] Regulation (EU) No 1382/2013 of the European Parliament and of the Council of December 17, 2013, establishing a Justice Programme for the period 2014 to 2020 [2013] OJ L 354/73.

[111] Regulation (EU) No 1381/2013 of the European Parliament and of the Council of December 17, 2013, establishing a Rights, Equality and Citizenship Programme for the period 2014 to 2020 [2013] OJ L 354/62.

While the EU Rights Clinic operates in a niche field in EU law, the breadth of EU law would certainly allow the establishment of specialized law clinics in many other fields, including, by way of example, cross-border family law, consumer law, and travel rights.

As universities become increasingly aware of the benefits of CLE – for which ENCLE deserves much praise – we should anticipate the emergence of further law clinics that specialize in the field of EU law. In order to encourage and sustain the further growth of law clinics in Europe, it is crucial that formal recognition of the value of CLE is achieved at the EU level.

PART IIC

Between Europe and the World

Exploring Internationalization within the European Clinical Movement

11

The Human Rights Law Clinic at Ghent University

Eva Brems and Stijn Smet

INTRODUCTION

It is fair to say that, even within Western Europe, which was not so long ago described as "the last holdout in the worldwide acceptance of clinical legal education,"[1] Belgium is somewhat of a late bloomer. Clinical legal education (CLE) has only really started burgeoning in Belgium in the past few years. Since 2014, in particular, legal clinics have sprouted at various Belgian universities.

At the moment of writing, three genuine legal clinics – defined as those that provide students with practice-based education in the form of experiential learning through work on real-life cases, supervised and evaluated by university staff – are in operation at Belgian universities: one human rights law clinic (at Ghent University) and two nondiscrimination law clinics (both at the Université Libre de Bruxelles). The academic year 2016/2017 should mark the start of two additional legal clinics: one migration law clinic (at the Université Libre de Bruxelles), and an ambitious clinical programme as a compulsory element, across all modules, of a newly established English-language Master in Laws (at Antwerp University).

Understood in a broader sense of introducing students to legal practice, something akin to CLE is also on offer at other Belgian universities. These are labelled "clinics" by the respective universities, but in practice either take the form of seminars with practitioners (at the Catholic University of Leuven [KULeuven]) or of externships (at the Free University of Brussels [VUB]).

At Ghent University's Law School, current clinical legal activities consist of a formal master's-level course (Human Rights Law Clinic) and an informal "Strasbourg Club" of PhD students at the Human Rights Centre who submit third-party interventions at the European Court of Human Rights (ECtHR). In the

---

[1] Richard J. Wilson, *Western Europe: Last Holdout in the Worldwide Acceptance of Clinical Legal Education*, 10 GERMAN LAW JOURNAL 823–46 (2009).

context of this contribution, we will focus primarily on the Human Rights Law Clinic course.

The Human Rights Law Clinic was founded in 2014. The Clinic is incorporated in the Law School's curriculum, at the master's degree level. It runs as a year-long course, currently worth four European Credit Transfer System (ECTS) credits. The Clinic provides CLE to a relatively small number of students, in the range of twelve to eighteen students annually. Most of our students are Belgian, but a growing number are European/international (e.g. British, Canadian, and Polish).[2] Nearly all of our students have a background in law. A small minority have a background in a discipline other than law.[3] Most students are enrolled in the Law School's Master in Law programme.[4] A few, however, are enrolled in one of the Law School's LLM programmes or are even pursuing a PhD.[5] The Clinic is staffed by a professor of human rights law (Eva Brems, Director), a postdoc (Stijn Smet, Coordinator), and two clinicians (a lawyer and a judge). Other Human Rights Centre researchers also supervise projects, on an ad hoc basis, where needed.

At present, the Clinic does not engage in direct service delivery (but see the later discussion of an exploratory live-client refugee law project). Instead, it cooperates with civil society partners who supply human rights–related projects to the Clinic. Like many human right clinics, our Clinic thus provides services to alleged victims of human rights violations *indirectly* by providing a range of services to the Clinic's partners.[6] Clinic students work on projects that vary from the strictly legal (aimed at litigation and legislative reform) to the more political (aimed at advocacy and lobbying). Projects cover a broad range of human rights issues, both domestic and international: disability, nondiscrimination, ill-treatment, academic freedom, and more. The Clinic's partners range from small Belgian nonprofit organizations, to larger nongovernmental organizations (NGOs) and international actors. Invariably, however, the final beneficiaries of the Clinic's projects are minorities and/or disadvantaged individuals in (Belgian) society: persons with disabilities, prisoners, transgender persons, Travellers, Muslim women, and the like.

---

[2] Out of the thirty students we have had over the course of the first two years of the Clinic's operation, twenty-six were Belgian and four non-Belgian. During the first year of operation, all eighteen students were Belgian. During the second year of operation, four out of twelve students were non-Belgian. This indicates a growing interest in (possibly coupled with a late discovery of) the Clinic among international students.
[3] Twenty-eight out of thirty students had a background in law, one in political science, and one in philosophy.
[4] Twenty-seven out of thirty (this figure includes Erasmus students).
[5] Respectively, one and two students. Enrolled PhD students take the Clinic purely out of personal interest.
[6] Deena R. Hurwitz, *Lawyering for Justice and the Inevitability of International Human Rights Clinics*' 28 YALE L. J. INT'L. L. 533(2003).

EMERGENCE OF CLE AT GHENT UNIVERSITY AND IN BELGIUM

Genesis and Context of the Human Rights Law Clinic at Ghent University

The Human Rights Law Clinic course started in the academic year 2014–2015. Its initiators, professors Eva Brems and Yves Haeck,[7] had long wished to establish a legal clinic in human rights and seized the opportunity to do so when a 2014 reform of the law school curriculum coincided with a fresh start in the career of Professor Brems. An important precursor to the Clinic's founding was the submission by the Human Rights Centre of its first third-party intervention at the ECtHR several years earlier, in May 2011.[8] The third-party interventions were an unplanned initiative emerging from the biweekly meetings of the Strasbourg Club, which brought together Professor Brems and six PhD researchers associated with an European Research Council (ERC)-funded research project[9] to discuss the progress of the research, as well as the recent case law of the ECtHR. Another spinoff of the Strasbourg Club is the blog "Strasbourg Observers," which publishes comments on recent ECtHR judgments.[10] Both the Strasbourg Club and its spinoffs continue to exist today (i.e. beyond the formal conclusion of the ERC project).[11] They remain linked, in the sense that the Strasbourg Club's practice of systematically scrutinizing all ECtHR judgments is the main method that leads to identifying suitable cases for third-party interventions.[12] In addition, the Human Rights Centre's third-party interventions are systematically announced and published on the blog, in addition to the Centre's website. The link between the Strasbourg Club and the Human Rights Law Clinic is probably strongest at the level of staff: Professor Brems is in charge of both, and, of the original members of the Strasbourg Club, one – Dr. Stijn Smet – became the coordinator of the Human Rights Law Clinic, while two others have been involved in supervising Clinic students. Additionally, in the academic year 2015–2016, one of the Clinic's projects involved the drafting of a third-party intervention before the ECtHR.[13]

---

[7] Professor Haeck left the project after the first academic year.

[8] Third Party Intervention of the Human Rights Centre at Ghent University in the Grand Chamber case of *Konstantin Markin v Russia*, May 17, 2011. All the Third Party Interventions of the Human Rights Centre are available at www.hrc.ugent.be/third-party-interventions-before-ecthr/.

[9] ERC Starting Grant of Professor Brems, "Strengthening the European Court of Human Rights: More Accountability through Better Legal Reasoning," 2009–2014.

[10] *See* htttp://strasbourgobservers.com

[11] The group since consists of Professor Brems and all interested postdoctoral or PhD researchers of the Human Rights Centre. In the academic year 2015–2016, these were three postdoctoral researchers and six PhD researchers.

[12] Yet, in some cases, an important additional factor was direct contact by persons involved in the case.

[13] Joint Third Party Intervention of the Human Rights Centre at Ghent University and the UN Special Rapporteur on the rights of freedom of peaceful assembly and of association in the case of *Mahammad Majidli v Azerbaijan (no. 3) and three other applications*, www.hrc.ugent.be/third-party-interventions-before-ecthr/.

In the remainder of this section, we will focus on the Human Rights Law Clinic course and leave the Strasbourg Club activities largely aside. We will begin by exploring the institutional context that facilitated the creation of the Human Rights Law Clinic course in more detail, as well as the main drivers behind its creation.

Institutional Context

A non-negligible factor that facilitated the creation of the Human Rights Law Clinic is the overall atmosphere at Ghent University and its self-branding as an institution that values social commitment[14] and encourages innovation in education. The internal and external identification of Ghent University with social commitment operated as a facilitating factor, in the first place at the level of personal motivation. Among the many ideas that any academic may have, she can only realize a few; hence she may feel more inclined to opt for those that are likely to meet with approval in the broader academic community than for those that she suspects might be met with scepticism or criticism. This effect is likely to be even stronger if the institution's principled commitment is translated into its concrete policies. In that respect, it is relevant that Ghent University adopted, in 2015, a policy plan on social value creation in research. One of the aims of the plan is to include social value creation among the criteria that are used for the evaluation of academic staff. Since legal clinics, like many other projects of social value creation, require a lot of time investment from academic staff, the valorization of this investment in terms of career prospects is an important factor that may facilitate future initiatives in CLE. The fact that Ghent University's policy on social value creation concerns research rather than education is not a problem in this respect. In fact, a unique feature of CLE is that it integrates all three of what – at least in Flanders – are considered to be the pillars of the academic job description: teaching, research, and services.[15] In the legal clinic at the Human Rights Centre of Ghent University, the third-party interventions are a straightforward example of social value creation of research as they flow directly from the expertise and insights that are acquired in the course of PhD research. In addition, the Human Rights Law Clinic course also has a strong research component.

Ghent University's commitment to innovation in education is translated among others in a funding scheme, in which small grants are handed out on a competitive basis. A grant of this type allowed the Human Rights Law Clinic to pay three clinicians – two attorneys and a judge – as part-time (20%) teaching assistants with the task of supervising student work during the Clinic's first year of operation.[16]

---

[14] See the first sentence of the Mission Statement of Ghent University: "Ghent University distinguishes itself as a socially committed and pluralistic university that is open to all students, regardless of their ideological, political, cultural or social background," www.ugent.be/en/ghentuniv/mission.htm.

[15] The term "services" or "academic services" comprises both internal services (participation in committees, etc.) and external services (in society at large).

[16] During the second and third year, two of these teaching assistants can be paid by the department; in addition, two senior researchers of the Human Rights Centre are also involved in student supervision

Another, earlier project of innovation in education at the Law School had examined the possibility of creating an ambitious CLE project that would service clients directly in a range of legal fields (i.e. a kind of law faculty "legal practice"). While this did not lead to any concrete initiative – negative reactions of the Bar to the idea seem to have played a role in this – it did prepare the ground in the Law School for the Human Rights Law Clinic. Moreover, an upcoming external visitation of the teaching programmes of all Flemish law schools also contributed to an environment in which the proposal to create a Human Rights Law Clinic – in the context of a small curriculum reform – was favourably received.

Hence, while the start of the legal clinic at Ghent University was an isolated event spurred by the personal motivations of its founders, it was at the same time facilitated by a relatively favourable institutional climate. Direct support from the university was limited to providing a small budget for the first year through the recognition of the clinic as a project of educational innovation, and direct support from the law faculty concerned only the inclusion of the Clinic in the curriculum as an optional course. Yet the overall climate at the university contributes to a widely shared perception that the Clinic is a laudable initiative and should be continued. This plays an important part in helping to sustain the enthusiasm for the project among the staff members directly involved in it. Indeed, given the significant workload, as well as the many frustrations that inevitably come with a pilot phase, keeping up enthusiasm is a crucial success factor.

Motivation

In the minds of its initiators, there are two strong motives behind the creation of the Human Rights Law Clinic: an educational motive and a societal motive. As is the case for many clinics, the Human Rights Law Clinic thus pursues a double aim, combining educational goals with a social justice mission.[17]

The educational motive concerns the integration into the Law School curriculum of a hands-on format that confronts students with the reality of the law outside the books. Such formats remain rare in Belgian legal education (as will be discussed later). The idea was to teach students useful skills and to open their eyes to real human rights issues and the role of the law in addressing these. In particular, Professor Brems, who is an alumna of Harvard Law School, has been following the expansion of the CLE programme at that school. The regular reports on students' clinical experiences in the *Harvard Law Bulletin* fuelled her determination to create a legal clinic at Ghent University.

> in the legal clinic master's course. At the time of writing, it is unclear whether there will be any further funding opportunities beyond that time.
>
> [17] Kris Gledhill, *Establishing an International Human Rights Clinic in the New Zealand Context*, 9 INT'L. J. CLINICAL LEGAL EDUC. 297(2013); Richard J. Wilson, *Western Europe: Last Holdout in the Worldwide Acceptance of Clinical Legal Education*, 10 GERMAN LAW JOURNAL 829(2009); Hurwitz, *supra* note 6 at 508, 522, and 527.

The social justice motive for establishing the Clinic was top of mind for Professor Brems (see also Chapter 8 by Nora Markard in this volume). Until 2010, Professor Brems had combined her full-time appointment at the law school with volunteering on the boards of several Belgian human rights organizations, most notably as the chair of the Flemish section of Amnesty International between 2006 and 2010. Between 2010 and 2014 she had been addressing human rights topics in Belgium and abroad as a member of the Belgian federal Chamber of Representatives while retaining a 50% appointment at the law school. The start of the Human Rights Law Clinic coincided with her return to full-time academics and, at a personal level, corresponded to a determination to integrate her societal commitment for human rights within her academic activities.

Professor Brems's familiarity with the main Belgian civil society actors in the field of human rights impacted on the legal clinic in two ways. In the first place, she wanted the legal clinic to support the work of these civil society actors who suffer from (sometimes extreme) scarcity of resources, in particular in terms of paid staff and legal expertise (see also Chapter 6 by Xavier Aurey in this volume). In addition, the preexisting network facilitated the establishment of the legal clinic in a format based on collaboration with partners. Thanks to personal contacts and preexisting trust, it was possible to establish a sufficient number of partnerships around a varied range of human rights topics to start up the Clinic in the autumn of 2014.

The Clinic's partners – past and present – include a broad range of civil society actors, ranging from small nonprofit organizations (e.g. the Belgian nonprofit Ouders voor Inclusie [Parents for Inclusion]) to larger NGOs (e.g. Amnesty International), independent governmental bodies (e.g. the Belgian equality body), and international actors (e.g. the United Nations Special Rapporteur on Freedom of Assembly and Association). The disparate nature of the Clinic's partners ensures potential exposure of students to a broad spectrum of human rights issues *and* actors. At their core, however, the Clinic's projects – no matter which partner supplies them – invariably address the human rights of minorities and/or disadvantaged members of society (e.g. prisoners, persons with a disability, transgender persons, Travellers, and Muslim women).

CLE in Belgium: Motivations, Catalysts, Incentives, and Obstacles

CLE is, by and large, a recent phenomenon in Belgium.[18] All Belgian law schools that claim to provide CLE founded their respective clinics in or after 2012. Some law

---

[18] For this section, we reached out to colleagues at six law schools in Belgium. We received responses from colleagues at five law schools. These include one law school that does not provide CLE (the Université de Liège) and four law schools that provide some form of CLE (Ghent University, Antwerp University, the Catholic University of Leuven [KULeuven], and the Université Libre de Bruxelles). Afterwards, we also heard of – and met with – a colleague who plans to start a migration law clinic at the Université Libre de Bruxelles.

schools employ a rather broad understanding of CLE, labelling as "clinic" what in reality amounts to either a seminar series with practitioners or externships.[19] CLE in the strict sense – understood here as providing students with practice-based education in the form of experiential learning through work on real-life cases, supervised and evaluated by university staff – is provided at three Belgian universities which host clinics in the areas of human rights law, nondiscrimination law, migration law, law and development, and law and business, among others.[20]

To the best of our knowledge, most Belgian clinics work with partner organizations rather than engaging in direct service delivery. The exception is the migration clinic at the Université Libre de Bruxelles, which is a live-client clinic. The other clinics' partners range from law firms to supranational organizations (e.g. the European Parliament), national institutions (e.g. the Belgian equality body), and national and international NGOs. Some clinics are incorporated into their law school's curriculum, while others are extracurricular.

At most Belgian law schools, legal clinics are a "pet project" of committed individual academic staff, introduced with or without explicit support from the broader faculty. Occasionally, however, CLE is provided as part of a deliberate cross-faculty strategy. The Law School at Antwerp University, in particular, has elected to incorporate legal clinics as a cross-cutting and compulsory element in the curriculum of a newly founded English-language Master in Laws, to start in the academic year 2016/2017. Legal clinics are a compulsory component across the master's modules, which include law and business and law and development, among others.

Motivations, Catalysts, and Incentives

In terms of motivations to establish a legal clinic, Belgian clinicians invariably cite a desire to provide practice-based education to law school students. They wish to bridge theory and practice, to introduce students to the field of human rights by allowing them to work on projects that are both legal and practical, and to (better) prepare students for their future professional career. Most, but not all clinicians, also identify social justice as a core objective in establishing their legal clinic. Through their clinic, they intend to support civil society and (indirectly) assist disadvantaged members of society. Yet a minority of clinicians only cite educational objectives as their motivation for providing CLE. They indicate that individual academic staff in charge of managing clinics *may* have a social justice goal, but that this is not part of the design of the clinical programme. In other words, at the level of the law school, the only aim is educational.

---

[19] The former at the Catholic University of Leuven (KULeuven), the latter at the Free University of Brussels (VUB).
[20] Ghent University, Antwerp University and the Université Libre de Bruxelles.

The desire to found a clinic often stems from a deep personal belief in the value of CLE. Many clinicians refer to their own experience with CLE – or the lack thereof[21] – as the primary catalyst to establish a clinic. Sometimes, however, the consideration is pragmatic. One law school, in particular, cited a difficulty in finding a sufficient number of English-language internships for their students in Belgium as the immediate catalyst for its choice to initiate a clinical programme as a feasible alternative.

When it comes to incentives for the establishment of legal clinics in Belgium, two factors might assist in explaining the current surge in CLE, beyond personal motivations of the academic staff involved. A first factor, cited by several clinicians, is the beneficial educational climate. Recent waves of internationalization, prompted by the Bologna reform process, have made law schools realize the importance of teaching practical and interdisciplinary skills to their students. There is also an increased demand on the part of students for such skills-based education. As one clinician noted, against the backdrop of internationalization, they "could not afford *not* to" embrace CLE (see also Chapter 13 by Lynn Welchman in this volume).[22] A second factor is the impact of funding policies on the research climate at Belgian law schools (cf. Chapter 13 by Lynn Welchman in this volume). This might not seem related to CLE at first glance, but an important indirect link exists to the establishment of legal clinics. As funding agencies are attaching increased importance to methodology, interdisciplinarity, and practical skills (such as converting research into policy proposals), a broader set of skills is needed to obtain all important research funding. By providing law school students with CLE, several law schools hope to prepare a greater pool of students able to write successful doctoral research proposals. This, in turn, would serve the law school's research agenda.

Obstacles

Despite the beneficial climate, important obstacles to the establishment of legal clinics nevertheless remain. Most Belgian clinicians cite resource constraints as one of the primary obstacles to the spread and future success of CLE in Belgium. When law schools refrain from engaging in CLE, the resource-intensive nature of CLE is generally the primary reason. Budgetary constraints sometimes have a direct impact on the kind of CLE provided to students at Belgian law schools. For instance, due to lack of financial support, it might sometimes only be possible to have clinic students provide supporting activities for the clinic's partners. The hope, in that case, is that once the clinic is more firmly established with the assistance of (additional) funding, students could offer a greater contribution to social justice objectives by undertaking more direct legal service provision, rather than indirect support work.

---

[21] In this case, the absence of CLE during their own formative years motivated clinicians to do things differently, i.e. to provide their students with opportunities they had themselves not received.
[22] Interview with Professor Koen De Feyter, Law School, Antwerp University (March 25, 2016).

Because funding for CLE is scarce, most – if not all – legal clinics in Belgium rely primarily (or even solely) on existing academic staff to perform the role of clinicians (see also Chapter 8 by Nora Markard in this volume). Because legal clinics in Belgium mostly rely on *existing* law school human resources to provide CLE in addition to their "day jobs," legal clinics often operate on a small scale. The lack of dedicated academic staff and the heavy workload of existing staff are also obstacles to the provision of the intensive supervision CLE requires. This has made some clinicians rather pessimistic. Although they are great advocates of the value of CLE, they see little future for (the further development of) CLE at Belgian universities without dedicated support in the form of academic staff specifically appointed to provide CLE.

The difference in academic "culture" to that in other countries is a final potential obstacle to the establishment of legal clinics at Belgian law schools, at which the conception of academic teaching may remain strongly based on theory and *ex cathedra* teaching to big groups of students, as opposed to the practice-based education CLE provides to small groups of students (see also Chapter 6 by Xavier Aurey in this volume). Academic "culture" can also have an impact on the social justice mission of legal clinics. The concern, here, is that having an explicit social justice objective for a clinical programme would be an obstacle to the acceptance of that clinical programme within the broader law school. When the law school, as a whole, does not share a single vision of the relationship between law and society (e.g. where part of the academic staff still embraces positivism), it is sometimes considered more prudent to focus solely on the educational objectives of CLE.

REFORMING THE TEACHING AND PRACTICE OF LAW IN EUROPE

Goals and Methods of Ghent University's Human Rights Law Clinic

The Human Rights Law Clinic: Aligned with Educational Goals, Challenging Educational Methods

Law school education in Belgium is aimed at forming competent lawyers who are prepared to function autonomously in a wide range of legal functions. Several law schools, including Ghent University Law School, in addition aim to form critical lawyers with a sense of societal responsibility (see also Chapter 13 by Lynn Welchman in this volume; cf. Chapter 6 by Xavier Aurey). Concretely, the Ghent University Law School distinguishes a number of "areas of competence" as objectives of its law curriculum.[23] These include academic competences, intellectual competences, competences in collaboration and communication, and societal

---

[23] See Self-evaluation report of the Ghent University Law Faculty for the 2014 Visitation, Faculteit Rechtsgeleerdheid Universiteit Gent, *Zelfevaluatierapport Opleiding Rechten*, June 2014, 220 p, at 15 ss.

competences. The Human Rights Law Clinic aligns itself with these competences by giving them concrete content. The Clinic thereby aims, first and foremost, to offer education that is *complementary* to the existing, more "traditional" human rights courses in the curriculum, which are taught at both Bachelor and Master level.

By working in the Clinic, students obtain many of the core educational competences identified by the Law School. Clinic students identify the relevant facts and law that will assist them in answering the complex legal questions put forth by the Clinic's partners. This aligns with concrete *academic* competences identified by the Law School, such as "formulate a well-founded legal argumentation for the analysis and solution of complex legal questions"; "detect and qualify relevant legal facts and in so doing formulate adequate and critical legal questions for complex cases."[24] In working for the Clinic's partners, students further provide creative answers to legal questions. They are encouraged to question existing legal rules and propose new legal solutions to existing human rights problems. This corresponds to the following *intellectual* competences put forth by the Law School: "dare to formulate a creative point of view vis-à-vis a legal question through scientifically founded analysis and logical legal reasoning"; "critically reflect on legal rules *de lege lata* and formulate proposals *de lege ferenda*."[25] Since teamwork is – by design – an inherent part of clinical work, students work together (in principle, in groups of three) and learn from each other through cooperative and critical engagement. When students are asked to draft information packages for directly affected individuals and/or work for partners who often do not have in-house legal expertise, they further learn how to write in clear, simple, and accessible language. Students thus gain some of the key *collaboration and communication* competences identified by the Law School: "work individually or in a team to scientifically analyse and synthesize a complex legal question with a sense of responsibility and deontology"; "draft a clear text destined for legal practice, adapted to the intended audience."[26] Finally, since the Clinic's projects invariably pursue a social justice objective and target disadvantaged members of society, students become aware of their social responsibility as lawyers-to-be and of the importance of integrating respect for diversity in their work. This parallels a number of *societal* competences emphasized by the Law School: "be aware of the social responsibility of lawyers and assess the legal implications of societal and technological evolutions for legal practice and legal science"; "creatively integrate societal commitment in scientific work and in functioning as a (starting) lawyer."[27] In short, the Clinic *aligns* itself with the Law School's educational objectives, rather than challenging them.

At the same time, however, the *methods* employed by the Clinic to achieve these objectives do challenge the "status quo." Most law school courses in Belgium are based on the study of primary sources (legislation and case law) and legal doctrine

[24] *Id.* [25] *Id.* [26] *Id.* [27] *Id.*

(see also Chapter 8 by Nora Markard and Chapter 6 Xavier Aurey in this volume).[28] Spurred on by the Bologna Process, several of these courses increasingly integrate group work, written work, and oral presentations, as well as working on fictional cases (see also Chapter 5 by Maria Marquès i Banqué in this volume). The Clinic, while also adopting these practices, crucially *transforms* them (see also Chapter 6). The parts of the curriculum that resemble the Clinic most closely are moot courts and internships. The similarity with moot courts consists in the fact that a small group of students work together over the course of several months in solving a complex legal problem. Yet, of course, the legal problem in the moot court remains a fictional one. In addition, the competitive context tends to dominate the moot court experience. Clinic students, conversely, work on real human rights issues, for real partners in a cooperative spirit. Clinical work also brings a level of unpredictability with it that is absent from the moot court experience. This unpredictability could be seen as a challenge, but also as an opportunity, since it will be a key feature of students' later professional lives. When internships are part of the curriculum, these include internships with human rights organizations. These may include the same organizations that are partners of the legal clinic (as noted earlier). One the key differences between collaborations in the context of an internship and in the context of a Clinic project is that the former entails individual work, while the latter requires group work. Students who join the Clinic work – per definition – collaboratively. A core objective of the Clinic is to have students learn how to work together, in a team, on real human rights issues. Students are moreover encouraged to take the lead: to the extent possible, students are put in charge of meetings with the partners, they divide the work, they lead the discussion of internal meetings (for instance readings of literature or giving feedback on their respective contributions to the project), and more. A further difference between the Clinic and internships is that the latter take place at the premises of the partner, are monitored by the partner, and are evaluated by the partner and the professor, whereas the former takes place at the university and is monitored and evaluated by university staff (including clinicians). In an internship, the partner moreover acts as an employer, whereas in the legal clinic, the partner is a client.

What ultimately sets the Clinic apart from other courses, thus, is this: Clinic students work collaboratively, in small groups and independently, but under intense supervision of clinicians, on real human rights issues for real clients, with concrete consequences and impact. The dedicated time students spend working in a 2:1 or 3:1 ratio with clinicians on real issues for a real partner is arguably what distinguishes the Clinic from most (if not all) other courses of Belgian law school curriculums.

---

[28] *See*, generally, Rob van Gestel and Hans-Wolfgang Micklitz, *Why Methods Matter in European Legal Scholarship*, 20 EUROPEAN LAW JOURNAL 292–316 (2014).

The Clinic's Core Innovation: Making Human Rights Real

Earlier, we described – in rather general terms – how the Clinic aligns itself with the Law School's educational objectives but subtly challenges the methods by which those objectives are pursued. Here, we will elaborate by discussing, in concrete terms, the core innovation of the Clinic: "making human rights real" for students.[29] Making human rights real entails three central elements: (1) exposing students to all aspects of human rights in practice, (2) making students aware of the promise of human rights *and* the obstacles to their realization, and (3) inducing empathy in students.

First, the Clinic exposes students to various aspects of human rights practice. Students learn that human rights are not confined to law in the strictest sense of litigation or legislative reform, but also include the political, in the form of policy and advocacy strategies (see also Chapter 13 by Lynn Welchman in this volume).[30] The Clinic takes on projects that reflect the diverse ways in which human rights function in practice. Clinic students may thus work on litigation (e.g. submitting a complaint to the European Committee of Social Rights or a third-party intervention at the ECtHR), legislative policy (e.g. drafting a federal Bill of law to amend the Belgian Criminal Code to comply with international human rights standards on the use of evidence obtained through ill-treatment during criminal trials), and/or advocacy (e.g. writing policy documents on the rights of transgender persons in the context of the Belgian health care system or drafting advocacy documents on the right to inclusive education for children with a disability). The strategy or route to pursue is identified not by the Clinic or its academic staff but by the Clinic's partners. Clinic students thus also learn, from the outset, that they are working *for* someone. They come to appreciate, often for the first time, what it means to put the client's interest centre stage. Given the different levels of legal expertise of the partner organizations in these projects, as well as the different target audiences, students moreover learn to adapt the style and content of their legal arguments and analyses to best fit the situation. They, in particular, learn to avoid complex, technical jargon and present things in an accessible and clear manner.

A second core objective of the Clinic in "making human rights real" is to create awareness in students of both the promise of human rights *and* the obstacles to their realization.[31] By working on Clinic projects, students invariably learn that there may be significant gaps between "the law on the books" and "law in practice." Students learn that accepted human rights standards, existing instruments, and established case law will often only take them so far. Partners, simultaneously, might have

---

[29] Hurwitz, *supra* note 6 at 528–29.
[30] *Id.* at 513; Caroline Bettinger-Lopez et al., *Redefining Human Rights Lawyering Through the Lens of Critical Theory: Lessons for Pedagogy and Practice*, 18 GEO. J. ON POVERTY LAW & POLICY 379 (2011).
[31] Hurwitz, *supra* note 6 at 516; Lydia Bleasdale-Hill and Paul Wragg, *Models of Clinic and Their Value to Students, Universities and the Community in the Post-2012 Fees Era*, 19 INT'L. J. CLINICAL LEGAL EDUC. 267(2013).

expectations that lie *beyond* the bounds of current human rights standards. For instance, in one of the Clinic's past projects, the partner wished to advocate for an absolute right to inclusive education for children with a disability. Throughout the project, however, the students became convinced that the partner's expectations were not entirely supported by current human rights standards. They thus realized the ambiguity and room for reasonable disagreement inherent in many human rights issues: How far does the law go, and how far *should* it go? In their commitment to provide the partner – *qua* client – with accurate advice, the students eventually opted to draft two documents. In the first, an external advocacy document, they put the argument for inclusive education as strongly as possible within the bounds of current human rights standards. In the second, an internal clarification document, they indicated to the partner which arguments were weaker and which strategies the partner might wish to pursue to nevertheless convince stakeholders of their salience.

A third and final aspect of "making human rights real" for the Clinic's students is to induce empathy towards the target group (i.e. the beneficiaries of the activities of the Clinic's partners).[32] Since the Clinic currently cooperates almost exclusively with civil society partners and thus does not engage in direct-service delivery (but see the later discussion about a live-client refugee law project), ensuring that students are aware of the real-world implications of their work is a particular concern. To the extent possible, the Clinic addresses this issue by organizing meetings with affected individuals. For instance, as part of a project on the inability of suspected war criminals from Afghanistan to obtain asylum in the Netherlands, students joined a meeting of the persons affected to hear their stories. Crucially, these persons could not be deported to Afghanistan due to their running a real risk of being tortured upon their return. A key aspect of the project was thus the "life in limbo" these suspected war criminals led in the Netherlands: trapped in a situation of insecurity they could not escape from. The tragic nature of their situation became very real to the students when they met the individuals in person. As one student later stated in an interview with the University's *Durf Denken* [Dare to Think] magazine:

> the most important experience, to me, was the contact with the Afghans. We could speak to the victims ourselves ... That made an inerasable impression and makes you immediately extremely motivated. In other courses, you work primarily for the marks and to learn something. In a clinic, you act in an engaged manner to help persons. That is a very different motivator.[33]

Beyond the Educational Goals

As explained earlier, the Human Rights Law Clinic combines education goals with a social justice mission. In terms of the latter, the Clinic's aim is to strengthen

---

[32] Hurwitz, *supra* note 6 at 522.
[33] X., "Recht in Real Life" [Law in Real Life], *Durf Denken* (January 2016), 23.

human rights activism in Belgium and potentially also abroad by providing free high-quality legal advice to human rights organizations and by building capacity for legal human rights activism in law students. In that respect, there is little doubt that a live-client clinic would be useful in Belgium, including in the field of human rights law. Indeed, the impression is that despite the existence of legal aid, some situations that may violate human rights or antidiscrimination law are not brought before a judge. This is partly due to the already mentioned limited resources of civil society organizations (CSOs), which moreover do not tend to prioritize litigation. It is not excluded that the Human Rights Law Clinic at Ghent University may evolve in this direction (in fact, an experiment with live clients in the field of refugee law has taken place in the Spring of 2016; as will be discussed later), yet, at the moment of writing, the focus is on legal advice to partner organizations in a range of practice-oriented formats (as noted earlier).

The primary impact of projects run by the Human Rights Law Clinic is, logically, confined to Belgium. Since our main social justice objective is to strengthen and assist Belgian civil society in the area of human rights, most of our partners are – by deliberate design – Belgian CSOs. These CSOs invariably raise questions and concerns about the human rights situation of persons living in Belgium. Hence, our projects tackle, in the first place, problems that arise in Belgium. Yet our Clinic's work also transcends Belgian borders. Several projects have been conducted for and with international partners, including the Scholars at Risk Network and the UN Special Rapporteur on the rights to freedom of peaceful assembly and of association. The geographical focus of these projects is, naturally, international and includes countries such as Azerbaijan, Nigeria, South Africa, and Thailand. But even our "Belgian" projects can have an international dimension. For instance, when projects involve submitting complaints to international or regional bodies such as the European Committee on Social Rights, they may have an impact on the future development of international/regional human rights standards.

One obstacle that we have encountered in our endeavour to support human rights activism in Belgium is that some of the organizations that need such support most – and that should therefore in principle be our priority partners – are in practice more difficult to work with. Indeed, the very lack of resources that motivates our desire to work with them may also stand in the way of efficient collaboration. This is the case, for example, when a partner organization is not able to identify a suitable or clearly delineated project for the Clinic, or when its staff is overburdened to such an extent as to not be able to communicate all necessary information to the legal clinic team. It should be noted, though, that in some cases a small organization that consists mainly of volunteers may nevertheless make an excellent partner.

For the third-party interventions, activism is mediated through scholarship. This practice commenced in the context of a project that had as its overall research objective the development of improved standards and techniques of legal reasoning, which might be used by the ECtHR. Most of the third-party interventions submitted by the Human Rights Centre have argued points of legal reasoning that were directly derived from research papers produced by Human Rights Centre scholars.

Summing up, it may be said that for the Human Rights Law Clinic course, supporting human rights activism is a primary goal, whereas for the Strasbourg Club third-party interventions the primary goal is to put scholarly expertise at the service of the ECtHR.

The Weight and Value of Internationalization

The salience of the interplay between domestic law and international/regional human rights law to CLE is frequently emphasized in the relevant literature. In highlighting the impact of the Europeanization and globalization of law on legal education in Europe, Miguel Poiares Maduro has noted that "[l]awyers increasingly need to operate in the context of a plurality of jurisdictions and legal sources," leading him to insist that "it is the teaching of law itself that must change" in the face of this new reality.[34] In relation to human rights clinics, in particular, Arturo Carrillo has argued that "human rights clinics are simply clinical legal education's natural response to the transnational exigencies of lawyering in the twenty-first century."[35]

Maduro's and Carrillo's findings are reflected in the daily practice of our Human Rights Law Clinic (see also Chapter 13 by Lynn Welchman, Chapter 10 by Anthony Valcke, and Chapter 9 by Alberto Alemanno and Lamin Khadar in this volume). In the Clinic, students are organically trained as lawyers who are keenly aware of the important interplays between different sources and levels of law. Many of the Clinic's projects require students to engage with both domestic law *and* regional/international human rights standards. International law undeniably has a great impact on how local human rights question are approached by the clinics' students. Which international/regional human rights instruments and legal forums students engage with depends on the nature of the project. Sometimes, students work directly for an international partner. In those projects, the focus is *ipso facto* on international/regional human rights standards. Students have, for instance, worked on projects for and with the UN Special Rapporteur on Freedom of Assembly and Association and the Scholars at Risk Network, an international network that advocates for academic freedom of expression on a global scale. For the UN Special Rapporteur, students drafted significant sections of a third-party intervention in an ECtHR case on freedom of assembly in Azerbaijan. This required deep engagement with the existing

---

[34] Miguel Poiares Maduro, Legal Education and the Europeanization and Globalisation of Law, *Contraditorio Policy Paper* 10/01 (February 2010), 3 and 10, www.contraditorio.pt/admin/source/files/1276200432-PolicyPaper10_01_LegalEducationandtheEuropeanizationandGlobalisationofLaw-Original.pdf (last visited July 8, 2016),

[35] Arturo J. Carrillo, *Bringing International Law Home: The Innovative Role of Human Rights Clinics in the Transnational Legal Process*, 35 COLUM. HUM. RTS. L. REV. 533 (2004).

case law of the ECtHR. In support of the Special Rapporteur's position, students deployed the existing case law strategically, where it was in line with the Rapporteur's position, and critiqued it where it failed to meet the Rapporteur's preferred standards. But the students also looked beyond the case law of the ECtHR. They, in particular, relied on comparative arguments drawn from the relevant standards in the Inter-American human rights system to strengthen their claims. Students who worked on the Scholars at Risk project, conversely, provided the partner with a database on global (UN) and regional (European, African, Inter-American) standards on academic freedom. They moreover prepared so-called incident reports, to be posted on the partner's dedicated advocacy website, on specific instances of violations of academic freedom in countries like Nigeria, Burundi, and Thailand.

But also when students work on projects for Belgian partners, international and regional human rights standards are often their first frame of reference. For instance, in the context of a project for Amnesty International, students drafted a federal bill of law on the exclusion of evidence obtained through ill-treatment from criminal trials in all circumstances, including terrorism. The case law of the ECtHR, the Human Rights Committee, and the UN Committee against Torture provided the framework within which the students developed their core arguments. Another project, for two Belgian human rights NGOs, concerned the alleged violation of the European Social Charter in relation to the social rights of prisoners in Belgium. For this project, students drafted significant sections of a complaint to be submitted to the European Committee of Social Rights by the Clinic's partners.

Crucial, from our perspective, is that the legal clinic experience allows students to deepen their knowledge of international human rights law in a bottom-up manner, starting not from norms or doctrine, but from the concrete facts of complex cases. An interesting feature of this experience is that it confronts students with the fragmented nature of international human rights law and obliges them to "integrate" human rights[36] from the perspective of the rights holders they are concerned with, bringing together the jigsaw pieces from different layers of human rights law. For example, the project on evidence obtained by ill-treatment for Amnesty International required the integration of sources from three distinct human rights bodies. In a traditional law school class, these remain separate sources, even if the approach of the course is thematic, as cases of supranational monitoring bodies by definition approach the matter from the perspective of a single instrument. Yet in many settings, such as lobbying, advocacy, or domestic litigation, a number of international human rights sources are simultaneously applicable and may all be

---

[36] This approach coincides with a scholarly interest at the Human Rights Centre. See the network project, The Global Challenge of Human Rights Integration; Toward a User Perspective, http://hrintegration.be/. *See also* Eva Brems, *Should Pluriform Human Rights Become One? Exploring the Benefits of Human Rights Integration*, 4 EUROPEAN JOURNAL OF HUMAN RIGHTS 447–70(2014).

invoked in the same case. The legal clinic exposes students, in a very concrete manner and often for the first time, to such a user-centred approach to human rights issues.

The students who choose to participate in the Human Rights Law Clinic course are generally those with a strong interest in international human rights law. In our experience, however, a very important lesson they learn in the legal clinic relates to the role of domestic law in the protection of human rights. Indeed, our experiences with projects submitted by Belgian CSOs is that they require not only a thorough study of international and regional human rights law, but also a study of – sometimes numerous – fields of domestic law, many of which the students may not have studied in detail in the course of their law school experience. For example, for a project about the social rights of Travellers, students had to engage with regional and municipal zoning rules, as well as with social assistance law, in addition to studying international and regional human rights law. Similarly, the above-mentioned project about inclusive education for children with disabilities required not only a thorough analysis of the UN Disability Rights Convention and EU nondiscrimination law, but also of the technicalities of Flemish regional legislation in the field of education. The salience of domestic law is not without challenges for the supervision of the Clinic's projects because the academic staff who are involved in the Human Rights Law Clinic consists of experts in human rights law and may thus know little about the field of domestic law at stake in a given project. Even the clinicians who are involved in directly supervising students' work are not always familiar with the details of all fields of law. One way we have tackled this challenge is by bringing in external expert input in the form of informal seminars for Clinic students.

Cooperation in CLE

Since our Human Rights Law Clinic has been established recently (2014) and given that CLE is only starting to genuinely emerge at Belgian universities (as noted earlier), we are still in the process of creating linkages and collaborations with other law schools. From our perspective, the beginning years of a Clinic involve a process of trial and error, whereby we – the academic staff – learn as much as the Clinic's students do about all the facets and implications of CLE. We have found great support, in this respect, in our membership of the European Network on Clinical Legal Education (ENCLE). The contacts we have made and discussions we have had at ENCLE events (conferences and trainings), in particular, have allowed us to shape our Clinic in ways that benefit the students. For instance, it was at an ENCLE event that one of us became convinced of the need to initiate a live-client refugee law project (discussed later). In terms of more institutionalized collaborations, we expect that, once the Clinic becomes more firmly established, we will be in a position to forge greater linkages and concrete collaborations with other law schools. The current emergence of clinics at other Belgian universities (as noted earlier) is a promising development in that respect.

Currently, the Clinic does, of course, cooperate with a number of international actors in the form of the Clinic's partners. None of these partners could be labelled strictly European, but some are global actors (for instance, the UN Special Rapporteur on Freedom of Assembly and Association and the Scholars at Risk Network). From our perspective, these collaborations benefit our students – in terms of both their legal education and future professional careers – in exactly the same manner as our collaboration with Belgian civil society partners does. Students learn what it means to work on concrete files for a partner-client. This exposes them to human rights law in practice and to the kinds of professional tasks they may perform in their future careers.

Diffusion of CLE

Legal clinics from abroad have played an important part in the genesis of the Human Rights Law Clinic at Ghent University. Contact with US universities and reverberations from the flourishing CLE movement in that context came first. In addition, the Human Rights Centre has been involved in several academic development projects in Sub-Saharan Africa, including projects in Ethiopia and Mozambique, which contained a clinical component. At some point, it appeared absurd to be promoting abroad a "best practice" that was not even applied at our own university. Finally, in the process of preparing for the creation of the Clinic, extensive online research documented existing legal clinics with a focus on human rights in Western Europe. Most of their coordinators were contacted with a view to obtaining more information. These exchanges were decisive in the choice to focus the legal clinic's approach, at least initially, on collaboration with civil society partners rather than on working with live clients (but see later discussion for future plans).

Since our Clinic is a (relatively) young one, we have not yet been actively involved in the spreading of CLE methods throughout Europe. In our personal capacities – as Director and as Coordinator of the Clinic – we have, however, participated in a number of national, European, and international events on CLE. These have included a number of ENCLE conferences, workshops, and trainings; a conference of the *International Journal of Clinical Legal Education*; and workshops in Belgium bringing together some of the Belgian academics involved or interested in CLE. These events have invariably been an occasion to exchange experiences, discuss obstacles and challenges, and identify best practices. From our perspective, our primary focus has thus far been on learning about the practical implications of CLE and, in particular, how we could implement and modify existing models to best suit our Clinic's objectives and philosophy.

The Future of CLE in Europe

When we consider, first, our own Clinic, we see a number of opportunities (and a need) for growth and transformation in the future.

First, we have identified a need to secure more ECTS for the Clinic within the Law School's curriculum. Currently, Clinic students obtain four ECTS or one-third of the credits awarded to moot court students while they perform at least the same intensity and amount of work. We have noticed that, particularly when projects are not defined sufficiently clearly by the partner and the communication between students and partner fails to provide the requisite clarity, students are prone to feel demotivated. Complaints by students about the amount of work involved in the Clinic relative to the credits earned are not uncommon. One of our immediate priorities is, thus, to attempt to raise the number of credits awarded to students for their work in the Clinic. If successful, this is expected to lead to further growth of the Clinic in terms of the number of students registering for the course. This, in turn, would create both the opportunity and challenge that comes with increased student interest. It would offer us an opportunity to select the most suitable students for the Clinic (e.g. those with a proven track record in human rights and who exhibit the greatest motivation). It would, however, also confront us with a challenge: Do we only select the best students (in the interest of our partners) or aim for a mix of students (in the interest of students' education)?

Second, we have identified a number of opportunities for growth of the Clinic. In particular, we have noticed great interest among international (Erasmus and LLM) students in joining the Clinic. We plan to further integrate international students' participation in the Clinic in the future. To that end, we have sought and obtained incorporation of the Clinic into the curriculum of the LLM on European and international law at the Law School. Yet this particular potential avenue for growth (i.e. making the Clinic available to international students) comes with a specific challenge: the need for more international – i.e. English language – projects.

Third, in terms of potential transformation of the Clinic, we are currently exploring the possibility of establishing a live-client Refugee Law Clinic. In response to the refugee crisis and students' clear interest in the issue – and inspired by a call at a recent ENCLE conference for European clinics to "do more" to assist in addressing the refugee crisis – we have initiated a trial Refugee Law Clinic project. In cooperation with the academic staff responsible for Migration Law at the Law School, we have set up a small-scale project under which three students – supervised by two migration lawyers – assist in preparing asylum seekers for their first interview and/or submitting judicial appeals against negative decisions. If the trial proves successful, we would look to establish a Refugee Law Clinic. Ideally, this would be done under the auspices of the Migration Law course, thereby becoming the second Clinic at our Law School.

If we turn our attention to the future of CLE in Europe, we see great potential in intensified networking among Europe's clinics. In establishing and developing our Clinic, the ability to learn from the experiences of others has been – and continues to be – invaluable. To give just one example, discussion with those involved in established Refugee Law Clinics has made us acutely aware of the opportunities, challenges, and obstacles involved, leading us to opt for a small-scale exploratory project focused on two strictly defined tasks for students. We personally do not see, however, a need for standardization of CLE in Europe. From our perspective, a major benefit of CLE is the room for creativity and contextualized learning which it grants in equal measure to students and academic staff. We thus see greater potential in maintaining the contextualized and creativity-driven nature of clinics, adapted to the personal needs of the country and legal system and the target groups, as well as to the motivations and vision of the academic staff. Where we *do* see a need for European-wide attention is in the area of funding. The sustainability of our Clinic, like that of most Belgian and European clinics, is by no means secured. To offer long-term viability of CLE in Belgium and Europe, dedicated funding is a prerequisite. We know this is a concern for the vast majority of clinics in Europe. It should, thus, be an absolute priority in changing the CLE landscape in Europe in the future.

CONCLUSION

At the time of writing, the Human Rights Law Clinic at Ghent University is completing its second year of operation. It is therefore too early for statements about the clinic's sustainability, its impact on students and civil society, or its contribution to the reform of legal education. If we nevertheless attempt to draw some broader conclusions from the pilot phase of our clinic, we suggest the following.

First, the clinic exemplifies the adaptation strategies of CLE to the Western European context. While the founders started from an American conception that assimilates CLE with live-client clinics, they reoriented the concept of the clinic towards one of consultancy for civil society partners and other human rights actors. This shift was the result of a context in which students cannot represent clients, and law faculties are anxious not to be perceived by bar associations as competitors in the market. In the case of the Ghent University Clinic, an exploration of the landscape of legal clinics in the human rights field in Western Europe indicated that this was by far the dominant model. At the same time, the clinic started experimenting almost immediately with the live-client format as an add-on to our core activities. This happened in response to the refugee crisis, which functioned both as a factor of necessity, tapping into the social commitment that motivated the creation of the legal clinic in the first place, and as an opportunity that revived the original image of what a clinic should look like.

Second, the clinic also responds to a European trend in which case files require students to delve simultaneously into international law and domestic law and to explore the connections between both. This is only in part due to the focus on human rights law, which is, in the European tradition, interpreted as including domestic civil rights law. An equally important factor is the fact that in EU Member States, layers of European and international law are very strongly interwoven with domestic law, both on account of the nature of EU law and because of the direct effect of international treaties (including Council of Europe treaties and UN treaties) in the domestic law of monist states such as Belgium.

Finally, it is worth noting that the clinic has benefited from a favourable institutional climate – although more in terms of rhetoric than in terms of actual support – with respect to both educational innovation and social value creation. For the founders who acted in the first place from a motivation for social justice, inserting the clinic into the discourse and programmes of educational innovation has been both a strategic move and a welcome avenue for generating additional benefits. Yet it is the institution's support for the social justice dimension of CLE that most sustains our enthusiasm and our determination to further develop the clinic.

12

Clinical Legal Education at Central European University, Budapest

A Small Project with Big Ambitions in a Supportive Institution

Renáta Uitz and Eszter Polgári

INTRODUCTION

The clinical specialization (as our clinic is known) at the Department of Legal Studies at Central European University (CEU), Budapest, Hungary was established in 2008. It is offered to students in the MA and LLM programs in human rights and comparative constitutional law. Our students arrive from more than thirty countries of the world, predominantly from Europe, North America, Sub-Saharan Africa, and South-East Asia. After graduation, many seek careers with human rights organizations and international organizations (such as the Council of Europe or the European Union [EU]), as well as in academia. Comparative reflection on the successes and limits of strategic litigation (or public interest litigation) to protect fundamental rights and to limit governmental powers has been a key component of our curriculum. During their year at CEU, students can choose from a wide range of experiential learning options (e.g. credited internships, in-house moot courts, advocacy projects, and the clinical specialization) embedded in the master curriculum which suit their current interests and future career needs.

Our course offering in the human rights and comparative constitutional law programs is defined by a strong comparative legal element taught by an international faculty and is built for an international student body. The curriculum takes into account the fact that legal education for the first law degree continues to be heavily tied to national legal systems. It is against this background that our courses and experiential learning components seek to explore legal and human rights problems beyond familiar national contexts and constraints. The Department's overall 7:1 student ratio and the clinical specialization's 4:1 student ratio permit our faculty to respond to students' individual interests throughout the academic year. Interactive, problem-based classes permit us to draw on the knowledge and experiences of a highly diverse student body. This approach is appealing to students who are interested in the legal architecture of human rights and government and are seeking an international or transnational career.

Due to the basic characteristics of our institutional and educational model, we cannot establish a live-client clinic. Instead, through cooperation with civil society partner organizations, we opted for an approach which permits our students to participate in strategic litigation through either preparing amicus briefs (interventions) and other submissions, or through providing research assistance for developing a litigation strategy to address human rights violations. Our faculty and the responsible litigators from the partner organization choose a problem or case jointly, carefully assessing the practical needs of our institutional partner as well as the education needs, goals, and benefits of a particular project for our students. The deliverables are benchmarked, taking into account the academic calendar as well as the needs of the project as seen by our partner organization. In addition to the activities of the clinical course itself, participating students are also required to take a number of designated courses from the MA and LLM course offerings of the Department (hence the name "clinical specialization"). This menu of courses comprises the clinical specialization, certifying student's participation in the clinic as well as proficiency in the broader context of the human rights problems covered by the clinical case. We decided to label this experiential learning option as a clinic because it shares some of the fundamental commitments of clinical legal education (CLE): students do *pro bono* work on a litigation project which is meant to trigger legal change in human rights cases involving vulnerable subjects (e.g. persons in detention). Their work product is based on comparative research and aims to contribute to litigation strategies in the European legal space.

The clinic has been a rewarding experience of institutional learning. Even with trusted partner organizations, selecting a suitable case or problem is a gamble. The more concrete the clinical case, the more the clinical course is exposed to twists and turns of real life, though the more gratifying the experience for students when they see the impact of their work in a real human rights problem. Based on student feedback,[1] we found that graduates of the clinical specialization find this opportunity rewarding when they receive direction and feedback from the clinical lawyer: students were much less satisfied with the clinical course when they had to brainstorm in general or develop alternative scenarios on a broad theme, while they benefited from the experience most when they worked on submissions which reached courts before the end of the academic year. Although sheer luck will always be part of a clinical project, we found that guidance from supervising faculty members and active cooperation between partner organizations and our own faculty are essential to creating a meaningful student experience. This is what makes a non–

---

[1] Alumni of the clinical specialization were surveyed in March 2016 for the purposes of this chapter. The survey comprised multiple-choice components and open-ended questions similar (but not identical) to surveys used in course evaluations and self-assessment surveys at the Department. Results on file with the authors.

live-client clinic distinct from a simple nongovernmental organization (NGO) internship, and this is how we seek to advance our own clinic in the future.

EMERGENCE OF CLE

Genesis and Context

CEU is a graduate institution of advanced research and teaching. It was established in 1991, received accreditation both in the United States and in Europe, and it offers master- and doctoral-level education primarily in the social sciences and humanities. CEU was established when transition to democracy from communism was taking off in Central Europe. Initially serving a student body mostly from post-Communist Central and Eastern Europe, the former Yugoslavia, and the former Soviet Union, by its twenty-fifth anniversary it has become a global university with a truly international student body and faculty reaching far beyond its initial region. The Department of Legal Studies has been among the founding departments of CEU. The initial LLM programs in comparative constitutional law and international business law were complemented in 1998 by an MA and in 2001 by an LLM program in human rights.

Building open societies, promoting their values, and encouraging self-reflective critical thinking have been central to CEU's institutional mission from the start and, together with enhanced civic engagement, remain focal points after several revisions of the mission. The initial LLM programs of the Department of Legal Studies were seeking to attract young law graduates from countries transitioning to democracy and a market economy. Catering for the target group of students, the Department's core mission in the early years was to educate lawyers for public administration and academia, as well as for civil society, who would become agents of democratic transformation in their home countries. With the admission of countries in the region to the Council of Europe in the mid-1990s and with European integration becoming central to their political realities, the Department opened new programs to explore the protection and promotion of human rights.

The opening of the human rights programs attracted applicants from well beyond the traditional CEU region and opened the possibility of closely cooperating with the Open Society Justice Initiative (OSJI) in providing academic training in human rights for mid-career professionals from all parts of the world. The MA program in human rights was specifically designed as an interdisciplinary degree, admitting students with different disciplinary backgrounds but with demonstrated commitment for human rights: while the curricula of the two human rights programs significantly overlap, founding a program for nonlawyers has substantially added to the diversity of the Department and resulted in an active conversation between human rights practitioners and activists across disciplines.

The Department of Legal Studies at CEU is not a full law school, it does not offer undergraduate degrees, and our programs are accredited only in the state of New York, and not in Hungary.[2] Students in our LLM programs typically are graduates of law schools in their native countries and received classical legal education, with a curriculum preparing graduates to practice law in a national legal system, with the occasional, specialized classes on international law and – in the case of European students – various EU-related subjects. The overwhelming majority of our students do not hold a law degree from Hungary and are not licensed to practice law in Hungary. In fact, the overwhelming majority of our students and faculty do not speak or read Hungarian. The one-year master's degrees require students to adhere to a rather strict course schedule during the academic year. Class attendance requires advance preparation, and students also have to submit written work based on individual research throughout the academic year. We were seeking a model for the clinical specialization that not only fitted the University's and the Department's institutional mission but also served the educational needs and interests of our students within the institutional constraints that apply to students and faculty alike.

By reason of its location at the heart of Central Europe, CEU is naturally exposed to Hungarian and regional sociopolitical changes, tendencies, and occasionally tensions. While being an English-language university with a truly international faculty and student body, the comparative constitutional law and the human rights programs continuously need to reflect on and respond to newly emerging human rights and constitutional challenges. At the same time, our curriculum is largely unaffected by reforms of legal education in Hungary: the degrees offered by the Department of Legal Studies are accredited only in the United States, chiefly due to the fact that, until 2013, Hungarian law did not recognize LLM degrees. In addition, our Department's master's degree programs are by far the most international in Hungary. In the past decade, the Department had students from thirty to forty countries each year. The gradual Europeanization or internationalization of Hungarian legal education, which may be the result of recent developments in the legal regulation of Hungarian legal education, do not directly affect the direction of curriculum development at our Department. International donors promoting CLE in Central Europe in the 1990s understandably focused on Hungarian law faculties which had hundreds of Hungarian students in their five-year Dr. iur. programs. As we only offer master's degrees to international students, and as our master's degrees are not accredited in Hungary, efforts of international donors to reform legal education in the law faculties of Central Europe understandably did not target CEU.

---

[2] CEU's legal status in Hungary is regulated by the Act no. CCIV of 2011 on higher education that lists the university among the institutions of higher education recognized by the Hungarian State. Several, bur far from all, master and doctoral programs at CEU hold Hungarian accreditation. For details, *see* https://www.ceu.edu/administration/accreditation.

The decision to establish a clinical specialization was driven by genuine curricular considerations endemic to our own LLM and MA programs in human rights and comparative constitutional law. Witnessing the educational benefits of the existing NGO–internship component of the human rights degrees, we sought to introduce an additional experiential learning opportunity for our students studying human rights and comparative constitutional law. We settled on a model which takes advantages of the Department's existing professional network and resources while also drawing in new ways on the strengths of the existing curriculum. The clinical specialization was meant to offer students an opportunity to participate in developing litigation strategies and to react to the changing circumstances and focus of an ongoing case, and thus participate in an experiential learning process. Enriching the curriculum and diversifying teaching methods, the clinical specialization serves broader social justice goals and priorities that are also shared in CEU's and the Department's own institutional mission.

Our clinical specialization fits into two clinical education models, depending on the need presented by the cooperating civil society organization (CSO): in some years, student work in a format that represents the characteristics of a litigation-based clinic, while in other years, our program resembles more the project model of clinical education.[3] In previous years, students prepared an application successfully litigated by our NGO partner before the European Court of Human Rights.[4] In other years, the findings of the clinical course formed the basis of developing the litigation strategy further or served as amicus briefs in ongoing procedures.[5]

In one year, the clinical course sought to assist a partner NGO in identifying the areas where legislative and policy reform was needed and to pinpoint the issues where litigation could be successfully pursued.[6] The complexity of the starting problem and the holistic approach that was expected from the students, however, did not yield creative solutions: while in principle the project offered a possibility to utilize a wide range of activities and strategies in order to trigger – both legal and social – change, students found that wide variety of options and measures confusing. For this reason, in recent years, we chose clinical projects which were more narrowly defined and had direct relevance for litigation.

---

[3] For a general overview of the different models and the reasons for opting for a particular set-up, see, Anna E. Carpenter, *The Project Model of Clinical Education: Eight Principles to Maximize Student Learning and Social Justice Impact*, 20 CLINICAL L. REV. 39 (2013).

[4] *Süveges v. Hungary* App no 50255/12 (ECHR, 5 January 2016). Our students helped the Hungarian Helsinki Committee (www.helsinki.hu/en/; last visited May 16, 2016) in preparing the application in the case.

[5] For example, our students assisted with thorough comparative background research on prison overcrowding and the applicable international standards that was later used in advocacy and litigation by the Polish Helsinki Foundation for Human Rights (www.hfhr.pl/en/, last visited: May 16, 2016).

[6] In 2011/2012, the clinical course working under the supervision of the director of the Mental Disability and Advocacy Centre (www.mdac.info/en, last visited: May 16, 2016) sought to identify ways to advance the rights of persons with psychosocial disabilities in Africa, including presenting briefs that potentially could support litigation.

In our experience, the clinic undoubtedly offers a genuine opportunity to combine formal education with actual practice and to develop transferable skills.[7] The motivation behind introducing clinical education in the curricula of our master's degree programs neatly corresponds with the expectation of the students who apply for the course. In a recent questionnaire, alumni emphasized that, as a result of working on a real human rights problem, the clinic equipped them with skills that were useful in their current position or constituted an advantage in the hiring process.

The well-articulated aim of founding a clinical specialization in collaboration with prominent civil society actors and known human rights experts was to train students who do not yet possess the full range of practical skills but share the underlying values of the clinic.[8] Working on real cases and pressing human rights issues exposes students to the problems of justice, fairness, and vulnerability – we find that no classroom environment can possibly deliver this on a similar scale and with a similar intensity.

Drivers

For an external observer, it may appear that Hungarian legal education is a poster child of clinical education.[9] Clinical projects rapidly developed after the transition to democracy in 1989/1990, when the Open Society Institute (OSI; now Open Society Foundations [OSF]) and the Soros Foundations started providing targeted grants for establishing legal clinics.[10] In 1997, the Constitutional and Legal Policy Institute operating under the auspices of OSI launched initiatives and provided technical support with the Public Interest Law Institute (now PILnet) across the region.[11] The first clinical program was established at the Eötvös Loránd University (ELTE) in February 1997, in cooperation with the Hungarian Helsinki Committee on the rights of refugees, and it primarily trained law students to represent and counsel refugees. It has been followed by several other similar clinics in other law schools, almost all focusing on human rights problems of marginalized groups. These efforts to develop clinics and infuse the law curriculum in Central Europe with interactive and clinical elements were not targeting CEU. CEU being a small,

---

[7] *See also*, Frank Dignan, *Bridging the Academic/Vocational Divide: the Creation of a Law Clinic in an Academic Law School*, 16 INT'L J. CLINICAL LEGAL EDUC. 75 (2011).

[8] *See also* Donald Nicolson, *Problematizing Competence in Clinical Legal Education: What Do We Mean by Competence and How Do We Assess Non-Skill Competencies?* 23 INT'L J. CLINICAL LEGAL EDUC. 66 (2016).

[9] Cf. Italy, where the first law clinics opened in 2010. Clelia Bartoli, *The Italian Legal Clinics Movement: Data and Prospects*, 22 INT'L J. CLINICAL LEGAL EDUC. I (2015) at 1.

[10] Mariana Berbec-Rostas, Arkady Gutnikov, and Barbara Namyslowska-Gabrysiak, *Clinical Legal Education in Central and Eastern Europe*, in THE GLOBAL CLINICAL MOVEMENT: EDUCATING LAWYERS FOR SOCIAL JUSTICE (Frank S. Bloch, ed., Oxford University Press 2010), 53–68.

[11] *See*, for more details, Edwin Rekosh, *Constructing Public Interest Law: Transnational Collaboration and Exchange in Central and Eastern Europe*, 13 UCLA J. INT'L L. & FOREIGN AFF. 55 (2008).

private, international institution understandably was not of interest for international donors who were seeking to reform national law schools that, at the time, were almost exclusively based at public universities.

In the fall of 2015, ELTE University hosted the third conference of the European Network of Clinical Legal Education (ENCLE),[12] while in May 2014 CEU hosted a major meeting of Hungarian legal clinics at an event convened by the OSJI and PILnet.[13] According to the description of Judit Tóth, who leads the highly successful legal clinic at Szeged University in southern Hungary, at the time, Szeged was the only law school with a fully operational legal clinic open to all students (including Erasmus students) throughout the academic year. At ELTE and in the University of Debrecen, the clinical program currently primarily follows a street law model, providing legal awareness training to secondary school students and occasional legal assistance, while the University of Pécs had just started a law clinic for start-up and small business entrepreneurs.

Despite their relatively long history, legal clinics are not fully integrated into Hungarian legal education. A clinic is typically an optional (elective) seminar with low credit value, taught by adjunct faculty members. As a result, clinics tend to attract students who already have a strong sense of justice, and participating students are more inclined to continue their professional careers in the civil sector: increasing their employability in the private sector is not their primary motivation. In fact, law students who are strongly committed to human rights causes tend to volunteer with CSOs directly, outside their law faculty's clinical program, doing much more work than required or possible in a clinical program.[14]

A major limitation on the sustainability of clinics in Hungarian universities is the lack of funding and proper academic supervision. It is difficult to secure the financial resources from tight institutional budgets, while external funding depends largely on donor priorities. At the same time, for supervising faculty members, a clinic is a burdensome occupation not yielding proportionate professional or financial results. In Hungarian law schools, even full-time professors hold various adjunct positions, and a time-consuming activity such as leading a clinic, no matter how noble the cause, is often beyond their capacities. Clinics largely depend on adjunct faculty members and external tutors.[15] Furthermore, adjunct faculty members do

---

[12] www.ajk.elte.hu/file/3rd_encle_conference_brochure.pdf (last visited: May 16, 2016).
[13] For a conference report in Hungarian by Judit Tóth, Jogklinikusok hálózata? [Network of Legal Clinician?], see www.juris.u-szeged.hu/oktatas/jogklinikusok-halozata/jogklinikusok-halozata (last visited: May 16, 2016). For a discussion of the state of play until 2010, see Balázs Fekete, *Practice Elements in the Hungarian Legal Education System*, 51(1) ACTA IURIDICA HUNGARICA 66 (2010), at 73–76 (describing a much more active clinical scene at ELTE law faculty) and Berbec-Rostas, Gutnikov, Namyslowska-Gabrysiak, *supra* note 11, at 59–60. As CEU is not a Hungarian law school, our clinic is not included in these English-language discussions.
[14] See, e.g., the bio of the co-president of the Hungarian Helsinki Committee, Dr Márta Pardavi (at www.helsinki.hu/kik-vagyunk/a-csapat/dr-pardavi-marta/) (in Hungarian).
[15] Tóth, *supra* note 14.

not carry sufficient institutional weight to influence curriculum reform – hardly a Hungarian specificity.

REFORMING THE TEACHING AND PRACTICE OF LAW IN EUROPE

Goals and Methods

The CEU clinic differs significantly from the clinical programs operating at other Hungarian universities due to the broader institutional environment it operates in. Our Department relies on interactive teaching in small groups (with class sizes on average ranging between eight and thirty students), focusing on a case- or problem-based teaching method. Our educational programs seek to foster intellectual independence and critical thinking; we invite our students to see complex legal problems in their broader historical, political, social, and economic context. Our master's degree programs share a commitment to comparative analysis. Based on feedback from our own students, the approach we take to legal education in our LLM programs differs from the routes followed by most law schools serving the needs of mostly students who seek a professional legal career in the country where they earn their primary law degree. Students in search of an international or transnational career, as well as students preparing for an academic career, appear to find our approach appealing. Since our classes are small (and often much smaller than the lecture halls of law schools), we are in a unique position to explore topics and problems close to individual students' interests, to provide personalized support for research projects as well as assist with career development advice. We are aware that, due to the unique institutional position of CEU in Hungary, as well as due to the advantages offered by our small class sizes, diverse student body, and faculty, our experience cannot be directly compared with that of the standard law school classroom and curriculum. We offer an educational option to international students which is not available to them in their home countries. This unique position allows us to develop a curriculum and experiment with teaching methods which are not readily available in the law schools where our students had graduated before coming to CEU.

The clinical specialization is part of an experiential learning component of our curriculum which has been gradually developed over time. Some experiential learning exercises rely on in-class simulation and are based on group work (i.e. mid-course mini-moot courts or mediation exercises, group presentations), while others require off-campus engagement in a professional environment (i.e. credited internship opportunities in NGOs). By integrating experiential learning components into the regular master's degree curriculum through emphasizing their significance among learning outcomes, as well as in the continuing assessment of student performance, CEU makes them part and parcel of the graduate learning experience. We find that these experiential learning components complement the classroom experience and permit students a controlled immersion into the practice of law while affording ample time for reflection on their engagement with practical legal problems outside the classroom. A feedback loop ensures that students share with their peers their experiences from such out-of-class activities. Through integrating experiential learning components into the taught curriculum, we seek to ingrain in our students a culture of self-reflection and continuous learning which we consider important building blocks of a professional career in law and human rights.

Applicants to our human rights and comparative constitutional law master's programs tend to have volunteer or professional experience beyond mandatory internship or apprenticeship requirements prescribed for their undergraduate law degrees. Typical student experiences would include volunteer work in soup kitchens for the homeless or refugees, organizing or assisting with public protests and appeals, advocacy campaigns on a wide range of human rights issues, participation in awareness-raising campaigns, and occasional experience with the work of legal clinics. Students typically engage in such activities coordinated by local NGOs or faith-based groups. Our students often draw on these experiences for their course work and research papers, and their contributions enrich in-class discussions. The curriculum offers ample opportunity to discuss student experiences with such advocacy and awareness-raising projects. Encouraging students to reflect on their field experience and to draw on their impressions and observations in their research is an essential component of various problem-based individual research tasks and regular course work throughout the academic year. Such assignments are meant to ensure that students engage with their subjects beyond the confines of the classroom and explore their subjects from multiple perspectives.

While many students already have some field or volunteer experience, the popularity of our various internship programs and the clinical specialization indicates that master's degree students value opportunities to gain work experience. Although such opportunities ideally should be part of the undergraduate curriculum in legal education, we find that our LLM and MA students actively seek such opportunities on the graduate level. This may be due to a number of factors: at CEU, our students are away from the comfort of their home environments and can thus test themselves in foreign and international NGOs, in a work culture which is likely to be different from what they are accustomed to. Students on the master's level are more mature than during their undergraduate years and look for inspiration for future employment. At the same time, students appreciate the quality control component which results from the selection of NGO partners, as well as feedback opportunities stemming from the fact that the clinical course is a credited one which is part of the regular LLM and MA curriculum (and is not simply a volunteer project they take up on their own).

Our vision of a lawyer is that of a socially responsible, engaged, and politically conscious professional who approaches legal problems in their broader context and explores potential alternatives while considering the international, regional, and comparative dimensions of a problem. This approach to legal education fits into the conception of legal education as a forum for teaching global citizens.[16] Martha Nussbaum grounds the concept of legal education for global citizenship in critical self-reflection, world citizenship, and what she calls narrative imagination: "the ability to think what it might be like to be in the shoes of a person different from oneself, to be an intelligent reader of that person's story, and to understand the emotions, wishes and desires that someone so placed might have."[17]

Beyond the Educational Goals?

At CEU, the goals of the clinical specialization resonate with the institutional mission of the university on many levels. The small universe of the clinic reflects the commitment of the university to build open societies, to engage in critical thinking, and to educate agents of change in emerging and established democracies. This institutional mission is unique around the world for a university and is certainly different from the missions of law schools in Hungary. As such, CEU as a whole and the master's programs of our Department offer a unique intellectual and professional opportunity for law students and students of human rights: those committed to social justice issues do not have to fight an institutional culture to implement their projects. When admitted to CEU, they become part of an institution which itself is committed to promoting social change.

While human rights students' commitment to social justice issues is rather deep already when they apply to CEU, we seek to further nurture and channel this commitment in the course of the academic year within the framework of the existing curriculum. From the student survey conducted for this chapter, we saw that students found that the opportunity to assist victims of human rights abuses in a concrete case provided a rewarding educational opportunity which students preferred over mock trials and internship opportunities. In years when the clinical course also included a field visit component, students were enthusiastic to join, although field visits largely depend on the nature of the clinical case and the partner NGO chosen by the faculty and our NGO partner.

Because our clinical specialization is not a live-client clinic, as our students do not speak Hungarian and are not admitted to practice in Hungary, we admittedly can do little on a daily basis to improve access to justice in Hungary. The approach we chose is more indirect, due to clearly recognized institutional limitations stemming from the fact that we work with international students who do not aspire to stay or work in Hungary after graduation. One of our regular NGO partners for the clinical

---

[16] Martha Nussbaum, *Cultivating Humanity in Legal Education*, 70 U. CHICAGO L. REV. 265 (2003); for drawing on this approach for the European context, *see* Jan Smits, *European Legal Education, Or How to Prepare Students for Global Citizenship*, in EDUCATING EUROPEAN LAWYERS (Aalt Willem Heringa, Bram Akkermans, eds., Intersentia 2011), 43–64.

[17] Nussbaum, *supra* note 17, at 270.

specialization, the Hungarian Helsinki Committee, is the best-known CSO promoting access to justice in Hungary and, through multiple successful cases before the ECtHR, in Europe. In years when we work with the Hungarian Helsinki Committee, students receive insight into how promoting access to justice is a gradual and multifaceted project, building on small steps, one case at a time. Strategic thinking and a forward looking approach are essential for any human rights organization which has limited resources (whether time, personnel, or funding). Through working on a case or brief, students get a better understanding on how a particular, seemingly technical or minor legal issue fits into an overall strategy to improve human rights guarantees in criminal justice. This enables students in their future career to think strategically about the projects they take on.

In terms of benefits for the NGO partners of our clinic, we understand that in the format of our clinic our students provide alternative perspectives, comparative insight, and research based on resources which are otherwise not available to our NGO partners. Through bringing international students – some lawyers and others studying human rights from diverse backgrounds – who are committed and are trained to conduct comparative research on complex human rights problems, we extend the resources of our NGO partners beyond what is otherwise available to them.

The Weight and Value of Internationalization

In Central Europe, clinics in law schools have received ample funding in the past three decades from generous donors. While CEU cooperates closely with the OSF (previously the OSI) and its various education and human rights programs, our clinic has not been supported by OSF. At the same time, while developing the concept, we have been in intense conversation with OSF's OSJI as well as the Higher Education Support Program (HESP), which both had ample experience with establishing and supporting clinics in the region. We studied carefully the models of clinical education promoted by OSF's various programs in different national educational environments. While the OSJI model is based on live-client clinics (an approach that we cannot pursue), we found the broader, community-based approaches pursued by HESP's human rights programs inspiring. The idea – connected to the clinical project pursued by OSF HESP at the time – of community outreach through cooperation with CSOs and a solid academic background in comprehensive course work and research supervision became key characteristics for our own project.

The regional and international dimension of our own clinical program primarily stems from the fact that our NGO partners are involved in human rights litigation and advocacy before European courts. This means that even when they are preparing cases before domestic fora they are looking for arguments and approaches which will enable them to bring the case to the European scene. Commitment to strategic litigation has been a staple of several human rights organizations in Hungary from the early days of transition to democracy. In this respect, these organizations adapt techniques familiar from the civil rights movement in the United States and have historically benefitted from the support of international donors to this effect.[18] Litigation is central to the efforts of these NGOs in seeking to trigger legal change: they go to court not simply to represent *pro bono* clients in individual cases, but in order to correct the structural shortcomings of the legal system which legal reform had not touched.

Our students are expected to provide insight on human rights problem with European and international minimum standards in mind. This approach is particularly beneficial for students who seek careers in human rights organizations or in human rights litigation and advocacy with a regional or international outlook. When selecting students for the clinical specialization, we do emphasize how involvement with the clinic provides some guidance for future careers. Based on survey responses, students value the insight the clinical experience provides for their future careers.

Diffusion of CLE

Our clinical specialization is admittedly small and tailored to fit the specificities of our own master's programs and the educational needs of our own students. As ours is not a live-client clinic, many of our experiences are not necessarily relevant to those European law schools which established successful live-client clinics in the past decades. Our experience is most valuable in explaining and exploring how a clinical project may be launched with particular institutional and systemic constraints in mind to ensure that a meaningful experiential learning component is introduced into the legal education curriculum. We find that a clinical experience is valuable to students when they get hands-on experience from experienced professionals who set tangible goals for the clinical project and make students see how the immediate project goals fit into a broader litigation or advocacy plan. This is a lesson which we value and seek to transfer through legal education reform projects conducted by our faculty members.

Our faculty members have been involved for decades in legal education reform projects in the former Soviet Union, and more recently in Myanmar, with grants from OSF. These projects aimed to make the law school classroom more interactive and more relevant to the needs of the legal profession. We found on more than one occasion that a clinical model is instantly appealing not only to students,[19] but also to

---

[18] Edwin Rekosh, *Constructing Public Interest Law: Transnational Collaboration and Exchange in Central and Eastern Europe*, 13 UCLA J. INT'L LAW& FOR. AFF. 55 (2008).

[19] A cautionary note: students' enthusiasm to be educated as revolutionaries in law clinics may easily make faculty members to get cold feet in transitional contexts where law school administration is less like to be enthused by a revolutionary flair in the classroom. Cf. Lee Dexter Schnasi, *Globalizing Clinical Legal Education: Successful Under-developed Country Experiences*, 6 T.M. COOLEY J. PRAC. & CLINICAL L. 129 (2003), at 183 et seq. and 197 et seq.

faculty members who seek to bring change to the classroom, yet – more often than not – this enthusiasm is not matched by the faculty's professional experience, institutional resources, professional networks, and, more generally, by the legal environment.[20] While a clinical model is only sustainable if it becomes an integral part of the law school curriculum, it cannot be the force which single handedly drives curriculum reform in legal education. Large-scale education reform provides momentum for introducing genuine experiential learning components into the law school curriculum. For a successful clinical component, however, the cooperation of the legal profession and civil society is also essential, especially at times of major legal and educational reforms. Finding a model which works will always be highly context dependent: even though we find that openness to new ideas and cooperation between legal academia and the legal profession are essential to building a sustainable clinical program, obstacles are numerous in practice and may often be impossible to overcome without legal change.

Future of CLE in Europe

According to its leading scholars and proponents, clinical education stands for a methodology (experiential learning) which is inseparable from a mission of advancing social justice.[21] The ultimate challenge for clinical education has been to be accepted as part of the regular law school curriculum. Gaining acceptance is a gradual process because the clinical movement seeks to redefine the relationship of the law school and its broader community while emphasizing the need for professional commitment to promote social justice.[22]

This process is not specific to Europe, although Europe may admittedly not be leading the way. The first hurdle involves ensuring that problem-based and experiential learning components become the more prevalent (preferably the defining) characteristics of legal education in Europe. It is worth recalling that this has been surprisingly difficult even in the United States, where the Langdellian method, though case-based, came to lose its practical orientation a long time ago. It was on what he saw as the ruins of the Langdellian edifice (an oversimplified academic exercise devoid of practical relevance) that Jerome Frank advocated a clinical approach to legal education in 1933.[23]

More recently, Todd Rakoff and Martha Minow argued for a non-Langdellian case method, describing the aims of legal education in the following terms.

---

[20] For insight into challenges, see Philip Genty, *Overcoming Cultural Blindness in International Clinical Collaboration*, 15 CLINICAL L. REV. 131 (2008).

[21] Frank S. Bloch and N. R. Madhava Menon, *The Global Clinical Movement*, in THE GLOBAL CLINICAL MOVEMENT: EDUCATING LAWYERS FOR SOCIAL JUSTICE (Frank S. Bloch and N. R. Madhava Menon, eds., Oxford University Press 2011), 267.

[22] Bloch and Menon, *supra* note 22, at 272.

[23] Jerome Frank, *Why Not A Clinical Lawyer-School?* 81(8) U. PENN. L. REV. 907 (1933).

Lawyers need to see how conflicting narratives might be built on the data, and to think about how those narratives might equilibrate in one setting or another. Lawyers need to be able to think about not only the specific version of a problem that presents itself, but also about the more general version of which it is but an instance. Lawyers need to be able to consider solving problems not just through litigation, but also through alternative forms of dispute resolution, through legislation, and through regulatory or executive action.[24]

They continue by saying that "[s]tudents who have a first-rate clinical experience probably learn a lot of what we are talking about, although they may be limited in the institutional mechanisms they are able to consider."[25] One hardly needs better reasons, and better advertisement, for integrating clinical methods into legal education more deeply and widely.

When integrating the clinical method into the curriculum, law schools need to address the institutional and curricular segmentation of the intellectual/academic and professional development aspects of legal education.[26] Reconsidering the significance of *all* experiential learning components in legal education, and including the clinical method in this broader context, may be a useful first step. This is all the more pressing as law schools are also facing a digital challenge: with increasing emphasis on electronic materials and e-learning platforms, the law school classroom needs to find and redefine its role in legal education. It has been suggested recently that clinical projects find competitors in video games as skill-building tools.[27] Thus, relocating methods in legal education with an appreciation of role of and ways of developing the interpersonal skills of future lawyers is all the more urgent.

The additional challenge is to ensure that, beyond the method, the mission of clinical education to improve awareness of social justice issues – or at least the social engagement of the law school – is also accepted. This latter step would require rethinking the mission of law faculties, and – possibly – undergraduate university education in Europe on a larger scale. If European universities are committed to educating global, or at least European citizens, then infusing social justice considerations, or at least a sense of civic responsibility, should not be a far cry.

In this respect, it is worth noting that demands to rethink legal education in Europe are certainly not new: European integration has become more than ever a force and a force to reckon with in law school curricula. Europeanization would mean more than adding the word "European" to course titles and boosting the course offering with "anything EU." Europeanization means reorienting legal

---

[24] Todd D. Rakoff and Martha Minow, *A Case for Another Case Method*, 60(2) VANDERBILT L. REV. 597 (2007), at 602.
[25] Rakoff and Minow, *supra* note 25, at 603.
[26] Susan Sturm and Lani Guinier, *The Law School Matrix: Reforming Legal Education in a Culture of Competition and Conformity*, 60(2) VANDERBILT L. REV. 515 (2007) at 534–537.
[27] Gregory Silveman, *Law Games: The Importance of Virtual Worlds and Serious Video Games for the Future of Legal Education*, in LEGAL EDUCATION IN THE DIGITAL AGE (Edward Rubin, ed., Cambridge University Press 2012), 130, at 151.

education already at the undergraduate level, from teaching legal rules of national legal systems to engaging with legal problems in a critical and self-reflexive manner in the European legal space. This would mean moving away from rules to exploring arguments, alternatives, and options through legal analysis. Experiential and problem-based learning methods are a clear match for approaches to denationalizing the law school curriculum on the undergraduate level. The next step is to take advantage of these methods, while the new frontier is to rethink the overall mission of legal education in an integrated Europe. This would entail a serious conversation about the relevance of social justice considerations and civic engagement when educating global citizens in European law schools.

At CEU, we are fortunate to work in an institutional environment where mission-driven education is in the fabric of the university and problem-based teaching has been the defining feature of the education we offer since the establishment of our master's programs. The clinical specialization in our human rights and comparative constitutional law programs complements a number of experiential learning components (simulated and real-life) which are integral to our curriculum. We intend to keep the clinic small, to ensure the enrollment of motivated and committed students and also to be able concentrate on legal problems which faculty members are keen to explore in cooperation with experienced NGO partners. We will continue to select clinical projects which keep our students engaged and that remain socially as well as intellectually relevant. This process creates a frame of reference which points beyond issues which are relevant for a Hungarian audience because our student body and faculty are highly international.

Because of its small scale, preserving the relevance and authenticity of our clinical project is not trivial. We understand, however, that, owing to the institutional specificities of our clinical project, room for cooperation with other clinics may be rather limited. We are mindful of experiences of cooperation between clinics in different legal systems and institutional cultures[28] which counsel us against seeking a clinical exchange partner. Since the clinical course runs across the academic year, students who are on a semester-long exchange cannot enroll in it (although other experiential learning options are open to them).

The curricula of our master's programs focus primarily on Europe and North America, due to CEU's location and accreditation. With the changing composition of the student body and the evolving research interests of our faculty, conscious attempts have been made in previous years to broaden the geographical coverage of courses to include Africa, South-East Asia, and Latin America. Despite these curricular developments, the clinic's focus – apart from one particular, relatively unsuccessful attempt – remained within the Council of Europe and the jurisdiction of the ECtHR. The diversity of the student body (which makes English the only

---

[28] See, e.g., William Berman, *Why Not an International Clinical Legal Exchange Program? It Is Worth the SHLEP*, 21 CLINICAL L. R. 171 (2014).

working language) and the length of the academic year do not allow the clinic to follow one particular case from the very beginning until the end many years later. For this reason, the students' involvement is usually limited to the initial stages of the procedures or a particular submission (NGO intervention or amicus brief).

Although students in the clinical specialization find the experience rewarding, we have yet to find the most suitable way to showcase their experience to a wider audience. This is all the more important as the clinical experience can be formative in students' career choices and may also influence them as future lawyers, advocates and human rights educators. Admittedly, sharing results and especially sharing experiences have been a challenge more generally to experiential learning components. We find that while students are intensely involved with these components, their experiences and lessons learnt from such projects are difficult to share with others. While this is not so much a problem with in-class group projects or moot courts (because the later are open to a more general audience), internship experiences and especially the clinic are much less visible to other students. One way to showcase students' experiences would be a tea house with a short presentation or poster session. The format should focus on sharing experiences and lessons learnt, thus differing from a project report or deliverable for end-of-course assessment.

CONCLUSION

The curriculum of our Department is built on encouraging critical thinking and a problem- (or case-) based approach to legal questions and is premised on comparative insight. The clinical specialization offers a special opportunity to activate these broad educational objectives within the framework of a well-defined and closely managed project. The clinical specialization offered to LLM and MA students in human rights and to LLM students in comparative constitutional law at CEU is the result of a faculty initiative to offer an opportunity to students with little or no work experience in human rights litigation and advocacy a chance to engage for an extended period of time with a legal problem under the guidance of an expert lawyer in the setting of a CSO.

The clinical course successfully demonstrates how complex a seemingly simple human rights problem may be in real life, how to respond to the needs of the supervising lawyer or the represented client, and how to develop a strategy that takes into account multiple variables and alternative scenarios. As the legal problem which is at the heart of each clinical course is disclosed in the call for applications for the clinical specialization early in the academic year, students are familiar with the broad outlines of the project which the clinical course will center on at the moment they apply. The emphasis on long-term commitment to explore solutions to a complex human rights problem (the clinic's project) is prevalent in our discussion of the clinic as well as in our recruitment of participants.

Although not a live-client clinic, our clinical specialization shares a strong commitment to address injustice through the instruments available to human rights professionals, to lawyers and nonlawyers alike. The clinical course, led jointly by a faculty member and an NGO lawyer, is part of a degree specialization which offers a solid academic background for clinical students to consider and address the legal issues that are at the core of the clinical project. CEU's own institutional mission is highly supportive of the clinical initiative. The moderate size of our clinical project is due to the overall size of our master's programs and the multiplicity of experiential learning options available to our students.

We find that through being able to offer relevant clinical projects to our highly international student body we make an important step toward educating our students as engaged and socially responsible individuals who think critically, place human rights issues in their broader social and political context, and address legal and human rights questions in a comparative, regional, and international perspective – just as we envision educating global citizens.

13

The International Human Rights Clinic at SOAS

Lynn Welchman

INTRODUCTION

The Clinic at the SOAS School of Law seems to have been the first international human rights clinic in the UK and has operated since 2007. I modelled it on human rights clinics in the United States, which are plentiful and come in different forms; according to Hurwitz, a human rights clinic is "a law school–based, credit-bearing course or program that combines clinical methodology around skills and values training with live case-project work, all or most of which takes place in the human rights context."[1] On the "learning-by-doing" principle of clinical legal education (CLE), the SOAS Clinic tries to have students experience, through working on a real brief with real partners from real human rights nongovernmental organizations (NGOs), something of what it is like to do human rights NGO research/advocacy work (including competing demands on their time). In this chapter, I present the experience of the SOAS Clinic as well as the broader CLE context in the UK, which mostly follows different models.

The SOAS Clinic is designed to build a skills set in practical legal research and desk-based "fact-finding," report/brief writing, teamwork, and negotiating and communications skills. Through their reflection on their work during and after the process, students are expected to develop a fine-grained appreciation and critique of human rights engagement in matters of social justice and their own potential in that space. Research and advocacy briefs agreed upon with our NGO partners cover areas of international human rights law, international humanitarian law, and international criminal law; most commonly, the focus will be on application and domestic implementation of the same and strategies for seeking correction or redress. Our project partners have also sought clinic input into the development of organizational policy and priorities on particular norms and/or geographical areas of

---

[1] Deena R. Hurwitz, *Lawyering for Justice and the Inevitability of International Human Rights Clinics.* 28 YALE J. INT'L L 505 (2003). *See also* Chapter 16 by Kjos and Nollkamper and Chapter 9 by Alemanno and Khadar in this volume. For the SOAS Clinic, *see* https://www.soas.ac.uk/law/international-humanrights-clinic/.

work. Clinic students thus have the opportunity to contribute in real terms to the work of the "human rights movement" and, by so doing, inter alia, to experience the tensions of theory and practice. In times of reduced resources for the NGO sector, the Clinic students bring their time, intellectual energy, and access to substantial academic resources to a cooperative endeavour for the benefit of the partners and, ultimately, the individuals and communities they seek to serve.

The Clinic is a full year postgraduate course running for credit for LLM and MA Law students as part of our human rights and international law specialisms.[2] Students in the Clinic work in small teams of up to four on research and advocacy briefs from UK- and overseas-based institutional partners engaged in international human rights work or domestic human rights work with an international and/or comparative dimension. The course is structured around a two-hour weekly seminar followed by a project hour. The seminar (Clinic "plenary") addresses a range of issues in human rights advocacy, strategies, and challenges and often involves practitioners engaged in different aspects and strategies of human rights work (mostly London-based project partners). Certain practical skills aspects are also addressed in the plenary, such as web-based research for human rights and human rights report-writing; there are structured project "rounds" sessions as well as less formal reflection periods. Students maintain a Project Diary and write a self-evaluation statement; formal assessment is conducted on the basis of a Project Portfolio, which includes these two items as well as a presentation of a selection of the student's project work (with the finished group project annexed); and, later, an end-of-course essay that has been the subject of a plenary presentation and discussion.

Over the years, our project partners have included mostly human rights organizations but also law firms with human rights specialization. Amongst others, we have worked on briefs for and with Amnesty International, REDRESS, Child Soldiers International, the Institute for Human Rights and Business, Lawyers for Justice in Libya, the Norwegian Refugee Council, Legal Action Worldwide, ASK (Dhaka), the Cairo Institute for Human Rights Studies, al-Haq and the Welfare Association (Palestine), and DC-CAM (Cambodia). Clinic project teams have addressed domestic violence legislation and policy, the protection of cultural property, violence against women, the right to water, corporal punishment, public health emergencies, disability rights, refugee and immigration detention, and a range of other matters invoking human rights as well as international humanitarian law. Clinic project teams meet with our partners for an initial briefing, with subsequent meetings agreed over the course of the project (in person or by Skype) and email

---

[2] LLM: Human Rights, Conflict and Justice, as well as the general LLM; MA Human Rights, and MA International and Comparative Studies. As of 2016, we have had more than 130 students pass through seven Clinics. Some of the narrative here may be out of date by publication as SOAS restructures its offerings to fit the Bologna criteria or may be overtaken as the sector overall adjusts to whatever comes after the "Brexit" vote on June 23, 2016.

correspondence in between. I supervise all the teams, with lead supervision provided for one or two teams by colleagues.[3] The teams conduct their work at SOAS, unless exceptionally they are required to work in situ by partners. The outcome briefs are delivered half way through the second term and may be delivered also in presentation at meetings organized by the project partners to a wider group of their colleagues.

EMERGENCE OF THE SOAS CLINIC AND THE CLE ENVIRONMENT IN UK

Genesis and Context

The SOAS Clinic hardly fits the model of CLE more generally recognized in the UK, but it does share key features of CLE as articulated by practitioner-scholars ("clinicians") in the relevant literature. It strikes me that asserting you are involved in (or setting up) a "clinic" is a little like asserting you are involved in a "human rights organization" in terms of the self-definition and assumptions that arise and the evolving practitioner/professional consensus around what qualities may rule you in or out. For his part, Richard Wilson, from 1990 the founding director of the International Human Rights Law Clinic at the American University's Washington College of Law, tells us that "a law school can call its clinical legal education activity by any name ... so long as the focus is on student experiential learning – learning by doing – for academic credit."[4]

The catalyst for my establishment of the Clinic at SOAS came directly from my continuing human rights engagement (mostly Middle East–related) after entering the academy following a decade and a half of international human rights practice working with Palestinian and international human rights NGOs (and once, for a very short stint, with the UN). As an academic I was able to respond to requests from human rights organizations to act as investigator, trial observer, and other such short-term and subject-specific tasks in the field, as well as taking on more ongoing responsibilities on different organizations' Boards. I was not, however, involved in teaching human rights courses. The year 2005 saw the end of a six-year multipartner, externally funded action-oriented research and advocacy project on strategies of response to "crimes of honour" as violence against women that I had coordinated with Sara Hossain from INTERIGHTS.[5] For me, this left a gap in institutional resources or structures through which to engage in sustained cooperation with individuals and organizations who had been our project partners, as well as others

---

[3] Iain Scobbie and Lutz Oette.
[4] Richard J. Wilson, *Western Europe: Last Holdout in the Worldwide Acceptance of Clinical Legal Education*, 10 (7)GERMAN LAW JOURNAL 823–46 (2009), at 829.
[5] *See* Lynn Welchman and Sara Hossain, eds. "HONOUR": CRIMES, PARADIGMS AND VIOLENCE AGAINST WOMEN (London: Zed Books 2005).

with whom I had established relationships. At the same time, like other colleagues, I was concerned by the increasing expectation on graduates that they secure unpaid internships in expensive capital cities if they were to position themselves most favourably for paid openings in human rights work. I took the actual decision to establish a Clinic at SOAS as the direct result of ruminations with an Amnesty friend in a hotel room in Sana'a in early 2006, waiting for a call from the authorities in Political Security to confirm a visit to detainees who had been returned to Yemen after extended periods in "black sites" under CIA authority, as part of the extrajudicial rendition programme in the "war on terror."[6]

Back in SOAS, I found solid support among some colleagues, particularly those themselves in positions of "engaged" or policy-related scholarship; volunteerism was and is very much a feature of the Clinic.[7] Friends and colleagues in and from the NGO human rights movement in the Middle East and South Asia were enthusiastic and interested in various forms of cooperation; colleagues running clinics gave advice on things to do and things to avoid,[8] and, while in Ramallah, I was further inspired by the energies of colleagues establishing the first human rights clinic in Palestine at the university of Al-Quds.[9] In terms of scholarship, I drew particularly on literature from human rights clinicians in the United States.[10] There is considerable reflection on "the deepening convergence of international law and clinical legal education in the United States" in the realm specifically of international human rights.[11] In 2010, Richard Wilson introduced "the first panel on clinical legal education in the Society's history" at the annual meeting of the American Society of International Law – again, emphasizing the relatively recent inclusion of CLE as

---

[6] See Amnesty International, *Below the Radar*, 5 April 2006. (AI Index AMR 51/051/2006), 9–17; and see *Al-Asad v Djibouti*, a complaint at the African Commission on Human and People's Rights, submitted following his release by one of these detainees through New York University's Global Justice Clinic and INTERIGHTS (the International Centre for the Protection of Human Rights), seeking relief for secret detention, ill-treatment, and *refoulement*.

[7] In particular, the team from the Hotung Project on Law, Human Rights, and Peace-Building in the Middle East: Iain Scobbie, Stephanie Koury, Ron Dudai, and Sarah Hibbin. Stephanie and I worked closely together in the establishment stage; Sarah volunteered with the Clinic until she left SOAS; and Iain still participates, as does Ron if he is in town. Joyce Song volunteered with the Clinic while in London as a New York lawyer.

[8] In particular, Deena Hurwitz, then at Virginia; I worked with Deena in Palestine in the mid-1990s.

[9] See David Chavkin, *Thinking/Practicing Clinical Legal Education from within the Palestinian-Israeli Conflict: Lessons from the Al-Quds Human Rights Clinic*, 18 HUMAN RIGHTS BRIEF 14–18 (2010); on legal clinics in Hebron and more generally, see Mutaz Qafisheh, *Modern Legal Education in Palestine: The Clinical Programs of Hebron University*, in EXPERIMENTAL LEGAL EDUCATION IN A GLOBALIZED WORLD. THE MIDDLE EAST AND BEYOND (Mutaz M. Qafisheh and Stephen A. Rosenbaum, eds. (Newcastle upon Tyne: Cambridge Scholars Publishing, 2016), 198–235.

[10] Notably, Deena Hurwitz, *Lawyering for Justice and Inevitability of International Human Rights Clinics*, 28 YALE J. INT'L. L. 505–50 (2003); Arturo J. Carillo, *Bringing International Law Home: The Innovative Role of Human Rights Clinics in the Transnational Legal Process*, 35 COLUM H. RTS. L. REV. 527–87 (2003–2004); Peter Rosenblum, *Teaching Human Rights: Ambivalent Activism, Multiple Discourses and Lingering Dilemmas*, 15 HARVARD HUMAN RIGHTS JOURNAL 301–15 (2002).

[11] Carillo, *supra* note 10 at 527.

a "method or philosophy of law teaching" and the "even more recent development within the clinical teaching movement" – that is, international law and, in particular, international human rights law. In his 2009 address in the *German Law Journal*, Wilson had suggested that "work in the area of human rights protection may provide a beachhead for clinical innovation" in parts of Europe that his title described as the "last holdout" against CLE.[12] He exempted the UK from these remarks, given that there has been a more or less active clinical movement here for a couple of decades, preceded by remarkable initial ventures in the 1970s.

We spent considerable effort trying to secure funding for a pilot phase of the Clinic at SOAS and drafting course proposals to be put through the various processes of approval. The proposal that was finally approved stated under "additional resources needed" that we were seeking external funding for a three-year post for one full-time staff member for the Clinic and that "the operation of the Clinic as of September 2007 will be dependent on securing this funding." We failed to secure funding, but external factors combined to prompt us to launch the Clinic anyway, and, happily, nobody who might have stopped us invoked the caveat about external funding. The University of London LLM was devolving to individual colleges and schools of the University, and, at SOAS, a comparatively small college, we were nervous about the impact on student recruitment when the attraction to students of being able to take two of their four LLM courses at other London colleges ceased to be a part of our offering. The decision on timing – that is, to proceed with existing resources and launch the Clinic that particular year – was part of an effort to enhance our profile for postgraduate students (both LLM and MA Law) in that context. In different ways then, the origins of the SOAS Clinic illustrate the observation that Clinics in the UK are "usually bespoke creations to meet the demands defined by individual Law Schools."[13]

Drivers

The editors of Britain's first student handbook on CLE are no doubt correct in saying that it is "in-house advice and representation clinics" that are "often viewed as the gold standard of law clinics" in the UK context.[14] Indeed, the fact that there *exists* a student handbook on CLE tells one part of the story of the current state of the field in the UK – the current diffusion and rise in CLE offerings, mainly to undergraduates but increasingly also to postgraduates. In 2015, Drummond found 102

---

[12] Wilson, *supra* 4 note at 828, and *see* 844.
[13] Orla Drummond and Gráinne McKeever, ACCESS TO JUSTICE THROUGH UNIVERSITY LAW CLINICS (Ulster: Ulster University Law School 2015), www.ulster.ac.uk/lawclinic/files/2014/06/Access-to-Justice-through-Uni-Law-Clinics-November-2015.pdf, 5.
[14] Kevin Kerrigan, *What Is Clinical Legal Education and Pro Bono?*, in A STUDENT GUIDE TO CLINICAL LEGAL EDUCATION AND PRO BONO (Kevin Kerrigan and Victoria Murray, eds., Houndmills: Palgrave Macmillan 2011), 1–20, at 1. The handbook chapters are contributed by staff members of the clinic (the Student Law Office) at the University of Northumbria's School of Law.

law schools in the UK, of which sixty-four had "clinic-related activities."[15] This was found to constitute an overall increase in university law clinics since the 1990s, with an acceleration from 2000–2010 and again from 2011–2015.[16] A 2014 LawWorks report which followed up previous surveys on law school clinical and *pro bono* work deduced from the responses to its survey that "at least 70% of all law schools are now involved in pro bono and/or clinical activity."[17] This was found to be a "marginal" increase (of 5%) over the findings from the previous 2006–2010 survey, which itself had shown an increase of 33% of the survey before that.[18] The increase may be predictably slowing, but it is surely indicative of a "mainstreaming" of CLE in UK university law schools that CLE pioneers here in the early 1970s might have aspired to, albeit without wishing upon us the attendant squeezes that appear to have given impetus to the current acceleration. These include severe reduction in government-funded legal aid provision and the imposition of undergraduate student fees (of up to £9,000 p/a from summer 2012)[19] along with significant austerity impacts in state funding of the higher education sector as a whole. Just shy of two decades of existence as an informal, umbrella grouping of those interested in CLE in the UK, in 2014 it was announced that the Clinical Legal Education Organization (CLEO) was applying for incorporation as a charitable organization, *inter alia* because "there is now ... a critical mass of law schools and individuals involved in clinic to make wider representation appropriate and feasible."[20]

On the scholarship side, there is a "surfeit of literature" on the "many different nuances of clinical legal education,"[21] despite the fact that one of the challenges facing CLE remains its scholarly place in the academy with a home discipline, law, that has had to struggle to establish its own intellectual corner recently enough to be prickly about developments that might appear to associate it too closely with "practice." And this relationship, between those involved with the "science of law" in the universities of England and Wales (a twentieth-century development)[22] and those practising it as barristers and solicitors, has been a key moulding factor in the

---

[15] Drummond and McKeever, *supra* note 13, at 16.   [16] *Id.*
[17] Damian Carney, Frank Dignan, Richard Grimes, Grace Kelly, Rebecca Parker. THE LAWWORKS LAW SCHOOL PRO BONO AND CLINIC REPORT 2014. LawWorks: LexisNexis (2014), https://www.lawworks.org.uk/sites/default/files/LawWorks-student-pro-bono-report%202014.pdf, 4.
[18] *See also* Lydia Bleasdale-Hill and Pail Wragg, *Models of Clinic and Their Value to Students, Universities and the Community in the post-2012 Fees Era*, 19 IJCLE 257–69 (2013), at 257.
[19] *Id.*
[20] Carney et al., *supra* note 17, at 43; *see* Richard Grimes, Joel Klaff, and Colleen Smith, *Legal Skills and Clinical Legal Education: A Survey of Undergraduate Law School Practice*, 30 THE LAW TEACHER 44–67 (1996) at 67, noting the formation of CLEO.
[21] Malcolm M. Combe, *Selling Intra-curricular Clinical Legal Education*, 48 (3) THE LAW TEACHER 281–95 (2014), at 282. *And see* Neil Gold and Philip Plowden, *Clinical Scholarship and the Development of the Global Clinical Movement*, in THE GLOBAL CLINICAL MOVEMENT (Frank Bloch, ed., New York: Oxford University Press 2011), 311–21.
[22] Anthony Bradney, *Ivory Towers and Satanic Mills: Choices for University Law Schools*, 17 (1) STUDIES IN HIGHER EDUCATION 5–20 (1992), at 7. *See also* Neil Gold, *Why Not an International Journal of Clinical Legal Education?*, 1 IJCLE 7–12 (2000), at 8.

development of CLE here. Bradney observes that the use of term "science of law" "indicates a belief that the academy should be divorced from the profession."[23] Legal scholarship had no intellectual tradition at universities and so the impetus was to insist on the academic content of law and to distance the discipline from the profession. Legal academics did not (and do not) have to be qualified to practise the law in order to teach it at university; law practitioners did not (and do not) have to have an undergraduate degree in law in order to practise the profession.[24] Indeed, they did not have to have an academic degree at all until the introduction of a "graduate entry" requirement for the vocational stages of legal education following the 1971 government-commissioned Report of the Committee on Legal Education (the "Ormrod Report" after the Committee's chair).[25] At the moment, the postgraduation route to qualification as a solicitor or barrister involves a year of vocational or practical training followed by a period of "apprenticeship" under the supervision of qualified practitioners and their regulatory authorities.[26] University students can opt for a non-law degree at undergraduate and then study law for a graduate diploma before proceeding to the vocational stage of practical training, or they can choose an undergraduate Qualifying Law Degree (its compulsory elements identified by the professional societies for certification) that qualifies them to pass directly to the vocational training stage after graduation.[27]

This means that there was (and is) "less focus on the 'practice gap' as a driver" for CLE in the British legal education system, as the vocational stage is precisely aimed

---

[23] Bradney, *supra* note 22, at 9.
[24] Twining says that some in other jurisdictions (still) find this "bizarre"; see William Twining, *LETR: The Role of Academics in Legal Education and Training: 10 Theses*, 48 (1) THE LAW TEACHER 94–103 (2014), at 99. Folsom and Roberts observe that this major recommendation by Ormrod was "accepted by the Bar and begrudgingly by the Law Society," continuing that "the most significant consequence of 'graduate entry' [...] is the initial selection of potential members of the legal profession through national competitive university admissions processes and the exposure of many of these students to legal academics"; see Ralph Folsom, and Neal Roberts, *The Warwick Story: Being Led Down the Contextual Path of the Law*, 30 JOURNAL OF LEGAL EDUCATION 166–83 (1979), at 169.
[25] Folsom and Roberts (*Id.* note 24 at 169). The year 2016 is seeing the introduction of (/reversion to) nongraduate entry to the profession of solicitor through Trailblazer Apprenticeships, described by the Law Society as "new legal apprenticeships" providing an "alternative to the traditional graduate route to qualification" and not requiring the apprentice to study for a degree. See www.lawsociety.org.uk/Law-careers/Becoming-a-solicitor/Routes-to-qualifying/.
[26] See Alemanno and Khadar, Chapter 9 in this volume, for Europe-wide comparison and also for the implications for the "social justice or public interest aspects of EU law" of the accelerated legal practice course being offered by "consortiums of large law firms" in the UK.
[27] The Solicitors Regulation Authority has been consulting on proposals to more broadly remove the requirements for graduate entry to the profession of solicitor (with a few exceptions). Critiques by Burrows and Bradney are published in *The Reporter*; see Anthony Bradney, *Professional Education for Solicitors and the Whimsical World of the Solicitors Regulation Authority*, 52 THE REPORTER: NEWSLETTER OF THE SOCIETY OF LEGAL SCHOLARS 4–5 (spring 2016). Bradney's opening paragraph (at 4) asks "Why continue with a system that most people are largely content with when you can have all the fun of introducing something that no-one understands and few want? That is what the SRA intend to do with their new scheme for the Solicitors Qualilfying Examination [...]".

at preparing incoming students for professional practice.[28] In 1971, the Ormrod Report held that "[t]he traditional antithesis between 'academic' and 'vocational', 'theoretical' and 'practical', which has divided the universities from the professions in the past, must be eliminated by adjustment on both sides."[29] Bradney, whose consideration of the relationship between universities and industry or the professions is a case study of the history of university law schools in this regard, concludes that despite other "vocational pressures" in the 1980s, and although some would disagree with him, "there is much ... to lead one to see the last few decades as a period in which university law schools have distanced themselves from the legal professions."[30] For his own part he holds "it is possible to argue that the course pursued by university law schools is the only principled path that they could have chosen."[31]

This is a slightly different part of the context of clinic, but still relevant given ongoing debates over the ethos of the CLE movement. A near-contemporary critique of curriculum reform and the early CLE programme at Warwick University School of Law insisted:

> some of the most strongly articulated demands for more relevant courses in law schools come from radical students. But the fact that in law at least, their demands are being met does not herald the increasing "radicalisation" of the law but rather its increasing *professionalisation*. This means that those who have as their aim radicalisation are, paradoxically, at one with the most austerely professional lawyers, whose orientation is anything but radical.[32]

The reader is referred here to the Ormrod Report, noting that *inter alia*, the Committee recommended "that the possibility of running legal aid clinics 'should be explored.'"[33] The critique just quoted was named for an earlier book-length comment considering the attempts by the founders of Warwick University (in the 1960s) "to make their institution 'useful' to 'business interests.'"[34] The Ormrod report was itself a product of a social and political context where, as described by Giddings et al., "[u]nmet legal need had become a rallying call for those seeking further welfare reform."[35] In the early seventies, the law schools of Warwick and Kent were

---

[28] Gold and Plowden, *supra* note 21, at 313. See also Jeff Giddings, Roger Burridge, Shelley A. M. Gavigan, and Catherine F. Klein, The First Wave of Clinical Legal Education. The United States, Britain, Canada and Australia, in THE GLOBAL CLINICAL MOVEMENT (Frank Bloch, ed., New York: Oxford University Press 2011), 3–22, at 14–15.

[29] Cmnd 4595 (Report of the Committee on Legal Education) 1971, para.85; cited by Bradney, *supra* note 27, at 9.

[30] *Id.*, at 12.   [31] *Id.*, at 15.

[32] Zenan Bankowski and Geoff Mungham, 'Warwick University Ltd.' (Continued), 1 BRITISH JOURNAL OF LAW AND SOCIETY 179–84 (1974), at 184 (emphasis in original).

[33] *Id.*, at 184; citing Cmnd. 4595 1971 para. 185.   [34] *Id.*, at 179.

[35] Giddings et al., *supra* note 28, at 6. Examining the latest (2013) report on legal education and training, Leighton notes that the 1971 Ormrod report "set the tone and structure for legal education in England and Wales that broadly operates today"; *see* Patricia Leighton, Back from the Future: Did the LETR Really Prepare Us for the Future?, 48 THE LAW TEACHER 79–93 (2014), at 79.

the first to embark upon CLE ventures in the UK, inspired according to Richard Grimes (for decades, a leader of CLE in the UK) by the examples being set in the USA, although Grimes stresses a significant difference in that "providing a service to meet legal need was not a driving force" even if much of the case work was "welfare-oriented." Rather, staff and students in these law schools, coming out of the energy of student activism in the sixties, were "driven both by recognition of the pedagogic value of this approach to study but also by the focus of the law schools in question on the importance of studying law in its political, social and economic context."[36] A 1979 analysis includes in the environment surrounding the creation of early clinics the recognition of law degrees from a substantial number of colleges and polytechnics and the establishment of a dozen new university law schools.[37] Both the polytechnics (which later became "new" universities) and what were then new universities came to be significant actors in the CLE movement in England and Wales.[38]

There are in-depth accounts of the programmes at Kent (the first to incorporate its Clinic into the undergraduate curriculum, in 1973) and at Warwick (1975).[39] The Kent clinic (built around the concept of "praxis") experienced internal political struggles, external concern (including from certain local legal practices concerned about prospective competition from the live-client advice programme at the clinic),[40] and also concern from the university authorities who were "unhappy with the political and public nature of the cases taken on by the clinic" as well as with the fact that some of them were directed against the university itself.[41] The clinic closed in 1976; Sherr observes that "[t]he reasons for this infant mortality were probably more closely related to the success of that enterprise, as intended, than

---

[36] Richard Grimes, *Learning Law by Doing Law in the UK*, 1 IJCLE 54–57 (2000), at 55. Sherr notes that the Warwick Legal Practice Programme explained its aims as "building on the existing Warwick emphasis of 'law in action' and 'law in context'"; see Avrom Sherr, *Clinical Legal Education at Warwick and the skills Movement: Was Clinic a Creature of Its Time*, in FRONTIERS OF LEGAL SCHOLARSHIP. TWENTY FIVE YEARS OF WARWICK LAW SCHOOL (Geoffrey P. Wilson, ed., Chichester: John Wiley and Sons 1995), 108–119 at 108. The "law in context" approach was also framed by its proponents in light of experiences in post-colonial African states as well as in the US and elsewhere: Id., at 114; Twining *supra* note 24, at 94; Folsom and Roberts, *supra* note 24, at 172–73. Twining (then at Warwick) describes himself as one of the "noisy young agitators" involved in this intellectual venture.

[37] Folsom and Roberts, *supra* note 24, at 171.

[38] *See* Kevin Kerrigan and Victoria Murray, eds. A STUDENT GUIDE TO CLINICAL LEGAL EDUCATION AND PRO BONO (Houndmills: Palgrave Macmillan 2011), at 10.

[39] *See* Giddings et al., *supra* note 28, at 6; William M. Rees, *Clinical Legal Education: An Analysis of the University of Kent Model*, 9 THE LAW TEACHER 125–40 (1975) (in part responding to Bankowski and Mungham, *supra* note 32); Folsom and Roberts, *supra* note 24; Sherr, *supra* note 36.

[40] *See* Frank Dignan, *Bridging the Academic/Vocational Divide: The Creation of a Law Clinic in an Academic Law School*, 16 IJCLE 75–84 (2011), at 83 on the "mutually advantageous" relationship that the Legal Advice Clinic at Hull has been careful to establish with "existing advice providers."

[41] Giddings et al., *supra* note 28, at 7, 11. *See*, by way of comparison, the website of the Essex University Law Clinic (offering "free initial legal advice"): "We also cannot assist any person wishing to pursue a claim against the University, its governors, employees or students": https://www.essex.ac.uk/law/about/clinic.aspx (last visited April 29, 2016).

its failure"[42] and goes on to note the different ways in which the Legal Practice Programme developed at Warwick (for example, according to Sherr, it was "less public and less openly principled").[43] The Kent clinic reopened in the 1990s, when Grimes reports there was a "flurry of activity on the clinical front," with leading roles played by the law schools at two more (then) new universities.[44] In 1995, Grimes wrote of "a discernible call for clinical legal education," noting a series of statements and positions from different government departments as well as the Law Society for further changes in the education of lawyers (this with a focus on skills, discussed further later) and the appointment of a review committee in 1994.[45] Grimes was involved in a survey on skills teaching in law schools carried out in 1994, in which 83% of those who responded indicated that they offered skills teaching, although only eight hosted real client clinics.[46] Consultations around legal education in the initial (academic) stage, under the auspices of the Lord Chancellor's Advisory Committee (ACLEC), were ongoing, and there was an early reference to "the value of clinical teaching, and how it might be funded."[47] The ACLEC's *First Report* was published in 1996, and Grimes wrote regretting its lack of attention to CLE as an "alternative but complementary" teaching method in law degrees.[48] Webb argued at the same time that the report's emphasis on ethics signalled a "significant opportunity" to promote CLE as a methodology, and Clubb identifies other emphases on legal education to which CLE could contribute distinctively; he credits this as a factor in the increased inclusion of CLE in the undergraduate curriculum.[49] The continuing increase in

---

[42] Sherr, *supra* note 36, at 108, citing Sherr, CLIENT INTERVIEWING FOR LAWYERS (Sweet and Maxwell 1986), vii.

[43] Sherr, *supra* note 36, at 113.

[44] Grimes, *supra* note 36, at 55. University of Northumbria at Newcastle and Sheffield Hallam; Grimes was himself involved with both at different times. He also refers to real-client clinics established in the 1990s in the Universities of Plymouth and Central England; Giddings et al., *supra* note 28, at 6, note "other early clinical ventures" at the polytechnics of South Bank and Trent and the University of Brunel.

[45] Richard Grimes, *Reflections on Clinical Legal Education*, 29 THE LAW TEACHER 169–88 (1995), at 169. This article mostly reflects on the establishment in 1993 and first two years' work of the Law Clinic at Sheffield Hallam University, but the first section responds to critiques of CLE by Bradney (*supra* note 27) among others which he includes as part of what he describes as a "lively (if not yet extensive) debate on the relevance and content of legal skills programmes."

[46] Grimes et al., *supra* note 29, at 48.

[47] ACLEC (Lord Chancellor's Advisory Committee on Legal Education and Conduct), ANNUAL REPORT FOR 1993–1994 (London: HMSO 1994), 28 para.10.3.vii.

[48] Richard Grimes, *The ACLEC Report – Meeting Legal Education Needs in the 21st Century?*, 7 (2) LEGAL EDUCATION REVIEW 281–89 (1996), at 289. Twining (*supra* note 24, at 94) opens his reflection on the 2013 LETR report by noting that "I have measured out my professional career with reports relating to legal education" which he says since he started teaching in the UK in 1966 "has been under almost continuous review."

[49] Julian Webb, *Inventing the Good: A Prospectus for Clinical Education and the Teaching of Legal Ethics in England*. 30 LAW TEACHER 270–94 (1996), at 271; Karen Clubb, *Masters of Our Destiny – The Integration of Law Clinic into Postgraduate Masters Provision*, 19 IJCLE 395–404 (2013), at 397. See also James Marson, Adam Wilson, and Mark Van Hoorebeck, *The Necessity of Clinical Legal Education in University Law Schools: A UK Perspective*, 7 IJCLE 29–43 (2005); Giddings et al., *supra* note 28.

the new century in the number of law schools offering "clinic-related activities" has already been noted.[50] In their 2011 overview of developments, Giddings et al. note the range of different activities that developed and were carried out as part of CLE in the UK; with CLE in its fifth decade here, they locate these as a result of "new blood, adjusted pedagogical objectives, resource pressures, educational policy and political expediency."[51]

Currently, there is significant support for the development of CLE activities and an emphasis on student (and practitioner) involvement in *pro bono* activities.[52] A set of prizes and awards recognize the work of student law clinics and *pro bono* work.[53] Encouragement of CLE has been traced *inter alia* to a focus on developing skills, to government's desire for cooperation between universities and industry, and to what Benneworth and Osborne identify as the Europe-wide and economic development-related "innovation imperative."[54] In the UK, the focus on "employability," undergraduate tuition fees, league tables, and consumerism trends at university[55] might support response to student demand if clinics are seen to increase employability, but they do not further the older "values" underpinning of CLE in England and Wales.[56] And certainly, a challenge remains in the fact that among subjects taught at university, law is still in the lowest funding band, and "[p]rofessional supervision of student case work by clinical teachers for large numbers of students has always fared badly in comparison with the traditional 'pile them high and teach them cheap' lecturing model."[57]

REFORMING THE TEACHING AND PRACTICE OF LAW IN EUROPE

Goals and Methods

In July 2015, the Quality Assurance Agency published its third iteration of the Subject Benchmark Statement for Law,[58] which titles the benchmark outcomes,

---

[50] Drummond and McKeever, *supra* note 13; Carney et al., *supra* note 17. *Infra* Section 2.
[51] Giddings et al., *supra* note 28, at 6. The most recent report of significance to legal education is the Legal Education and Training Review (J. Webb, J. Ching, P. Maharg and A. Sherr, SETTING STANDARDS: THE FUTURE OF LEGAL SERVICES EDUCATION AND TRAINING REGULATION IN ENGLAND AND WALES (London: Legal Education and Training Review 2013); *see* examination in Leighton, *supra* note 35.
[52] Giddings et al., *supra* note 28, at 10.
[53] For example, the LawWorks and Attorney-General Student Pro Bono Awards.
[54] Paul Benneworth and Michael Osborne, *Knowledge, Engagement and Higher Education: Contributing to Social Change*, in HIGHER EDUCATION IN THE WORLD 5 (Global University Network for Innovation 2014), 219–32, at 221.
[55] *See* Leighton, *supra* note 35, at 88.
[56] *See* Marson et al., *supra* note 49; Drummond and McKeever, *supra* note 13, at 13; Leighton, *supra* note 35, at 80.
[57] Giddings et al., *supra* note 28, at 10. *See also* Drummond and McKeever, *supra* note 13, at 6; and Marson et al., *supra* note 49, at 41–42 on arguments for rebanding. Compare Uitz and Polgári, Chapter 12 in this volume, on clinic demands on faculty.
[58] This time covering Scotland as well. *See* www.qaa.ac.uk/publications/information-and-guidance/publication?PubID=2966#.VyNoLu1wbIU.

for the first time, as "a law student's skills and qualities of mind." The statement continues:

> By qualities of mind, we mean the intellectual abilities and attributes of graduates in law including but not limited to legal knowledge and understanding. Accordingly, we have kept references to knowledge and understanding from previous Law Subject Benchmark Statements, but we have added references to self-management and academic integrity.[59]

Law schools across the UK will be considering the revisions made to the Benchmark Statement and its implications for the likely quality assessment of their provision in the coming years. For law schools offering clinical options, the inclusion in qualities of mind of "self-management, including an ability to reflect on their own learning, make effective use of feedback, a willingness to acknowledge and correct errors and an ability to work collaboratively" are all potentially relevant. In their 2011 guide to CLE, Kerrigan and Murray spend several pages explaining to the undergraduate student reader how a clinical experience can enhance their learning and help them to meet the goals set out by the quality controllers of undergraduate law degrees.[60] Of particular significance in the 2015 Statement is the explicit inclusion of "experiential learning" as one among other possible teaching methods for students of law.[61]

Since the Statements apply to undergraduate degrees, they are not directly relevant to the goals we set for the SOAS Clinic. I set out earlier (in the Introduction) what we hope the students will experience and achieve in taking the Clinic as one of their courses. We do not teach the fundamentals, the substance, of international human rights law.[62] Students participating are normally expected to already have a familiarity with international law or human rights law, or to be acquiring such familiarity through other School of Law courses during their degree. Our "learning outcomes" are formally identified as the following:

> [by the end of the course] students should have an understanding of the rigours and challenges involved in international human rights practice and be equipped to research and write on this area; understand the dynamics of team work; be able to conduct research, individually and in teams, on case-specific themes and country situations, through a variety of media and sources, including web-based resources; understand, and be able to analyse, the application of international human rights instruments in and to specific situations; and be able to reflect constructively on the

---

[59] Id., 4–5.   [60] Kerrigan and Murray, *supra* note 38, at 13–15.
[61] QAA Subject Benchmark Statement Law 2015 8 para.3.3. Clubb notes that the Joint Academic Stage Board (JASB) Handbook (for 2011) does not prescribe methodologies through which law courses are to be delivered by certified institutions; and thus "although clinical legal education is valued as an experiential learning model it is not currently a mandatory requirement of qualifying law degrees in England and Wales"; see Clubb, *supra* note 49, at 396. This remains the case under the more recent Handbook (BSB and SRA 2014, 4 para. 2.a).
[62] Whether or not to attempt to do this is a discussion among US international human rights clinicians, who take different approaches. See Hurwitz, *supra* note 10, and Rosenblum, *supra* note 10.

dynamics involved in building and sustaining relationships with partners in a variety of countries and situations.[63]

In specific regard to human rights, my aim is that my students, enrolled as they are on postgraduate programmes of international (human rights) law, learn the prospects for empowerment and remedy that the law may offer alongside "the limited value of legal action"[64] and the complexities involved in developing advocacy strategies to access legal as well as other forms of remedy. The methodologies through which the SOAS Clinic seeks to have its students achieve the goals combine a number of established clinical practices, and we have also had to make decisions about challenges that have faced other clinics and have been resolved in different ways. I will consider three issues here: the composition of the Clinic, teamwork, and assessment and reflection.

To start at the beginning, it is usually not possible to accommodate in the Clinic each year all the students who wish to take it as part of their LLM/MA. Class size limitation has been discussed since early clinic days in England and Wales and often applies whether or not participation is assessed.[65] In Clinic 1, we set a maximum of fifteen students; in my most recent class (Clinic 7), the largest to date, I had twenty-four students, assigned to six project teams of four.[66] Considerable flexibility has been required from SOAS central and faculty support in order to exempt the Clinic from the preterm online sign-up procedures that now otherwise apply; online sign-up is taken as an expression of interest in taking the course but does not guarantee a place in the Clinic. After the first class of term, where I have introduced the concept of CLE, the SOAS Clinic, and the projects for that year, I make available on the Clinic's electronic learning site a form for application and return by those who wish to sign up for the class. The form includes a statement as to motivation as well as space to detail previous or ongoing voluntary commitments and/or human rights experience (broadly writ).[67] Also in that first class, I invite graduates from the previous year's Clinic to address prospective Clinic students in a question-and-answer session (from which I withdraw), which has proved very popular and which I have found to enhance diversity in the composition of the incoming class.[68] On receipt of the applications, I assign students to teams on the basis of

---

[63] International Human Rights Clinic – Introduction 2015–16, https://www.soas.ac.uk/law/international-humanrights-clinic/.
[64] Grimes, *supra* note 45, at 171.
[65] See Rees, *supra* note 39, at 138–39. Dignan, *supra* note 40, at 79 (assessed); Cardiff Law School Law Clinic (extracurricular, *see* website).
[66] Undergraduate Clinics may use the designation "firms." *See* Dignan, *supra* note 40, at 79; Elaine Campbell, *Transferring Power: A Reflective Exploration of Authentic Student-Centred Small Group Work in Clinical Legal Education*, 22 IJCLE 1–31 (2015).
[67] Compare Chapter 16 by Nollkaemper and Kjos and Chapter 12 by Uitz and Polgári in this volume.
[68] Clinic students have come from majority and BME communities in the UK and from states in Europe and North America, as well as from Middle Eastern, African, South Asian, East Asian, and Australasian states.

the fit with the project briefs, having regard as far as I can to a set of variables including proportionate LLM/MA representation, individual student's interests and background, and abilities in languages other than English; on gender diversity, I have to report that only rarely have men applied in sufficient numbers to have one in each team.

The expansion in SOAS Clinic numbers has been due to student demand and growing interest among partners and to the fact that my line managers have allocated me a certain number of weekly "tutorial" hours in recognition of the amount of time spent in project supervision. This does not match the actual time spent (this Clinic is as labour intensive as all others appear to be),[69] but it does formally account for enough of my time to release me from other teaching during the first term when the project work is most intense.[70] In 2000, in the opening practice note contributed to the first edition of the *International Journal of Clinical Legal Education*, published at Northumbria, Richard Grimes reported on "a significant shift in attitude" in regards to the obstacles that law school lecturers perceived in establishing programmes of CLE:

> Those who did not run clinics thought that set up and running costs would be the principal difficulty. Those that did have clinics operating saw the amount of staff time as the major cause for concern. ... The hard fought battles over pedagogic relevance of clinical education may now be largely a thing of the past. The debate seems to have moved on to resources and funding issues and to ensuring that the maximum benefit is extracted from clinical activity for all relevant stakeholders.[71]

A second critical issue is that of teamwork and the management of that process by the clinical supervisor.[72] The research and advocacy brief that I have agreed with the project partner before term starts is, for each team, the basis of the first engagement with the partner and may involve negotiation as well as clarification in the first meeting. Usually, the team members do not already know each other, and they work in a flat structure: there is no designated "team leader" (except, in various capacities, myself). Working in this team, they learn to negotiate with each other and with the partner, to order and minute meetings and follow-up action agreed upon, and the other skills that come from working collaboratively and intensively together over a period of some four months. Every few weeks, the Clinic plenary is given over to

---

[69] For examples, see Chapter 12 by Uitz and Polgári in this volume.
[70] Two colleagues are also allocated a one-hour tutorial a week over the period of project work.
[71] Grimes, *supra* note 36, at 56.
[72] See McAllister (1997) 53–59, summarized in Judith Gowland and Paul McKeown, *Working with Your Supervisor and Others*, in A STUDENT GUIDE TO CLINICAL LEGAL EDUCATION AND PRO BONO (Kevin Kerrigan and Victoria Murray, eds., Houndmills: Palgrave Macmillan 2011), 88–106, at 89, for an insightful consideration of the different and sometimes conflicting roles of the clinic supervisor, and the importance of the role model. See further Jeff Giddings, *The Assumption of Responsibility: Supervision Practices in Experiential Legal Education*, in EXPERIMENTAL LEGAL EDUCATION IN A GLOBALIZED WORLD. THE MIDDLE EAST AND BEYOND (Mutaz M. Qafisheh and Stephen A. Rosenbaum, eds., Newcastle upon Tyne: Cambridge Scholars Publishing 2016), 29–52.

Project Rounds, with each team presenting and reflecting on the progress on their work (including the relationship with their project partner) and receiving feedback from the Clinic as a whole. In between, they meet with me and with the project partner or follow up meetings by email and/or Skype. In depth feedback is provided on all drafts of the project work. Although by now I can predict fairly accurately at what point(s) project teams will begin to regret having signed up for the Clinic, overall and certainly by the end "[m]ost students find the experience more intense and engaging than other law school coursework."[73] The explicit idea of commitment (to the project, the team, the partner, and the Clinic as a whole) drives the Clinic for the best part of two terms.

The third issue is that of assessment and credit. Increasingly in common with other university law schools, SOAS has *pro bono* options for both undergraduate and postgraduate students. But the Clinic is different: it is a fully integrated part of the School of Law's postgraduate curriculum, credit bearing and running over the two teaching terms. Giving students credit for their work is seen by some as critical to clinic development; in 2000, Grimes identified this as one of the issues remaining as a challenge for the integration of clinics across the wider curriculum in the UK.[74] In an earlier piece, he had reflected that "students both demand and deserve credit for their efforts"; clinic teachers find formal assessment good for engaging and sustaining commitment, and, in my case, NGO project partners preferred on principle that the students' work was done for formal credit.[75] The question for me, then, was not whether to assess the students, but how to do it; assessment of CLE work is recognized as extremely challenging.[76] I assessed by long essay for the first two years but, in response to student feedback, switched to include a mark for the student's Project Portfolio. This Portfolio includes a reflective presentation of the project and excerpts of the student's individual writing contribution to the final project outcome brief and annexes the full project document or report, a self-evaluation statement from the first term, and the student's Project Diary.

---

[73] Jeff Giddings and Jennifer Lyman, *Bridging Different Interests. The Contributions of Clinics to Legal Education*, in THE GLOBAL CLINICAL MOVEMENT (Frank Bloch, ed., New York: Oxford University Press 2011), 297–309, at 307. *See* Campbell, *supra* note 66, on small group work in clinic as a "paradigm of student-centred teaching." And *see* Dignan, *supra* note 40, at 76: "Collaborative work based learning enhances employability"; it is also one of the QAA "law student qualities."

[74] Grimes, *supra* note 36, at 57. *See also* Combe, *supra* note 21, at 282; Giddings et al., *supra* note 28, at 10. Kerrigan and Murray (*supra* note 38, at 12) say that "it is becoming increasingly common for clinic modules to be formal and assessed."

[75] Grimes, *supra* note 45, at 175; Rees, *supra* note 39, at n6. Carney et al., *supra* note 17, estimated that 25% of clinical work by students was assessed, compared to 10% in 2010.

[76] *See* the Special Issue of the IJLCE (Vol.23/1 2016) comprising papers from a workshop on "Problematizing Assessment in Clinical Legal Education" and introduced by Hall Elaine Hall, *The Special Issue: Problematising Assessment in Clinical Legal Education*, 23 (1) IJCLE 11–4 (2016). The seminar was funded by a seminar prize awarded by the Association of Law Teachers to the University of Northumbria's clinic.

Reflective journals are a standard of CLE practice;[77] I encourage my students to use the Project Diary to log hours, activities, and ideas, as well as for reflection on the nature of the project and its place in "human rights work," but engagement with it can be uneven and making it part of the formal assessment is inevitable. The opportunity to review and radically restructure assessment is presented by SOAS's preparations to switch to the common credit framework for postgraduate courses (the European Credit and Transfer Units associated with the Bologna Process).

Kerrigan and Murray identify for the UK law student a good range of clinical and *pro bono* activities available at different law schools, with a focus on undergraduates.[78] The key feature of a particular activity being a practice of CLE for them is that it includes reflection on the activity, and they include the following as examples of CLE: in-house advice and representation clinics, advice-only/gateway clinics, placements and externships, street law projects,[79] simulation activities, and specialist clinical projects such as Innocence Projects[80] and "policy/law reform clinics."[81] At the SOAS human rights clinic, we have once placed a student team in a law firm to work on a brief, at the firm's request, but mostly the teams work from SOAS.[82] We integrate skills-building classes into the weekly plenary, but we do not attempt to explicitly cover the "DRAIN" lawyering skills that may be focussed on in undergraduate CLE programmes.[83] Clubb discusses

---

[77] *See* for example Dignan, *supra* note 40, at 79; Richard Grimes, David McQuoid-Mason, Ed O'Brien, and Judy Zimmer, *Street Law and Social Justice Education*, in THE GLOBAL CLINICAL MOVEMENT (Frank Bloch, ed., New York: Oxford University Press 2011), 225–40, at 234.

[78] Twining *supra* note 24, and *see* also *Let's Talk: Framing Enquiry and Discussions about "Legal Education,"* 49 (3) THE LAW TEACHER 388–98 (2015) has criticized what he perceives as the "absence of emphasis on postgraduate and advanced studies" in discussions of legal education and training, of the postgraduate stage.

[79] On Street Law in the UK, *see* Richard Grimes, *Legal Literacy, Community Empowerment and Law Schools – Some Lessons from a Working Model in the UK*, 37 THE LAW TEACHER 273–84 (2003); and Grimes et al., *supra* note 77.

[80] Towards the end of March 2016, *The Justice Gap* posted an interview with Richard Foster, chair of the Criminal Cases Review Commission (CCRC), which included the following: "A few years ago it was claimed that university innocence projects were looking at over 100 cases. The Commission points out that in the 12 years of the innocence movement they have only received around 25 applications from universities – and half of them from one university (Cardiff). With an analogy that is not going to go down well with university innocent projects, Foster says: 'If you think that you have a terminal illness, would you rather have your case considered by medical students in the bar on Friday night – or would you rather send it to a consultant oncologist?'" *See* http://thejusticegap.com/2016/03/way-back-court-appeal/ (last visited April 30, 2016). Notice was promptly drawn to this on the CLEO mailing list, and *The Justice Gap* has a number of posts in response, many from clinic supervisors.

[81] Kerrigan and Murray, *supra* note 38, at 7, 2–3. Other particular clinical projects presented on the website of different UK law schools include the Essex Law Clinic's Miscarriage of Justice Project and Cardiff University's Legal Advice Scheme's partnership with the Welsh Rugby Union.

[82] On this occasion, the team members were asked to sign a confidentiality agreement with the firm; compare Chapter 16 by Nollkaemper and Kjos in this volume.

[83] Drafting, Research, Advocacy, Interviewing and Negotiation; *see* et al. *supra* note 49, at 37–38.

some of the challenges that exist in a clinic such as ours at SOAS at postgraduate level and including students from different jurisdictions and non-law backgrounds; she proposes an "action research type model as a basis for the provision of postgraduate law clinic."[84] In addition to Clubb's own offering at Derby, there are recently-created LLM programmes in CLE at Ulster and in the Theory and Practice of CLE at York.

Beyond the Educational Goals

The Ulster LLM programme is framed as "access to justice through legal education,"[85] signalling its positioning within the older "skills v. values" debate in CLE.[86] A major research publication co-authored by a director of the Ulster University Law Clinic investigates precisely the issue of access to justice through clinics at university law schools and begins by noting the changes made over the past thirty years in publicly funded legal aid provision in the UK, from a system "that was regarded as one of the most generous in the world, to a rationalised provision that has seen significant reductions to both the scope of work that comes within legal aid schemes and the remuneration available to cover it."[87] Indeed, many CLE and *pro bono*-related publications over recent years affirm the reduction in state-funded legal aid provision (including reduced funding for local advice centres and the introduction of certain court and tribunal fees) as among the contextual factors supporting the need for increased provision by university CLE programmes and *pro bono* commitments by the professions and those aspiring to join them, commitments that Giddings et al. note are being "vigorously promot[ed]" by the Attorney General, city law firms, and the bar, as well as by the government.[88] According to Martin Barnes, Chief Executive of LawWorks, announcing the tenth round of LawWorks and Attorney General Student Pro Bono Awards in 2016:

> Restrictions in legal aid and cuts in funding for local law centres have significantly reduced people's ability to access legal advice and representation, putting greater demand and pressure on pro bono services. While pro bono is not, and should not be seen as, an alternative to legal aid, law students and law schools make an

---

[84] Clubb, *supra* note 49, at 400.
[85] https://www.ulster.ac.uk/courses/course-finder/2016r/clinical-legal-education-908/.
[86] According to Gold and Plowden (*supra* note 21, at 314) "a proxy for the debate over the heart and soul of the clinical movement."
[87] Drummond and McKeever, *supra* note 13, at 8.
[88] Giddings et al., *supra* note 28, at 10. See Martin Barnes, Foreword. In *LawWorks Clinics Network Report April 2014–March 2015*. LawWorks 2015, https://www.lawworks.org.uk/solicitors-and-volunteers/resources/lawworks-clinics-network-report-april-2014-march-2015 (last visited April 30, 2016); the foreword by Baroness Scotland to Kerrigan and Murray's (*supra* note 38) Student Guide at xviii; and Bleasdale-Hill and Wragg, *supra* note 18, at 257. For a direct impact *see*, Dignan, *supra* note 40, at 76 on the ending of £700,000 of local authority funding to the Humberside Law Centre ("now closed").

important contribution to enabling people to access the advice and support they need.[89]

Drummond and McKeever propose that such context can in part be responded to by the academy providing students with "a learning-by-doing approach to understanding the barriers to justice, and the student/lawyer role in helping to overcome these barriers."[90] Previously, better state-funded access to justice and legal aid provision in the UK slowed the impetus for CLE programmes;[91] and while "radical" students and staff (e.g. in Kent and Warwick in the early 1970s) saw an improved equality agenda to be realized through clinics (and law more generally), Drummond and McKeever agree that from the 1990s:

> the motivation for clinic creation has been focussed on "employability" through the acquisition of practical legal skills, and the conceptual basis of social justice has been superseded by a focus on educational priorities. While social justice can still be delivered, it tends to be as a consequence of a pedagogically focussed initiative rather than as its mission.[92]

In summarizing the findings from their research and based on responses from thirty-two UK university law school clinics in a survey carried out in the summer of 2015, they note that clinics "prioritise the objectives of improving student employability and developing professional capacity in law students over assisting local communities and delivering access to justice."[93] Kerrigan and Murray take a more engaged approach than that consensus would suggest: explaining to the student readers why "the relationship between clinic and social justice is ... long-standing and deeply entrenched," they say that, in a general law degree, "students may fail to grasp the reality that legal rules and legal processes are not separate from social, political and economic relationships, but are an intrinsic part of the unequal distribution of power and resources in society."[94]

Internationalization, Cooperation, and Diffusion

In the SOAS Clinic, the framing of international human rights law already pronounces something of a built-in social justice purpose – even if, for critics of human

---

[89] https://www.lawworks.org.uk/about-us/news/nominations-open-pro-bono-lawworks-and-attorney-general-student-awards-2016 (last visited April 14, 2016).
[90] Drummond and McKeever, *supra* note 13, at 8. *See* more generally Frank S. Bloch and Mary Anne Noone, *Legal Aid Origins of Clinical Legal Education*, in THE GLOBAL CLINICAL MOVEMENT (Frank S. Bloch, ed., New York: Oxford University Press 2011), 153–66.
[91] Drummond and McKeever, *supra* note 13, at 12.
[92] *Id.*, at 12–13. They cite here Dignan, *supra* note 40, and Grimes, *supra* note 36.
[93] Drummond and McKeever, *supra* note 13, at 5. They did however find agreement that CLE programmes can and do provide access to justice, a consequence of which students are a part (at 6).
[94] Kerrigan and Murray, *supra* note 38, at 18.

rights, its proponents are inextricably bound up in power dynamics.[95] In a human rights clinic, much as is to be expected, the thrust of most work will be taking on governments (or certain "authorities") in some way or another, in some forum or another, or at least preparing the ground for this. If it is not aimed at preparing the ground for an intervention in an international or regional forum, it may be a direct contribution to the research and advocacy work of a domestic human right group seeking legislative or policy change to bring national government(s) into greater compliance with international commitments. The partners and projects that have come to the SOAS Clinic have largely been a result of my own networks and those of close (and like-minded) friends and colleagues from the human rights movement. In the early debates over CLE in the UK, Rees identified one of the critiques made by Bankowski and Mungham of developments at the universities of Warwick and Kent as being that "the theory of society and community underlying these new developments is seldom made explicit by the harbingers of clinical training."[96] And Sherr, looking back in the mid-nineties, asked "Is it right that the clinical teachers clandestinely operated their own political agenda?"[97] In the United States at the end of 2014, participants in the International Human Rights Clinicians email list[98] were responding to noisy critique by Eric Posner – *inter alia*, that international human rights law clinics "have no pedagogic value and do nothing more than engage in 'left-wing' political activism."[99] A post by a more sympathetic reader of Posner's critique found it healthy to be reminded that such clinics "are outside the traditional box of law school clinics and that they do risk becoming a platform for pure political advocacy (and training students in pure political advocacy)." "Should law students really be training to do the same kind of stuff," Ku asks, as that done "within the orbit of the larger universe of UN-affiliated NGOs and UN human rights institutions?"[100]

[95] See David Kennedy, *The International Human Rights Movement: Part of the Problem?*, 15 HARV. HUM. RTS. J. 101–25 (2002); *The International Human Rights Regime: Still Part of the Problem?*, in EXAMINING CRITICAL PERSPECTIVES ON HUMAN RIGHTS (Rob Dickinson, Elena Katselli, Colin Murray and Ole W. Pederson, eds., Cambridge: Cambridge University Press 2012) 19–34; and, for one of many responses from a scholar-activist, *see* Christine Bell, *Human Rights and the Struggle for Change: A Study in Self-Critical Legal Thought*, in EXAMINING CRITICAL PERSPECTIVES ON HUMAN RIGHTS (Rob Dickinson, Elena Katselli, Colin Murray and Ole W. Pederson, eds., Cambridge: Cambridge University Press 2012), 217–46.
[96] Rees, *supra* note 39, at 131.   [97] Sherr, *supra* note 36, at 119.
[98] My thanks to Professor Stephanie Farrior, Director of the Center of Applied Human Rights at Vermont Law School, for getting me on to this list.
[99] As summarized by Sitai Kalantry, Eric Posner Has a Narrow Understanding of Human Rights Clinics, *Chronicle of Higher Education* November 24, 2014, http://chronicle.com/blogs/conversation/2014/11/24/eric-posner-doesnt-understand-human-rights/; and Eric Posner, The Human Rights Charade, *The Chronicle of Higher Education* November 17, 2014.
[100] Ku, Julian. "Eric Posner's Not Completely Wrong Critique of International Human Rights Law Clinics." *Opinio Juris*, December 3, 2014. On line at: http://opiniojuris.org/192014/12/03/eric-posners-not-completely-wrong-critique-international-human-rights-law-clinics/?utm_source=feedburner&utm_medium=email&utm_campaign=Feed%3A+opiniojurisfeed+%28Opinio+Juris%29.

In the SOAS Clinic, students' reflection on their project work – and more generally on the work of human rights NGOs into which this broadens – often invokes Peter Rosenblum's argument for an "ambivalent activism": "committed to action, but alert to the multiple consequences; ... more sympathetic to the plight of people trying to do good, while at the same time more critical of those who do it without reflecting on the possible negative consequences."[101] This kind of personal reflection may or may not be underpinned by broader scholarship more critical of the human rights enterprise generally, including that of my SOAS colleague Stephen Hopgood, who holds a seminar with my Clinic students every year.[102] The Critical Legal Studies tradition is quite established in the SOAS School of Law, and my students over the years appear to be increasingly tending towards the underlying critique of the power dynamics of international human rights as a starting point; many of them focus on the co-optation of human rights discourse in neo-liberal agendas and neo-imperial military ventures, and some find it hard to believe that "human rights" ever held, or ever could hold, radical promise of change. In 1995, Sherr speculated that the same "ethos" and "original political objectives" that underpinned early CLE efforts and matched the "anti-authoritarian views" of that era's students "probably also gave rise to the critical legal studies movement."[103] Pondering the subsequent CLE focus on skills teaching, Sherr wondered:

> Is it possible to take the politics out of clinical legal education? Can they be left with the theoreticians of the critical legal studies movement and can legal skills be taught, sanitised of the ideology and devoid of the emotion?[104]

The recent furore around US human rights clinics might suggest not. The weight of clinic students' critique is not directed at the aspiration for change and for "social justice" but at how we might get there; the engagement with a specific project and a specific organization opens the way for application of the critique and back again to reflection, all the while fulfilling commitment to the partner by completing the work to the highest standard possible.[105] The manner of the partner's engagement with the team's work is critical to the student experience. In turn, the partners' cooperation with the Clinic is based on an expectation of a serious contribution to

---

[101] Rosenblum, *supra* note 19, at 304–05.
[102] *See* Stephen Hopgood, KEEPERS OF THE FLAME. UNDERSTANDING AMNESTY INTERNATIONAL (Cornell: Cornell University Press 2006); THE ENDTIMES OF HUMAN RIGHTS (New York: Cornell University Press 2013).
[103] Sherr, *supra* note 36, at 118.
[104] *Id.*, at 119. *See* Caroline Bettinger-Lopez, Davida Finger, Meetali Jain, JoNel Newman, Sarah Paoletti, Deborah M. Weissman, *Redefining Human Rights Lawyering through the Lens of Critical Theory: Lessons for Pedagogy and Practice*, 18 (3) GEORGETOWN J. POVERTY L. & POL. 337–97 (2011), for an account of the recent scholarly cooperation of a set of human rights and poverty clinicians and poverty law clinicians in examining the utility and implications of applying critical legal theory to their work.
[105] Where appropriate, the Clinic teams' work is acknowledged in publications by the partners.

their work by the Clinic team and, in some cases at least, of an engagement with potential future colleagues in the human rights movement.

CONCLUSION

At the time of writing, after the victory of the "Brexit" campaign in the referendum,[106] the medium- and long-term implications of a withdrawal of the UK (or parts of it) from the EU for the higher education sector in general and for legal education and training in particular are as yet unclear. Even before the referendum, for undergraduate clinics in the UK, Campbell and Boothby find the future to be "far from clear" in light of consumerism-driven changes to legal services provision and the ramifications of registering as Alternative Business Structures.[107] As already noted, Richard Wilson has suggested that human rights might be the area of law in which clinical work might take off in Council of Europe countries.[108] A question for international human rights clinics in Europe is whether we have sufficient "critical mass" to begin to work together in cooperative ventures in scholarship as well as, possibly, in practice – perhaps in praxis! The issue of scholarship is key. In the UK, a number of clinical scholars have commented on the fact that in the last two Research Assessment/Excellence Exercises, on the basis of which the government decides its allocation of research funding to individual universities, publications on legal education, including scholarship on CLE, have generally not received a strong rating. According to Gold and Plowden, this illustrates a continuing "antipathy to practice-based and pedagogic materials in law."[109] In the most recent exercise, the subpanel in law said that it was "pleased to receive submissions relating to legal education but the methodological rigour and significance exhibited by some of these outputs was uneven."[110] Twining notes a "switch of emphasis in general law school culture from teaching to research" which he holds to be "largely attributable" to Research Excellence Framework (REF) exercises.[111] The increasing attention to the "impact" of scholarship in such exercises is not straightforwardly applicable (linkable) to the work of Clinic students, no matter how demonstrable that "impact" might be. The risks here include that teaching a clinic will be detrimental to an academic lawyer's career, given the demands on the teacher, if the associated scholarship arising from the clinical experience is not "rated."[112] Drummond and McKeever have suggestions as to how to take the scholarship forward, as do Gold and Plowden,[113] and, possibly, cooperation between clinic

---

[106] On June 23, 2016.
[107] Under the Legal Services Act 2007. ## Elaine Campbell and Carol Boothby, *University Law Clinics as Alternative Business Structures: More Questions than Answers?*, 50 (1) THE LAW TEACHER 132–37 (2016), at 137; Leighton, *supra* note 35, at 80.
[108] Wilson, *supra* note 4, at 828.   [109] Gold and Plowden, *supra* note 21, at 316.
[110] *Research Excellence Framework 2014: Overview Report*, Sub-Panel 20: Law, 71, para. 6
[111] Twining, *supra* note 28, at 389 n3.   [112] See Giddings et al., *supra* note 28, at 16.
[113] Drummond and McKeever, *supra* note 13, at 13; Gold and Plowden, *supra* note 21, at 316–20.

convenors in different parts of Europe might have contributions to make here. In the UK, a more recent governmental initiative in the field of surveillance of academic effort, the Teaching Excellence Framework (TEF), might be expected to rate CLE programmes quite healthily, and an earlier optimistic projection suggested that more university law schools would start to offer clinical options of some sort because those not doing so would find themselves disadvantaged in the increasingly competitive market of law student recruitment.[114] However, this by no means implies a reconciliation between the demands of teaching and the expectations of research for the individual clinic teacher.

References

ACLEC (Lord Chancellor's Advisory Committee on Legal Education and Conduct). *Annual Report for 1993–1994*. London: HMSO, 1994.

Amnesty International, *Below the Radar*, 5 April 2006 (AI Index AMR 51/051/2006).

Bankowski, Zenan, and Geoff Mungham. "'Warwick University Ltd.' (Continued)." 1 *British Journal of Law and Society* 1974 179–84.

Bar Standards Board and Solicitors Regulation Authority. *Academic Stage Handbook* (v. 1.4). July 2014 [on line].

Barnes, Martin. "Foreword." In *LawWorks Clinics Network Report April 2014–March 2015*. LawWorks 2015: available at https://www.lawworks.org.uk/solicitors-and-volunteers/resources/lawworks-clinics-network-report-april-2014-march-2015 [last accessed 30 April 2016]

Bell, Christine. "Human Rights and the Struggle for Change: A Study in Self-Critical Legal Thought." In *Examining Critical Perspectives on Human Rights*, eds. Rob Dickinson, Elena Katselli, Colin Murray and Ole W. Pederson, 217–46. Cambridge: CUP, 2012.

Benneworth, Paul and Michael Osborne. Knowledge, Engagement and Higher Education: Contributing to Social Change. In *Higher Education in the World* 5, 219–32. Global University Network for Innovation, 2014.

Bettinger-Lopez, Caroline, Davida Finger, Meetali Jain, JoNel Newman, Sarah Paoletti, Deborah M. Weissman. "Redefining Human Rights Lawyering through the Lens of Critical Theory: Lessons for Pedagogy and Practice." *Georgetown Journal on Poverty Law and Policy* XVIII/3 (2011) 337–397.

Bleasdale-Hill, Lydia and Pail Wragg. "Models of Clinic and Their Value to Students, Universities and the Community in the post-2012 Fees Era." IJCLE 19 (2013) 257–69.

Bloch, Frank S. and Mary Anne Noone. "Legal Aid Origins of Clinical Legal Education." In *The Global Clinical Movement*, ed. Frank S. Bloch, 153–66. New York: OUP 2011.

Bradney, Anthony. "Ivory Towers and Satanic Mills: Choices for University Law Schools." *Studies in Higher Education* 17/1 (1992) 5–20.

Campbell, Elaine. "Transferring Power: A Reflective Exploration of Authentic Student-Centred Small Group Work in Clinical Legal Education." IJCLE 22 (2015) 1–31.

Campbell, Elaine and Carol Boothby. "University Law Clinics as Alternative Business Structures: More Questions than Answers?" *The Law Teacher* 50:1 (2016) 132–37.

Carillo, Arturo J. "Bringing International Law Home: The Innovative Role of Human Rights Clinics in the Transnational Legal Process." *Colum H. Rts. L. Rev.* 35 (2003–2004) 527–87.

---

[114] Marson et al., *supra* note 49.

Carney, Damian, Frank Dignan, Richard Grimes, Grace Kelly, Rebecca Parker. *The LawWorks Law School Pro Bono and Clinic Report 2014*. LawWorks: LexisNexis (2014) on-line at: https://www.lawworks.org.uk/sites/default/files/LawWorks-student-pro-bono-report%202014.pdf

Chavkin, David. "Thinking/Practicing Clinical Legal Education from within the Palestinian-Israeli Conflict: Lessons from the Al-Quds Human Rights Clinic." *Human Rights Brief* 18 (2010) 14–18.

Clubb, Karen. "Masters of Our Destiny – The Integration of Law Clinic into Postgraduate Masters Provision." IJCLE 19 (2013) 395–404.

CMND 4595 1971. Report of the Committee on Legal Education.

Combe, Malcolm M. "Selling Intra-curricular Clinical Legal Education." *The Law Teacher* 48:3 (2014) 281–95.

Dignan, Frank. "Bridging the Academic/Vocational Divide: The Creation of a Law Clinic in an Academic Law School." IJCLE 16 (2011) 75–84.

Drummond, Orla and Gráinne McKeever. *Access to Justice through University Law Clinics*. Ulster: Ulster University Law School, 2015. On-line at: www.ulster.ac.uk/lawclinic/files/2014/06/Access-to-Justice-through-Uni-Law-Clinics-November-2015.pdf

Folsom, Ralph and Neal Roberts. "The Warwick Story: Being Led down the Contextual Path of the Law." *Journal of Legal Education* 30 (1979) 166–83.

Giddings, Jeff. "The Assumption of Responsibility: Supervision Practices in Experiential Legal Education." In *Experimental Legal Education in a Globalized World. The Middle East and Beyond*, ed. Mutaz M. Qafisheh and Stephen A. Rosenbaum, 29–52. Newcastle upon Tyne: Cambridge Scholars Publishing, 2016.

Giddings, Jeff, Roger Burridge, Shelley A.M. Gavigan and Catherine F. Klein. "The First Wave of Clinical Legal Education. The United States, Britain, Canada and Australia." In *The Global Clinical Movement*, ed. Frank Bloch, 3–22. New York: OUP, 2011.

Giddings, Jeff and Jennifer Lyman. "Bridging Different Interests. The Contributions of Clinics to Legal Education." In *The Global Clinical Movement*, ed. Frank Bloch, 297–309. New York: OUP, 2011.

Gold, Neil. "Why Not an International Journal of Clinical Legal Education?" IJCLE 1 (2000) 7–12.

Gold, Neil and Philip Plowden. "Clinical Scholarship and the Development of the Global Clinical Movement." In *The Global Clinical Movement*, ed. Frank Bloch, 311–21. New York: OUP, 2011.

Gowland, Judith and Paul McKeown. "Working with Your Supervisor and Others." In *A Student Guide to Clinical Legal Education and Pro Bono*, eds. Kevin Kerrigan and Victoria Murray, 88–106. Houndmills: Palgrave Macmillan, 2011.

Grimes, Richard. "Reflections on Clinical Legal Education." *The Law Teacher* 29 (1995) 169–88.

"The ACLEC Report – Meeting Legal Education Needs in the 21st Century?" *Legal Education Review* 7: 2 (1996) 281–89.

"Learning Law by Doing Law in the UK." IJCLE 1 (2000) 54–57.

"Legal Literacy, Community Empowerment and Law Schools – Some Lessons from a Working Model in the UK." *The Law Teacher* 37 (2003) 273–84.

Grimes, Richard, Joel Klaff and Colleen Smith. "Legal Skills and Clinical Legal Education – A Survey of Undergraduate Law School Practice." *The Law Teacher* 30 (1996) 44–67.

Grimes, Richard, David McQuoid-Mason, Ed O'Brien and Judy Zimmer. "Street Law and Social Justice Education." In *The Global Clinical Movement*, ed. Frank Bloch, 225–40. New York: OUP, 2011.

Hall, Elaine. "The Special Issue: Problematising Assessment in Clinical Legal Education." IJCLE 23/1 (2016) 11–4.

Hopgood, Stephen. *Keepers of the Flame. Understanding Amnesty International*. Cornell: Cornell University Press, 2006.

The Endtimes of Human Rights. New York: Cornell University Press, 2013.

Hurwitz, Deena. "Lawyering for Justice and Inevitability of International Human Rights Clinics." *Yale Journal of International Law* 28 (2003) 505–550.

Kalantry, Sitai. "Eric Posner Has a Narrow Understanding of Human Rights Clinics." *Chronicle of Higher Education* 24 November 2014: on-line at http://chronicle.com/blogs/conversation/2014/11/24/eric-posner-doesnt-understand-human-rights/

Kennedy, David. "The International Human Rights Movement: Part of the Problem?" 15 *Harvard Human Rights Journal* (2002) 101–25.

"The International Human Rights Regime: Still Part of the Problem?" In *Examining Critical Perspectives on Human Rights*, eds. Rob Dickinson, Elena Katselli, Colin Murray and Ole W. Pederson, 19–34. Cambridge: CUP, 2012.

Kerrigan, Kevin and Victoria Murray, eds. *A Student Guide to Clinical Legal Education and Pro Bono*. Houndmills: Palgrave Macmillan, 2011.

Kerrigan, Kevin. "What Is Clinical Legal Education and Pro Bono?" in *A Student Guide to Clinical Legal Education and Pro Bono*, ed. Kevin Kerrigan and Victoria Murray, 1–20. Houndmills: Palgrave Macmillan, 2011.

Ku, Julian. "Eric Posner's Not Completely Wrong Critique of International Human Rights Law Clinics." *Opinio Juris*, 3 December 2014. On line at: http://opiniojuris.org/192014/12/03/eric-posners-not-completely-wrong-critique-international-human-rights-law-clinics/?utm_source=feedburner&utm_medium=email&utm_campaign=Feed%3A+opiniojurisfeed+%28Opinio+Juris%29

Leighton, Patricia. "Back from the Future: Did the LETR Really Prepare Us for the Future?" *The Law Teacher* 48 (2014) 79–93.

Marson, James, Adam Wilson, Mark Van Hoorebeck. "The Necessity of Clinical Legal Education in University Law Schools: A UK Perspective." IJCLE 7 (2005) 29–43.

McAllister, Lindy, Michelle Lincoln, Sharyne McLeod, Diana Maloney (eds.). *Facilitating Learning in Clinical Settings*. Cheltenham: Nelson Thornes Ltd 2001 (original print 1997).

Posner, Eric. *The Twilight of International Human Rights Law*. New York: OUP, 2014.

Qafisheh, Mutaz. "Modern Legal Education in Palestine: The Clinical Programs of Hebron University." In *Experimental Legal Education in a Globalized World. The Middle East and Beyond*, ed. Mutaz M. Qafisheh and Stephen A. Rosenbaum, 198–235. Newcastle upon Tyne: Cambridge Scholars Publishing, 2016.

Rees, William M. "Clinical Legal Education: An Analysis of the University of Kent Model." *The Law Teacher* 9 (1975) 125–40.

Research Excellence Framework 2014. *Overview Report by Main Panel C and Sub-Panels 16–26*. January 2014.

Rosenblum, Peter. "Teaching Human Rights: Ambivalent Activism, Multiple Discourses and Lingering Dilemmas." *Harvard Human Rights Journal* 15 (2002) 301–15.

Sherr, Avrom. Clinical Legal Education at Warwick and the skills Movement: Was Clinic a Creature of its Time." In *Frontiers of Legal Scholarship. Twenty Five Years of Warwick Law School*, ed. Geoffrey P. Wilson, 108–19. Chichester: John Wiley and Sons, 1995.

Twining, William. "LETR: The Role of Academics in Legal Education and Training: 10 Theses." *The Law Teacher* 48:1 (2014) 94–103.

"Let's Talk: Framing Enquiry and Discussions about 'Legal Education'." *The Law Teacher* 49: 3 (2015) 388–98.

Webb, Julian. "Inventing the Good: A Prospectus for Clinical Education and the Teaching of Legal Ethics in England." 30 *Law Teacher* (1996) 270–94.

Webb, J., J. Ching, P. Maharg and A. Sherr, Setting Standards: *The Future of Legal Services Education and Training Regulation in England and Wales*. London: Legal Education and Training Review, 2013.

Welchman, Lynn and Sara Hossain, eds. *"Honour": Crimes, Paradigms and Violence Against Women*. London: Zed Books, 2005.

Wilson, Richard J. "Western Europe: Last Holdout in the Worldwide Acceptance of Clinical Legal Education." *German Law Journal* 10:7 (2009) 823–46.

"Introductory Remarks." *American Society of International Law Proceedings* 2010 "Teaching International Law: Lessons from Clinical Education" 87–88.

14

The Experience of the Åbo Akademi University International Human Rights Law Clinic, Finland

Juan-Pablo Pérez-León-Acevedo

INTRODUCTION

Finnish legal education has traditionally been characterized by a doctrinal, theoretical, and research-oriented approach. It exemplifies European legal education in which the implementation of clinical legal education (CLE) has faced a number of challenges relating to *inter alia* opposition from the legal profession, an incompatible conception of law, the nature/status of the professoriate, and heavy state control over legal education.[1] This explains why there was no CLE in Finland until 2012 and that there is currently only one pilot initiative. The academic and legal environment in Finland has delayed the emergence of CLE and prevented its expansion.

In March 2012, the project to create the first Finnish legal clinic, i.e. the Åbo Akademi University International Human Rights Law Clinic (ÅAIHRLC), was presented to the Åbo Akademi University Institute for Human Rights (ÅAIHR) authorities.[*] Upon discussion and approval, the ÅAIHR hosted the ÅAIHRLC from September 2012 to June 2014. Upon my departure from Åbo, the ÅAIHRLC was no longer continued. As an ÅAIHR researcher and a lecturer, I planned, led, and ran the ÅAIHRLC during its existence.

The ÅAIHRLC members were master's degree-level students – between four and eight per academic semester – recruited based on a competitive process from mainly students registered in our master's degree programme on international human rights law (IHRL). Selected students received up to ten European Credit Transfer System (ECTS) credits per academic year.

From Åbo and following an externship/seminar format, students provided *pro bono* legal services to two overseas partner organizations/individuals: (1) the legal team(s) led by Barrister Richard Harvey, Chairperson of Garden Court International at the Garden Court Chambers (London), lead defence counsel at the International

---

[*] Åbo Akademi University International Human Rights Law Clinic, Founding Supervisor (2012–2104). The views expressed herein are the author's own and not necessarily those of the persons, organizations, and entities mentioned.

[1] See Richard Wilson, *Western Europe: Last Holdout in the Worldwide Acceptance of Clinical Legal Education* 10 GERMAN LAW JOURNAL 823, 830–39(2009).

Criminal Tribunal for the Former Yugoslavia (ICTY), member of the Association of Defence Counsel Practising Before the ICTY (ADC-ICTY), and a lawyer/legal adviser in cases litigated before domestic jurisdictions; and (2) HURINET-U, a Ugandan umbrella human rights nongovernmental organization (NGO) that works on diverse human rights issues including international criminal law (ICL).

By networking with our partners, the ÅAIHRLC students worked on issues concerning mainly ICL and related areas such as international humanitarian law, IHRL, transitional justice, international/regional courts proceedings and litigation, and domestic implementation of international law. The ÅAIHRLC course included weekly seminars to organize tasks and discuss the progress of the students. Under my close supervision and coordination, students expanded their legal knowledge and put it into practice in applied research and drafting of legal documents such as reports, memoranda of law, and working papers according to the specific demands and feedback from our partner organizations when litigating cases or performing other legal functions.

Students provided legal advice and research on *inter alia*: (1) modes of criminal liability of senior leaders (ICTY); (2) the principle of proportionality in war crimes litigation (ICTY); (3) legal elements of international crimes (ICTY); (4) civil compensation for alleged victims of NATO strikes in Libya; (5) national legislation assessment (the Philippines, Uganda) under ICL and related areas; (6) the reparations programme for international crimes/serious human rights violations (Uganda); (7) impact and implementation of the International Criminal Court (ICC)'s decisions in Africa; (8) the relationship between the African Union (AU) and the ICC; (9) the ICC admissibility test; (10) drone attacks under ICL and international humanitarian law; (11) Colombia's transitional justice process and the ICC; and (12) European Court of Human Rights (ECtHR) admissibility proceedings.

EMERGENCE OF CLE

Genesis and Context

In establishing the ÅAIHRLC, the following considerations were taken into account.

Institutional Considerations
First, it was desired to provide our master's level students a legal practice opportunity without leaving Åbo and simultaneously with their course intake. The ÅAIHR Director and Deputy Director welcomed and supported the ÅAIHRLC. They, alongside ÅAIHR researchers and alumni, found the ÅAIHRLC to be a good way in which to modernize and reform teaching and education practices as well as to provide public legal services.

Second, the ÅAIHRLC emerged and worked in fulfilment of the ÅAIHR's mandate "to promote research, provide education and disseminate information relating to the protection of human rights."[2] The ÅAIHRLC was also an avenue to disseminate information about the ÅAIHR and draw attention to the ÅAIHR's academic, training, and research activities among our partner organizations and those individuals and organizations that received legal advice and/or were represented by them. Thus, dissemination and/or consolidation of the ÅAIHR's profile in the (international) human rights law community was borne in mind. The addition of partner organizations and their clients to the ÅAIHR's network of academic and institutional partners and related institutional benefits were considered.

Third, the introduction of a legal clinic was also regarded as a distinctive feature to make the ÅAIHR master's IHRL programme stand out when compared to similar Scandinavian and Nordic programmes. Indeed, the quite limited presence of (international) legal clinics at regional law schools increased the need for introducing the ÅAIHRLC, which in turn enhanced the comparative advantages of our academic offer.

Educational Considerations

First, the ÅAIHRLC was part of a series of projects at the ÅAIHR intended to offer our master's level students a wider set of elective courses and complement theoretical courses and seminars with an eminently practical course and, importantly, pioneer CLE in Finland.

Second, the ÅAIHRLC was considered an interesting initiative to introduce CLE methods, previously unknown in Finland, to Åbo Akademi University and other Finnish universities. Thus, the ÅAIHRLC was, for the ÅAIHR and the closely related Åbo Akademi Law Department, an effort at pioneering (international) CLE in Finland. In turn, the ÅAIHRLC exemplified the ÅAIHRLC's interest in and actions taken with respect to continuously reviewing its curricula qualitatively and quantitatively. Precisely, the Bologna Process shed light on the need to strengthen quality assurance and the need to approach higher education with a view to employability within Europe and beyond.[3] By involving students in international law advice and research as applied to real cases and situations, the ÅAIHRLC arguably contributed to enhancing our students' qualifications and prospects when applying for jobs or academic programmes in the context of an increased compatibility among higher education systems as sought by the Bologna Process.[4] Simultaneously, the creation of the ÅAIHRLC paid heed to the goal of making European and particularly Finnish universities more competitive and

---

[2] See ÅAIHR, www.abo.fi/fakultet/en/humanrights (last visited March 1, 2016).
[3] European Commission, The Bologna Process and the European Higher Education Area, http://ec.europa.eu/education/policy/higher-education/bologna-process_en.htm (last visited March 1, 2016).
[4] Id.

attractive worldwide, as envisioned by the Bologna reforms.[5] Additionally, the ÅAIHRLC was perfectly in sync with the process of modernization of education and training systems tailored to the demands and needs of a continuously changing labour market that increasingly requires highs levels of skills, innovation, and entrepreneurship.[6] All of these considerations, strongly promoted and justified by the Bologna Process, led to the creation and work of the ÅAIHRLC.

Beyond the ÅAIHRLC, the Bologna Process has influenced Finnish CLE. Although the Helsinki Law Clinic (HLC) does not mention it explicitly, it seeks to *inter alia* create a learning experience for law students where they can put their theoretical knowledge into practice by advising real clients.[7] It could be argued that Finnish CLE has been guided by the analytical, personal, cognitive, and managerial competencies that the Bologna Process encourages academic institutions to instil in law students so that they may become effective lawyers.[8]

Third, the eminently international character of the ÅAIHRLC fitted into the trend to internationalize and globalize legal studies in Finnish law schools. The decision to focus the ÅAIHR on ICL and related areas and make the ÅAIHR part of the ÅAIHRLC master's IHRL degree was part and parcel of a trend resulting in a substantial increase in international and European law courses in legal education on offer at (especially postgraduate) Finnish universities. Indeed, the ÅAIHR's said master's level programme came to existence in the academic year 2006–2007. Also, the other Finnish master's degrees with important international and European law concentrations – namely, the Law and Information Society Programme (Turku University Law School) and the International Business Law and Public International Law Programme (Helsinki Law School) – were introduced in the past decade.[9] Another example of the internationalization of legal studies in Finland is the Turku Law School, which combines the academic and teaching resources of the ÅAIHR/Åbo Akademi Law Department and Turku University Law School to offer mainly international and European law courses to postgraduate, undergraduate, and exchange students.[10] These programmes and initiatives have arguably become the flagships of their respective institutions. Thus, not only setting up the ÅAIHRLC but also and, importantly, endowing it with an international law profile were greatly influenced by the globalization and regionalization of Finnish legal education. Moreover, a feature common to the ÅAIHRLC and the above-mentioned programmes is the use of English as the working language and the language of

[5] *Id.* [6] *Id.*
[7] HLC, Report of Activities-Spring 2016, 2016,www.helsinki.fi/helsinki-law-clinic/Report%20Helsinki%20Law%20Clinic%20Spring%202016.pdf (last visited July 5, 2016).
[8] *See*, for discussion, Wilson, *supra* note 1 at 839–44.
[9] *See*, respectively: www.utu.fi/en/units/law/studying/masters-degree-program/Pages/home.aspx (last visited January 15, 2016).
    www.helsinki.fi/law/studies/mdp/Programme.html (last visited January 15, 2016).
[10] *See* https://nettiopsu.utu.fi/opas/opintoKokonaisuus.htm?rid=20718&uiLang=en&lang=en&lvv=2015 (last visited January 15, 2016).

instruction, which corresponds to the conception of these initiatives as platforms to teach international and/or European law to an international audience. Additionally, that Finnish CLE has been part of postgraduate legal education corresponds to the international/European law–oriented focus expected during master's-level studies under the Bologna Process.[11]

Field of Law Considerations
As noted, ICL was the main legal field for the ÅAIHRLC's work. ICL is relatively new compared to other branches of international law and yet to be fully fledged in some areas.[12] However, ICL has increasingly drawn much attention in the past two decades. This is explained by the establishment of international criminal tribunals and national implementations of the ICC Statute. Thus, the relative novelty and dramatic expansion of ICL constituted powerful reasons to link the ÅAIHRLC's work to ICL. The novel nature of many ICL topics foreseeably offered new challenges to our students as they provided legal advice on issues about which legal sources (case law included) had not come up with clear answers yet or had even remained silent. Being part of the ICL expansion, from an academic standpoint, was also deemed important.

Second, setting up a legal clinic primarily focused on ICL and related areas was perceived as part of a necessary effort to fill a gap in legal education and, more specifically, among legal clinics. Although there is an important and increasing number of legal clinics addressing (international) human rights law cases and topics, they normally tackle a wide variety of human rights subareas or human rights subareas other than ICL. Barring a few exceptions,[13] ICL is not typically the main focus of legal clinics and rather forms just a part of their workload.[14] Therefore, at the ÅAIHRLC, ICL was understood as a fertile yet not fully explored ground for CLE.

---

[11] See Miguel Poiares Maduro, *Legal Education and the Europeanisation and Globalisation of Law*, 4 CROATIAN YEARBOOK OF EUROPEAN LAW & POLICY, vii. xiii (2008).
[12] See Antonio Cassese, INTERNATIONAL CRIMINAL LAW, 2nd ed. (Oxford University Press 2008), 4–10.
[13] E.g., clinics/similar projects at Geneva, Utrecht (discontinued), Case Western, American University, Melbourne, and Rosario University (Colombia) law schools:
www.cassese-initiative.org/global-activity/law-clinic.html (last visited January 15, 2016);
www.schoolofhumanrights.org/index.php?id=42&tx_ttnews%5Btt_news%5D=36&cHash=b2ae4222b6 (last visited January 15, 2016);
http://law.case.edu/Academics/Academic-Centers/Cox-International-Law-Center/Henry-T-King-Jr-War-Crimes-Research-Office (last visited January 15, 2016);
https://www.wcl.american.edu/warcrimes/activities.cfm (last visited January 15, 2016);
http://law.unimelb.edu.au/students/jd/enrichment/pili/subjects/international-criminal-justice-clinic
www.urosario.edu.co/Clinica-Juridica-Internacional/Que-hacemos/ (last visited January 15, 2016).
[14] E.g., legal clinics at Amsterdam, Northwestern, Emory, and Berkeley universities:
http://ailc.uva.nl/for-students (last visited January 15, 2016);
www.law.northwestern.edu/legalclinic/humanrights/projects/ (last visited January 15, 2016);
http://law.emory.edu/academics/clinics/international-humanitarian-law-clinic.html (last visited January 15, 2016);

Third, ICL has mainly been developed at the international level by international and hybrid criminal courts. Nevertheless, the application of ICL is not the exclusive preserve of such courts; also – and importantly – domestic courts and agencies apply ICL. This scope of application should not be underestimated by legal clinics working on ICL (i.e. it is advisable not to focus exclusively on either the national or international level and neglect the other altogether). These points were considered in the design and work of the ÅAIHRLC. Thus, the ÅAIHRLC was conceived to support ICL litigation and applied research at international courts (mainly ICTY) as well as legal advice in national and regional scenarios. This led to drawing a fine workload balance between the two levels.

Therefore, the ÅAIHRLC demonstrated that ICL can be an important/new substantive area for the development of CLE. ICL provides a wide range of opportunities to apply CLE methods and approaches. This is because cases in which ICL is applied are litigated at international/hybrid criminal courts and in national criminal jurisdictions. CLE also benefits from the opportunity provided by ICL to advise a diverse range of actors, from victims to defendants, and on topics that integrate international, criminal, and comparative law. Like other law clinics, the ÅAIHRLC's experience evidences that certain areas of law not (fully) explored by CLE present an important opportunity for the development of CLE.[15]

Sociopolitical Field Considerations

The ÅAIHRLC was conceived to serve not only one particular community or the local community (i.e. Finland). Conversely, the ÅAIHRLC was structured to legally contribute to specific topics of interest to the international community as a whole and, more specifically, to diverse national communities according to the requests made by our partner organizations. Therefore, the ÅAIHRLC members provided legal services on matters relating to the former Yugoslavia, Uganda, the Philippines, Colombia, and Libya, among others.

When selecting our partner organizations and, thus, clients, attention was paid to particularly challenging sociopolitical contexts. This was specially the case with HURINET-U, the leading Ugandan NGO and one of the most prominent African human rights NGOs. The ÅAIHRLC was designed to provide specialized and in-depth legal research and advice on highly technical and complex matters of ICL and related areas. Thus, the ÅAIHRLC aimed to successfully complement HURINET-U's expertise with respect to the local and regional legal and sociopolitical contexts. In turn, this resulted in an efficient synergy of efforts. The ÅAIHRLC was satisfied with this cooperation due to the fact that highly

https://www.law.berkeley.edu/experiential/clinics/international-human-rights-law-clinic/resources-and-publications/ (last visited January 15, 2016).
[15] See Chapter 15 by Joost Pauwelyn and Mattia Salamanca Orrego in this volume.

specialized knowledge of ICL and related areas in Uganda – and most of the Sub-Saharan region – is yet to fully develop among lawyers and civil society organizations (despite the exponential number of international crimes perpetrated there). Additionally, this skill gap affects a large number of victims of serious human rights violations who cannot afford legal representation or advice. Against a background context of limited financial resources and sociopolitical constraints under which HURINET-U works, the ÅAIHRLC assisted it to better conduct a wide array of activities ranging from litigation to dissemination and thus especially benefitted the most vulnerable and dispossessed in Ugandan and African society.

There is, of course, an increasingly tense relationship between Uganda, an important number of African countries, and the ICC. When designing the ÅAIHRLC and when already working for HURINET-U, important challenges emerging out of the African political context came into play. Certainly, the sociopolitical landscape in Uganda and Africa in general in many cases triggered HURINET-U's requests for legal advice. Some examples include (1) AU initiatives to create a regional body with jurisdiction overlapping that of the ICC and promote mass withdrawal from the ICC's jurisdiction, (2) African States Parties to the ICC Statute not enforcing the ICC arrest warrants against Sudan's President Al-Bashir, (3) the lack of national reparations programmes and other transitional justice projects related to international crimes, and (4) the tension between the need for amnesties for international crimes to bring and keep peace on the one hand and, on the other, the need to fight against impunity for such crimes in order to secure democracy. The ÅAIHRLC had been aware of these upcoming challenges and problems related to the sociopolitical context in Uganda and Africa. Indeed, this was one of the main factors leading to the decision to assist HURINET-U.

Concerning the other partner organization (i.e. the international teams led by Barrister Harvey [Garden Court International-Chambers/ADC-ICTY]), similar considerations of sociopolitical contexts surrounding the cases and situations to be advised on were taken into account. Thus, concerning defence litigation at the ICTY, contribution to legal advice relating to the facts and events in *Karadzic* was considered by the ÅAIHRLC to be important in helping to solidify the still fragile postwar, transitional justice and reconciliation efforts in the Balkan region. Other cases also involved highly sensitive sociopolitical issues, such as discussion of amnesties and/or pardons for non-state armed group members in internal armed conflicts in Colombia and the Philippines.

Therefore, the ÅAIHRLC students had to approach the law in context, paying attention to the sociopolitical scenarios in which our cases and projects were situated. The ÅAIHRLC prepared argumentation tailored to the requests from and interests of our partner organizations and their clients. However, the ÅAIHRLC's legal services were always delivered in a technical manner, considering the sociopolitical situations but without political bias.

Drivers

Based on my own experience and those of other clinicians and researchers in Finland,[16] three main drivers behind the recent emergence of CLE in Finland may be identified. First was a desire to offer more practically oriented and proactive methods to teach law to Finnish law students so that they could be better prepared for successful legal practice upon graduation. This was missing in Finnish legal education until very recently as evidenced by the fact that, prior to the ÅAIHRLC (2012–2014) and the HLC (started in 2015–2016), no Finnish legal clinic had existed. This scarcity is, of course, not exclusive to Finland or a specific legal field.[17] Second was a desire to provide high-quality legal assistance to actors of the international community, such as lawyers at international and domestic courts, human rights NGOs, and, through them, other clients including victims and defendants (ÅAIHRLC) or those not covered by the Finnish legal aid schemes, such as EU citizens, migrants, and students who begin to establish start-ups (HLC).[18] Third was a desire to answer the calls from Finnish institutions such as the Supreme Court and Bar Association to equip law students with more practical education.

However, CLE still has a long road to go to achieve consolidation and sustainability in Finland. Institutional support at Finnish law schools has yet to (substantially) increase (or materialize at all) in a sustained manner beyond pilot projects. Limited time and human and financial resources have hindered the expansion of Finnish CLE and explain why CLE has so far only been present at two universities. The two legal clinics that recently emerged in Finland were created mainly because of individual initiatives of some researchers. However, Finnish law schools and universities should also adopt a top-down approach to enhance and consolidate bottom-up initiatives and projects in CLE.

With regard to what fellow clinicians, or those who potentially become clinicians, and myself hope(d) to achieve, the following may be observed. First, it is hoped that we have raised awareness of the importance of CLE across Finnish law schools. Second, it is hoped that the importance of CLE becomes evident both to members of the (international) society who benefit from legal aid and to students who are taught law via a practice-oriented approach which may better prepare them for future legal practice in public and private sectors and at the international or national levels. Third, it is hoped that there will strengthened cooperation and cohesion within law schools and legal clinics, among teachers, students, and other university community members, and concerning external relationships between academia and actors and institutions of the national and/or international community.

---

[16] Information from communications with Helsinki and Turku Law Schools colleagues.
[17] *See* Lamin Khadar, University Law Clinics and the Growing Demand for EU Law (OPEN SOCIETY FOUNDATION VOICES, October 30, 2014), https://www.opensocietyfoundations.org/voices/university-law-clinics-and-growing-demand-eu-law (last visited March 5, 2016).
[18] HLC: https://weboodi.helsinki.fi/hy/frame.jsp?Kieli=6&valittuKieli=6 (last visited March 5, 2016).

Generally speaking, I consider that Finnish CLE also reflects an emerging trend in response to broader social, political, or economic changes taking place beyond academia and law. For example, the scope and activities of ÅAIHRLC directly stemmed from increasing initiatives to foster global governance and accountability mechanisms in the context of mass atrocities. In turn, HLC's scope arguably responds to challenges linked to migration and economic recession/crisis which have recently ensnared Europe.

REFORMING THE TEACHING AND PRACTICE OF LAW IN EUROPE

Goals and Methods

The status quo of ICL teaching in terms of educational goals is to introduce students to ICL foundations as applied at international/hybrid criminal courts and/or at the national level. Depending on the level (i.e. graduate/postgraduate) and length of the programme, ICL teaching covers substantive and procedural issues and develops critical and analytical skills which aim to prepare students for international and/or national practice and research.[19] Practice-oriented goals of ICL teaching have been enhanced through mooting; however, this is limited to the ICC proceedings and not yet widespread.[20] Thus, traditional lecture courses and seminars had been the main ICL teaching formats. As mentioned, few legal clinics in Europe and beyond undertake ICL cases and advice as part of their workload, and even fewer primarily focus on ICL. Accordingly, the ÅAIHRLC, by introducing CLE in ICL teaching, may be considered an example of adding more practical and problem-solving educational goals and, unlike mooting, in a professional context, tackling real cases and situations. Thus, the ÅAIHRLC complemented the traditional educational goals by aiming to educate and train students in ICL using a much more pragmatic and practice-oriented approach.

The ÅAIHRLC aimed to fulfil and arguably exemplify the functions of CLE not only in terms of filling a gap in legal education but also by serving as a vehicle to reform legal education more broadly. Concerning the latter, the ÅAIHRLC represented an avenue to pursue new trends in legal education, including the development and enhancement of experiential and practical training methods.[21] Moreover,

---

[19] E.g., international criminal law programmes at Amsterdam/Columbia and Leiden: http://als.uva.nl/programmes/content2/international-criminal-law.html (last visited February 1, 2016); http://en.mastersinleiden.nl/programmes/international-criminal-law/en/introduction (last visited February 1, 2016).

[20] E.g., ICC moot court courses at Vrije Universiteit Amsterdam and Helsinki law schools: https://vu.nl/en/study-guide/2015-2016/master/h-l/international-crimes-and-criminology/index.aspx?view=module&origin=51102892&id=51102849 (last visited February 15, 2016); https://weboodi.helsinki.fi/hy/frame.jsp?Kieli=6&valittuKieli=6 (last visited February 15, 2016).

[21] Claudio Grossman, *Building the World Community Through Legal Education*, in THE INTERNATIONALIZATION OF LAW AND LEGAL EDUCATION (Jan Klabbers and Mortimer Sellers, eds., Springer 2009), 21, 30.

due to its international law orientation, the ÅAIHRLC aligned with efforts to reform legal education by implementing an innovative model of legal education.[22] This model relies on, among other things, fostering international awareness, establishing strong links between the study of domestic law and international law, and focusing on different legal systems.[23] Like other law clinics,[24] the ÅAIHRLC was aware of CLE's potential to challenge and transform the status quo of (local) legal education and the institutional environment.

The ÅAIHRLC, in pursuing academic reform, was one among a range of efforts to respond to major challenges in European legal education. These challenges relate to changes in the way that law is taught, changes in the profile of the lawyer sought by the market, and increasing competition among European law schools in the European academic market.[25]

Therefore, the ÅAIHRLC fulfilled its educational goals to enhance knowledge in specific human rights issues; train students in drafting the memoranda of law, reports, and other papers used in litigation and legal advice; deepen specialist knowledge in specific areas; strengthen drafting, analytical, and research skills; apply abstract knowledge to concrete situations; and instil legal professional ethics, including strict respect for professional secrets and confidential matters.

Concerning ICL teaching methods, these have been mainly confined to those traditionally applied in lectures. These, especially in Europe, have been normally passive, formalistic, hierarchical, and/or doctrinal. As other authors in this volume have noted, this model of legal education has to a greater or lesser extent been characteristic of European legal education.[26] More dynamic and proactive methods have been offered in seminars and, when available, mooting and CLE. At the ÅAIHRLC, diverse teaching methods were used, particularly dynamic, proactive, and collaborative teaching and learning. This combination arguably challenged the status quo of ICL teaching. The ÅAIHRLC relied on assigning in-advance and post-class readings (i.e. selected case law, instruments, and academic literature); however, students were also asked to identify legal sources to prepare themselves individually and/or in teams for their tasks and to comment on them at weekly seminars. These seminars were quite dynamic and interactive because the students had to provide mutual feedback. The supervisor guided students and lectured on and/or provided information in relation to specific points and commented on student presentations. Students – individually and occasionally in teams – submitted draft reports and/or memoranda of law reviewed by the supervisor who provided feedback on contents and style. Then, the finalized documents were submitted to our partner organizations, which followed up with questions and clarification requests. This process was conducted subject to demanding deadlines and ad hoc requests from our partner organizations, sometimes changing the scope of the work.

---

[22] *Id.* [23] *Id.*, at 30–33. [24] *E.g., see* Chapter 5 by Maria Marquès i Banqué in this volume.
[25] Maduro, *supra* note 12 at xiii. [26] *E.g., see* Chapter 8 by Nora Markard in this volume.

This prepared students to expect the "unexpected," as occurs in legal practice. Overall, the ÅAIHRLC methods encouraged and required students to become much more proactive and assume centre stage in their legal education. Some interdisciplinary approaches and methods were also considered when, for example, examining the ICC's impact on victims and their communities in Africa.

The ÅAIHRLC promoted a conception of "the lawyer" as a professional role that challenged the status quo in ICL since the topics and cases handled pushed students to think "outside the box." As previously noted, ICL is relatively new. A large number of substantive and procedural matters that have not yet been (fully) developed provided fertile ground for our students to creatively approach legal advice and research requests from our partner organizations. Furthermore, when advising them, the ÅAIHR members critically examined legal instruments by revisiting well-established case law and mainstream academic work to propose consistent arguments tailored to the interests, legal status as defence or victim lawyers, and legal strategies of our partner organizations.

Beyond the Educational Goals

Concerning service-learning or the more socially oriented goals of the ÅAIHR, the ÅAIHRLC constituted part thereof and enhanced them. The ÅAIHRLC fitted into the goals of the ÅAIHR IHRL master programme, namely by equipping and preparing graduates for "demanding human rights law assignments in international organizations, non-governmental organizations and in public administration" and "advanced human rights law research."[27] Moreover, by undertaking real cases, the ÅAIHRLC strengthened the ÅAIHR's integration into the community and the development of socially significant knowledge.[28] Due to the ÅAIHRLC's international profile, "community" meant both the "international community" and diverse national communities.

The primary justice-related and service-related goals of the ÅAIHRLC were to actively participate in the application of ICL instruments in cases and applied research at the international and national levels. Thus, it was aimed to support and serve some international community actors dealing with procedural, institutional, and substantive law challenges in ICL and related areas. Also, the ÅAIHRLC aimed to contribute towards the consolidation of the international rule of law concerning, especially, the application of legal instruments and efficient work of individuals and organizations participating in cases and activities involving serious international crimes.

---

[27] See www.abo.fi/fakultet/en/humanrightsmaster (last visited July 4, 2016).
[28] See Paul Benneworth and Michael Osborne, *Knowledge Engagement and Higher Education in Europe*, in HIGHER EDUCATION IN THE WORLD 5: KNOWLEDGE, ENGAGEMENT & HIGHER EDUCATION: CONTRIBUTING TO SOCIAL CHANGE (Global University Network for Innovation 2014), 219, 222.

To what extent those goals pursued by the ÅAIHRLC challenged the status quo of ICL teaching and thus differed from typical ICL teaching could be understood as follows. The ÅAIHR put a lot of emphasis on justice-related and service-related goals. These goals rendered the ÅAIHRLC substantially unique as compared to traditional ICL courses and seminars whose main, if not exclusive goals, are educational. This is particularly the case when ICL is only offered as an optional course among many others at undergraduate and postgraduate levels or when law schools and/or university institutes solely undertake academic research. Only if law schools and/or institutes undertake applied ICL research (potentially) benefitting national and international community actors such as victims, defendants, and lawyers, does ICL legal education truly go beyond educational goals. The ÅAIHRLC illustrated the need for, and feasibility of, incorporating justice-related and service-related goals into the objectives typically defining ICL legal education.

Limiting ICL teaching to educational goals was not an option at the ÅAIHRLC. The need to challenge the status quo came from the fact that ICL is applied in difficult and urgent contexts involving large numbers of individuals, victims, and institutions ranging from international courts to human rights NGOs. To contribute in a timely manner towards meeting the deterrent, punitive, and restorative goals pursued by international criminal justice, the ÅAIHRLC found it necessary to supplement legal educational goals with the goal of serving a number of actors in order to achieve justice. The ÅAIHRLC considered that ICL teaching must pursue educational and justice-/service-related goals. This is because serious international crimes and related degradations of justice are urgent issues and underpin the very existence of ICL, developed and expanded from Nuremberg to the ICC. The ÅAIHRLC humbly illustrated that legal education in the context of ICL should not neglect or undermine the importance of these ulterior goals.

In the context of access to justice, the status quo in legal service provision in ICL may be briefly summarized as follows. At the level of international and hybrid criminal courts, legal aid for victims and defendants (when found indigent) is provided by the respective international organizations (e.g. the ICC Office of Public Counsel for Victims) or through associated offices (e.g. the ADC-ICTY). Depending on the legal framework, funding comes from obligatory state contributions and/or international community donations. However, defence teams, especially compared to the Prosecution, tend to face funding problems which result in inter alia understaffing and less state cooperation. In this regard, the added value of the ÅAIHRLC concerning legal service provision was to assist the appointed standby defence team in *Karadzic* (ICTY) and, hence, contribute to the goals of full equality of arms and legitimacy of international criminal justice institutions. Thus, our partner organization/team was able to better handle its large workload and focus on litigation, in-court, and managerial activities. This support was crucial given the overwhelming number of witnesses/evidence and complex factual and legal issues at stake. The ÅAIHRLC tasks focused on applied research, legal memoranda drafting, and legal advice provision as requested. This maximized our contribution because our partner organization/team relied on our advice/research to back up its argumentation and thus saved time which could then be deployed towards examining witnesses, evidence, and the like.

At the domestic level, depending on the national financial and human resources, there may be some public counsel offices for victims and defendants.[29] Law firms normally do not litigate ICL cases. Generally, human rights NGOs and, in some common law countries, some barrister chambers undertake ICL litigation and advice.[30] Nevertheless, due to the highly specialized nature of ICL, few lawyers at the national level are familiarized with the particular challenges of ICL and substantive and/or procedural technicalities. Additionally, lawyers who are ICL experts do not necessarily provide *pro bono* services, and, if so, they may be understaffed or face other limitations. The ÅAIHRLC occupied this vacuum, focusing on ICL as applied nationally, especially assisting HURINET-U in Uganda and across Africa. In this regard, the added value of the ÅAIHRLC concerning legal service provision was to deliver highly specialized *pro bono* legal advice to HURINET-U. This collaboration was worthy because HURINET-U needed legal assistance considering, on the one hand, the large number of victims, lawyers, and activists represented and/or advised by it and, on the other, its limited financial, expertise, and human resources.

The Weight and Value of Internationalization

Inspired by initiatives of bringing international law to CLE[31] and due to our international profile and orientation, ÅAIHRLC students were constantly engaging with international law sources. They studied and analysed the international legal framework applicable to our cases and/or applied research requests. They identified international law provisions applicable to specific and complex facts and related legal problems and then employed general international law interpretation methods as complemented by specific interpretation methods from ICL and related legal fields.

International treaties, statutes, and rules of procedure and evidence were first considered, followed by case law and the practice of international courts, particularly the ICTY, the ICC, other international criminal tribunals, and international/regional human rights bodies and/or courts. Additionally, upon request by our partner organizations or for our own needs, our students conducted extensive research into national practice (i.e. as evidenced by legislation and case law) to see

---

[29] HiiL, Legal Aid in Europe: Nine Different Ways to Guarantee Access to Justice? (HiiL 2014),www.hiil.org/data/sitemanagement/media/Report_legal_aid_in_Europe.pdf (last visited March 1, 2016).
[30] E.g., respectively, HURINET-U and Garden Court International-Chambers.
[31] *See* Frank Bloch, *International Clinics and the Global Clinical Movement*, 26 (1) MARYLAND J. INT'L. L. 1–7 (2011).

whether there was a general legal principle or an (emerging) customary international law rule. In addition to those international law sources and methods, our students examined related academic literature and reports by NGOs and university institutes.

Interaction with international forums was a continuous feature of the ÅAIHRLC. As noted, the ÅAIHRLC assisted an international legal team led by Barrister Richard Harvey in *Karadzic* at the ICTY. Additionally, our legal research for and advice to other teams, also led by Barrister Harvey, related to potential proceedings and/or ongoing cases at other international judicial forums (the ICC and ECtHR) and diverse national forums (e.g. the Philippines, Belgium, and Colombia). Regarding HURINET-U, some of ÅAIHRLC's work involved assisting HURINET-U in its preparations for submissions before the African human rights system, including the African Commission on Human and People's Rights, and also the AU. Involvement with international forums was also necessitated by our work beyond Uganda, concerning the whole African continent, particularly the tense relationship between the ICC and the AU States in recent years.

The ÅAIHRLC's international profile enhanced the legal education of our students as most of them provided international law advice to international organizations and/or institutions for the first time. The volume and complexity of international law material examined, highly technical international legal questions addressed, pressing deadlines, and challenges of quick familiarization with (originally) unknown contexts strengthened the legal education of our students. They certainly gained a great deal of confidence using international law methods and sources applied to complex international cases subject to international quality standards. They were also fully aware of confidentiality and professional ethics when handling quite sensitive issues involving *inter alia* international criminal justice. This whole international experience meaningfully complemented the national practice background of some students and/or their knowledge of international law.

Since most of our students want(ed) to pursue careers at international organizations and/or national state and non-state organizations dealing with international law issues, the ÅAIHRLC's international law profile proved or may prove to be beneficial. First, our clinic alumni acquired practical analytical skills that enable them to undertake internships and/or legal positions more professionally and confidently, and, importantly, they acquired this during their master's-level studies rather than only afterwards, thus maximizing their time. Due to *inter alia* financial limitations, some students could not afford to undertake internships at international organizations in expensive cities. By bringing international-level work to Åbo, the ÅAIHRLC to some extent recreated the internship experience, providing students with valuable international legal practical experience regardless of their financial capacity. Second, as recruitment for internships and legal positions, internationally and nationally, has increasingly become more competitive, participation in the

ÅAIHRLC may help the applications and resumes of our alumni to stand out vis-à-vis other applicants who lack international legal clinical training.

Cooperation in CLE

When designing the ÅAIHRLC, preliminary contact with some relevant organizations and lawyers was made to find suitable institutional partners who could provide a source of meaningful and sustained clinical work for more than two years. Our two partner organizations constituted key allies for European and global collaboration. As explained, considering the ÅAIHRLC externship/seminar format, our clinic depended on our partner organizations' legal advice requests. Thus, there was a symbiotic relationship. Other law clinics have also used this institutional model based on external partner cooperation rather than on a live-client approach.[32] Since our partner organizations were based in Europe (The Hague/London) and in Uganda, and also because of the international scope of their activities, the nature and extent of this collaboration acquired a European and global character. Via our partner organizations, which in turn advise in and/or litigate cases on behalf of an important number of clients across the world (Barrister Harvey's teams at Garden Court International-Chambers/ADC-ICTY) and in Uganda and Africa (HURINET-U), the ÅAIHRLC collaborated with organizations and individuals in major regions worldwide, including Europe. For instance, legal research and advice provided to Barrister Harvey's teams benefitted lawyers of alleged Libyan victims litigating before Belgian courts civil compensation claims for damages caused by NATO's strikes in Tripoli. Another example was legal research and advice on the impact and implementation of the ICC's decisions in Africa submitted to HURINET-U. Considering the HURINET-U's network, this meant an (indirect) collaboration with other Ugandan/African human rights NGOs, lawyers, and victims.

The impact and scope of our collaboration went much further than serving our two direct partner organizations because our legal advice and research also assisted organizations and individuals directly advised or legally represented by the above-mentioned partners. In turn, this large group of clients and lawyers collaborated with us, via our partner organizations, by asking complex legal questions. This collaboration was quite useful for our students as our partner organizations and third parties advised and/or represented by them continuously requested us to undertake relevant legal work on ICL and related areas at the international and national levels. Such an exposure to a wide array of legal problems arising from diverse factual scenarios encouraged and required our students to be seriously committed to CLE. Their efforts, fed by the said collaboration, certainly benefitted the students and, arguably, their career prospects because they acquired specialized legal knowledge and factual

---

[32] E.g., see Chapter 12 by Renáta Uitz and Eszter Polgári in this volume.

information about prominent international criminal justice topics and cases litigated and/or researched in several countries and at international courts and organizations.

Regarding collaboration with other European law schools, due to the novelty, duration, and scope of the ÅAIHRLC, no concrete partnership materialized. However, the ÅAIHRLC was approached, and we also approached other legal clinics to explore avenues of collaboration, mainly experience and know-how exchange. At a meeting of Nordic law schools deans and other authorities in Turku, Finland (2013), I met Gothenburg University Law School representatives who were planning to launch a legal clinic. I was happy to share experiences and expertise accumulated at the ÅAIHRLC, especially concerning methods and course planning. I was also contacted by Russian legal clinics for potential collaboration; however, because of quite different legal practice fields, collaboration options were not explored further.

Diffusion of CLE

As the ÅAIHRLC's founder, I was mainly inspired by the teaching practices that, as a student, I had been exposed to and also by other teaching practices I came across. As a master's-level student at Columbia University Law School, I did an externship at the UN Office of Legal Affairs as a component of a UN seminar. This externship format meant meeting a supervisor for two hours at the UN office every other week between January and April 2011, combined with weekly seminars at Columbia Law School. This experience gave me some preliminary ideas about how to create a legal clinic under an externship format. This format, combined with seminar sessions, was indeed much needed at the ÅAIHRLC to afford our students the opportunity to work on cases litigated before an international criminal tribunal and on ICL applied research. There is neither an international criminal court nor a human rights NGO dealing with these issues in Finland.

Exposure to the Socratic method, as used at the above-mentioned UN seminar, provided guidance on how to better coordinate the work of the ÅAIHRLC, conduct weekly sessions, and give feedback to the students.[33]

The American model of CLE was adapted to the methods and teaching of the ÅAIHRLC, leading to a hybrid outcome. The adaptation was necessary because, unlike mainstream American CLE, the ÅAIHRLC was not based on a live-client approach and was implemented via seminar sessions intended to discuss the practical work conducted by ÅAIHRLC members. Inspired by American CLE, those seminar sessions involved students' active engagement when presenting their progress and giving feedback to and receiving feedback from other students. The European lecture-oriented approach was also present and complemented the American CLE features.

---

[33] Concerning the Socratic method, *see, e.g.*, Grossman, *supra* note 22 at 23–26.

This corresponded to the externship format of the ÅAIHRLC and its existence within a European master's degree course and Finnish legal education. The ÅAIHRLC illustrated that CLE provides a model which might be adaptable to European legal education, especially in view of the Bologna Process.[34]

Paying attention to the importance of interdisciplinary analysis present at American law schools, some empirical methodology was occasionally included in few of ÅAIHRLC's projects. For example, when examining the ICC's impact on victims in Africa, in addition to traditional legal sources, analysis of empirical data collected and published by other institutions was examined to test our own argumentation and conclusions.

Additionally, hybrid teaching methods (i.e. lecture-oriented but with features borrowed from the Socratic method) learnt from my experiences in Peruvian law schools were also applied. Considering that most ÅAIHRLC students came from European law schools where there is a prevalence of conference/lecture teaching, I deemed it convenient to combine the said methods. The outcome was characterized by active student participation during the weekly seminars when they reported their progress and/or discussed assigned readings. In any event, I always made sure to reinforce the main points and expected results. This last point was necessary as, unlike traditional classes graded via exams and/or papers, the ÅAIHRLC students provided legal advice in real cases and, therefore, had impact beyond the classroom.

Accordingly, the teaching methods employed at the ÅAIHRLC drew a lot of inspiration from American law schools as complemented by some features from European and Latin American legal education.

The dissemination of teaching methods employed at the ÅAIHRLC was achieved in two ways: first, through participation in conferences or academic events at which other clinicians shared their experiences and/or presented legal clinic research. For example, I participated in the New York University Clinical Law Review Writers' Annual Workshop in 2012. I also shared thoughts about ÅAIHRLC teaching methods with Gothenburg Law School representatives in 2013 as they were planning to establish a legal clinic. Second, while in Åbo and during the ÅAIHR's advance courses, I spread the word about the existence of teaching methods and legal services at the ÅAIHRLC. Considering the alumni of these advanced courses (experienced attorneys, law professors, and researchers from all continents), information about the work at the ÅAIHRLC was well-disseminated. For instance, a report on CLE put forth the ÅAIHRLC as the example of CLE in Finland, providing general information about the clinic itself and an overview of the methods used, as explained on our website.[35]

---

[34] Wilson, *supra* note 1 at 829.
[35] Emil Winkler, CLINICAL LEGAL EDUCATION: A REPORT ON THE CONCEPT OF LAW CLINICS (Gothenburg University 2013), 14–15, http://law.handels.gu.se/digitalAssets/1500/1500268_law-clinic-rapport.pdf (last visited February 15, 2016).

Future of CLE in Europe

The ÅAIHRLC could be reinstalled at the ÅAIHR in months or years to come. Should the ÅAIHR decide to do so and continue the externship/seminar format, two points must be addressed. First, an ÅAIHR full-time researcher/lecturer must step in to lead the ÅAIHRLC. Second, this new supervisor must identify suitable organizations and/or individuals based in Finland and/or overseas and reach cooperation agreements similar to those achieved in 2012 when the ÅAIHRLC was set up. The legal fields to be explored in a new edition of the ÅAIHRLC would certainly be determined by the supervisor's expertise and the legal work conducted by new partner organizations/individuals. As the ÅAIHR would again host the ÅAIHRLC, IHRL will still be, broadly speaking, the working legal field. Thus, the ÅAIHR's research areas that may provide grounds for CLE are migration, minorities, international/European criminal law, and/or economic and social rights.

Other legal clinic formats may certainly be explored. However, depending on how large and ambitious new projects are, attention must be paid to funding. This aspect is crucial as Finnish universities have faced recent challenges related to state funding. This situation is also illustrated by the progressive introduction of tuition fees for non-EU students by some Finnish universities. Thus, considering the current financial situation of most Finnish and other European universities, the externship format for legal clinics could be considered as a good option to offer students access to meaningful international law cases litigated at the international and/or national levels but without bearing high budgetary expenses.

Regarding how CLE teaching and practice may change in Europe in the next five to ten years, I foresee four potential main trends. First, an increased specialization of the legal fields at university law clinics, which corresponds to trends of offering specialized undergraduate/postgraduate courses at European law schools. This reflects the in-depth specialization that legal practice has acquired in Europe and beyond. I believe that legal clinics will progressively become more "specialist": legal clinics would/should only focus on areas in which supervisors possess expertise to guarantee high legal service standards. Second, in addition to traditional CLE areas such as human rights, immigration, international law, and public law, legal clinics working on other areas such as tax or business law may increase in number. Additionally, new and emerging legal areas related to technological and scientific developments may also become more common. Third, clinical teaching may increasingly incorporate a more interdisciplinary approach. This would mirror the increasing trend of interdisciplinary legal education and research worldwide. Depending on the legal fields practised at the respective legal clinic, nonlegal areas of knowledge could be particularly useful. Fourth, to guarantee the viability and expansion of CLE in Europe, institutional involvement of the respective law schools, including but not limited to regular funding, will be pivotal as the Finnish experience illustrates.

Provided that there is a change in the academic focus of European legal education from a theoretical to an increasingly practice-oriented approach as institutionally and financially supported, CLE in ICL and related areas such as (international) human rights law have strong chances to develop due to, *inter alia*, an "incredibly strong culture of human rights within Europe."[36]

CONCLUSION

The ÅAIHRLC and the European Network for Clinical Legal Education (ENCLE), which aims to unite legal clinics across Europe,[37] were established in 2012. This is not just a simple coincidence but illustrates the situation of CLE as a European trend in legal education which is increasingly gaining strength.

During its existence, the experience of the ÅAIHRLC demonstrated that it managed to fulfil its CLE goals by equipping students (who came from around the world) with or enhancing their professional legal skills. Thus, our students can arguably better face challenges arising in legal practice in a professional context which is increasingly characterized by the use of two or more working languages; digital literacy; and international, supranational, or multinational jurisdictional links.[38] This corresponds to the increase in the multinational character of both cases and the demand for legal services, which is ushering in an emerging European/global legal education market.[39]

The experience of the ÅAIHRLC constitutes a good example of how CLE is reforming the teaching and practice of law in Europe, particularly in Finland and the legal field of ICL. With regard to the teaching of law, the ÅAIHRLC meant the introduction of the legal clinic concept at a Finnish law school and also joined the very few (European) legal clinics which mainly or to some extent work on ICL cases and applied research. Importantly, the ÅAIHRLC also challenged the status quo of legal education in ICL by effectively combining different law teaching methods. The outcome of this exercise brought an important quota of dynamism, based on real cases and experiential learning, to the traditionally passive and doctrinal teaching of ICL still predominant, to a greater or a lesser extent, at law schools in Europe and worldwide.

With regard to the practice of law, the ÅAIHRLC sought and managed to train students in professional settings that are not limited to one jurisdiction, language, or familiar context. Indeed, the profile and activities of the ÅAIHRLC followed the current trend which has seen the rise of the global or international legal practitioner and, in that regard, made our alumni better prepared to handle cases involving international, regional, or foreign jurisdictions during their professional careers.

---

[36] Wilson, *supra* note 1 at 845.   [37] ENCLE, http://encle.org/ (last visited February 29, 2016).
[38] Aalt Heringa, *European Legal Education or Legal Education in Europe*, 18(3) MAASTRICHT JOURNAL OF EUROPEAN AND COMPARATIVE LAW 221, 221–22 (2011).
[39] *See* Maduro, *supra* note 12 at ix–xii.

However, the use of CLE in ICL, CLE in Europe, and, particularly, in Finland still needs to travel quite some distance to become a quintessential component of, respectively, ICL teaching and Finnish (European) legal education. Institutional and financial commitment of law schools and universities is pivotal to provide legal clinic initiatives with sustainability of time and resources and also to progressively introduce legal clinics specialized in ICL or at least working on ICL and related areas. Concerning the very limited presence of CLE in Finland, this could become the Achilles' heel of the Finnish legal education system when compared to European and, especially, American law schools. These limitations may to some extent undermine the manner of practicing law by those graduating from law schools in years to come and thus need to be addressed via continuously institutionally backed CLE projects.

15

The International Economic Law Clinic at the Graduate Institute in Geneva

Joost Pauwelyn and Mattia Salamanca Orrego

INTRODUCTION

The Graduate Institute of International and Development Studies in Geneva has hosted the Clinic in International Economic Law[1] since 2008. Its intent is to empower countries and smaller stakeholders to reap the full development benefits of global trade and investment rules. The Clinic is designed to connect students and experienced legal professionals to public officials (especially in developing countries), small and medium-sized enterprises, and civil society to build lasting legal capacity.

Projects range from advice on treaty negotiations and preparing a claim or amicus brief in World Trade Organization (WTO) dispute settlement to assessments of compliance under trade or investment agreements of proposed or actual legislation and drafting of model laws or legislative text to address specific trade or environmental problems. Project topics may include WTO law, international investment law and arbitration, and any subfield of international economic law (which includes fields such as intellectual property, tax, and finance). The final output is, in most cases, a legal memorandum or draft treaty chapter or model law. It can be public or fully confidential (e.g. when preparing legislative or treaty proposals or briefs in actual disputes).

The Clinic operates on a semester basis, currently with four legal projects per Clinic edition. Master's and Ph.D. students in law and any of the other disciplines at the Institute may apply with a CV and a motivation letter. Their academic curriculum must include at least one successfully completed course on international trade or investment law. Through "learning by doing" the Clinic wants to train and promote the next generation of trade and investment lawyers. Students work in groups of two to four under close supervision of a professor and teaching assistant (TA). Locally based economic law experts are brought into the Clinic as mentors to give guest seminars on topics related to the projects and review drafts. The Clinic also offers skills sessions focused on how to conduct legal research, legal writing, and oral presentation skills.

---

[1] *See* http://graduateinstitute.ch/trade-law-clinic; all links last visited March 29, 2016.

Beyond education, the Clinic's aim is to make available a pool of knowledge and expertise to less resource-rich countries and stakeholders, with the ultimate goal of supporting their legal capacity building (LCB) efforts. The Clinic is part of a broader network of legal clinics and LCB efforts – operating under the umbrella organization TradeLab.org – with sister clinics operating or being established in Europe, North America, Africa, and the Middle East.

EMERGENCE OF THE CLINIC

Clinical legal education (CLE) is not common, certainly not in continental Europe. The International Economic Law (IEL) Clinic at the Graduate Institute emerged bottom-up, as the initiative of one of the authors (Joost Pauwelyn, a law professor at the Institute) who had been teaching earlier in a US law school. The main drivers were (1) to better prepare law students by providing them with hands-on legal experience, (2) to take full advantage of the many international organizations and embassies based in Geneva so as to offer both faculty and students a unique experience, and (3) to offer *pro bono* legal information and research to the many stakeholders in global economic affairs who are affected by international trade and investment agreements and dispute settlement but do not have the resources to fully engage in this field. The Clinic started informally, by means of a few practical projects as part of a more traditional seminar before it was transformed into a projects-only clinic for which both the professor and students obtained credit. While initially no other institutional incentives were provided, the institutional set-up at the Graduate Institute was flexible enough to quickly set up and support the Clinic.

Institutional Factors

The nature and unique characteristics of the Clinic host institution have been key factors in the development and success of the programme. The Graduate Institute, founded in 1927, is the oldest international relations institution in continental Europe[2] and is strongly oriented towards public service and service learning. Its mission is to foster international cooperation and development through the promotion of graduate studies[3] in relevant fields. For instance, it is dedicated to analysing contemporary world challenges[4] by emphasizing the

---

[2] Aberystwyth University, in Wales, was founded in 1919.
[3] Article 3.1 of the English version of the Memorandum of Association for the Foundation for the Study of International Relations and Development (Memorandum), signed in Geneva on September 20, 2007, and modified by the Foundation Board on February 28, 2014: "through the aforementioned Institute, the mission of the Foundation is to promote international and development graduate studies in an effort to foster international cooperation and to make an academic contribution to the development of less privileged societies."
[4] Article 3.2 of the Memorandum: "the Institute's objective is to analyse contemporary world challenges with independence. . . ."

links between the intersecting fields of international relations and issues in international development. Students benefit from considerable academic independence while being simultaneously supported by the international, collaborative network nurtured by the Graduate Institute.[5] In this sense, the Clinic is an ideal match for the mission of its host institution because it gives students the opportunity to engage with cutting-edge issues involving interdisciplinary components, mainly but not exclusively in law and economics. The Institute also receives new opportunities to develop lasting relationships with other institutions and state agencies, especially from developing countries. Furthermore, less resource-rich stakeholders get a voice and the chance to benefit from the IEL system.

The educational policy of the Graduate Institute[6] marries intellectual rigour with a practical approach. Since 1927, to enrich a core curriculum of more traditional mandatory classes held by leading scholars,[7] highly regarded professionals and intellectuals[8] have delivered a number of "temporary courses and special lessons" (*Cours temporaires et leçons spéciales*). Many of the special classes took into account the state of world affairs of the period and produced a number of tailored and focused scientific works in support of peace[9] in a way not too dissimilar from modern clinics. With time, this approach led to strong ties with the network of the international community in Geneva.[10] Being particularly conducive to innovation, the teaching environment created a context which nurtured the gradual growth of the Clinic.

Since its foundation, the Institute kept adapting its structure to the growing complexity of international relations. The creation and the growth of the eight

---

[5] Article 3.2 of the Memorandum: "... in cooperation with the University of Geneva and in collaboration with other academic institutions in Switzerland and worldwide."

[6] Message of Director Philippe Burrin (*Graduateinstitute.ch*, 2016), http://graduateinstitute.ch/home/about-us/message.html (last visited March 8, 2016).

[7] For example, Hans Kelsen was nominated *professeur ordinaire* in 1933. He completed *Pure Theory of Law* the following year. Other professors who held mandatory courses were Guggenheim, Lalive, Meessen, Marek.

[8] Among many others, Eugène Borel, Luigi Einaudi, René Cassin, and William Rappard.

[9] Already in the late 1930s, the Graduate Institute produced a number of publications that reflected upon the state of world affairs, such as William E. Rappard and Paul Mantoux, *THE WORLD CRISIS* [Collection D'études Publ. À L'occasion Du Dixième Anniversaire De L'institut Universitaire De Hautes Études Internationales] (1937). In addition, in 1939, the professors of the HEI (the Graduate Institute) began planning a series of scientific endeavours. In the following years, they produced numerous scientific publications that analysed (1) the experience of the League of Nations and other international cooperation instances and (2) possible legal settings and other relevant issues for the establishment of new multilateral system. They clearly understood the relevance of their experience in Geneva and their close ties to the existing multilateral organizations. Rapport du Conseil Exécutif HEI 286/1/1939, Graduate Institute of International and Development Studies Archives.

[10] To be understood as the network comprising all actors operating in the field of international relations that have a presence in the greater Geneva area. This includes IOs, law firms, NGOs, interest representation firms and consultancies, universities, countries missions, representations, and delegations.

academic departments[11] was a gradual process. Such development followed the growth in the number of enrolled students and the expansion of courses necessary to accommodate their increasingly varied interests. More recently, a number of research centres were established within the Graduate Institute. The centres brought scholars from various disciplines under one roof, to avoid working in silos and to allow the unfettered study of interdisciplinary issues. Within centres, professors benefit from a significant degree of flexibility while pursuing their research because they are able, with the technical and administrative support offered by the Centre, to compete for external funding and dispose of means to conduct their research projects independently of the constraints of the Institute's general budget. This greater degree of autonomy fostered the development of events, seminars, and highly specialized courses. Indeed, the IEL Clinic was conceived within and continues to be supported by the Centre for Trade and Economic Integration (CTEI).

The Institute adapted its academic offerings to the Bologna standards in 1999.[12] Thus, the structure of the academic programme progressively became module- and credit-based, but these changes had a limited impact on the Institute's overall educational policy. Indeed, the Bologna Process has given students more international exchange opportunities, opening the courses of the Institute to visiting students in return for allowing its own students to follow courses in other European institutions. Yet the composition of the student body and of the faculty at the Institute has not significantly changed, being already very diverse and international.[13] At present, the Institute's professors and visiting and research personnel come from more than thirty different countries, and the Institute's approximately eight hundred students come from more than one hundred countries (2016 data). The Institute's faculty members have diverse academic and professional experiences, as well as strong ties to the business, international relations, and academic communities. In addition, a diverse student body may have facilitated the development of new teaching methods since the students do not share a single "national" approach to course participation or expectations regarding how a course should be delivered. In fact, this diversity may have paved the way towards a greater acceptance of unconventional teaching methods. In addition, a multilingual student body from all over the globe has also facilitated communication and outreach

---

[11] International Affairs, Development Studies, Anthropology and Sociology of Development, International Economics, International History, International Law, International Relations – Political Sciences. Academic Departments and Programmes (*Graduateinstitute.ch*, 2015), http://graduateinstitute.ch/home/study/academicdepartments.html (last visited March 9, 2016).

[12] Switzerland has been a full member of the European Higher Education Area (EHEA) since 1999. In this context, the Graduate Institute has experienced several changes: (1) a modularization of its study programmes with corresponding adaptations of the examination system; and (2) an ECTS-compliant credit system based on the *Empfehlungen der CRUS für die Anwendung von ECTS an den universitären Hochschulen der Schweiz*, Rektorenkonferenz der Schweizer Universitäten, 23. August 2004.

[13] Based on internal data that cover the period 1990–2015.

to stakeholder-clients from different backgrounds and has allowed the Clinic to digest materials in multiple languages.

Educational Considerations

A number of educational considerations have influenced the decision to establish the Clinic. First and foremost, the goal was to offer students a unique experience, working with "real clients" on actual legal problems of high concern in the real world of global economic affairs. This opportunity better prepares students for a legal career.[14]

At the Graduate Institute, international law students benefit from the unique location; the strong ties of the Institute with international organizations, not-for-profit, and business actors; the renown of its faculty; and its research environment.[15] Yet the Institute operates in a highly competitive environment. Most of its competitors,[16] especially those in the United States, have some form of learning-by-doing experience in their curriculum. Although many US law schools have permanent clinical programmes well integrated into their curricular offering, very few were offering clinics in international law,[17] the area of specialization of the Graduate Institute. Until 2008, IEL was a niche underserved by clinical education despite its growing relevance. The establishment of a long-term clinical programme in a yet unserved area of law, such as IEL, required significant financial resources, human capital, and time to develop a pilot programme that could take into account the particular characteristics of IEL, promote clinical education to largely unaware stakeholders, and, most importantly, have the ability to deliver.

With the establishment of CTEI in 2007, co-founded by Professors Joost Pauwelyn (law) and Richard Baldwin (economics), the Graduate Institute decided to devote significant resources to IEL and CLE. The CTEI became the Graduate Institute's centre of excellence for research on international economic issues, bringing together the Institute's research activities in the areas of trade, investment, economic integration, and globalization. The Centre provided a platform for developing the clinical programme, supporting it in kind and through competitively obtained third-party funding. The CTEI made experts available for clinical projects, took charge of the promotion of the Clinic, and involved new stakeholders in the programme. It worked with the Institute to facilitate the integration of the Clinic in

---

[14] See the later section on Goals and Methods.
[15] Based on the internal 2015 student satisfaction survey data.
[16] This statement is based on internal data. It is determined by looking at the students' alternative choices for those who were accepted and those who dropped their applications to pursue graduate studies elsewhere. A similar exercise on clinical students only confirms the trend while exhibiting a greater bias towards North American institutions.
[17] As noted also by Acevedo in Chapter 14 of this volume: "indeed, the quite limited presence of (international) legal clinics at regional law schools increased the need for introducing the AAIHRLC, which in turn enhanced the comparative advantages of our academic offer."

its curricula and to reward students with credits for their participation.[18] After seven years, clinical education is taking root in IEL as the overall costs involved in establishing IEL clinics are diminishing. The Graduate Institute is sharing its know-how with other leading institutions. Seven IEL clinics around the world have been or are being established.[19] The value of clinical education is no longer disputed within the field of IEL. Clinics are a win-win for all involved: beneficiaries get expert work done for free and build capacity, students learn by doing, obtain academic credits and expand their network, faculty and expert supervisors share their knowledge of cutting-edge issues and are able to attract or hire top students with proven skills.

Special Characteristics of International Economic Law

IEL specificities have played a significant role in the decision to establish the Clinic. The domain has a broad social impact, and it has undergone a transformation in the past thirty years. Cross-border trade and investment flows indiscriminately affect consumers, businesses, government officials, and citizens. Yet international trade and investment rules have become so complex that only the most resource-rich companies and governments can really follow, influence, and take advantage of those rules. Today, beyond the WTO, World Bank, and UNCTAD, there are also hundreds of bilateral investment treaties (BITs) and free trade arrangements ranging from Generalized System of Preferences (GSP), EU economic partnership agreements (EPAs), and Common Market for Eastern and Southern Africa (COMESA) issues to Association of Southeast Asian Nations (ASEAN), Central America Free Trade Agreement (CAFTA), and Trans-Pacific Partnership (TPP), each with its own negotiation, implementation, and dispute settlement system. John Jackson, regarded by many as the father of modern IEL, considered it the responsibility of practitioners and academics "to reflect on [the law], to explain it, to advocate for change to it, and always to look ahead."[20] Since its inception, the Clinic has nurtured links between various actors in the IEL community, linking in particular experienced academics and practitioners with students new to the field and stakeholders in need of legal information and help. The Clinic aims to engage stakeholders with limited resources, such as developing countries, smaller trade associations, businesses, or nongovernmental organizations (NGOs), with leading experts and ad hoc teams of students, allowing them to participate in the development of IEL as well as to benefit

---

[18] In accordance with the *Directives du Conseil des hautes écoles pour la mise en œuvre de la déclaration de Bologne dans les hautes écoles spécialisées et pédagogiques, Conférence des Recteurs des Universités Suisses*, May 28, 2015.

[19] Graduate Institute, Georgetown University, Ottawa University, Qatar University, IELPO, TRAPCA, and Jindal Global Law School.

[20] Donald McRae, *International Economic Law and Public International Law: The Past and the Future*, 17 J. INT'L. ECON. L. (2014), 10.1093/jiel/jgu036 (last visited March 10, 2016).

from international trade and investment regimes. The Clinic aspires to contribute to a more transparent, inclusive, and ultimately better IEL system.

Until the turn of the twentieth century, much of the public international law literature[21] barely considered IEL one of its canons. Today, there are "still ongoing efforts to develop a theory of IEL to explain its purpose in regulating the global economy and achieving a world public order of human dignity."[22] For a long time, IEL was beyond the scope of many law departments around the world. Confronted with limited departmental and clinical resources, as well as the greater popularity of other branches of international law, IEL failed to receive the attention that it may have deserved. This trend has seen a reversal in the past three decades because of the entry into force of a significant number of IEL treaties, in particular the WTO treaty in 1995 and the coming of age of investor-state treaty arbitration in the past five to ten years and the burgeoning growth of IEL, arguably thanks to the efforts of a few notable scholars like John Jackson, Ernst-Ulrich Petersmann, and Robert Hudec. According to Cottier, contemporary IEL goes well beyond negative integration or, simply put, tariff barriers, and pursues trade regulation by positive integration through behind the border measures.[23] "Modern trade rules harness and shape ... domestic law" (Cottier) in many fields, such as trade, investment, labour, finance, and monetary affairs, and many are topics potentially within the purview of IEL, from processes and production methods (PPMs) and climate change and mitigation to taxation and food security and migration. IEL's relevance was undisputed, despite unresolved theoretical issues. For practitioners and experts, it became apparent how a "precious global public good" IEL was "in the pursuit of peace and welfare" (Cottier).

By the late 2000s, the importance of IEL became evident to civil society, governments, the private sector, and academia. Globalization and IEL has had a strong impact on the general public. Protectionist tendencies and widespread scepticism[24] about trade originated because of, among others factors, the greater complexity of IEL, the extensive "intrusion" of current IEL rules into domestic policy-making, the not always clear *ex-ante* full impact of IEL rules, and the perceived democratic gap and lack of national debate.[25] This active sociopolitical environment led to a skyrocketing increase in the demand of IEL professionals as well as the popularity of IEL among students and, consequently, to the allocation of more resources for research programmes and the training of more people, thereby laying the

---

[21] Steve Charnovitz, The Field of International Economic Law, 17 J. INT'L. ECON. L. (2014), 10.1093/jiel/jgu030 (last visited March 13, 2016).

[22] Id.

[23] Cottier refers to this process as "underlying changes in the [IEL] normative structure." Thomas Cottier, *International Economic Law in Transition from Trade Liberalization to Trade Regulation*, 17(2) J. INT'L. ECON. L. (2014), 10.1093/jiel/jgu029 (last visited March 13, 2016).

[24] Dani Rodrik, THE GLOBALIZATION PARADOX (WW Norton & Co. 2011), 51.

[25] For an extensive overview: Simon Lester, The Role of the International Trade Regime in Global Governance, 209 UCLA J. INT'L L. & FOREIGN AFF. 223–74 (2011).

foundation for clinical programmes. It also stimulated the action of LCB programmes aimed at improving the ability of all stakeholders in having a say in IEL matters. Additionally, international actors established initiatives to reach out to civil society directly.[26]

Goals and Methods

The educational objective of the International Economic Law Clinic is to enable students to analyse IEL and jurisprudence through a combination of practice and theory. By examining a particular problem and presenting a proposed solution, students learn how to think critically, how to write a legal brief, and how to work in groups and interact with clients.

As in many other legal fields, traditional IEL teaching methods are largely based on the relationship between legal concepts.[27] During lectures, case facts may be reported and WTO Appellate body reports and Arbitral Tribunal decisions also mentioned, but they are often analysed in ways that stress the specific doctrinal issues.[28] In addition to that, classes are given in a conference setting, and although student participation is limited, it is not entirely confined to passive listening and note-taking.

The clinic setting differs greatly from traditional classes. Clinic projects are selected on the basis of need, available resources, and practical relevance. Prospective students must have already completed a course on international trade or investment law or both and must submit a motivation letter and a curriculum vitae.[29] Two to four selected students are assigned to each project. Students are teamed up with Geneva-based expert mentors from law firms and other organizations (all assisting the Clinic *pro bono*) and are carefully prepped and supervised by professors and teaching assistants. Students in the same project team work together to fulfil the deadlines and requirements of their project as specified in the project proposal. They benefit from skills building expert sessions, do detailed legal

---

[26] For instance, the WTO created new channels of cooperation with civil society (like the WTO public forum, the acceptance of *amicus curiae* briefs during litigation) and businesses (e.g. the creation of the International Trade Centre, together with UNCTAD, aims at the direct support of the internationalization of small and medium-sized enterprises).

[27] The issue is discussed more in Chapter 12 by Renáta Uitz and Eszter Polgári in this volume. In addition, according to Grossman, "Exclusive reliance on the Langdellian ideology, which treats law as a science in which legal principles are derived by studying selected cases, will not adequately prepare law students for the contemporary world." Claudio Grossman, *Building the World Community through Legal Education*, in THE INTERNATIONALIZATION OF LAW AND LEGAL EDUCATION, IUS GENTIUM: COMPARATIVE PERSPECTIVES ON LAW AND JUSTICE, 1st ed. (Springer Science 2008), 29.

[28] Walter Otto Weyrauch, *Fact Consciousness*, 46J(263) J. LEGAL EDUC. (1996).

[29] As noted in Chapter 13 by Welchman in this volume, "we don't aim to teach the fundamentals of international human rights law" but "by the end of the course we expect students to have an understanding of the rigours and challenges involved in international human rights practice and be equipped to research and write on this area."

research, and work on several drafts shared with supervisors, mentors, and the beneficiary for comments and feedback. To foster participation and share best practices, each student is also allocated to another "shadow" project. Students must follow the progress of their shadow project and are required to provide questions and comments when their shadow project is being presented in class, thus increasing the overall exposure of participants to the variety of legal questions and problems faced by the other groups. The Clinic culminates in a polished legal memorandum, brief, draft law, treaty text, or other output tailored to the project's needs. Clinics deliver in three to four months. Work and output can be public or fully confidential, as when preparing legislative or treaty proposals or briefs in actual disputes. Grading depends on both class attendance and participation and on the work submitted and its presentation.

The scope of the Clinic's work in IEL is wide-ranging, going beyond the traditional disciplinary silos typically associated with, for example, "trade" or "investment" issues. The students participating in the Clinic come from diverse fields of study, with most coming from the legal field but others from economics or international relations. While working on a project, the students are required to apply their previously acquired knowledge and experience to the project's particular fact pattern. Critical and innovative thinking is required in order to fully address beneficiaries' concerns. Active participation and group discussion facilitates collaborative learning and opens surprising doors to new ways of facing and solving problems.

Most of the students of the Clinic intend to take up a career in legal practice, be it with a law firm, government, international organization, company, or NGO. By the time they start their graduate studies at the Graduate Institute, they already have many years of legal training behind them. But, for most students, this training is limited to theoretical course work because most law schools, especially in Europe, do not emphasize practical legal skills. This translates into higher training and hiring costs for law firms that are then passed on to clients. However, the legal services market has been undergoing significant and permanent changes since the financial crisis of 2008. "Law firm clients have increasingly demanded more efficiency, predictability, and cost effectiveness in the delivery of the legal services they purchase."[30] Yet the response of legal education to changing market conditions has mostly been passive. CLE has a role to play in responding to market trends by training more effective and, ultimately, better lawyers. Traditionally, clients outsourced many if not all key decisions regarding "the organization, staffing, scheduling, and pricing of legal matters" to one vertically integrated and large law firm. Today, clients are much more involved and "in active control of all of those decisions,"[31] which has provided new opportunities for smaller providers of legal

[30] Georgetown Law Centre for the Study of Legal Profession, 2016 Report on the State of the Legal Market (GEORGETOWN LAW 2016), www.law.georgetown.edu/news/upload/2016_PM_GT_Final-Report.pdf (last visited March 3, 2016).
[31] Id.

services. Tailor-made legal teams can offer high-quality legal services for a price competitive with vertically integrated firms. However, this opportunity also requires flexibility and the ability to effectively work in groups and with high professional standards. These three skills are the largest component of evaluating the students' participation in the Clinic. Technology also plays a role in making lawyers more efficient and legal services more accessible. The Clinic is therefore a valuable opportunity to get acquainted with research, project management, and writing tools.[32] These tools can help professionals in focusing on high-value activities while reducing the time spent on ancillary activities, as well as reducing the delivery time and improving the consistency of the final product.

Beyond the Educational Goals

Developing countries are party to a multitude of international agreements in the field of trade, investment, and economic cooperation. Most of these treaties seek to foster economic growth and human development. The negotiation, implementation, and settlement of disputes under these treaties are increasingly complex and very costly. Without enhancing the pool of stakeholders that have access to IEL knowledge and expertise, only the most resource-rich companies and governments are able to really follow, influence, and benefit from IEL rules. The Clinic is a service learning endeavour. Its primary objective, beyond education, is making available its pool of knowledge and expertise to less resource-rich countries and stakeholders (e.g. SMEs or NGOs in both developing and developed countries), with the ultimate goal of supporting their LCB efforts. To this end, the Clinic combines and makes use of advancements in LCB practices, legal education, and innovations in legal services related technologies.

LCB can be understood as any effort aimed at enhancing the pool of stakeholders who have access to legal knowledge in the field of IEL. To address the complex and often rapidly evolving problems that arise from intensified international interdependence, a high degree of technical expertise is required by governments and all interested parties. The more knowledgeable government officials and other stakeholders' representatives are about IEL, the more effective they can be in the definition of their international economic policy; treaty negotiations; and conflict prevention, mitigation, and resolution strategies. They gain the tools necessary to interact with experts in IEL and with other legal professionals.

The contemporary LCB landscape is the result of decades of work by international actors, academic institutions, and private firms. On the supply side, there are a number of active and varied LCB providers. Some are large organizations, with

---

[32] For instance, use of databases for information gathering and organization, reference management software, encryption and secure information sharing, automation and communication software, videoconferencing and remote presentation, computer-based text analysis tools.

thousands of employees worldwide; others are smaller and more focused institutions. They may be international organizations (IOs), public development agencies, universities, consulting, or law firms, and they operate as not-for-profit and for-profit. Some may rely on external consultants to provide LCB; others rely exclusively on their own internal expertise. On the demand side, most beneficiaries are public-sector entities.[33] Yet, in the past twenty years, businesses, civil society, and universities have managed to become recipients as well in a more limited number of LCB programmes.

There are different ways in which the supply and demand of LCB services meet. When a programme is either financed by a third party or directly by a provider, as is often the case when IOs are involved, beneficiaries are actively selected by the provider. The selection process may include bidding and participating in competitions, recurrent invitations, or beneficiaries selected through specialized agencies and NGOs. When a recipient finances its own LCB efforts, it selects the provider either directly or through public procurement competitions. The content of LCB programmes varies, from training on IEL principles, support and advice in IEL negotiations, and domestic implementation and litigation. A large part of LCB programmes are rather short term (seven days or less) and have limited follow-up facilities. In addition, most LCB programmes still rely on travelling to a specified location, and technology is mostly used for communication and organizational purposes, with limited use of e-learning tools.

In the past twenty-five years, a great amount of resources has been devoted to LCB.[34] Indeed, a number of indicators[35] have shown improved participation of developing countries in the system. Larger providers share a lot of human, financial, and technical resources through their LCB programmes. Smaller providers may play a role, as paid external experts, as part of their *pro bono* activities, or as part of their academic/governing body engagements. Yet it is hard to actually quantify the impact of these efforts beyond the number of programmes delivered or treaties signed. During a multiprovider exercise organized by the CTEI,[36] three main issues

---

[33] For instance, the WTO capacity-building and training exercises focus primarily on government officials, but there are ongoing efforts to expand its scope to other civil society stakeholders. For more information, see Committee on Trade and Development, Biennial Technical Assistance and Training Plan – 2016–2017, at 28 (World Trade Organization 2015). Other IOs, like the International Trade Centre, may have broader mandates and target businesses and civil society.

[34] For example, the United Nations Conference on Trade and Development (UNCTAD) alone secured US$5,552,109.75 for "Capacity Building on Trade Policy, Trade Negotiations and Commercial Diplomacy." United Nations Conference on Trade and Development, Indicative List of Requests for UNCTAD Technical Cooperation Activities Received in 2013–2015, at 3 (United Nations 2016), http://unctad.org/en/PublicationsLibrary/dommisc2013d1_en.pdf (last visited February 29, 2016).

[35] United Nations Conference on Trade and Development, World Investment Report 2015 (United Nations 2016), http://unctad.org/en/PublicationsLibrary/wir2015_en.pdf (last visited March 19, 2016).

[36] Legal Capacity Building in International Trade and Investment Law: Taking Stock and Opportunities Ahead, March 6–7, 2014, held at the Graduate Institute of International and Development Studies. The data gathered are confidential but some considerations can be found in

were identified in the traditional, top-down approach to LCB. A first predicament concerns the limited extent of LCB programmes in terms of participation since, historically, most top-down programmes have been confined to government officials. A second issue relates to the theoretical nature of LCB programmes, which can be ill-suited to the needs and realities of beneficiaries. A third concern pertains to the limited duration of LCB initiatives, often confined to seven days or less, with limited follow-up and monitoring. Given the complexity of IEL, the shorter the training, the harder it is to assimilate and make the knowledge actionable.

The evolution of LCB, legal services, and technology has allowed the entry of new smaller players in the LCB sector that have been able to address at least one of the critical issues as identified with the top-down approach to LCB. Clearly, a large part of relevant economic information is held by businesses, trade associations, trade unions, and NGOs, not governments. When these actors have access to the tools that enable them to bring up issues concerning trade, investment, or other topics within the scope of IEL with governments and in international fora, they can be very effective in identifying trade distortive behaviours, policy violations, or gaps and are able to propose innovative and practical solutions. Local actors and their legal counsellors do work together with their governmental counterparts on a daily basis. But their ability to act varies widely, and their legal expertise in IEL may be limited. It takes time, varying from country to country, to acquire the ability to interact with authorities in a constructive way, providing quality inputs and without undermining government legitimacy.

Based on the nature of the work done and of its project partners, the International Economic Law Clinic can indeed be understood as a small LCB provider, clearly focused on targeting less resource-rich stakeholders in IEL matters. Since spring 2009, the Geneva Clinic has produced forty-eight memoranda on diverse IEL issues for a range of interested parties including IOs and NGOs, Geneva-based missions, public institutions, and small and medium-sized enterprises (SMEs). More specifically, almost half of the papers (twenty-two) were written for NGOs and SMEs, with the rest equally distributed among different countries' national bodies (fourteen) and international specialized agencies (twelve). Some examples include the drafting of an amicus curiae brief for environmental NGOs in a WTO subsidies dispute, research on illicit trade and IEL, advising an SME land owner about possible expropriation rights, assisting African nations in the reform of investment treaties, and analysing IEL implications of the United Kingdom leaving the European Union for a UK-based NGO. Progressively, partnerships have shifted from solely Geneva-based organizations during the first years of activity to various beneficiaries across the globe, such as stakeholder coalitions, small ad hoc legal teams working for

the report Legal Capacity Building in International Trade and Investment Law: Taking Stock and Opportunities Ahead (Graduate Institute of International and Development Studies 2016), http://graduateinstitute.ch/files/live/sites/iheid/files/sites/ctei/users/Mattia/LCB_workshop_report.pdf (last visited March 2, 2016).

less resource-rich countries, and small companies. The Clinic has also had the opportunity to collaborate with larger, inclusive LCB projects. As such, in the past three years, more than half of the Clinic's project partners were sourced from outside the larger Geneva area.

Diffusion and Cooperation
CLE is not standard in the IEL field and certainly is not widespread in continental Europe. While US CLE provided a reference point for the Clinic, designing a CLE initiative in a field devoid of any significant CLE experience was a daunting task. Where CLE is already established, creating a new clinic is, cost-wise, a more predictable effort. In addition, such CLE endeavours benefit from the well-established standing of the home institution in the local legal service market, and they commonly provide legal services in fields well understood by their beneficiaries, like civil, family, or criminal law. IEL had no previously established CLE practice. Most of the potential beneficiaries were scattered around the globe, far from the Graduate Institute. They were not generally aware of what a clinic was, what could be done for them, or even that they had an IEL-related problem. The clinic format had to be adapted to the IEL specificities, at a significant cost in both human and financial terms.

Proper resources were devoted towards the adaptation of the CLE format to the specificities of IEL; the identification and contact of beneficiaries that could profit from clinical work and of LCB programmes the clinic could contribute to; the creation of a professional network of experts and LCB providers active in Geneva, Washington DC, and around the world; and the organization of LCB events and workshops for LCB providers. All this knowledge was converged into TradeLab.

TradeLab is a community of clinics and IEL professionals that want IEL to work for everyone. TradeLab has been an active promoter of CLE. It has been instrumental in the creation of four new clinics in North America and in the Middle East, including one in the making in Europe. TradeLab has worked alongside academic institutions in establishing CLE by assisting with (1) the understanding of resource requirements and quality standards; (2) the supporting of the actual establishment of a clinic, where intense cooperation is put in place to adapt the clinical format to the specificities of the recipient institution's academic and administrative structure; and (3) the launch of the clinic, including student selection, providing candidate pilot projects, and the identification and involvement of suitable mentors tasked to guide the students' group work in addition to the supervising professor(s). Throughout the process, TradeLab ensures high quality standards and confidentiality, where required. After a successful run, and if the host institution decides to permanently establish its IEL clinic, TradeLab continues to provide projects and helps to identify supervising experts/mentors with relevant expertise.

Another area of cooperation, in lieu of mounting a full clinic, is project-specific partnerships. With the support of TradeLab, the Georgetown Practicum and the Graduate Institute Clinic have partnered with the Trade Policy Training Centre in Africa (TRAPCA), based in Arusha, Tanzania. The partnership involves a team of two students from the home institution and two students from TRAPCA to work jointly on a project. It is a challenging setting for all involved because time, language, and cultural differences may affect the work of the team. However, this interaction also allows for excellent real-world training opportunities for all students involved, and these foster their project management abilities, communication skills, and critical and unconventional thinking. The partnering institution has only to provide supporting faculty members and put in place an appropriate reward scheme for participating students. In the long term, project-based cooperation could help the partnering institution in building the necessary capacity for an independent and sustainable CLE programme.

TradeLab provides the computer infrastructure to build, maintain, and promote the clinic and expert network and to gather new projects. The website is a projects intake channel so that everyone with Internet access can go online and describe his or her IEL issue. If the question can be answered rapidly, the clinic personnel or volunteering experts can provide a quick answer. The match is made by an algorithm supervised by the TradeLab managers, and only members with the appropriate expertise are notified. If the problem is more complex, it is directed to a clinic. As of early 2016, more than sixty legal memoranda have been delivered by TradeLab clinics to beneficiaries from around the world.

The Weight and Value of Internationalization

The Clinic not only deals with international law and is an international LCB actor – albeit small – but it also has a very diverse and international participating student body. Since spring 2009, one hundred and thirty-three students have taken part in the Clinic, with 42% coming from developing countries. More than half of those came from only six developing[37] countries: China, Brazil, India, Russia, Ukraine, and Mexico. From developed countries, students predominately come from the EU (with Germany leading) and the United States. We lack exhaustive data about the careers students pursued after graduation, but, based on a sample of our developing countries pool, we have verified that many have returned to their home countries and have remained active in the field of IEL, either in the private sector or serving as public officials. In those countries, there is indeed a high demand for IEL experts due to increasingly complex global economic relations and the need for corresponding expertise in economic law and policy. Clinic students may be more successful early in their career compared to their peers who did not undergo CLE because they

---

[37] In this text, the country status refers to that followed in the WTO. Andrew T Guzman and Joost Pauwelyn, INTERNATIONAL TRADE LAW (Wolters Kluwer Law & Business 2012), 670.

are already acquainted with managing international legal sources, contacting and working with international issues, and mastering the inherent cross-cutting nature of IEL. In practical terms, the Clinic experience exposes students to modern workplace settings. While the students often work for a remote beneficiary, sometimes groups themselves are geographically dispersed. Thus, they rely on technology to gather and process data, to ensure a proper and consistent output, and to share information and communicate with teammates and beneficiaries. Finally, by the end of the course, students are not only technically savvy, but they are also made aware of the security concerns that technology has introduced in the daily work of lawyers.

Future of CLE in IEL

The future of CLE in IEL will depend on the ability of further developing clinic structures and budgets. The IEL community of institutions, beneficiaries, students, and professionals is global. To make a lasting impact, CLE in IEL should undergo a process of institutionalization. This means adopting a long-term action and perspective. Only a proven track record will allow clinics to build trust among globally dispersed beneficiaries and to be considered as reputable LCB providers by other LCB actors. In order to do so, we suspect that, in the IEL field, CLE will emulate the development process that has characterized US clinics. For instance, IEL Clinics will have to strengthen their structure by having professors, supervising personnel, and supporting staff largely or exclusively devoted to clinical activities and on a long-term basis. But this also means that funding schemes have to be rethought to acquire long term sustainability. In the United States, law schools have an established approach to clinical funding, and resources are regularly allocated to clinical programmes.[38] Some US clinics, like the Harrison Institute for Public Law at Georgetown Law Center, are also able to attract considerable donations[39] and benefit from a favourable fiscal environment. In fact, institutional donors were "instrumental in jump-starting clinical legal education in most of the law schools in the United States"[40] during the twentieth century.

Because of IEL specificities, increasing the financial capacity of clinics and their further institutionalization seem to be a necessary precondition to the usefulness and long-term sustainability of CLE within the field of IEL. A long-term setting will allow for further integration of clinics into existing LCB programmes in IEL, and it would justify higher rewards and longer involvement of students in the clinical exercise.

[38] For a comprehensive perspective on the funding and development of CLE in the US, C. Dubin, and Peter A. Joy. Clinical Education for This Millennium: The Third Wave, 7 CLIN. L. REV. 1 (2000).

[39] Mattia Salamanca Orrego, Interview with Robert Stumberg, The Clinical Experience of The Harrison Institute for Public Law – Georgetown Law (2016). For more information about the Institute: www.law.georgetown.edu/academics/academic-programs/clinical-programs/our-clinics /HIP/.

[40] Dubin and Joy, *supra* note 38 at 19.

Since IEL clinics engage with beneficiaries that are not served by most LCB providers and are able to provide capacity to a diversity of stakeholders (both students and beneficiaries), public and institutional donors (including national research funds) could represent possible funding opportunities, either directly or in the context of large LCB programmes. Considering the expansion of the IEL field, its widespread real-world impact, and increased public awareness as to the importance of IEL, finding additional funding sources should be feasible.

An element of adaptation of the traditional clinical model to IEL is the enhanced cooperation among clinical actors. Now and in the future, it will be key to make CLE in IEL an established reality. Cooperation is needed to spread the CLE model to other institutions teaching IEL. The CTEI and TradeLab are sharing their know-how and projects with other institutions and offer a centralized project intake aimed at consolidating the global demand of IEL advice and LCB. Having CLE operations acting in concert is leading to greater trust and recognition among the global communities of beneficiaries and LCB actors. We also believe clinics will be able to root themselves in the regional landscapes and further engage with local communities. But because of IEL's features, only a prolonged engagement with local actors could lead to meaningful result.

CONCLUSION

IEL rules are increasingly complex. Beyond the WTO, the World Bank, and UNCTAD, there are also hundreds of BITs and free-trade arrangements, each with its own negotiation, implementation, and dispute settlement system. Everyone is affected, but few have the time and resources to fully engage. The negotiation, implementation, and settlement of disputes under IEL treaties are increasingly complex and very costly. Without enhancing the pool of stakeholders who have access to IEL knowledge and expertise, only the most resource-rich companies and governments are able to really follow, influence, and benefit from IEL rules. The Clinic in International Economic Law makes its pool of knowledge and expertise available to less resource-rich countries and stakeholders (e.g. SMEs or NGOs in both developing and developed countries), empowering them to reap the full development benefits of global economic rules.

Since 2008, the Clinic has expanded from its original focus on questions of WTO law to include projects on international investment law and arbitration and, more recently, on any subfield of IEL (including fields such as intellectual property, tax, and finance). The Clinic enables students to analyse IEL and jurisprudence through a combination of practice and theory. Small groups of highly qualified and carefully selected Graduate Institute students work under the close supervision of faculty and other professionals with long-standing experience in the field. To date, the Clinic has delivered forty-eight memoranda on diverse IEL issues for a range of interested parties. Progressively, partnerships have shifted from solely Geneva-based organizations to beneficiaries scattered around the world, such as stakeholder coalitions, small ad-hoc legal teams working for less resourceful countries, and small companies. The Clinic has also had the opportunity to collaborate with larger, inclusive LCB projects.

The Clinic is an ideal match for the mission of its host institution, the Graduate Institute, which is situated at the intersection of the various actors in the IEL community, linking in particular experienced academics and practitioners with students new to the field and stakeholders in need of legal information and help. The Institute also gains new opportunities to develop lasting relationships with other institutions and state agencies, especially from developing countries. The establishment of a long-term clinical programme in a yet underserved area of law such as IEL required significant financial resources, human capital, and time. Especially important was the development of a pilot programme that could take into account the particular characteristics of IEL and promote clinical education to largely unaware stakeholders and, most importantly, have the ability to deliver. After seven years of groundwork made possible by the support of the CTEI and the Graduate Institute, clinical education is taking root in IEL as the overall costs involved in establishing IEL clinics are diminishing.

Finally, the Graduate Institute is sharing its know-how with other higher education institutions in both developed and developing countries through TradeLab. TradeLab is a community of Clinics and IEL professionals that want IEL to work for everyone. TradeLab has been an active promoter of CLE and has been instrumental in the creation of four new clinics in North America and in the Middle East, one in the making in Europe, and the joint programme with TRAPCA, in Arusha, Tanzania. TradeLab maintains and promotes the clinic and expert network, gathers new projects, and provides the technological infrastructure. At this stage, further developments of CLE in the IEL field will depend on the ability of CLE programmes to further institutionalize by means of having permanent staff; to become financially self-sustainable, as is the case for non-IEL clinics in North America, instead of being reliant on the budget of the home institution; and to work in concert with other IEL clinics and LCB actors active around the world.

Despite the significant efforts required to establish a viable CLE model for IEL, we consider that it is here to stay because it is an outstanding value and a clear win-win for all involved: beneficiaries get expert work done for free and build legal capacity; students learn by doing, obtain academic credits and expand their network; and faculty and expert supervisors share their knowledge on cutting-edge issues and are able to attract or hire top students with proven skills.

16

The Amsterdam International Law Clinic

Hege Elisabeth Kjos and André Nollkaemper

INTRODUCTION

The Amsterdam International Law Clinic (AILC or Clinic) at the University of Amsterdam (UvA) was set up in 1999, and, since then, it has been providing legal advice on questions of international and European law for an equitable fee.[1] The legal issues are of a broad variety, including international human rights law, international criminal law, international environmental law, the law of immunities, and international trade and investment law, as well as a range of European Union law issues. Clients include law firms, nongovernmental organizations (NGOs), (staff unions of) international NGOs, government ministries, companies, and private individuals. Also in view of its low fees, in these respects, the Clinic can be seen to complement the Dutch legal aid system.

The legal advice is provided by law students in their final years of study. The AILC is an elective course in the master's degree-level programmes "Public International Law", "European Union Law," and "International Trade and Investment Law." It is open also to students from other LLM tracks and to exchange students. Successful participation for one semester provides six European Credit Transfer System (ECTS) credits. For shorter assignments, three ECTS can be awarded. The AILC is coordinated by co-author Dr. Hege Elisabeth Kjos, who also serves as Acting Director. The overall responsibility rests with the other co-author, Professor Dr. André Nollkaemper.

On average, the AILC has taken on about five to six cases each semester. The students generally work in teams of two to three members per assignment, and the number of students per semester is linked to the number of cases. Students are invited to apply twice a year, at the start of each semester. The AILC receives many applications; in the academic year 2015–2016 there were about forty-five applications. When applying, students are asked to submit a motivation letter, a curriculum vitae (CV), a list of courses and grades, and a sample paper. We also interview applicants. Due to the competitive nature of the application process, the AILC is able to select the

---

[1] University of Amsterdam, Faculty of Law, Amsterdam International Law Clinic http://ailc.uva.nl/.

best students and match their interest and qualifications with the various legal issues involved in the cases that we are working on each semester.

As a rule, the students and their supervisor(s) all meet with our clients, and, in the case of law firms, the lawyers' clients. The legal advice is provided under close supervision of staff members of the Department of Public International Law and European Law[2] and the Amsterdam Center for International Law[3] at the UvA Faculty of Law. We appoint one or two faculty supervisors per case, depending on the nature of the case and the expertise required. The subject matter of the case forms a key criterion for supervision, and staff supervisors can include professors, assistant and associate professors, and, at times, also doctoral researchers. The students work in the Clinic Office made available at the Faculty, and they meet with their supervisors on a regular basis.

Emphasis is placed on respect for confidentiality, professionalism, and team work; before students are admitted, they must sign a contract of confidentiality that covers current and past cases. The students receive intensive, hands-on guidance on how to conduct legal research and to write legal opinions for our clients. For that purpose, there is also a compulsory Clinic course in which staff and guest speakers deal with various aspects of the legal profession, including the client–attorney relationship. Furthermore, the UvA Law Library offers a course in legal research specifically designed for the AILC. The course is tailored for the nature of cases taken on each semester. Thus, when one of the cases deals with European human rights law, extra attention will be paid to, for example, the HUDOC database of the European Court of Human Rights;[4] or, for international investment law, the Investor-State Law Guide.[5]

Following this introduction, we proceed to relate our experience with the Amsterdam International Law Clinic to the emergence of clinical legal education (CLE) in general (discussed in the next section). Next, we reflect on CLE as a means of reforming the teaching and practice of law in Europe, after which general conclusions are offered.

EMERGENCE OF CLINICAL LEGAL EDUCATION

Genesis and Context

The AILC was set up by Professor Nollkaemper shortly after accepting the Chair of Public International Law at the University of Amsterdam. Prior to coming to

---

[2] University of Amsterdam, Faculty of Law, Department of Public International Law and European law, www.uva.nl/en/about-the-uva/organisation/organisational-structure/content/faculties/faculty-of-law/department-of-public-international-law-and-european-law/department-of-public-international-law-and-european-law.html.
[3] University of Amsterdam, Faculty of Law, Amsterdam Center for International law http://acil.uva.nl/.
[4] European Court of Human Rights, HUDOC database, http://hudoc.echr.coe.int/.
[5] Investor-State Law Guide, www.investorstatelawguide.com/.

Amsterdam, Nollkaemper had visited several law schools in the United States, including the University of Washington School of Law in 1993–1994. During these visits, he became familiar with the key role that CLE can play in law schools. After taking up his position in Amsterdam, he decided to introduce this type of education, specifically in the context of international law.

Nollkaemper succeeded in establishing the AILC at the beginning of the academic year 1999–2000, and it was officially made an elective course on January 2, 2000. At that time, cooperation between external clients on the one hand and law students and professors on the other hand was new in Dutch legal practice, at least as concerns its focus on international and European law.[6] Especially the integration of the AILC in a university education programme sets it apart from the Dutch tradition of *rechtwinkels* ("law shops") – institutions where clients can get legal advice at very low or no cost and generally supported by students who participate in these *rechtswinkels* during their study.[7]

It is noted in this context that the Dutch rules regulating the qualifications required for the rendering of legal advice appear to be more flexible than those in other countries. As Kolb observes, "[r]emarkably, the *advocaats* have no monopoly on giving legal advice. It is therefore permitted for a *rechtskundig adviseur* to give legal advice without a formal qualification or indeed a law degree."[8] It is likely that these more liberal rules facilitated the development of *rechtswinkels* as well as the faculty's approval of the Clinic.[9]

The AILC further benefits from another comparative advantage: for its focus on public international law and EU law, the Netherlands offers fertile soil. The Dutch legal system is especially open to international law,[10] and its location in the "global legal capital" can be seen to provide easier access to clients seeking expertise in

---

[6] Richard J. Wilson, Clinical Legal Education in Dutch Legal Culture: Clashes of Tradition, Tolerance, and Progress in Global Law's Capital (2010) 31–32, http://ssrn.com/abstract=1695137 (noting that the Maastricht Legal Clinic opened in 1988).

[7] *Id.* at 30–31. For an overview of "law shops" in the Netherlands, see e.g., Platform Rechtwinkels! Nederland, www.platformrechtswinkels.nl/page.php?12 (observing that there are about eighty law shops in the Netherlands).

[8] Christian Kolb, How to Qualify as a Lawyer in Netherlands, www.ibanet.org/PPID/Constituent/Student_Committee/qualify_lawyer_Netherlands.aspx. *See also*, Lycaeus Juridisch Woordenboek, www.juridischwoordenboek.nl/woordenboekrechtsh.html#17726 (*Rechtskundig adviseur* is defined as a "person who gives advice in legal cases. This can be a lawyer or jurist, or anyone. The title is namely not protected. The *rechtskundig* adviseur does not have to have a law degree. After all, a person can be knowledgeable about the law without *having* attended law school" [translation by authors]).

[9] Kolb, *supra* note 8. (The liberal rules have "led to the commendable development of a substantial number of law centres (*rechtswinkels*) and law clinics, which in turn have brought down the costs for legal advice, particularly for smaller cases.")

[10] *See e.g.*, C. M. Brölmann and E. W. Vierdag, *International Law and European Community Law in the Netherlands*, in THE INTEGRATION OF INTERNATIONAL AND EUROPEAN COMMUNITY LAW INTO THE NATIONAL LEGAL ORDER (P. M. Eisemann, ed., Kluwer Law International 1996) 433.

matters pertaining to international criminal law and the law of immunities of international organizations, for instance.[11]

Drivers

Six drivers in particular can explain the genesis and continued support for the AILC, and, to some extent, these can be considered to be drivers behind this type of clinic more generally.

First, the emergence of clinics has been driven by an increasing recognition that legal education has been too doctrinal and theoretical and may insufficiently prepare students for what is required of them once they enter the legal profession. After the Bologna reform process,[12] Dutch legal education, like that in many European countries, was divided into a three-year bachelor of laws degree, followed by a one- or two-year master of laws degree.[13] Most students seek to obtain "civil effect," which allows them to be admitted to the bar. In order to do so, students must take a required set of courses at the University,[14] after which follows a three-year legal apprenticeship.[15]

The emphasis placed on theory versus practice has been criticized.[16] Learning about legal systems, rules, and doctrine in a classroom setting does not adequately train students for interaction with clients, team members, and supervisors; for providing legal advice in support of specific interests of clients (rather than formulating the "best exam answers"); and for analyses of a variety of factual and legal situations of a cross-cutting nature that require knowledge stemming from separate areas of law. Thus, commenting on the Dutch system, Wilson argues:

---

[11] Wilson, *supra* note 6, at 1–2, 8–10.

[12] On the Bologna Process, see European Commission, The Bologna Process and the European Higher Education Area, http://ec.europa.eu/education/policy/higher-education/bologna-process_en. *See also*, The Bologna Declaration of June 19, 1999, a joint declaration of the European Ministers of Education, http://media.ehea.info/file/Ministerial_conferences/02/8/1999_Bologna_Declaration_English_553028.pdf.

[13] Kolb, *supra* note 8. *See also* Wilson *supra* note 6, at 26; Nederlandse orde van advocaten [Dutch Bar Association], Juridische bachelor en master met civiel effect, https://www.advocatenorde.nl/258/studenten/juridische-bachelor-en-master.html.

[14] Wilson, *supra* note 6, at 20; Nederlandse orde van advocaten, *supra* note 13); Convenant inzake het civiel effect, March 22, 2016, https://www.advocatenorde.nl/11848/20160322-convenant-civiel-effect. For an example of required courses, see Faculty of Law, University of Amsterdam, Civiel effect, http://student.uva.nl/rechten/az/content/civiel-effect/civiel-effect.html.

[15] Kolb, *supra* note 8. *See also* Richard Wilson, *Practical Training in Law in the Netherlands: Big Law Model or Clinical Model, and the Call of Public Interest Law*, 8 (1) UTRECHT LAW REVIEW 177–80 (2012); Wilson, *supra* note 6, at 22–24; Nederlandse orde van advocaten, *supra* note 13.

[16] Wilson, *supra* note 6, at 20. (Dutch academic legal education has maintained a "profoundly conservative character," characterized by "its heavy reliance on required courses; a conservative professoriate who are products of a system that emphasizes theory over practice; and the rigid segregation of legal training into academic and practical tracks controlled by the academy and the profession or the courts, respectively."); *Id.*, at 26–27 (referring also to remarks by Prof. Rob van Otterloo, former Dutch Bar official).

Neither law school nor practical training in the Netherlands, as currently conceived, adequately prepare practicing lawyers with the problem-solving skills, and perhaps more importantly, with the ethics and the values that all lawyers need for effective interaction with their clients and communities as professionals.[17]

For law schools, CLE can be seen to answer the call of the Bologna reform process for universities to give increased attention to competencies and skills required for a successful career and active participation in the economy and society.[18] The AILC not only shares these aspirations, as elaborated later in the section on goals and methods, they also are to a large extent its raison d'être. When in 2003–2004 the Faculty adopted the bachelor-master structure following the Bologna reform process,[19] the AILC had already successfully run as a course for a number of years. Thus, it was easy to integrate it into the new structure not only from an educational point of view but also practically. At the same time, it should be noted that the AILC teaches students to understand the law in the various contexts in which it is to be applied. This means that the Clinic is not just a course that connects legal education to practice. Placing the law in context also contributes to the students' academic development.[20]

Second, the work of the AILC is part of a quest for innovation in legal education that places the individual student more in the centre – in contrast to the traditional modes of legal education dominated by large class settings, often hundreds of students.[21] When participating in the Clinic, students are assessed individually in the light of demands that are placed upon them.[22] Students are evaluated not only on their end product, but also on their application of the skills they acquire on the road towards delivering the final product.

Third, in an increasingly competitive market for students, law schools perceive the need to distinguish themselves by offering specialized courses, *inter alia* with a strong link to practice. This development goes hand in hand with a challenging job

---

[17] Wilson, *supra* note 15, at 170.
[18] *Id.*, at 27; Andreas Bücker and William A. Woodruff, *The Bologna Process and German Legal Education: Developing Professional Competence Through Clinical Experiences*, 9 GERMAN LAW JOURNAL 575, 614 (2008), http://ssrn.com/abstract=1375457; see also Alberto Alemanno and Lamin Khadar, Chapter 9 in this volume.
[19] On the Bologna Process, see *supra* note 6.
[20] Cf. International Legal Center, LEGAL EDUCATION IN A CHANGING WORLD: REPORT OF THE COMMITTEE ON LEGAL EDUCATION IN THE DEVELOPING COUNTRIES (Nordic Africa Institute 1975) 62: "Much evidence seems to indicate that students who are given opportunity to engage in applied legal work (even when it is simulated) *while* they are engaged in 'academic' studies become better motived and often better oriented towards law study."
[21] Cf. Wilson, *supra* note 6, at 21: "Courses throughout undergraduate study tend to be taught in large classrooms with many students and in a very theoretical, code-based style."
[22] Cf. American Bar Association, ABA Standards and Rules of Procedure for Approval of Law Schools 2016–2017, Interpretation 303-2: "Factors to be considered in evaluating the rigor of a writing experience include the number and nature of writing projects assigned to students, the form and extent of individualized assessment of a student's written products, and the number of drafts that a student must produce for any writing experience."

market for graduates, who more and more need to excel vis-à-vis other job seekers. As noted earlier in this section, legal education in the Netherlands is highly regulated by demands (laid down in the law) of the legal profession.[23] This means that the programmes of Dutch law schools are all largely similar in terms of core courses. Correspondingly, there is only a relatively limited space for expressing a law school's unique identity. CLE is one means to create an exclusive profile both for law schools who provide and for students who participate in such education. In fact, it is our experience that many students apply to the master's programme in international and European Law at the University of Amsterdam precisely because of our clinical programme.

Fourth, the establishment of the AILC has been driven by the fact that, in an increasing number of cases, lawyers, NGOs, and other institutions are facing questions of international law for which they do not have expertise in house. Also, prior to the Clinic coming into existence, staff members at our Department were regularly contacted for advice on various legal issues involving international and European Union law. The AILC provides a means by which these institutions acquire expert knowledge on questions of law to which they otherwise would have little or no access.

There continues to be a growing interest in and need for lawyers with a deeper understanding of the functioning and application of international and EU law and with experience in handling arguments based on these sources of law. Since staff members have limited time for engaging in requests for advice, the establishment of the Clinic offered the possibility to provide legal advice and, at the same time, let students gain important experience. This created a "win-win" situation: students could acquire important skills that allowed them to make contact with their future profession in a direct manner and prepared them for their future as lawyers, and, for a reasonable fee, clients could receive legal advice, the quality of which was guaranteed through the supervision of faculty members who were experts in the field. In this respect, reference should also be made to the Dutch legal aid system, which has been characterized as comparatively "expansive and generously funded."[24] Indeed, several of the Clinic reports have been written for lawyers offering legal advice to clients on the basis of legal aid.

A fifth and related driver concerns the increasing attention being paid to knowledge valorization or social value creation. As stated by the Dutch Association of Universities:

> The social responsibility of the Dutch universities is three-fold. In addition to educating almost 250,000 students and carrying out high quality scientific and

---

[23] Cf. Nederlandse orde van advocaten, *supra* note 13.
[24] Wilson, *supra* note 6, at 10. *See also* the Dutch Legal Aid Board [Raad voor Rechtsbijstand], Legal Aid in the Netherlands: A Broad Outline (2015), www.rvr.org/binaries/content/assets/rvrorg/informatie-over-de-raad/legalaid-brochure_online–2015.pdf.

academic research, the universities are making this scientific and academic knowledge valuable to society. The Dutch term "valorisatie" translates into valorisation, a concept also referred to in an international context as "knowledge transfer." Since 2000 valorisation has gained a prominent place on the European agenda. At the start of the millennium it even became an additional core task of Dutch universities, alongside education and research.[25]

Valorization is high on the agenda of the University of Amsterdam.[26] Because staff members are appointed based on their expertise in the various cases, Clinic supervision also allows researchers at our University to contribute to the valorization of (legal) research in a broader societal setting. All reports are in principle confidential, unless confidentiality is explicitly waived. If this is not the case, valorization is limited to the client, although this is often a (larger) organization/firm. At times, however, confidentiality is waived, such as when the client seeks a broader audience/attention for its cause. In these situations, the report may be published online either by the client[27] and/or on the Clinic's website.[28] Clinic research has also been published in law journals, such as an article on accountability of international organizations vis-à-vis their staff members which built on a report commissioned by the Staff Union of the European Patent Organization.[29] Further means of dissemination of research are discussed later in the section on cooperation in clinical legal education.

Sixth and finally, the existence of the AILC is seen to support the aim of placing education generally (and legal education in particular) in the context of internationalization (of the law). We discuss this driver in more detail later, in the section concerning the weight and value of internationalisation.

---

[25] VSNU [Association of Universities], Research at Dutch Universities, www.vsnu.nl/nl_NL/research-at-dutch-universities-en.html.

[26] Louise J. Gunning-Schepers, Foreword, in *Valorisation at the University of Amsterdam* (2014), www.uva.nl/binaries/content/assets/uva/en/about-the-uva/uva-profile/rules-and-regulations/uva_eng_valorisatie_bij_de_uva_final.pdf?2845731035267. ("[T]he UvA strives to have the greatest possible impact with the knowledge it develops and the way in which it shares this knowledge.")

[27] See e.g., Center for Civilians in Conflict, Amsterdam International Law Clinic: Monetary Payments for Civilian Harm in International and National Practice (2013), http://civiliansinconflict.org/uploads/files/publications/Valuation_Final_Oct_2013pdf.pdf; Friends of the Earth Netherlands, Amsterdam International Law Clinic, Michael G. Faure and André Nollkaemper, Climate Change Litigation Cases (2007), www.banktrack.org/download/climate_change_litigation_cases_analyses_of_issues_to_be_addressed/0_071215_climate_change_litigation_cases.pdf ; Staff Union of the European Patent Office, Amsterdam International Law Clinic: Application of European Community Law to (Staff Members of) the European Patent Organisation (2007), https://suepo.org/documents/42584/53721.pdf.

[28] Amsterdam International Law Clinic, Completed Reports, http://ailc.uva.nl/legal-services/recent-reports/completed-reports.html.

[29] R. Boryslawska, L. Martinez Lopez, and V. Skoric, *Identifying the Actors Responsible for Human Rights Violations Committed Against Staff Members of International Organizations: An Impossible Quest for Justice?* 1(2) HUMAN RIGHTS & INTERNATIONAL LEGAL DISCOURSE 381 (2007).

REFORMING THE TEACHING AND PRACTICE OF LAW IN EUROPE

Goals and Methods

In terms of educational goals, the AILC strives to accomplish two main goals that challenge the traditional mode of legal education. First, the Clinic aims to teach students how the law operates in an international setting. As Kornet observes, due to the processes of European integration and globalization, "[l]egal problems are no longer neatly confined to national jurisdictions, exclusively subject to law originating from the nation-state."[30] Our Clinic responds to her assessment that legal education that continues to treat the law as a nationally oriented discipline "does not prepare the future generation of legal professionals to function in this complex, ever-changing, globalized legal world."[31] The focus on international and European law ensures that the great majority of cases on which the AILC works concern global issues with a cross-border dimension.

Second, through problem-based learning, the Clinic programme seeks to help students understand the law in the context in which it is to be applied and to "think outside the box" in a way that serves our clients' needs.[32] This requires consideration of legal questions in their particular factual contexts, as well as an openness to consider legal arguments from different fields of law. Clinic reports are generally written in the form of comprehensive studies, often of a cross-cutting nature. They are designed to be balanced, and in length they are usually between fifty and one hundred pages. Yet, on occasion, clients have requested a report supporting only one side of potential arguments, for example, when preparing an appeal.[33]

In terms of educational methods, AILC students are trained and evaluated not only with their end result ("exam") in mind, but also during the process in which they interact with clients, team members, and supervisors in working towards the final report to be submitted to the clients. The meetings between the students and their supervisor(s), on the one hand, and the clients, on the other hand, serve a key role in this respect. While most of the meetings take place either in the client's offices or at our Faculty, for international clients, we have made use of Skype. At times, clients have invited us to their offices abroad. Clinic students and supervisors have, for instance, been invited to meet with and also present their research for staff unions of international organizations in Germany and Switzerland.

Through meetings, we gain knowledge about the background context to the client request; thereby, the Clinic is in a better position to understand and serve the specific needs of the client. In particular, conversations with clients allow a "meeting of the minds" as concerns the discrete questions of law to be addressed by the students. These questions are included in a contract entered into between the

---

[30] Nicole Kornet, *Future-Minded Legal Education in Europe: The European Law School*, 3 CHINA-EU LAW JOURNAL 23 (2014).
[31] Id.   [32] Cf. Juan Pérez-Léon, Chapter 14 in this volume.   [33] Cf. Wilson, *supra* note 6, at 34.

Clinic and each client, and the students and their supervisor(s) spend time (re-)drafting the contract to ensure feasibility in the scope and timing of the report.

In terms of a conception of the lawyer, the AILC is premised on and contributes to the formation of lawyers who work in an international arena rather than in a purely domestic one. This applies to both the substantive areas of law covered in the Clinic as well as to the network of Clinic alumni around the globe. By virtue of the nature of the various assignments taken on by the Clinic, students are also exposed to the frequent interconnectedness of different fields of law in concrete cases. In addition, the AILC recognizes the importance of legal research, legal writing, and teamwork and the duty of confidentiality for the legal profession. Hence, these aspects and corresponding skills receive particular attention throughout the Clinic course.

Beyond the Educational Goals

The AILC first and foremost seeks to realize educational goals for its students. However, beyond this, its establishment was driven by the aim to contribute to the internationalization of the law, and, more particularly, to the proper application of public international law and EU law in the Netherlands. As the Dutch legal system is open to international law, an increasing number of areas of law and practice are influenced by international law.[34] As the knowledge and understanding of international law generally and its modes of interaction with domestic law in particular often remain limited, conflicts and tensions are likely to occur between legal systems. Behind this formal notion of legal conflicts there lies a question of legal protection of rights by multiple layers of governance. The AILC is part of a broader set of institutions and processes that seek to reconcile such layers and to position its clients in a new internationalized legal environment.

In the context of access to justice, in the large majority of its cases, the AILC has advised clients with few or no means to get access to professional legal advice, which, as a rule, is quite expensive. Typical cases involved questions put by NGOs or lawyers acting on the basis of legal aid. As concerns the latter cases, the Dutch legal aid system provides legal aid to persons of limited means. Anyone in need of professional legal aid but unable to (fully) bear the costs is entitled to call upon the provisions as set down in the Dutch Legal Aid Act.[35] As noted earlier in the section on drivers, a significant number of the cases that come to the Clinic have originated in cases brought by persons or institutions who depended on legal aid. The AILC has set its fees low so that it is accessible for these type of clients. This is also based on the consideration that precisely this category of clients will otherwise have difficulty in accessing expert knowledge on matters of international and EU law.

The AILC has developed several partnerships with law firms and institutions that seek specifically to provide legal services for persons relying on legal aid. It has

[34] See e.g., Brölmann and Vierdag, *supra* note 10.   [35] Dutch Legal Aid Board, *supra* note 24.

established close cooperation the law firm Prakken d'Oliveira (previously Van den Biesen Prakken Böhler)[36] and, in the past, the Liga voor de Rechten van de Mens, an NGO providing legal support in cases where victims have difficulty in getting access to justice.[37] The private sector has made relatively little use of the Clinic. There is reason to presume that this sector has access to other means for securing expert knowledge on matters of international and EU law.

The Weight and Value of Internationalization

The need for internationalization has been embraced in the strategic plans of the University of Amsterdam.[38] The aim is further reflected in the Faculty of Law's curriculum and research,[39] but also in the establishment of legal master's programmes taught in English, the recruitment of international staff, and increasing collaboration in teaching and research with universities in other states. With the opening of the Clinic for international students, the AILC fits with this international profile.

The same can be said about the AILC's focus on international and EU law. Some cases are purely of an international or EU law nature, whereas in other cases questions of international and/or EU law connect to domestic law. However, also in the latter type of cases, AILC's contribution concerns questions of international and/or EU law. As observed earlier in the introductory section, this covers a wide variety of areas, including human rights law, refugee law, international criminal law, international environmental law, international trade law, and the law of (immunities of) international organizations, as well as numerous EU law topics.

The Clinic is also international in terms of its orientation for students. Students from the Netherlands and abroad work together with staff members who are from both the Netherlands and abroad. The connection of different legal backgrounds of students and staff provides an internationalized setting in which students learn from each other and their backgrounds and experiences.

---

[36] Advocatenkantoor Prakken d'Oliveira, www.prakkendoliveira.nl/en/home/.
[37] Liga voor de Rechten van de Mens, www.ligarechtenvandemens.nl/.
[38] The strategic plans of the University of Amsterdam for the periods 2007–2011 ("Learning to Excel"), 2011–2014 ("An Eye for Talent") and 2015–2020 ("Boundless Curiosity") are available at www.uva.nl/en/about-the-uva/uva-profile/identity/aims-and-ambitions/strategic-plan/strategic-plan.html. Internationalization features as a central theme in all three plans. On internationalization in particular, see also University of Amsterdam, Internationalisation, www.uva.nl/en/about-the-uva/uva-profile/identity/internationalisation/internationalisation.html.
[39] University of Amsterdam, Faculty of Law, Education, www.uva.nl/en/about-the-uva/organisation/faculties/faculties/faculties/content/folder/faculteit-der-rechtsgeleerdheid/education/education.html. ("The Faculty of Law prides itself on integrating international law across the faculty's entire curriculum, not only in the international law master's programmes."); *Id.*, Research, www.uva.nl/en/about-the-uva/organisation/faculties/faculties/faculties/content/folder/faculteit-der-rechtsgeleerdheid/research/research.html.

The rise in the number of international students is not only a result of the Bologna reform process[40]; the EU law on mobility of lawyers also plays a crucial role.[41] Furthermore, the learning experience and skills related to public international law and EU law are adaptable for legal careers abroad. In this respect, we note that the AILC has been instrumental in helping students seeking employment. While it is not possible to attribute success solely to the Clinic, a sizable number of Dutch and foreign Clinic students have been successful in finding employment at international (non-)governmental organizations and/or international law firms or other institutions at home and abroad. Some of these employers have also been using the services of the Clinic, and, in this sense, the AILC is building bridges between the University and legal practice beyond the concrete cases on which it is working.

Cooperation in Clinical Legal Education

The AILC has established relations with international clients, such as staff unions for international organizations, and, as a consequence thereof, it has taken up several cases for the same client. It has also been working together with institutions such as the Centre for Accountability of International Organizations in Geneva[42] and the Center for Civilians in Conflict in Washington DC[43]; sometimes, together with these institutions, Clinic staff and students have presented Clinic work at conferences or workshops.[44]

At the AILC, we strive to keep in contact with our alumni, *inter alia* through a separate LinkedIn Group. We have received cases and leads from former students. Former students have also given presentations to current students on various aspects of the legal profession.

---

[40] On the Bologna reform process, see *supra* note 12.
[41] Wilson, *supra* note 6, at 17–18; Anne-Lise Sibony, *Internationalising Legal Education in Belgium: Why Are We Doing It?* in THE INTERNATIONALISATION OF LEGAL EDUCATION (Christophe Jamin and William van Gaenegem eds., Springer 2016) 47, 58 (referring to Council Directive 77/249/EEC of March 22, 1977; Directive 98/5/EC of the European Parliament and of the Council of February 16, 1998; and Directive 2005/36/EC of the European Parliament and of the Council of September 7, 2005).
[42] Centre for Accountability of International Organisations, www.caio-ch.org/.
[43] Center for Civilians in Conflict, http://civiliansinconflict.org/. Cf. Lynn Welchman, Chapter 13 in this volume(on SOAS's institutional partners in the UK and overseas).
[44] See e.g., Amsterdam International Law Clinic, Law Students Research the Value of a Human Life (October 11, 2013), http://ailc.uva.nl/sample-projects/content/2013/10/law-students-research-the-value-of-human-life.html; Hege Elisabeth Kjos, Does the Administrative Tribunal for the International Labour Organization Offer an Adequate Level of Protection for Staff Members of International Organizations?, Brussels, March 17, 2007, Human Rights & International Legal Discourse, International Conference: Accountability for Human Rights Violations by International Organizations, https://www.law.kuleuven.be/iir/nl/activiteiten/documentatie/OldActivities/HRILD-kleur-international%20conferrence.pdf.

Diffusion of Clinical Legal Education

As noted earlier, in the section on the genesis of our Clinic, the decision to establish the AILC was to a great extent inspired by the practice of CLE in the United States.[45] This practice indicated that clinics are instrumental in allowing students to get hands-on experience in the application of international law in practice and in context. This not only enhances their technical legal skills, but also informs their understanding of the law as such.

In Europe – and this also held for the University of Amsterdam – international law was taught in a rather abstract, doctrinal way. Introducing CLE in the style taught in the United States allowed legal education to become more practical and hence more relevant. As a result, it also greatly benefited the engagement of students in their studies of the law.

In the context of the yearly congress of law schools in the Netherlands, the AILC has presented on its work to staff from other Dutch universities.[46] Furthermore, the Clinic has received questions from other law schools both at home and abroad on the nature of its work. In this context, the present authors are grateful for the opportunities for cooperation and dissemination of knowledge made possible through the conference organized by the editors and the subsequent publication of this volume.

Future of Clinic Legal Education in Europe

There is every reason to expect CLE to play a larger role at the University of Amsterdam and more widely in the Netherlands. This expectation is supported by three complementary developments. First, in an increasingly competitive international market for legal education, universities increasingly design programmes that allow individual students to engage and excel. The AILC has demonstrated that CLE has the potential to significantly increase the engagement of students and thereby their legal understanding and skills. Second, there is an increasing demand to connect legal studies to legal practice and to prepare students better for the requirements that the legal profession will make on them. Third, in an increasingly competitive job market, it will be necessary that students are provided with opportunities to make their individual mark and distinguish themselves. Working with real-life clients in the setting of clinics is one of the means by which this can be realized.

It is difficult to predict with any certainty to what extent CLE will develop more widely in Europe. Yet, judging from the testimonies given by the authors of the other

---

[45] Cf. Philip M. Genty, Chapter 1 in this volume.
[46] See e.g., Jaarcongres der Juridische Faculteiten [Yearly Congress of Law Faculties], January 28, 2011, University of Utrecht, https://www.rechtenonline.nl/upload/20116117108384820818go.pdf.

contributions in this edited volume, there is reason to believe that not only are clinics here to stay, but that they will grow in number.

CONCLUSION

From a European perspective, the AILC has been operating successfully for a relatively long time. Its establishment was made possible through the initiative of one person who had drawn inspiration from US law clinics. Yet, the faculty and its staff members have continued to support the Clinic. Without doubt, this is because they realize the positive effects of the Clinic for the students, the clients, the staff, and also the University. CLE is a unique way to prepare students for their future profession. In addition to gaining expertise in various areas of international and/or EU law, they acquire skills pertaining to teamwork, legal research, and writing. Perhaps most importantly, they also learn to identify and apply the law to the facts in a way that serves the client's needs.

The Clinic as a University course is time intensive,[47] and, in budget discussions, this can be its drawback. Yet, CLE should be embraced for its larger significance beyond student credits. Its existence prepares law faculties and students for the future as it dovetails with an increased recognition of the importance of practical legal education and the symbiosis that can be realized between the universities and society in general. Considering our own experience with the AILC, we would applaud increasing attention to and use of law clinics in Europe and across the world.

---

[47] International Legal Center, *supra* note 20, at 65. (Clinical legal education is "usually costly requiring intensive teach or other supervisory ratios and other resources as well."). See also Welchman, Chapter 13 in this volume.

Conclusion

Alberto Alemanno and Lamin Khadar

As a brief reminder, in this volume, we have set out to explore how clinical legal education (CLE) is reforming the teaching and practice of law in Europe. We noted at the outset a number of transformations taking place within the legal systems of Europe linked chiefly to processes of Europeanization and internationalization. We remarked that these transformations to European legal practice and culture were not, for the most part, being met by corresponding transformations in legal education (beyond superficial transformations to teaching content – adding a course reading here or a module there). We suggested that this stagnation may likely be a consequence of the reticence of the European legal academy (contrary to our American cousins) to engage in self-reflection about the nature of our craft. We have concerned ourselves more with *what* we are teaching than with *how* we are teaching. We pondered to what extent CLE should be understood as yet another minor reform in a largely conservative system of legal education or, rather, might be part of a broader awaking of a more self-reflective brand of European legal education. We speculated that, whatever the case, CLE may be intimately bound up in, and revealing of, the broader transformations to European legal systems (beyond legal education), and we set out to find out how.

Here, we will first engage in a theme-by-theme analysis of the different transformations that we hypothesized were, in one way or another, linked to the emergence of CLE in Europe. We will explore to what extent our hypotheses have been proved accurate and, if not, what else we have discovered. Following that, we will try to answer two core questions that we posed in the introduction: How is the practice and theory of clinical legal education adapting in European soil (*adaptation*)? And, what are the fruits of the emerging, "Europeanized" practice of CLE (*blossoming*)? We will then briefly conclude this edited volume with broad reflections on what we have learned and proposals for a future research agenda.

THE TRANSFORMATION OF EUROPEAN LEGAL EDUCATION: THEME-BY-THEME ANALYSIS OF OUR ORIGINAL HYPOTHESES

In the introduction, we hypothesized that CLE in Europe had emerged as a result of:

a) The Europeanization and Internationalization of domestic legal fields (i.e. law and legal practice);
b) The emergence of supranational and international jurisdictions and tribunals;
c) The emergence of a European and a global market for legal education;
d) Increasing demands for relevance in law school education (due to the changing political and social climate);
e) The emergence of a CSR/service learning/community engagement ethic within European higher education institutions;
f) Increased focus on innovation and practical skill–based education within European higher education institutions.

The Europeanization and Internationalization of Domestic Legal Fields

In the introduction, we hypothesized that CLE in Europe had emerged in part as a response to the process of Europeanization and internationalization of domestic legal fields. By "internationalization" and "Europeanization" we implied both the intrusion of international and European law into an increasing array of substantive legal fields and the convergence of domestic legal systems. For instance, as European Union (EU) law has come to affect virtually all areas of national legal systems, including constitutional, administrative, and private law, as well as criminal law, this has simultaneously had the effect of harmonizing national legal systems. However, by "internationalization" we also implied changes in the structure of legal practice, such as the rapid global expansion of the world's largest law firms over the past three decades and the emergence of a range of new legal professionals: compliance officers, regulatory affairs specialists, policy-makers and legal consultants (e.g. tax experts, lobbyists, nongovernmental organization [NGO] advocates).

We noted, however, that the progressive internationalization of the European legal fields has not been as rapidly followed-up by a parallel internationalization of legal education.[1] In other words, we continue training German, French, Czech, Polish, and Dutch lawyers as opposed to legal professionals capable of understanding the increasingly global and multilayered legal system across Europe and beyond. Only a few universities can legitimately claim – as the University of Amsterdam

---

[1] Jürgen Basedow, *Breeding Lawyers for the Global Village – The Internationalisation of Law and Legal Education*, in THE INTERNATIONALISATION OF LEGAL EDUCATION, THE FUTURE PRACTICE OF LAW (William van Caenegem and Mary Hiscock, Edward Elgar, 2015).

does – that "The need for internationalisation has been embraced in the strategic plans of our university [since at least 2007]."[2]

On the contrary, the vast majority of our contributors have confirmed that, as a result of a dominant nationally oriented and historically rooted attitude towards legal education, European and International law are subjects often ghettoized in legal education across Europe.[3]

However, as highlighted by Veronika Tomoszková and Maxim Tomoszek in Chapter 4 of this volume, there is also a risk that clinical education itself might fall victim of this phenomenon (merely reproducing or reflecting the historical and nationally oriented model of legal education prevalent across many European law schools). In their experience, the level of engagement with international and EU law in clinical teaching varies considerably depending on the focus of a given clinic, and some of their clinics focusing on labour law or other predominantly national disciplines remain rather insulated from international influence. However, this might have more to do with the particularly broad scope and offering of clinical education at Olomouc Law School than with CLE per se. Indeed, the vast majority of the clinics that we have examined in this volume instead suggest a deep awareness of and often involvement with, International and/or EU law.

The clinical experience documented in most EU countries, such as Germany, Belgium, Spain, and France, suggests an inherent ability of CLE (and desire on the part of clinicians themselves) to transcend a vision of law construed along national and disciplinary boundaries. In particular, as highlighted in Chapter 9 by Alemanno and Khadar, CLE may act as a bridge between EU law as a discipline and the Europeanized *practice* of law. This is true also for international law – as argued by Nora Markard in Chapter 8 – who, based on her clinical experience in German asylum law – shows how both international law and EU law seem particularly well-placed to lend themselves to CLE.

As recognized by Veronika Tomoszková and Maxim Tomoszek, while CLE is not the forum in which students are supposed to acquire basic knowledge of European

---

[2] The strategic plans of the University of Amsterdam for the periods 2007–2011 ("Learning to Excel"), 2011–2014 ("An Eye for Talent") and 2015–2020 ("Boundless Curiosity") are available at www.uva.nl/en /about-the-uva/uva-profile/identity/aims-and-ambitions/strategic-plan/strategic-plan.html.
Internationalization features as a central theme in all three plans. On internationalization in particular, see also University of Amsterdam, "Internationalisation," www.uva.nl/en/about-the-uva/uva profile/identity/internationalisation/internationalisation.html. This is reflected not only in the opening of the Amsterdam International Law Clinic but also in a thorough review of the Faculty of Law's curriculum and research, University of Amsterdam, Faculty of Law, "Education," www.uva.nl/en /about-the-uva/organisation/faculties/faculties/faculties/content/folder/faculteit-der-rechtsgeleerdheid /education/education.html ("The Faculty of Law prides itself on integrating international law across the faculty's entire curriculum, not only in the international law master's programmes"); ibid., "Research" www.uva.nl/en/about-the-uva/organisation/faculties/faculties/faculties/content/folder /faculteit-der-rechtsgeleerdheid/research/research.html.

[3] See, in particular, Chapter 10 by Anthony Valcke; Chapter 4 by Veronika Tomoszková and Maxim Tomoszek; and Chapter 11 by Eva Brems and Stijn Smet, as well as Chapter 7 by Ulrich Stege and Maurizio Veglio to explore this theme further.

and international law, in the clinical setting, students are confronted with and forced to develop a more realistic and complex understanding of the law in its polygenetic and multilayered European glory. This exposure promotes advanced knowledge and skills related to nondomestic sources of law. Students learn how to apply the theoretical knowledge about supranational law that they have gained in their compulsory courses to complex real-life scenarios. This is a welcome development insofar as it proves the ability of CLE to fill the gap between the realities of legal practice and those of education in the uniquely European context.

As highlighted by Nora Markard in Chapter 8, it appears undisputed that, for a contemporary lawyer, it is indispensable

> to be familiar with the relevant instruments at supranational level, to be able to put them to effect in domestic settings, and to be able to mobilize their enforcement structures where domestic remedies prove fruitless or where this is strategically advisable.

Our hypothesis, which our individual contributors agreed to explore in this volume and according to which CLE in Europe has emerged in part as a response of an incremental awareness of such a process of internationalization, has been largely confirmed. CLE both emerges from and responds to these developments. This is evident both from the way in which the contributors to this volume talk of the added value of CLE (in a similar fashion to Markard), but also in how they are actively deploying this teaching method. By confronting their law students with the reality of contemporary European legal practice in all its complexity, European clinicians are placing CLE at the forefront of a progressive internationalization of legal education.

Yet, CLE has not yet prompted a denationalization of the law curriculum. For this to happen, we must expose students to an increasingly multisource and transdisciplinary "law in action." As argued by several of our contributors, we believe that CLE is particularly well-placed to effect such a transformation. This will in turn entail the mainstreaming and integrating of CLE across the whole teaching curriculum by embedding its methodology, techniques, and overall attitude to the legal world in mainstream courses.

As highlighted by Anthony Valcke in Chapter 10 of this volume, CLE is not a one-way-street in relation to internationalization and Europeanization. Neither international nor EU law operate in a vacuum, and therefore clinical students, even when heavily exposed to nondomestic sources of law, will still be required to engage with national law. Insofar as any lawyer today still requires an anchor to a domestic legal order, any orthodox form of internationalization of legal education through CLE must be resisted.

The Emergence of Supranational and International Jurisdictions and Tribunals

In the introduction, we hypothesized that CLE in Europe was embracing the emergence of supranational and international jurisdictions and tribunals by exposing students to a multiplicity of fora. We noted that the rapid proliferation of international courts was, in some respects, democratizing the practice of international law and, with this, making it incumbent on lawyers – beyond the historic international or Euro-elite – to engage with and have some understandings of the procedures and doctrine of international tribunals. In particular, by pursuing interactions with public authorities and supranational and international bodies, and thus prompting strategic thinking on legal remedies and avenues, we posited that CLE could render students more comfortable with an increasingly multilayered and, as a result, multijurisdictional legal landscape.

Our contributors, most of whom engage in their clinics with supranational courts and fora, tested our hypothesis. In so doing, they provide insightful ideas largely confirming our intuition and direct experience.

The Åbo Akademi University International Human Rights Law Clinic (ÅAIHRLC), the Amsterdam International Law Clinic, the CEU Clinic, the SOAS Clinic, the Kent EU Rights Clinic, the Human Rights Law Clinic at Ghent, and the EU Public Interest Clinic at HEC /NYU have deliberately decided to situate the scope of their clinical action in relation to preexisting international courts.

For some of them, such as the CEU Clinic, the SOAS Clinic, and the Kent EU Rights Clinic, their international dimension primarily stems from the fact that their NGO partners/clients are involved in human rights litigation and/or advocacy before European and international courts. In other words, their ecosystem demands them to engage with and facilitate access to international fora. Thus, for instance, as Renáta Uitz and Eszter Polgári write in Chapter 12 of this volume – in the case of CEU Clinic – a commitment to strategic litigation is embedded in the legal culture of their NGO partners. In this respect, these organizations embrace techniques familiar from the civil rights movement in the United States and have historically benefitted from the support of international donors to this effect.[4] Litigation is central to the efforts of these NGOs in seeking to trigger legal change: they go to court not simply to represent *pro bono* clients in individual cases, but to correct the structural shortcomings of the legal system which legal reform had not touched.

For others, such as the Amsterdam International Law Clinic and the ÅAIHRLC in Finland, their involvement with international courts has to do with a deliberate choice to expose their students to those supranational legal systems.

Yet, regardless of whether their initial driver has been to improve access to international courts or to train students to interact with those courts, the ultimate aim and result that all these clinical programmes pursue is the same. They all play a pivotal role in improving law students' literacy vis-à-vis international litigation/ judicial engagement while at the same time improving access to those courts for less privileged actors.

---

[4] Edwin Rekosh, *Constructing Public Interest Law: Transnational Collaboration and Exchange in Central and Eastern Europe*, 13 UCLA J. INT'L LAW& FOR. AFF. 55 (2008).

This is due to the first common feature shared by these clinics: that they place themselves at the service of preexisting organizations (NGOs) whose institutional ecosystem requires the intervention of supporting and often equalizing actors, such as *pro bono* lawyers, clinical students, or other forms of skill-sharing capacity builders.

As André Nollkamper and Hege Elisabeth Kjos in Chapter 16 observe:

> the establishment of the AILC has been driven by the fact that in an increasing number of cases, lawyers, non-governmental organisations and other institutions are facing questions of international law for which they do not have expertise in-house ... The AILC provides a means by which these institutions acquire expert knowledge on questions of law to which they otherwise would have little or no access.

Along similar lines, in Chapter 9, Alberto Alemanno and Lamin Khadar recognize that, due to the multiplication of channels of participation in the EU space, NGOs struggle to keep pace, in particular with the ever-increasing number of public consultations. Moreover, NGOs often lack the skills and resources to effectively advocate for the interests of their European constituents.[5] As a result, the EU Public Interest Clinic seeks to expand access to the policy process as well as justice by working for NGOs that aim to hold the EU institutions to account and provide a countervailing force to undue business influence by representing diffuse public interests.[6]

Similarly, Joost Pauwelyn and Mattia Salamanca Orrego underline that the law governing international trade and investments is increasingly complex. Thus, behind the World Trade Organization (WTO), the World Bank, and UNCTAD, there are hundreds of bilateral investment treaties (BITs) and free trade arrangements, each with its own negotiation, implementation, and dispute settlement system. As a result of this multiplication of systems and sources of law, they argue that, "[e]veryone is affected but few have the time and resources to fully engage."[7]

That's the *raison d'être* of the Graduate Institute Clinic. Similarly to the EU Public Interest Clinic, the Geneva-based Clinic also takes leave from a procedural-based (or substantively neutral) vision of social justice (i.e. focused predominantly on ensuring a more equal access to the negotiating table) and engages in various policy areas, ranging from public health to the environment, while serving different typologies of actors, be they small states or NGOs.

On this point, one must observe how some of the European-based clinics, such as the Human Rights and Migration Law Clinic (HRMLC) in Turin, SOAS, the

---

[5] The Good Lobby, Survey of the Legal and Advocacy Needs of NGOs active in the EU policy space, June 2017, edited by Lamin Khadar and Alberto Alemanno, and available at www.thegoodlobby.eu

[6] For a broader theory of change putting forward the need for equalizing forces in our societies, see Alberto Alemanno, LOBBYING FOR CHANGE: FIND YOUR VOICE TO CREATE A BETTER SOCIETY (London: Iconbooks, 2017).

[7] Chapter 15 by Joost Pauwelyn and Mattia Salamanca Orrego in this volume.

Graduate Institute, CEU, and the EU Public Interest Clinic at HEC/NYU, act fully autonomously, picking their causes and representing them, sometimes on their own (i.e. without any NGO partners/clients).

In this context, it is worth highlighting the unique role played by SOAS (described in Chapter 13 of this volume) in the context of international and domestic human rights litigation. The SOAS programme is not a conventional human rights law clinic. It instead focuses on fact-finding activities that might be required to support pending human rights litigation, be they international (such as the International Criminal Court [ICC]) or domestic. As such, its diverse body of students engage in field investigation in Africa and the Middle East. Sometimes they also mobilize investigative reporters to be used in front of courts, thus strengthening the case against alleged human rights perpetrators.

In sum, the clinical journeys embarked upon by our contributors confirm our hypothesis. The international dimension of many clinical programmes primarily stems from a deliberate choice to embrace internationalization as an opportunity to meet the goals of clinical education (a richer and more impactful law teaching) while at the same time improving access to justice to a new, complex set of international courts and adjudicatory mechanisms.

The Emergence of a European and a Global Market for Legal Education

In the introduction, we hypothesized that CLE in Europe emerged in part as a consequence of the increasingly internationalized and Europeanized markets for legal education. We referred to the common practice across Europe according to which the master's degree-level legal education is oriented towards the European and international markets for students. We noted the increasing mobility of European law students and law teachers both within Europe and internationally. We suggested that CLE in Europe was both a consequence of and response to this process.

Virtually all our contributors confirmed – through their direct experience and reflections – this hypothesis. It is indeed a truism to state that the impact of globalization did not limit itself to economic processes. Inevitably, it has also affected legal education and that despite the traditional reticence of the latter to transform. According to Marzia Barbera in Chapter 3 of this volume, legal clinics offer a paradigmatic example of the incipient structural transformations that are taking place on a macro level, reconfiguring the classic legal curriculum. Indeed, the emergence and diffusion of CLE across Europe must be contextualized in the broader transnational circulation of legal models that are largely affecting every aspect of the law, including structures of legal expertise and education. This process is largely prompted by academic and professional *élites* who – due to their increasingly mobile nature – give rise to a number of academic and professional networks. Although these networks are largely informal and tend not to operate in a targeted manner, they are the result of a series of migrations of both students and scholars who take part in doctoral or LLM programmes or are involved in academic or research project exchanges. While these informal networks have existed for several decades, with European scholars studying in other European countries and many of them crossing the channel or the Atlantic, the number of students and faculty involved in these processes has increased significantly in recent years. Inevitably, this has resulted in an expanding transnational practice and a growing standardization of professional requirements.[8] Thus, for instance, international law firms across European capitals de facto require an LLM degree of anyone seeking a job with them.

While we are far from witnessing the emergence of a global – or even European – legal education market, the progressive internationalization of the legal profession has been highlighting the need to educate lawyers capable of adapting to and acting in different legal contexts. This is not so much with reference to knowledge of the law of each national legal system, but rather in terms of skills and working methods. That sought-after quality is often referred to as "global fluency."[9] From that perspective, the study and teaching of EU law played a unique role. Given the pervasiveness of EU law in so many fields of law, being able to study, research, and play with EU sources and their national implementation has provided a wonderful laboratory of experimentation for European legal education.

From this perspective, the clinical approach also allows students to demystify nondomestic sources of law[10] by illustrating that the implementation of the law is not the exclusive preserve of *"often remote and inaccessible institutions."*[11] The progressive convergence of domestic and international regimes inevitably reflects a more globalized international legal market for education.

As illustratively demonstrated by Xavier Aurey in Chapter 6 of this volume, the emergence of national and international academic competition in the market for legal education shook up a teaching model that was rooted in a secular tradition.[12] Indeed, today offering a clinical experience to internationally mobile students can

---

[8] See Robert Lutz, *Reforming Approaches to Educating Transnational Lawyers: Observations from America*, 61 J. LEGAL EDUC. 449 (2012); more generally, Jane Knight, *Internationalization Remodelled: Definition, Approaches, and Rationales*, 8 J. STUDIES INT'L. EDUC. 5 (2004).

[9] The NYU Law Abroad Program is designed to help students develop global fluency: sensitivity to different legal cultures and contexts, linguistic ability, and the flexibility to work effectively across jurisdictions; see Frank Bloch, N.R. Madava Menon, *The Global Clinical Movement*, in THE GLOBAL CLINICAL MOVEMENT. EDUCATING LAWYERS FOR SOCIAL JUSTICE (Frank Bloch ed., Oxford University Press 2011), 267.

[10] Bernard Duhaime, La pertinence de l'approche clinique pour enseigner le droit international des droits de la personne, in *Les cliniques juridiques* (Xavier Aurey and Marie-Joëlle Redor-Fichot, dir., Presses universitaires de Caen, 2015), 129.

[11] *Id.*

[12] As highlighted by Yves Gaudemet, today universities are the heirs of reforms from the nineteenth century: Yves Gaudemet, *Les facultés de droit dans la réforme universitaire*, 3 REVUE DU DROIT PUBLIC 680 (2008).

indeed be a differentiating factor in an increasingly globalized, or at least international, legal education market. This has been expressly recognized and directly experienced by the clinicians at SOAS, Ghent, and the Graduate Institute, as well as the Kent EU Rights Clinic. As argued by Veronika Tomoszková and Maxim Tomoszek in Chapter 4, clinics in European law schools provide a "unique forum in which future lawyers can learn to see the whole picture of the cases they are working on, including their supranational dimension. ... In this way, students also learn what it means to be part of the EU as well as of the international community and which instruments of law enforcement derive from this."

Largely as a result of such a drive, some schools, such as the Graduate School in Geneva, CEU in Budapest, UvA in Amsterdam, and Tarragona, introduced CLE at the master's level. The specialized nature of a large number of Europe-based clinics means that clinics extensively engage with both EU and international law. But this is not the only feature that renders European CLE "international" in scope. Most of the clinics examined do not only integrate the cross-national dimension of law, but they also count on a very diverse and international participating student body. This is certainly the case for the Graduate Institute in Geneva, where 42% of its participants come from developing countries. Likewise, the EU Public Interest Clinic at HEC/NYU counts on several nationalities among its clinical students, with a predominance of EU and US citizens. This is also the case for the CEU Clinic, as well as for Åbo Akademi University International Human Rights Law Clinic (ÅAIHRLC) and the Kent EU Rights Clinic.

The internationalization of legal education as a result of the globalization of the profession, however, is not only a market-driven process. Indeed, many of the clinics that have emerged in Europe, such as Abo, CEU, the Graduate Institute, and the EU Public Interest at HEC/NYU, are vanguard, boutique, and often value-based schools. As a result, these clinical programmes tend to target only graduate, typically international, well-selected students, and do not entail the study of domestic law. Thus, there is a risk that their inherently international dimension may render them insulated from local influence insofar as their impact typically transcends the local realities. Yet there is evidence that these programmes have been playing a key role in adapting CLE in Europe and in potentially turning them into scalable educational models to be mainstreamed into legal education more broadly.[13]

Increasing Demands for Relevance in Law School Education

In the introduction, we hypothesized that CLE in Europe may be arising in response to growing demands for greater relevance in law school education or, at the very least, capitalizing on such demands for its growth. We suggested that, in Europe, at least since the end of the past decade, there is a heightened sense of crisis which has

---

[13] *See, e.g.,* Chapter 9 by Alberto Alemanno and Lamin Khadar.

begun to penetrate our law schools. We spoke of the crises *in* Europe and the crisis *of* Europe – the sovereign debt crisis, the migrant crisis, the terror threat, and the constant threat (now partial reality) of European disintegration. We suggested that this sense of crisis may be catalysing the development of CLE by motivating job-hungry law students to get practical experience, or socially conscious students and law teachers to get off the side-lines, out of their armchairs, and pitch in and help out.

A number of our contributors proved this hypothesis to be at least partially valid. First, several contributors revealed the significance of the so-called migrant crisis to the founding and missions of their clinics. Chapter 8 by Nora Markard, in particular, sheds much light on this theme. Markard describes in some detail the emergence across Germany of a student-led "Refugee Law Clinic movement" (there were twenty-some such clinics by 2016/17). This movement was apparently a direct consequence of the 2014–2015 refugee protests in Germany. These protests against the Dublin system and restrictions on freedom of movement garnered support from civil society and students who collectively "started volunteering in soup kitchens, sorting through the tons of donated clothes, offering language classes [and] activities for children or supporting individual refugee families in reception centres ... in their daily lives and bureaucratic struggles." For law students, this type of volunteering naturally evolved into providing more law-oriented forms of support and into the founding of student-run legal clinics for the benefit of refugees and asylum seekers. The students relied on local lawyers and select faculty members to provide them with training, and so the clinics were, at least initially, largely autonomous from their relevant law schools. However, they have subsequently received sanction from the law schools and been institutionalized to one degree or another.

Markard's chapter neatly reveals how students, confronted by pressing social challenges, seek to make their legal education relevant and useful by deploying it through skilled volunteering in the public interest. Talking of the founding of her own clinics, Markard comments that:

> we knew of the frustration of many students who had chosen law school in order to help change the world, and who found themselves trapped by exam requirements, textbooks, flashcards, and prep courses without a glimpse of how they might ever be able to use all of this detailed, but largely theoretical knowledge for the public interest work they yearned to get into.

The Refugee Law Clinic in Hamburg (which Markard now helps to supervise) was itself a student-initiated project. Similarly, students of the Human Rights and Migration Law Clinic in Turin are so passionate about the social justice aspect of the programme (providing legal support to refugees in the Turin area) that they remain involved as volunteers following graduation.[14]

---

[14] *See* Chapter 8 by Nora Markard in this volume.

Interestingly though, demands for greater relevance in law school teaching dovetail with demands for a greater emphasis on CV-building, employability, and professionalization.[15] Students, to be sure, are not one-dimensional and they appear to view legal clinics simultaneously as a forum in which to act out their desires for social activism and impact and also to build skills or networks and add lines to their CVs that may help them to secure jobs in – increasingly – competitive employment markets upon graduation.[16]

Of course, the desire to put a legal education and legal training to social use is not the preserve of law students alone. Law teachers, too, may yearn to make an impact in their communities and play a positive role in the social challenges making headline news. Indeed, while not student-founded, the clinics in Turin and Brescia, discussed in Chapter 7 by Stege and Veglio and Chapter 3 by Barbera, respectively, similarly take leave from the migrant crisis (or, in any event, the increased migration flows to Italy in recent years). When speaking of their aims and drivers, the authors all write passionately about the growing migration to Italy consequent upon war and political instability in neighbouring regions and about the rising number of deaths on the Mediterranean. The authors seem to view CLE as a vehicle for channelling their sense of social outrage (e.g.) at the way that migrants are treated, into (hopefully) useful legal responses.

However, it is not only the migrant crisis in Europe that has served as inspiration or justification for CLE. The financial crisis also has spurred some to call for greater support for law school clinics. In Chapter 10, Anthony Valcke explains that the economic crisis in Europe (over the past decade or so) has made it more difficult for EU citizens and their family members to access legal advice and representation in relation to EU free movement issues. This, he explains, is consequent upon the reduction of legal aid budgets in a number of member states, meaning decreased availability of legal aid in cases concerning residence rights (and, thus, often, EU free movement rights). Accordingly, Valcke views the EU Rights Clinic as a means to meet some of these unmet legal needs by working with EU citizens and their family members right across Europe and helping them to access their rights. Similarly, Welchman, in Chapter 13 of this volume, reveals how, in the UK in particular, legal aid cuts and austerity may have been drivers for the "mainstreaming" of CLE at UK university law schools.

However, both Chapter 10 by Valcke and Chapter 9 by Alemanno and Khadar reveal how clinics are also responding to a deeper and more uniquely European challenge: the crisis *of* Europe. The authors all talk, in one way or another, about a EU system that is broken or of threats to the values that underpin that system. While Valcke talks of rising populism and anti-EU sentiment, specifically taking aim at the free movement of persons (in the form of Brexit), Alemanno and Khadar

---

[15] *See* Chapter 13 by Welchman in this volume.
[16] For a critique, *see* Alberto Alemanno, LOBBYING FOR CHANGE: FIND YOUR VOICE TO CREATE A BETTER SOCIETY (London: Iconbooks, 2017).

speak of the growing influence of private corporations over the EU policy process and attendant concerns with transparency and accountability within the EU institutional system. These authors see CLE (among other forms of public interest lawyering) as a response to the legitimacy and existential challenges facing the EU politico-legal order. CLE, the authors suggest, may play a role in nurturing informed and active citizens, empowered to engage with the EU system (either as individuals or in the form of civil society organizations) so as to influence the policy process or defend their rights, as the case may be.

With respect to all the chapters discussed in this section, whether CLE can live up to the hopes and expectations of the authors remains to be seen. However, what is clear is that these clinicians, in establishing and running legal clinics, are reacting personally and emotionally to the political and social issues of contemporary European society through a kind of *socially informed, skilled activism*. Indeed, it seems that CLE in Europe, when viewed holistically, may be a form of collective action, of law students and teachers seeking to place law and their experience of the law at the heart of the social and political challenges gripping twenty-first-century Europe.

The Emergence of a CSR/Service Learning/Community Engagement Ethic within European Higher Education Institutions

In the introduction, we hypothesized that the idea of community engagement can and has in some cases served as a narrative to justify CLE in Europe and win support from university administrations. We noted that, since around the turn of the last century, the imperative to engage with local communities and civil society in a constructive way has filtered into the objectives of universities at both regional and domestic levels across Europe. Whether you call it the "third mission," "community engagement," or even "CSR," we posited that certain academics may be strategically making use of such narratives to win support for CLE at their respective institutions.

While this hypothesis was not universally confirmed, our contributors nonetheless shed light on the ways in which the European CLE movement has managed, in certain instances, to cruise in the tailwind of institutional objectives related to the third mission of higher education institutions. In some cases, clinics have even served as inspiration for mainstreaming community engagement activities beyond the law faculty and across the university.

The Environmental Law Clinic at Rovira i Virgili University was established in 2005. By 2010, the founder of the clinic, Maria Marquès i Banqué had been appointed Vice-rector for Teaching and the European Higher Education Area. In this capacity, she played a pivotal role in establishing, in 2012, a programme aimed at institutionalizing service-learning throughout the entire university. By positioning the clinics at Rovira i Virgili University institutionally within the service learning programme and aligning the clinics to the social responsibility mission of the university, Marquès i Banqué managed to secure institutional recognition for CLE that is still lacking in many of the legal clinics across Europe, where clinics are more of a voluntary add-on lacking institutional backing. Marquès i Banqué, convinced of this strategy, believes that clinics across Europe should take advantage of the growing emphasis placed by higher education institutions on their so-called third mission and use this to secure institutional recognition. This is already happening in Italy, where, as Stege and Veglio discuss in Chapter 7, as of 2015, universities are subject to evaluation on the basis of their performance with respect to their third mission ("terza missione") by the National Agency for the Evaluation of Universities and Research Centers. Clinicians across Italy are already seizing upon this as an opportunity to seek institutional recognition and, ultimately, further institutionalization. Marquès i Banqué believes that by institutionalizing CLE in this fashion, we may also be able to address concerns about quality control by subjecting all clinics to internally established minimum requirements regarding their operating procedures.

Meanwhile, in Belgium, the rebranding of Ghent University with a focus on "social commitment" both served as inspiration for the founding of the clinic and provided an institutional lens through which the clinic could be understood and supported. In Chapter 11, Brems and Smet explain that, in Flanders, the three pillars of academic work are teaching, research, and "services" (implying both services within the institution and *services to the community*). The clinic, focused on applied human rights research for the benefit of local nonprofit organizations, is perfectly aligned with this triple mission. In 2015, Ghent University adopted a policy on "social value creation in research." One of the objectives of this policy is to include social value creation among the criteria used for the evaluation of academic staff. This policy served as both a catalyst and as kindling for the clinic. First, as Brems and Smet suggest, creating a relationship between the significant investment required to establish and run a clinic and academic career progression (through the inclusion of social value creation in academic performance evaluation), no doubt provides incentives and rewards to (would-be) clinicians. Second, having an institutional commitment to social value creation in research provides a supportive framework for the clinic which helps to sustain the clinic over time. It is easy to give up on a clinic when one feels (as is often the case in Europe) institutionally isolated, labouring in a battle that, in the best case, nobody else perceives and, in the worst case, people actively oppose. In a supportive institutional environment, even where that support is only verbal, it's easier to remain committed over time. Similarly, in the Netherlands, a broad commitment, evidenced in a statement of the Dutch Association of Universities to the "valorization" of academic research (understood as rendering academic research useful to society) has helped to provide institutional recognition to the work of the International Law Clinic at the University of Amsterdam.

What is clear from these examples, and has been broadly confirmed across this edited volume, is that in order to achieve long-term success and sustainability, European legal clinicians need to operate strategically, translating their clinical ambitions and activities into institutional agendas, targets, and funding priorities. Canny European clinicians have managed to secure resources (whether recognition, prestige, funding, facilities, or staff) and so to institutionalize their clinics to one degree or another. This sort of entrepreneurial and strategic operating seems to be a key part of the necessary tool-kit of European legal clinicians.

Growing Frustration with Traditional Legal Teaching Methods and Increased Demand for Innovation and Practical-Skill-Based Education within European Higher Education Institutions

In the Introduction, we hypothesized that the Bologna Process and its associated calls for innovation and practical skill-based education may have helped to create fertile ground for CLE in Europe. At the very least, we suggested, clinicians may have been relying on the frameworks and narratives ushered in by the Bologna Process to justify and promote CLE in their institutions.

A key finding in this regard, one emerging from the contribution of Maria Marquès i Banqué (Chapter 5), is that "the Bologna Process seems to be, almost universally, the primary catalyst for the emergence of Clinical Legal Education in Spain." In Spain, it seems that the Bologna Process "led all Spanish Faculties of Law to adopt a more skill-oriented and student-centred approach to learning." Clinical legal education was one tool, among others, in the arsenal of Spanish legal educators responding to the call of the Bologna declaration for a greater emphasis on employability through the development of skills and competencies. Also in Chapter 1 by Philip Genty, the author draws compelling links between Bologna and the growth CLE during the second wave (i.e. the resurgence of CLE from the mid-2000s). However, with the exception of Spain, while many authors mentioned the Bologna Process (either as part of the broader context of transformation in legal education or as a useful narrative that clinicians may rely on to garner institutional support), there was little evidence of causality between Bologna and the emergence of CLE. The Bologna Process seems to have either been actively opposed by European law schools or otherwise experienced by them in a rather passive way. There is some evidence of the Bologna Process sparking debates about the extent to which law schools effectively prepare students for legal practice but little evidence of this process serving as *inspiration* (as opposed to *justification* after the fact) for CLE.

What emerged instead from the chapters was a broad dissatisfaction with the *status quo* of legal teaching in Europe. Legal education is described variously as *dogmatic and positivist* (Aurey), *formalist* (Barbera and Markard), *backwards-looking and historical* (Tomoszek and Tomoszek), *doctrinal and theoretical* (Nollkaemper and Kjos), and *academic* (Markard). Many authors also complain of what

Welchman, in Chapter 13, refers to as the "pile them high and teach them cheap" model of legal education prevalent across Europe. That is, a lecture-based and textbook-dependent model of legal teaching that has very little student interaction and places the teacher and the textbook at the centre of the educational experience. As Welchman's turn of phrase suggests, and as our authors confirm, this model of teaching is often necessitated by funding constraints on law schools. There may also be a generational aspect to this dissatisfaction as the authors seem to complain not only about the state of legal education in general but more specifically about the state of legal education when they were in law school.

The authors almost universally present CLE as a challenge to this status quo and as the antithesis of all that ails contemporary legal education (or the legal education of their day). This insofar as CLE is *instrumentalist, applied, interactive, practical, present-oriented, context-bound*, and the like. This is not to say that CLE is accepted uncritically. Authors acknowledge the structural and financial limitations of CLE (i.e. the limited number students who can take part in a clinic and the greater demands on faculty time and resources). However, it is clear that clinicians are deploying law clinics instrumentally to fix a system of education that they perceive as broken and out of touch. Perhaps this is a similar impulse to the new parent wanting to avoid the perceived mistakes of their own parents, but perhaps it signals something more profound than this. Perhaps it signals a broader discontent with legal education across Europe and is indicative of a transformation taking place in legal education. A number of the chapters certainly provide some evidence of this. Authors talk of universities in general and law school in particular increasingly prioritizing innovation in legal education. This imperative for innovation may be couched in terms of the need for practice-oriented education, for employability, teaching quality, enhanced competitiveness (of legal education, as discussed further earlier), or greater community engagement (also discussed earlier), but at any rate represents a welcome change to a model of legal education that has remained (largely) unchanged in Europe for centuries. In this sense, we can say that CLE in Europe emerges out of and must be construed in light of a broad *reflective turn* in European legal education.

ADAPTATION: HOW IS CLE ADAPTING IN EUROPEAN SOIL?

Having reviewed our hypotheses and some of the key findings emerging from the contributions to this volume, we can now return to two of our central research questions. First, how is the practice and theory of CLE adapting in European soil (*adaptation*)? And, second, what are the fruits of the emerging, "Europeanized" CLE practice (*blossoming*)?

We begin here with the question of adaptation. The question is how CLE, which at least historically, is not a European practice, is transforming itself in order to thrive in Europe. In particular, how have/are European clinics adopting aims, models, structures, or methods or engaging in issues which are context-specific (meaning endogenous to or unique to Europe)? Are they embracing European institutions and European issues? Are they forming European networks and pursing Pan-European collaboration? How are they adapting CLE to fit the demands of European legal education? Is the resulting model(s) of CLE characterized by convergence, divergence, or hybridization?

We suggested in the Introduction to this volume that the first wave of CLE in Europe (from the mid-1990s to the early 2000s, in Central and Eastern Europe) was a US-led transplant.[17] Meanwhile, the second wave (from the mid-2000s to the present) has been more of a bottom-up, idiosyncratic phenomenon. The contributions to this volume have largely confirmed this view. However, a few caveats must be added. First, the reflective chapters by Philip Genty (Chapter 1) and Katarzyna Ważyńska-Finck (Chapter 2), and also the chapter by Veronika Tomoszková and Maxim Tomoszek (Chapter 4) reveal a slightly more nuanced picture of the first wave. Ważyńska-Finck reveals that, although the early clinical initiatives in Poland were indeed US-funded, the Polish academics involved were far from passive recipients of a US model. There was (also owing to the recent political transformations in Central and Eastern Europe) genuine frustration with historical teaching methods in Poland and a real thirst for something new. Tomoszková and Tomoszek paint a similar picture in relation to the early clinical projects in the Czech Republic. Ważyńska-Finck further notes that some of the clinical projects may have arisen at the initiative of Polish academics themselves, following study trips to the United States and conversations with American peers. Moreover, in Poland, it seems there was an authentic "heterogeneous and yet coherent [clinical] movement, composed of students (often members of the European Law Students Association), young legal scholars, and well-established law professors, who shared, at least to some extent, the same ideas and convictions."[18] Ważyńska-Finck also reveals that, in Poland, the local clinicians took a "proactive" approach to the US clinical model which "involved the development of a pedagogical methodology that could fit with the local realities."[19]

Genty sheds further light on the first wave when he suggests that, to the extent that there was an attempt (on the part of US funders) to affect a direct transplant of the US model, it largely failed. Genty suggests that "the American models that were

---

[17] See, e.g., Richard J. Wilson, *Beyond Legal Imperialism: US Clinical Legal Education and New Law and Development*, in Bloch, *supra* note 12 at 135; Leah Wortham, *Aiding Clinical Education Abroad: What Can Be Gained and the Learning Curve on How to Do So Effectively*, 12 CLIN. L. REV. 615 (2006); Steven Austermiller, *ABA/CEELI's Law Clinic Programs in Croatia*, INT'L. J. CLIN. LEGAL EDUC. 3 (2003); John M. Burman, *The Role of Clinical Legal Education in Developing the Rule of Law in Russia*, 2 WYO. L. REV. 89 (2002); Rodney J. Uphoff, *Why in-House Live Client Clinics Won't Work in Romania: Confessions of a Clinician Educator*, 6 CLIN. L. REV. 315 (1999); James C. May, *Creating Russia's First Law School Legal Clinic*, 23 VERMONT BAR J. L. DIGEST 43 (Aug. 1997); and C. Nicholas Revelos, *Teaching Law in Transylvania: Notes from a Different Planet*, 45 J. LEGAL EDUC. 597 (1995).

[18] See Chapter 2 in this volume. [19] *Id.*

'transplanted' failed to take account of the significant structural and cultural differences between the US and Europe."[20] These differences include:

- European rules that prohibit law students from practising law or making submissions to and appear before national courts
- The differences between common law and civil law legal practice and the consequent need to focus less on skills related to the lawyer–client relationship and the intricacies of the adversarial legal process and more on legal research and the drafting of documents, which are far more important skills in the inquisitorial legal process
- Larger class sizes, heavier teaching loads in European law schools, and the lack of formal recognition (credit, remuneration, teaching time) for both students and teachers taking part in clinics
- The fact that many European law professors are not admitted to practise law; as a consequence, given the emphasis placed by funders on "live-client"[21] clinics, there was a need to hire private lawyers into the clinic to actually formally represent clients
- The much more limited budgets of European law schools as compared to US law schools; this meant once the funders withdrew in the mid-2000s, any staff they had retained for the clinics they were funding were not kept on by the relevant institutions.

Ultimately, Genty concludes, as we suggest in the Introduction, that:

[t]he most visible sources of potential US influence – funding and educational consultants – failed to have a direct, lasting impact on European legal education. Much of the early growth of European clinical education that occurred in the 1990s and 2000s was reversed once the outside foundation funding moved to other regions.[22]

However, Genty suggests, and Ważyńska-Finck, Tomoszková, and Tomoszek demonstrate, that the efforts were not a complete failure. In the words of Genty, "seeds had been planted, and these soon began to bear fruit."[23] The communities of clinicians, the clinical know-how, the passion for CLE, and even some of the infrastructure survived the departure of the US funders in the mid-2000s. It seems that the flourishing of the clinical movement in Poland (and to a lesser extent in Russia) continued to serve as an inspiration (through conferences and study visits) to other would-be and fledgling clinicians across the region and beyond.

This brings us to the second wave, where, again, the contributions add some nuance to the picture we painted in the Introduction. There are perhaps five trends that we might remark upon. First, some European legal clinics have in fact emerged

---

[20] See Chapter 1 in this volume.
[21] These are clinics in which students directly represent individual clients in judicial proceedings.
[22] See Chapter 1 in this volume.   [23] Id.

from the seeds planted during the first wave. For example, the HRMLC in Turin drew on inspiration from the Polish and Czech clinical movements and in turn (alongside the Clinic at Brescia Law School) ignited a vibrant clinical movement right across Italy. Second, and much more common than the first trend, several clinics have resulted from the exposure of European academics to US legal education and their subsequent return home to set up clinics at their respective institutions (often with very little institutional support). This is the case for the Amsterdam International Law Clinic, the Clinic at Ghent Law School, and the clinic at the Graduate Institute in Geneva. Third, in some cases, there is clear US institutional support, such as with EU Public Interest Clinic co-hosted by NYU and HEC Paris. Even the HRMLC in Turin has received some support from the Open Society Foundations (although it was not launched at their initiative). Fourth, in some cases (as with the Tarragona Clinic and the Brescia Clinic), it is clear that clinics are set up by European academics without any prior exposure to the US model of CLE and, moreover, without any knowledge that the enterprise being engaged in might even be identified as a "clinic." However, even in this case, once these clinicians become aware of the broader clinical movement, study visits to the US and from US clinicians to Europe usually follow. Fifth, it should be noted that all it seems to take is two or three clinics in a given country to spark a broader clinical movement. This appears to have been the case in Spain, Italy, the Netherlands, Belgium, Germany, and France. And these follow-up clinics (which we might call the "third wave") seem to take inspiration primarily from their national forerunners (rather than from contact with US legal education).

What emerges then is a rather complex picture of the origins of the contemporary European clinical movement: a picture from which we cannot fully extricate the US but, at the same time, a picture that is very much the result of European effort and innovation.

This brings us to the next question: How is CLE transforming itself in order to thrive in Europe? Earlier, we noted the differences, identified by Genty, between the European and US context, which accounted for the failure of the transplants of the first wave. What is distinctive of the second wave is the extent to which these differences *have* been accounted for (not entirely but to a much larger extent). This is no doubt a consequence of Europeans, rather than Americans, being in the driving seat during the second wave.

In contrast to the first wave, there is now a much greater focus on what Genty describes a "limited scope" model of CLE. This is to say that, acutely aware of limitations imposed both by student practice rules and by the fact that European clinicians themselves are often not admitted to the bar, the clinicians have embraced alternative models of CLE departing from the archetypal US live-client model. For example, students may provide information (rather than representation) to individual clients (as is the case in the Polish legal clinics), or they might help asylum seekers to prepare for interviews or prepare "know your rights" guides (as the

HRMLC in Turin has done). Much more common, and perhaps a defining characteristic of the European clinical movement, is the model whereby clinics work directly for NGO clients, producing memos, reports, amicus briefs, UN submissions, ombudsman complaints and submitting FOIA requests or carrying out human rights fact-finding. Historically, US counterparts might have criticized such activities as not constituting "authentic" CLE. However, it should be noted here that NGOs in Europe are historically far less legally sophisticated than their counterparts in the US. Europe has not benefited from a "public interest law movement," which in America gave birth to hundreds of "public interest law firms" (i.e. NGOs with a large legal staff embracing complex legal advocacy strategies, such as the Environmental Defense Fund, the Mexican American Legal Defense and Education Fund, the National Women's Law Center, or the NAACP Legal Defense Fund).[24] The public interest law movement placed lawyers and legal strategies at the forefront of civil society advocacy all across the nation and has had a long-lasting impact on US civil society, on how issues are framed, on what constitutes impactful advocacy, and on who nonprofits hire.[25] To an extent, the global human rights movement, the influence of the European Court of Human Rights (ECtHR), and the emergence of the supranational EU legal system and the increasingly technocratic and law-oriented nature of EU policy are all, at least since the 1990s, having a similar impact on European civil society. However, the argument can be made that NGOs in Europe, often lacking full-time legal staff,[26] can benefit from the kind of legal services that clinical students are well equipped to provide, more so than their US equivalents. To this extent, the second wave of CLE in Europe is arguably taking a shape which emerges from the necessities of the local ecosystem, which, as discussed at length earlier, is characterized by a complex polygenetic and multilayered legal landscape in which advocacy-oriented (rather than law-oriented) NGOs often need support to make an impact.

Moreover, the work that clinic students carry out for nonprofits, and even for individual clients where legal information is provided, places a far greater emphasis on legal research and legal drafting than was placed on these skills during the first wave. The strong emphasis on the lawyer–client relationship and adversarial oral advocacy skills, which Genty notes was characteristic of the first wave, is almost nowhere to be found in the contributions to this volume. Again, it seems that when European academics are left to their own devices to design legal clinics from scratch, they design clinics that are in harmony with the norms of local legal practice (i.e. the greater emphasis placed on researching, drafting, and presenting legal submissions

---

[24] *See*, generally, Burton Allen Weisbrod, Joel F. Handler, and Neil K. Komesar. PUBLIC INTEREST LAW: AN ECONOMIC AND INSTITUTIONAL ANALYSIS (University of California Press 1978).

[25] *See*, generally, Louise G. Trubek, Public Interest Law: Facing the Problems of Maturity. U. ARK. LITTLE ROCK L. REV. 33 (2011).

[26] The Good Lobby, Survey of the Legal and Advocacy Needs of NGOs active in the EU policy space, June 2017, edited by L. Khadar and A. Alemanno, and available at www.thegoodlobby.eu.

in continental legal practice where combative oral advocacy is rare, even at Europe's highest courts in Strasbourg, Luxembourg, Geneva, and The Hague).

Another distinctive feature of clinics during the second wave of CLE in Europe is their resourcefulness. No longer can the clinics rely on generous financing from outside funders, and so, typically, the clinics represented in this volume do not have more than one (often relatively junior) full-time staff member, if they have any at all. They rely on energetic professors (often working unremunerated and beyond the formal curriculum) and on volunteer (or poorly remunerated) PhD or master's degree students to staff and run the clinics.

A final point to note is the extent to which clinics in the second wave are taking on a distinctly European identity. They are, as noted earlier, engaging in fundamentally European challenges, such as the migrant crisis, Roma rights, and European integration, and they are interacting with and taking shape in relation to the European institutional environment (the Council of Europe and the EU). Of course, much of this infrastructure, although present during the first wave of CLE, was relatively untapped as a venue for public interest lawyering. It is interesting to note here that, until 2005, the number of NGO third-party interventions per year at the ECtHR was less than ten (averaging around 5 per year between 1998 and 2003) and did not reach forty until 2010.[27] Moreover, many of the countries targeted during the first wave were only just becoming part of or had not yet joined to the Court of Europe and EU systems. So it is impossible to say whether the first wave of legal clinics would have fully embraced this ecosystem had it been more readily accessible to them.

Ultimately, we can quite confidently conclude that CLE in its second European wave is adapting to European soil in multiple ways, resulting in a very rich clinical practice. This practice is perhaps best described as a hybrid of the US clinical model and various heterogeneous European models. However, whether this implies that clinics will have more staying power this time around is a separate question which we will delve into in the following section.

BLOSSOMING: UNDER WHICH CONDITIONS IS CLE SPREADING?

After having seen how CLE has been adapting in European soil, the time has come to examine its fruits thus far. In other words, is European CLE blossoming? Is it changing what it means to be a lawyer today? Is it transforming the role and self-identity of European law schools and European legal teaching? Is it instilling values, such as social justice, in students in a way that was not done in the past?

Most contributors suggest that Europe is witnessing a "burgeoning" – rather than a blossoming – of CLE. In other words, while there are more clinics than in the past

---

[27] Laura Van den Eynde, *An Empirical Look at the Amicus Curiae Practice of Human Rights NGOs Before the European Court of Human Rights.* 31 NETHERLANDS QUARTERLY OF HUMAN RIGHTS 280 (2013).

across European jurisdictions, CLE has not necessarily gone mainstream yet. For instance, as suggested in Chapter 11 by Brems and Smet as well as in Chapter 10 by Valcke, while several legal clinics are sprouting across Europe, only few of them are genuinely embracing clinical education methods and qualify as such as legal clinics. Often, the self-proclaimed clinics are often mere seminars that host legal practitioners.

Moreover, as previously highlighted, most of the clinics involve – due to their vanguard nature– only a small (often international) number of students, rather than reaching out to the general law student body. In these circumstances, European CLE is not deepening but widening, with more and more universities embarking on the creation of new clinical – or clinic-inspired – programmes. In the absence of a critical mass of legal clinics having reached maturity, we agree with our contributors, according to whom it would not appear accurate to describe the rapid development of European CLE as a "blossoming."

But what are the major obstacles faced by CLE in its blossoming journey across Europe?

First, many contributors suggest that the establishment and rapid diffusion of CLE in Europe has not been prompted or accompanied by institutionalization. Although clearly influenced by the American experience, European CLE has predominantly been driven by endogenous (academic and cultural) forces. This is exemplified by the emergence of informal networks of scholars and master's degree students who have borrowed the idea from the other side of the Atlantic before adapting it to European soil. While our contributors agree that the sudden emergence of clinics in the Western European space must be ascribed to the progressive globalization of the legal market, CLE has broadly failed – at least thus far – to receive any form of institutional – not to mention financial – support.

Although individual European clinics have received investment both from EU and private philanthropic sources (e.g. the Olomouc Clinic, the Kent EU Rights Clinic, and the HRMLC in Turin, to name a few), neither domestic authorities nor EU institutions have endorsed CLE in systematic or wholesale fashion as an enterprise worth investing in. The general institutional framework of the university system has remained unchanged. This, in turn, has required new legal clinics to cope with a series of institutional, financial, and bureaucratic constraints. In addition to the financial difficulties – which seem to be a common challenge to most European clinics – clinics do not typically exist in the bureaucratic organization of the university. As a result, teachers involved in the clinical programme cannot expect to be recognized with any official status. Nor can they expect to receive any salary as "clinicians," being generally adjunct professors or teaching extra hours on top of their standard teaching load.

Also, the bar associations have been reticent to endorse CLE and have often resisted the idea by perceiving clinical students as "competitors" in both the legal aid and commercial markets. A recent exception is the Haeri Report on the future of the legal profession that was solicited by the French Minister of Justice.[28] This report recommends that all French law schools establish legal clinics to provide hands-on experiences to French law students before they enter the legal market.

To secure formal recognition of the value of CLE from public authorities at the national and/or EU level, as well as by the European and national bar associations, is a prerequisite for the development and therefore the blossoming of European CLE. If institutionalization requires both top-down and bottom-up interventions, what European CLE needs to consolidate is the proactive support of the institutional apparatus.

As argued by Anthony Valcke in Chapter 10, institutionalization – either prompted by public authorities or bar associations – would be a first step towards the possibility of procuring long-term funding for law clinics in Europe, which is necessary to sustain the future and growth of CLE in Europe. We agree that such recognition would pave the way for encouraging further access by law clinics to existing sources of EU funding, such as the Erasmus+[29]; Justice[30]; and Rights, Equality, and Citizenship[31] programmes, which remain inaccessible to us as European clinicians. There are, of course, exceptions, for example as experienced by the Law School in Olomouc which succeeded in funding (at least initially) its clinical programme via a grant from the European Social Fund. This is interesting to observe because that external funding opportunity boosted the reputation and, as a result, the attractiveness of the Law School in Olomouc.[32]

Second, most contributors suggest that another obstacle currently obstructing the blossoming of CLE in Europe is the lack of cooperation among the various clinical education realities. There is an almost unanimous call for more cross-border cooperation between clinicians, not only on pedagogical issues but also on systemic political and social issues which they all seem to commit to. The European Network for Clinical Education (ENCLE) pursues both objectives and hosts an annual event to gather the growing number of clinicians in Europe. The positive response to our call for contributions to our edited volume proved how keen – not to say enthusiastic – the emerging European CLE community is on

---

[28] Rapport sur l'avenir de la profession d'avocat : rapp., 2 févr. 2017, confié par le garde des Sceaux à Me Kami Haeri. See A. Alemanno and Alexandre Biard, *L'enseignement clinique du droit : une réponse aux nouveaux défis de nos sociétés*, 22 LA SEMAINE JURIDIQUE (22 mai 2017).

[29] Regulation (EU) No 1288/2013 of the European Parliament and of the Council of December 11, 2013, establishing "Erasmus+": the Union programme for education, training, youth and sport [2013] OJ L 347/50.

[30] Regulation (EU) No 1382/2013 of the European Parliament and of the Council of December 17, 2013, establishing a Justice Programme for the period 2014 to 2020 [2013] OJ L 354/73.

[31] Regulation (EU) No 1381/2013 of the European Parliament and of the Council of December 17, 2013 establishing a Rights, Equality and Citizenship Programme for the period 2014 to 2020 [2013] OJ L 354/62.

[32] According to an unpublished survey conducted among the first-year students of Palacký Law School in 2015, approximately 10.5% of them chose the Palacký Law School over other Czech law schools because of the clinical programme and the overall practical focus of the curriculum.

cooperating, not only on the day-to-day operation of their respective clinics but also in deeper conversations on future directions. There is a clear need to create more opportunities for informed conversations that transcend the pedagogical and material challenges faced by CLE. In the absence of institutionalization, there is a clear convergence among European clinicians towards building a case for CLE at both the national and European levels.

Third, a related significant impediment to the development of an effective clinical journey for European law students and teachers is the absence of a literature *on* clinical education and *for* clinical education as well as well-crafted material for the classroom. As observed by Marzia Barbera in Chapter 3:

> such literature is abundant in the United States, where it developed at the same time as the clinical movement, yet it is sporadic at best in most European countries, where there are just a few journals providing systematic reflection on clinical work, and the number of articles published that describe, criticize, or set normative standards relating to clinical work is quite small.

It is against this backdrop that our contributors suggest that, for CLE to blossom in Europe, there is an urgent need for its institutionalization, both through university reform and the intervention of bar associations. Yet there is not agreement on how to actually make it happen. The ongoing debate on whether CLE should become mandatory is part of such a broad conversation.[33] The examples provided by experiences gained in Olumuc, Brescia, and Tarragona show that a full integration of clinical education in the curriculum is possible. The 2017 Haeri Report suggests that this might also be the future direction in the French education system. Yet, even if universities should embrace and mainstream CLE, it is likely – as argued by Valcke – that differences in clinical structures, fields of interest, and national legal education will prevent a drive towards standardization of CLE at both the European and national levels. In his view, such standardization could even be considered "to hamper the creativity and diversity of law clinics in Europe."

Indeed, there appears to be some consensus that, in the current stage of the European project, CLE in Europe must adapt to the local, national level to thrive. But for this transformation to occur, what is needed is a cultural transformation that can and should be initiated by the nascent networks of both national and European clinics.

As a result, a more nuanced approach towards institutionalization of CLE might be offered by the progressive formal and informal networks of existing and soon-to-appear clinics. In particular, the ENCLE network is expected to play a proactive role in disseminating best practices and prompting and sharing teaching resources, as well as facilitating the establishment of new clinics across the continent.

---

[33] For a US perspective, see Rima Sirota, *Making CLE Voluntary and Pro Bono Mandatory : A Law Faculty Test Case*. LOUISIANA L. REV. (forthcoming).

CONCLUSION

CLE in Europe seems to suffer from a kind of frustration: it carries the right solution to many problems of legal education in Europe (it is professionalizing, experiential, socially relevant, and increases employability), but is struggling to convince the world (academic institutions and public authorities) of its genius. As such, it mirrors the difficulties of the European project to gain the degree of acceptance that it deserves based on its sixty years of contribution to European societies.

Legal education is a subject that is more often practised than reflected upon. This is all the more so in Europe, where legal academia showed an historical reticence to engage in self-questioning and soul-searching. "Who should I be? Who should I become?" are questions that have traditionally been set aside in European legal education in favour of "what should I learn?"

Despite the rapidly changing landscape, European legal academia has proved extremely resilient in preserving the traditional legal curriculum and teaching methods from disrupting and pervasive phenomena such as digitalization. There is an evident tension between the inherently safe environment of education versus the inherently unpredictable clinical environment. Facing this alternative, the average university manager and professor opts for the status quo.

Yet, as nicely narrated by each of our contributors, some transformations are occurring in the legal curricula which suggest that times are ripe for more introspection in European legal education. The developments are not fortuitous, and they seem to respond to significant changes in the European academic and professional legal fields that we have tried to deconstruct in our volume. We have witnessed the ascendance of powerful and highly legalized supranational European and international institutions that seem capable of providing solutions but often remain distant, undecipherable, and apparently unaccountable to ordinary citizens and those at the bottom of the power pyramid. This dynamic has fostered (and perhaps demands) a new brand of European legal practitioners and academics who are more inclined towards seeing legal practice and scholarship as a form of civic engagement or political activism, mediating between ordinary citizens (and noncitizens) and pressing political and social issues and the power centres in Brussels, Strasbourg, Luxembourg, and Geneva.[34]

On the demand side, the internationalization and Europeanization of national legal orders in Europe and the attendant regionalization and globalization of legal practice is drastically changing what it means to be a practicing lawyer in Europe and the requisite skill-set that is needed (e.g. multilingualism/multijurisdictionalism).[35]

---

[34] Lamin Khadar, University Law Clinics and the Growing Demand for EU Law, Open Society Foundation Voices, www.opensocietyfoundations.org/voices/university-law-clinics-and-growing-demand-eu-law; and Alberto Alemanno, Public Interest Lawyering as Vocation, *1st Falcon Public Lecture*, Leuven University, December 2014.

[35] Miguel Poiares Maduro, *Legal Education and the Europeanisation and Globalisation of Law* [editorial note], 4 CROATIAN YEARBOOK OF EUROPEAN LAW & POLICY (2008), Aalt Willem Heringa,

The globalization of legal education in Europe is placing pressure on law schools to revise their teaching practices and student offerings to stay competitive on the international market.[36] Within the academic job market, this process has resulted in intensified competition, especially at the top schools, which has given rise to a highly cosmopolitan, innovative, and entrepreneurial class of legal academics who are keen to learn from other parts of the globe and experiment with novel pedagogies.

While there seems to be consensus that CLE was partly driven by the search for relevance in a world of legal education that aspires to internationalize, it remains unclear to what extent such a dynamic must be ascribed to the Bologna Process per se. Even though the Bologna Process's influence is rather minor, it can still be seen as an important piece of the puzzle, leading to an overall shift from theoretical to practical higher education, which can be observed in many contexts in Europe.

Simultaneously, there is increasing salience in the public consciences of complex legal and political issues (environmental degradation, global trade inequity, mass migration, corporate crime and corruption, the closing space for civil society, genocide and war crimes, etc.) that defy borders and demand global or regional responses.[37]

We submitted at the beginning of this volume that all of these processes and structural adjustments are central to understanding the emergence of the European CLE movement. They both sustain the movement and offer glimpses of what it could achieve. Growing out of this context, Europe's new legal clinics seem capable of radically reinventing traditional European approaches to legal education and practice. Through the European clinical movement, spurred on by this restructuring of the European legal field, European legal teaching – historically formalistic, doctrinal, hierarchical, and passive (lecture- and textbook-based)[38] – has come

---

European Legal Education or Legal Education in Europe [editorial], 18 (3), MAASTRICHT JOURNAL OF EUROPEAN AND COMPARATIVE LAW 221–22 (2011).

[36] See Karsten Schmidt, *New Challenges for Law Faculties: The View of a Private Law School*, 6 (1) EUROPEAN JOURNAL OF LEGAL EDUCATION 4, 5 (2011); Vincenzo Ferrari, *Doctoral Education in an International Perspective*, 5 (2) EUROPEAN JOURNAL OF LEGAL EDUCATION 10 (2009); Marie-Luce Paris-Dobozy, *Challenging Exchange Programs: Studying the Common Law and Civil Law Systems in a Joint Law Degree*, 5 (1) EUROPEAN JOURNAL OF LEGAL EDUCATION 47, 49, 56 (2009); Simon Marginson and Marijk van der Wende. *Europeanisation, International Rankings and Faculty Mobility: Three Cases in Higher Education Globalisation*, in OECD CENTRE FOR EDUCATIONAL RESEARCH AND INNOVATION, HIGHER EDUCATION TO 2030, vol. 2: Globalization (Paris 2009), 110; and Carel Stolker, RETHINKING THE LAW SCHOOL: EDUCATION, RESEARCH, OUTREACH AND GOVERNANCE (Cambridge University Press 2014), 267–68.

[37] James Goldston, *The Rule of Law at Home and Abroad*, 1 HAGUE JOURNAL ON THE RULE OF LAW 38–45 (2009).

[38] Richard Ball and Christian Dadomo. UKCLE Law Subject Survey: European Union Law (2010) at 89 and 104. This survey related to EU law teaching in the UK and found that such teaching (at least at universities) was primarily conservative and doctrinal. However, anecdotal evidence suggests that this would be even more so for continental Europe, which is traditionally far more conservative in its approach to legal education.

under increasing pressure to reimagine itself as pragmatic, policy-aware, and action-oriented.

As CLE is rapidly emerging as a badly needed bridge between the teaching and practice of law across Europe, one may wonder to what extent it may also deliver in better connecting academia with European society.

At a time of unprecedented citizen awakening, one may wonder to what extent CLE may actually leave the legendary ivory tower typical of the university setting and bond with the multifarious forms of activism and do-it-yourself citizenship. In other words, can European legal clinics not merely pursue their dual mission of pedagogical and social justice goals but also connect with national and transnational legal activism and support social movements? Are these two enterprises complementary or disjointed, harmonious or antagonistic?

As online petition platforms, grassroots movements with transnational ambitions, and new forms of citizen engagement multiply, the question is whether law schools and their legal clinics can support the emergence of both domestic and pan-European diverse forms of activism.

That is the experience that we – as co-editors of this volume – have gained with the establishment of The Good Lobby, a skill-sharing community connecting academics and lawyers with civil society organizations who need their advice. Our ambition is to adapt and scale-up the clinical educational model to match the high demand for *pro bono* advice from civil society and grassroots activists with an increasingly available supply of *pro bono* advice by academics and lawyers.

While it is too early to provide conclusive insights, we have already successfully experimented with several new forms of collaboration. Most importantly, through the offering of educational trainings and simulations, we have begun instilling a culture of *pro bono* work across and beyond the legal profession. While no formal links exist between the EU Public Interest Clinic and The Good Lobby, both the methodology and the networks that we have mobilized largely owe a debt to CLE.

Based on this early experience, we believe that European CLE carries the potential to eventually bridge the gap between academia and society. It is for these reasons that we support the idea of coordinated action to be taken by European legal clinics together with NGOs and a network of professionals at local and European levels. This may build up cross-border cooperation between clinicians not only on pedagogical issues but also on systemic political and social issues.

Today, a growing number of EU-based civil society organizations working on environmental protection, anticorruption, democracy, rule of law, human rights, ethnic minorities, LGBTI, women's rights, and migrants are facing unprecedented obstacles to their daily operation by state action. As the civic space for civil society continues to narrow,[39] CLE is expected to play a key role in defending such a space.

---

[39] Civic Space in Europe Survey, Civicus and Civil Society Europe, 2016, https://civilsocietyeuropedo teu.files.wordpress.com/2016/10/civicspaceineuropesurveyreport_final251015.pdf.

What we should work out is a road map for creating coordinated and interconnected human rights- and social rights-oriented CLE programmes across Europe, which might include individual actions, group actions, proposals for law reform, policy and case support, reporting, and so on.

As CLE is emerging as a badly needed bridge between teaching and the practice of the law, as well as between academia and society, this volume provides a sense of the new directions undertaken by a growing community of entrepreneurial academics.